William and Sarah Biddle,

1633 – 1711

Planting a Seed of Democracy

in America

A 1710 map of New Jersey adapted from Map #12, page 33 of *The Story of New Jersey Civil Boundaries 1606 - 1968,* created by John P. Snyder showing the errant Keith Line of 1687 and its extension by the Coxe - Barclay Agreement of 1688 (described on page 159 of this book). This was the division line between East and West New Jersey that was used by the proprietors in William Biddle's time. The map is used with the permission of the New Jersey State Archival Library which now owns the John Snyder maps.

William and Sarah Biddle, 1633 – 1711

Planting a Seed of Democracy in America

C. Miller Biddle

by C. Miller Biddle, M.D.

Published by
C. Miller Biddle, M.D.
Moorestown, New Jersey

ISBN 978-0-9848616-0-6
Edited and prepared for publication by Jane Fletcher Fiske, FASG
Printed by McNaughton & Gunn, Inc., Saline, Michigan

Copies of this book may be obtained from:
Biddle Biography
P.O. Box 714
Moorestown, N.J. 08057

TABLE OF CONTENTS

Prologue

The Biddle Family 300th Reunion was held at the historic Biddle home, Andalusia, situated on the Delaware River north of Philadelphia, in October 1981. With close to 400 family members gathered together that day I began to think about the ancestors who preceded us and especially about William and Sarah Biddle who were the progenitors of our family here in America.

I found out that the house that they built and lived in was still standing in Mansfield, New Jersey, and before a week had gone by I visited it. When I explained my interest in the house to the current residents, they let me tour through the basement and rooms on the first floor. It was a strange feeling to know that I was standing in a place that my ancestors of ten generations before had lived from 1684 to 1711.

Then I began to go to the archival libraries in this area and found that there was extensive material about their lives here and in England. Early in my research I came upon the articles written by a distant cousin, Lydia Rickman, who had moved to England and had researched the ancestors of William Biddle and Sarah Kempe, his wife. This information was inspiring and helpful and it convinced me later to visit Birlingham, England, where William was born. I found the church where he was baptized and the graveyard where his brother and parents were buried. Back in London, I walked the streets where they lived, trying to find landmarks they might have known when they lived there.

Back home I spent many hours in the archival library collections of the State of New Jersey, Burlington County, Burlington City, Moorestown, New Jersey, Swarthmore College, Haverford College and the Historical Society of Pennsylvania. Reading hundreds of documents and books relating to that period, I gained a deeper understanding of their lives in England and in the New World of New Jersey.

William, the second son of an illiterate farmer in rural England, was sent to London as an apprentice to learn to be a shoemaker. He found himself in the midst of a group of people who were among the earliest Quakers in London. He soon became a member of the Religious Society of Friends (Quakers) and he experienced the persecution of the Anglican government, serving time in jail for standing firm on his beliefs. He married his wife, Sarah, and they began to raise their family in London as a part of the growing Quaker movement there.

Left
The author, C. Miller Biddle

The Quakers kept meticulous records in London and in West New Jersey where William and Sarah eventually settled in 1681. The couple became part of the group planning to settle a new territory in America with a new constitution that would give them the ability to own land, to form a government and practice their religion, all without fear of arrest or injury.

Four years after the original settlers from London arrived in Burlington, William and Sarah joined them along with their young family. From the very beginning of his life in America William played a leadership role in the government, the court system, in the matters concerning the settling of land and in his Quaker religion. The records for each of these areas confirm the important contributions that William and Sarah made to their new country.

This book is an attempt to pull together the vast amount of information on their experiences from 1633 in England to their deaths here. I have tried to describe for the reader the incredible lives that they lived out in West Jersey—which became the State of New Jersey—and in the Delaware Valley, which includes Philadelphia and Eastern Pennsylvania.

I am fascinated by their story and I have tried to record it in a manner that will let others understand it and enjoy it as well.

C. Miller Biddle, M.D.

CHAPTER 1

Birlingham, Worcestershire, England, 1633–1650

Birlingham was a country parish in Worcestershire, England, on one of the manors of Lord Thomas Russell, partially encircled by a loop of the River Avon and surrounded by lowland meadows. It was still in the grip of the late winter chill on Sunday, March 10, 1633/4 when Edward and Penelope Biddle left their home with their children, Thomas, age four, Elizabeth, age two, and William, an infant, heavily bundled in his mother's arms to protect him from the swirling wind coming across the river. The parish church bell was calling the townspeople from their homes. Each family made their way by their own paths to the common roadway which led to the town center and the parish church. William Biddle was to be baptized on that day.[1]

Edward Biddle, as the second son in his family, had moved to Birlingham from nearby Bushley, Worcestershire, in 1623. His farming background would have to be sufficient for him to support his family. Like many of the rural people in England at that time, Edward could not read or write. There was no effort or need to educate the common people, for the aristocracy and the clergy took care of any transactions affecting them that may have required an education. The person who remained illiterate continued in the bondage of these propertied and educated classes.[2]

Edward purchased a messuage (a dwelling house) in Birlingham in 1626, and the following year he married Penelope Goodale of that parish.[3] Penelope had been educated and thus would be able to help Edward avoid the risks he might encounter because of his illiteracy. She would also see that their children received a basic education at home.

After the birth of William in 1633 the family continued to grow. Jane was born in 1634, Edward in 1638, Mary in 1641, Joseph in 1644, and Richard in 1647.[4]

The Biddle family had resided in Bushley, Worcestershire for at least three generations before the birth of Edward in 1602, son of John and Elizabeth (Higgins) Biddle. As the law and custom of inheritance of real estate interests was by primogeniture and entail in England, undoubtedly the majority of the estate of John Biddle passed on to the older brother of Edward, William Biddle, when his father died in 1626 intestate. Edward's mother, Elizabeth, administered the estate, and she herself died in 1639.[5]

The grandfather of Edward Biddle was Edward Byddyll, born in Bushley in 1539. His wife, the grandmother of Edward Biddle of

Birlingham, was Elizabeth Wyett, sister of the Vicar of Bushley. Edward was the eldest son of John Byddyl of Bushley, born about 1500. It is uncertain if John Byddyl was born in Bushley; he may have come from Upton-on-Severn, about five miles distant from Bushley, where there are records of Biddles (or Byddylls) dating back to 1298. John Byddyl was listed as a bowman on the Muster Call Roll of 1539-42, indicating that he had served in the military in allegiance to the Lord of his Manor, as was the custom throughout England. Edward Byddyll was the eldest son of John Byddyl, entitling him to the majority of the estate of his father, as meager as it may have been.[6]

The home of Edward and Penelope in Birlingham, one of many homesteads of the parish, was situated on ground high enough to be safe from flooding of the River Avon. The parish was rural and its economy was oriented toward agriculture. Yeomen had to be as self sufficient as possible, and even tradesmen such as blacksmiths, butchers, cordwainers and chandlers, while serving the needs of others in the town, had to know enough farming to maintain their families. Inns and boarding houses fed and housed farm workers, and served as meeting places for townspeople as well as stopping-over places for travelers passing by from Bristol or London.

The Edward Biddle homestead consisted of the dwelling house, an adjacent orchard and garden, a twelve-acre field behind the house, a two-acre meadow and eight acres of pastureland. Barns, sheds and pens housed sheep, hogs, oxen and cows, and protected tools and grain.[7] Outside of the village, Edward, as a freeholder, or as a copyhold tenant, controlled additional arable land. He also had rights to the common meadows and pastureland near the river, land that flooded part of the year, but served as a useful pasturage and forage resource for the manor during the rest of the year.

The River Avon was a valuable resource to the parish of Birlingham. A wharf constructed on the riverbank accommodated the ferry and other vessels that used the river. The ferry allowed goods, livestock and passengers to be carried across the river to Nafford,[8] or transported down the river to markets as distant as Bristol. The yeomen and tradesmen of Birlingham were thus able to find buyers for their wares more easily than those who did not have such a river available to them. The streams emptying into the river were harnessed by waterwheels to power mills for processing the corn and other grains grown by the yeomen of Birlingham.

The manor of Birlingham had been purchased by the Russell family in 1562.[9] It may have included monastery lands before the reformation, but by 1625 there was little or no religious turmoil in this part of England. The

Church of England was the only religion of the area. The local church leadership was chosen by the church authorities, probably in consultation with the Lord of the Manor, Sir Thomas Russell. The townspeople participated in the business affairs of the church. Edward and his oldest son, Thomas, served as church wardens for many years.[10] Tithing, though an added form of taxation, was an accepted practice of the members of this religious community.

Land tenure for the yeomen of Birlingham, as well as for all yeomen on manors elsewhere in England, was dependent upon the will of the lord of the manor, and beyond that authority it was dependent upon the will of the Royal Crown. Although the feudal age had ended a century before, there remained vestiges of the feudal system in all English land tenure. Lord Russell owed allegiance by oath to the Crown and thereby retained ownership of the lands of the manor. If the Crown demanded, he would owe money to the Crown derived from the benefits of the ownership of the land. Thus, a yeoman or others in the manor did not have complete ownership of their lands. There was always a clause in the ownership agreement that under certain circumstances allowed the land to revert to the lord of the manor. All lands were held by the lord of the manor either through a tenant or lease agreement, or by freehold, an agreement that was secured by a yearly quitrent paid to the lord of the manor.

Edward was a freeholder of land and a copyhold tenant of the manor. Though he controlled these lands and made them as productive as possible, each year he paid Lord Russell a sum of money for the quitrent of the freehold lands, and a sum of money or a percentage of the production from the lands held by tenancy or lease.

Until 1660 these agreements for the use of the lands of the manor also included an allegiance to the lord of the manor for military support in times of war. Therefore, a yeoman could be told to leave his family and estate at the will of the lord of the manor for military purposes. Although this situation may not have happened very often, it was a possibility that threatened the security of a yeoman like Edward in rural England.

While the freeholders and copyhold tenants of the manors of England paid rent for their lands, there was no reciprocal agreement with the lord of the manor that these funds would be used for the benefit of the people of the manor, or for the maintenance of manor roadways or bridges or other projects for the public good.

Besides having very little to say about the amounts of rents and quitrents and church tithes, inhabitants of the manors were taxed by the Crown, through the lord of the manor, whenever it was decided by the Crown that money was needed. They might be taxed on their lands, or on the results of their labor or business, or by a head tax, or by elements of their homes, such as a tax on hearths. The common person had to establish savings in one form or another to be prepared to meet this unpredictable method of taxation, for if they could not pay, they would face seizure of all of their possessions.

The electorate was entirely male and was determined by landholder status, or by the level of personal income. Edward, as a freeholder yeoman with an income of greater than forty shillings per year, was able to vote for his parliamentary representative, but he had little or no voice in the selection of the slate of candidates running for office.

The judicial system of Birlingham consisted of the County Court, the Worcestershire Quarter Court and the Manorial Court. The latter court existed for the resolution of petty matters of the parish and manor, to see that the business of the manor was completed efficiently. The justices of the peace were appointed by the Crown from the country gentry.

The Russell family owned several manors in Worcestershire, including Strensham, located just to the west of Birlingham. It was there that Thomas Russell, Esquire, the uncle of Sir Thomas Russell had lived. Sir Thomas Russell was an appointed Justice of the Peace of the Worcestershire Quarter Court and was the Justice of the Peace for the Birlingham Manor Court. His uncle, Thomas Russell, Esquire, had been a friend of William Shakespeare.[11]

The laws and customs of the manor varied slightly from one manor to another, but since the manorial courts were under the control of the Crown, the laws of the manor could not be contradictory to the laws of England. The Poor Laws, which defined the responsibility of the manor and parish in the care of their poor people, and the Statute of Artificers of 1563, which defined the rules of apprenticeship, were national laws both enacted during the reign of Queen Elizabeth (1558-1603). These laws and others clearly dictated to the rural courts how cases were to be decided when matters of this kind came before the court.

Not all persons could sit on a jury. Yeomen and other townspeople would qualify for jury duty if their income or property holdings were sufficiently large. Edward, as a yeoman, and later his oldest son, Thomas, did qualify and did sit on juries in the courts. The legal process was dominated by the Justice of the Peace, with the jury playing a minor role in decisions reached.

All other officials of the county, the manor and the parish were appointed by either the Crown or the lord of the manor. These appointed officials—such as the coroner, the sheriff and the constable—administered the laws as they interpreted them from their positions of power, no matter how their actions might jeopardize the rights of others. The system of justice placed considerable power in the hands of appointed individuals, without a sufficient influence on these non-elected people to see that they were qualified, just, or humane. The common person living under this system had every reason to remain on good terms with all other persons with whom they would come in contact. The justice system forced the average person into a conservative and traditional lifestyle.

In rural England, homesteads were clustered in the towns, with the fields surrounding. It required much effort and cooperation by the townspeople to maintain the health and prosperity of the town. Many orders were issued by the manor court, controlling almost every aspect of the environment. There were rules concerning the use of common lands, the clearing of drainage ditches, maintaining roads and bridges and cleaning up of debris to prevent contamination of well water and the growth of insects and spread of disease. The court would decide on the marks that each individual would use to identify his livestock, for problems perpetually arose concerning the damage done by stray beasts. Rotation of crops on common lands was practiced in order to maintain the fertility of the soil.

The manor courts assigned committees to oversee all these problems of communal living. Edward was assigned tasks for the public good a number of times through the court of the manor.[12]

William Biddle spent the first sixteen years of his life in Birlingham, Worcestershire with his parents and seven siblings. In this environment he knew only the practices of the Church of England. He learned to read and write with his brothers and sisters, taught probably by his mother and perhaps with the help of the local minister. Reading materials were scarce, the main textbook being the Bible, so he developed a good knowledge of Christianity while he became literate.

William had mastered the skills of a yeoman, growing crops, tending to animals, shearing sheep, assisting the blacksmith and helping to butcher the livestock for food. He knew how to handle himself in a boat and he realized the value of the river to the town. All of this knowledge would come to good use later in his life.

He had watched his father work hard to develop a prosperous and successful homestead for his large family, but he knew that his father's main possessions would be left to his older brother Thomas. William, therefore, faced a choice. He could seek his own livelihood elsewhere in rural Worcestershire, as his father had done, or he could move on to a completely different trade somewhere else. At the age of sixteen it was time to make that decision.

John Byddyl (b.1500)

m.

Margaret (d. 1549)

Edward Byddyll (1539–1578) m. **Elizabeth Wyett** (d. 1590/1)	Ann b.1541	Richard 1543–1547	Joan b. & d. 1548	Alice b.1548

Richard b.1563	Katherine b. 1565	**John Biddle** (d.1626) m. **Elizabeth Higgins** (d.1639)	Syble b.1570	William b.1572

Elizabeth b.1600	William b.1601	**Edward** (1602–1672) m. **Penelope Goodale** (d. 1677)	Richard b.1604	Margaret b.1605

Thomas b. 1629 m. Mary	Elizabeth b. 1631 m. — Stone	**William Biddle** (1633–1711) m. 2/7/1665/6 **Sarah Kempe** (1637/8 – 4/27/17)	Jane b.1634 m. Taylor	Edward b.1638	Mary b.1641	Joseph b.1644	Richard b.1647

Sarah b&d.1667	Elizabeth (1668-69)	**William Biddle** (1669-1743) m. 1695 **Lydia Wardell**	John (1670-73)	Joseph (1672-74)	Child d. at b.	*Sarah Biddle* (1678-8/17/1705) m. (1) *W. Righton* (2) *C. Plumstead*

William Biddle (1697-1756) m. (1)Anne Newbold m. (2) Mary Scull	Elizabeth b.1699	Sarah b.1701	Penelope b. 1703 m. James Whitehead	Lydia b.1704 m. Peter Imlay

Joseph Biddle b.1705 m. (1) — Arney (2) — Rodgers	John Biddle (1707-1789) m. Sarah Owen

CHAPTER 2

London, Apprenticeship as a Cordwainer, Conversion to Quakerism, 1650-1660

England under the reign of Queen Elizabeth (1558-1603) had changed dramatically from a predominantly rural society to a country oriented toward trade and manufacturing. In order to provide skilled craftsmen many of the young people of the country were placed in apprenticeships that had been defined by the Satute of Artificers of 1563 as a period of seven years, from about the age of sixteen to twenty-three. Under an apprenticeship agreement, a boy or girl would be placed, usually by his or her parents, under the strict supervision of a master or mistress, who promised to teach him or her a trade and often to provide some formal education and a new suit of clothes at the end of the apprenticeship. This system removed many adolescents from their homes and families at an age when they might normally be rebellious, placing them in an environment where they were expected to respond to the discipline of their master. For children who could not hope to inherit property, this arrangement provided an opportunity to learn a trade that would offer them a living. Marriage during the period of apprenticeship was generally forbidden.

For some time the nation had been in turmoil. Following a civil war, King Charles I had been beheaded in January 1648/9 and the country was now without a sovereign, governed under the Protectorate of Oliver Cromwell. The religious differences that had caused so many Puritans to emigrate to New England seemed to be resolved, at least for the time being.

Edward and William agreed that it would be in William's best interests for the boy to go to London to be trained by Thomas Biddle, a cordwainer (leather worker), who was probably the boy's uncle.[1] An apprenticeship was arranged; Edward paid Thomas £5 and Thomas agreed to take William as an apprentice for a period of seven years, commencing July 18, 1650.[2]

William moved from Birlingham to Old Change, Exchange Alley, London, the home of Thomas Biddle and his wife Esther. Thomas Biddle was a respected, honest, citizen and freeholder of London. William was immediately exposed to the industriousness of this home and business in the crowded city of London. Esther had come from Oxford, a center of learning, and as a very educated person she would exert considerable influence on the household. At that time the household may have been traditional in its religion, but many ideas both political and religious that were circulating about London were obviously introduced into the conversations held at this home.[3]

With the establishment of the Commonwealth of Oliver Cromwell and under the growing influence of the Puritans, education began to spread to the common people of England. This freed a great many people of middle and lower class England, urban and rural, from the chains of illiteracy that had been inherited from the feudal age. The clergy could no longer keep the secrets of the bible to themselves. The Bible was the principal textbook of the Puritan infiltrators of the national churches, and people began to learn to read and to make their own interpretations of religion. Under the influence of John Milton, Cromwell allowed a greater degree of freedom of the press than had existed before this time. A great number of pamphlets and books on religion and other similarly serious subjects became available to the now literate English people.

England, especially the city of London, was experiencing a barrage of new religious, political and social ideas. Numerous non-conformist and separatist religious groups and sects were being formed. However, the Church of England was still predominant, and there was no clear separation of Church and State. While the national church was weakened by the intrusion of the Puritans, Cromwell knew he would be unable to hold a clear majority of the people in his favor unless he continued a relative toleration of all religions.

It was to this dynamic, changing city of London that William was introduced in 1650. It was a city full of ideas, with pamphlets and books and discussions about religious alternatives. If his own powers of observation and his own curiosity were not enough, William was sure to have been further prodded by the energetic and intellectual Esther Biddle.

It was in this setting in England that the teachings of George Fox, the founder of Quakerism (the Religious Society of Friends) took root in 1652, first in the rural north country, and later in the more populated cities of Bristol and London. Quakerism seems to have been a natural outgrowth of Puritanism. Under the Puritans there was a great simplification of church doctrine and of church symbolism as exhibited in the church buildings themselves. Puritanism demanded that its members lead a religious and moral life and there was a strong emphasis on education. As a result of this effort to educate, there was a growth of new ideas and an encouragement of the advancement of scientific knowledge. New ideas from outside England were being introduced and studied in London because of the increase in overseas trade.

Under the Puritans, the seed ideas for social awareness and social conscience were allowed to develop. Thoughts and debates concerning alternative forms of government, and the need for government to be responsible and responsive to the people were permitted expression. The Puritans had encouraged the unleashing of these forces, but, while doing this, they did not completely separate themselves from traditional religious practices. They still worshipped in simplified churches with steeples, and they continued to practice some of the symbolism traditional to the Church of England. In addition they retained a hired ministry. But they still had limits on their toleration of other's beliefs on religious matters.

George Fox, unfulfilled by these Puritan modifications in religious practice, subjected himself to a prolonged period of study of religion, using his own intuition and experiences as a guide in reading and interpreting the Bible. His studies focused on the features of primitive Christianity; Christianity untainted by the interpretations of the organized church institutions. He tested his theses by entering into debate with numerous religious officials and authorities.

Out of this study came the revelation, mystical or not, that all men and women could be in touch with God, without the need of intermediaries or of the symbolism of the church institution. This experience had precedent in the recorded life and experience of Jesus. The desires of God, concerning how a Christian should conduct themselves, were also well recorded in the Bible. Direct communication with God was not to be limited to any man or woman for any reason such as social position or wealth since all men and women were equal in value in God's sight. It was because of this learning that Fox opposed the use of rank and title.

With all people living truly Christian lives as "friends" in brotherhood, there would be no need for war, nor for anyone to be subjected to humiliating subservience to religious or governmental authorities. However, Fox felt that there should remain a respect for the ruling authority that had been established for the public good. In a society where all individuals were to be complete Christian beings, Fox believed groups of people could honestly formulate the rules needed to live together, and they could fairly and justly govern themselves.

Upon the completion of his studies, George Fox began to share his experience and learning with those of other religions, often on the premises of their churches, either during or after their religious ceremonies. He was imprisoned several times for this expression of his non-traditional ideas and for his frequent intrusions on others religious territory.

It was not until 1652 that he was successful in convincing others to experience "Quakerism," as his religion was called because its followers trembled in the presence of God. As people converted to Quakerism, a group of ministers was formed called Publishers of the Truth; a group that eventually included about sixty persons. These ministers traveled throughout England and the world telling others of the beliefs of George Fox. Thus a period of "convincement" was begun.

Under the able leadership of George Fox, a method of worship was developed: a silent Meeting for Worship which could take place in the simplest environment, indoors, or outdoors; a type of Meeting for Worship in which each individual present would have the opportunity to communicate with God and to express themselves if they desired; a Meeting for Worship which practiced democracy in religion. In this period of convincement, from 1652 to 1660, approximately one percent of the population of England, or about sixty thousand people, became members of the developing "Religious Society of Friends" and regular places of worship were established.

In these early years the business of the religion was overseen by the Two Weeks Meeting which was established by Quaker leaders in London. The decisions reached in these meetings by the leaders of the Friends were debated by looking at all sides of the issue and decided by concensus of the group.

In 1654 Quakerism was formally introduced to London. The first Meetings for Worship were held at the home of Simon Dring on Watling Street, around the corner from the home of Thomas Biddle. Esther Biddle, then aged twenty five and disillusioned with the Church of England, attended these meetings. When exposed to the preaching of Francis Howgill, one of the traveling ministers, she became convinced of the truth of Quakerism. She brought this convincement home to Thomas and to William Biddle and other members of her household.

Esther had found, as did many women of England, that the newly established Society of Friends allowed her a greater liberty, a greater freedom of self expression and a greater freedom of conscience than she could find in any other civil or religious institution in England. She became a traveling Quaker minister herself, traveling to Newfoundland and The Netherlands in 1656, Barbados in 1657, and later to the Mediterranean region. She used her writing abilities when, in 1655, she published the first of many articles and pamphlets.

Her ministry continued into the 1690s. In 1694 she confronted Queen Mary II, asking her to put an end to the war between Christians that was being waged between France and England. Apparently with the Queen's permission, she traveled to France that same year to meet with King Louis XIV to deliver the same message. She died in London in 1697, at the age of

67, a pauper, living on a pension on the grounds of one of the London Monthly Meetings. She had been imprisoned by the civil authorities fourteen times for her religious convictions and her near-fanatical expression of them.[4]

William, having been exposed to this environment during the seven years of his apprenticeship, had improved his education and had become increasingly aware of the exciting world around him. He remained in London at the completion of his training to continue participating in the shoemaking business with Thomas Biddle and to continue his involvement in his new religion.

CHAPTER 3

London and Early Persecution, 1660-1665

The persecution of the Quakers and other non-conformist religions began during the last years of the Commonwealth under Oliver Cromwell. The non-traditional methods of the Quakers, their plain dress and their speech, set them apart from others. Moreover, the ideas that they championed and the behavior that they demanded of the governing authorities seemed threatening because they were not understood by the more traditional English people.

It seems understandable that Quakers were arrested for disrupting the church services of other religions, for in doing so they were intruding on the rights of others. However, they were imprisoned also for objecting to civil rules, such as the requirement to take an oath based on the sacraments of the Church of England, or to pay tithes to the Church of England, or to pay fines that they felt were administered unjustly. Quakers believed these requirements of the civil and religious authorities were incursions upon their own rights.

The intense emotion of the traveling ministers caused Quakerism to spread rapidly in England and abroad. Many of these religious emissaries, both men and women, traveled outside of England to deliver their religious messages, usually in an appropriate but convincing manner. In Bristol, however, the intensity of one of the missions became inappropriate. An almost blasphemous event occurred there when the Quaker minister James Naylor was led into the city on a horse, surrounded by people chanting and cheering, conveying the impression that he was more than just a minister, perhaps even a sacred person himself.[1]

However, even the most appropriate missionary methods and messages of the Quakers were believed to be seditious by the English civil and religious authorities. Those in government were still convinced that there must be a uniform religion for the nation and consequently a unity of church with state.

The Commonwealth essentially ended with the death of Oliver Cromwell in September of 1658. For almost two years after his death attempts were made to try to continue the Protectorate government. There were debates about the re-establishment of the sovereignty and the conformist Church of England. Military forces remained under the control of General Monk, who had served under Cromwell, so the religious and political opinions of this General were respectfully considered by Parliament.

Initially General Monk had little tolerance for the Quakers, and his troops had severely beaten a group of them in London. In that group was Edward Byllynge, a past officer in Cromwell's army, who was now publicly expressing new political ideas as a very active Quaker.[2]

In Parliament, the traditionalists' ideas won out and preparations began for the re-establishment of the Church of England. In the summer of 1660 Charles II was returned to the English throne from exile in The Netherlands. Puritan ministers were removed from the churches and their places taken by priests.

King Charles II returned to London with his brother James, the Duke of York. He had expressed sympathy for toleration of the religious non-conformists in his Declaration of October 1660. While the legislative act prepared for Parliament had included a proviso for religious toleration for Catholics and Quakers, political circumstances did not allow for the passage of this act into law.[3]

On January 7, 1660/1 an uprising of the so-called Fifth Monarchy Men spread fear into the citizenry of London, ending any further thought of toleration of non-conformist religions. On Thursday, January 10, 1660/1 a proclamation was issued forbidding meetings of Quakers, Fifth Monarchy Men and Anababtists. Even though the Quakers had not been involved in the uprising, they were included in the restriction.[4] London Mayor Richard Brown swiftly imprisoned all Quakers who attended meetings for worship in London. He continued their imprisonment in Newgate Prison despite the strong statements of protest by George Fox reminding authorities of the fact that Quakers practiced non-violence, and that they did not fight with "outward weapons."[5]

During the early 1660s William, Thomas, and Esther Biddle were jailed in Newgate Prison in London, remaining there for several months. Among other Quakers jailed with them were a number of people (or their relatives) with whom William would associate later in his lifetime. These included Thomas Hooton, Henry Salter, Francis Collins, William Harding, John Hinde, Thomas Mathews and Christopher White.[6]

Charles II and his council, dominated by Parliament and led by Lord Clarendon, continued to pass legislation that assured the re-establishment of a strong conformist Church of England, purged of Puritan influences. The first of these laws was the Corporation Act of 1661, which made it necessary for all officials and members of municipalities to take an oath based on the sacraments of the Church of England. Because of their beliefs, this act excluded the Quakers from their rights as Englishmen in all of the municipalities of England.[7]

An almost identical act, The Quaker Act, was passed on May 2, 1662. It sought out Quakers who would not take oaths and it prohibited more than five Quakers from meeting together outside of their homes for religious purposes. This act gave London officials the right to disrupt meetings and to destroy the public meetinghouses of the Quakers; they could also arrest the worshippers. The brutalities and arrests which followed the passage of this act, including some at the Bull and Mouth Meetinghouse (where Esther attended Meetings for Worship) are well recorded, for the Quaker leaders saw to it that each of the sufferings of the Quakers was accurately described and preserved in minute books.[8]

The second major act of persecution, the Act of Uniformity, passed by Parliament on May 19, 1662, established the supremacy of the Book of Common Prayer. This act reversed the efforts of John Milton in his plea for freedom of the press, and diminished any freedom that might have existed to publish religious books and pamphlets.[9]

The Conventicle Act, passed in 1664 and renewed in 1670, again limited all non-conformist religious meetings of more than five people. In 1665 Parliament carried the restrictions further by passing the Five Mile Act which prevented non-conformist clergy and schoolmasters from practicing their professions within five miles of their previously assigned parishes or work locations. This act particularly disrupted the gains of the Puritans in religious educational institutions in England.[10]

The return of the sovereign, the Acts of Parliament, and the dominance of the Church of England were not enough to fully suppress the influence of Puritanism on England.

London continued as a highly sophisticated capitol city. The art and literature of the world were available to its citizens. The city had an active theater schedule, partially supported by the royal family, with performances of works of English origin, including the plays of William Shakespeare, as well as those of foreign playwrights. For people who could afford it there were many inns and restaurants for dining out. There was even a gaming house, the equivalent of a gambling casino. Intellectuals were stimulated by the formation of the Royal Society, where such diverse persons as Sir Isaac Newton, Thomas Sydenham, John Locke, Christopher Wren and others would gather to present their ideas and the results of their experiments. London, as recorded by Samuel Pepys, was an exciting city.[11]

The Quaker community of London was excluded from the social and intellectual glamour of the city, but largely by choice. These people preferred the simple, industrious life that they had created for themselves.

They were deprived of their rights as Englishmen by the acts of Parliament. They defended themselves by non-violent protest, and they persisted in expressing and living by their convictions. They also continued to demonstrate their displeasure of the authorities, including the Crown, whenever opportunity arose.

An excellent communication system developed among Quakers throughout England, as their traveling ministers continued to visit meeting groups. Highly industrious and well-trained in trades, many became prosperous and the financial stature of the Quaker community began to reflect this success. As Friends were banished from England to Barbados and Jamaica, overseas markets developed, and a group of mariners emerged who were either Quakers, or sympathetic to the Quaker movement. As this unique religious community gained strength, Quakerism began to make its mark on both England and the New World

William, Thomas, and Esther Biddle found themselves in the midst of this network of communication and trade. Four boys were born to Thomas and Esther starting in 1660, but only one of the children lived to adult life — Benjamin, born on September 7, 1663.[12] William stayed in close contact with Thomas and Esther, but sometime after his apprenticeship ended he moved from their home and took up residence on Bishopsgate Street Without, a neighborhood heavily populated by Quakers.[13]

The Quakers were especially interested in the colonization of America. Their mariners carried traveling Quaker ministers to America on their trips to trade with the islands — Barbados, Jamaica and Bermuda — settled by banished Quakers. These ministers delivered the message of Quakerism effectively in America, and a number of small Quaker communities were founded in the colonies, including towns in Massachusetts, Rhode Island, New York, New Jersey, Maryland and Virginia.

These scattered American Quaker communities were at times subjected to religious persecution. The extreme occurred in Boston in 1660 and 1661 when four Quaker martyrs (one of them Mary Barrett Dyer) suffered death by hanging for their religious convictions.[15] Although the Massachusetts Bay Colony had been founded by people seeking religious freedom, its leaders were now practicing persecution as dire as any they had fled in England. The Quakers thereby learned an early lesson about the continuing need to preserve religious toleration for all faiths.

Those Friends in England who were beginning to think about founding a Quaker colony in America took careful note of the persecution and tragedy in Massachusetts. A few London Quakers went so far as to commission Josiah Coale in 1660 to travel to the lands of the Susquehanna

Indians to attempt to purchase land from them. The mission was unsuccessful.[16]

But Quakers in England were still hoping for reform in the government there. In 1659 Edward Byllynge wrote a pamphlet entitled *A Mite of Affection*, in which he advocated a number of government reforms.[17] George Fox wrote a letter in 1660 to both houses of Parliament, proposing a number of reforms in government, such as speedy trials, proper qualifications for all persons bearing office, simplification of laws so that they could be understood by the common man, and of course religious toleration.[18] At this early point in the founding of their religion, Quaker leaders were already beginning to develop ideas for an experiment in government, a plan and a project that would take many more years to fully work out and implement.

The conflicts that were taking place between the Dutch and the English over ownership of lands in America were particularly interesting to the Quakers. The Dutch controlled New Amsterdam, but the English claimed ownership based on the discoveries of Sebastian Cabot in 1497. On March 12, 1663/4 Charles II granted to his brother James, Duke of York, a royal patent for lands extending from Connecticut to Maryland. On June 24, 1664 James, Duke of York, granted to John, Lord Berkeley and Sir George Carteret, members of the Privy Council and loyal friends of the Stuart rulers during the years of civil war, the territory that now comprises New Jersey.

Later, on September 7, 1664, the English fleet took control of New York and all of the Dutch claims in America. During this period of time Admiral Penn accomplished victories on the seas that left King Charles II indebted to him — a debt that was subsequently collected by the Admiral's son, William Penn, in the form of a grant for the lands of Pennsylvania.

During this time the Carolina Provinces were also established. Berkeley and Carteret were included in these grants as well. Constitutions were developed for the Carolina territories with the aid of John Locke. A constitution was written also for the Carteret half of the New Jersey territory, called *Nova Caesaria*.

William Biddle meanwhile was still living in London, presumably employed in his trade, perhaps having become self-employed. He undoubtedly gave assistance to Thomas in his business, for due to the multiple arrests of Esther and Thomas and the seizure of their possessions, their business was beginning to suffer losses. They all remained under the threat of persecution, fine and imprisonment.

William was not imprisoned again, but many of his friends were victims of the persecution. They were fined for attending religious meetings, or for failure to pay tithes to the Church of England, or for refusing to take an oath when requested by a justice. Percivale Towle of nearby Radcliffe Meeting was imprisoned in 1663 for refusing to give "hat service" to Alderman Richard Brown.[19]

The laws were so written that informers would receive a reasonable portion of a fine. Therefore, Friends were placed at the mercy of the informers, some of whom would give false information to the officials so that they might profit from their testimony. Quakers persisting in their beliefs and fined or imprisoned multiple times were subjected to "praemuniring," the loss of estate and the loss of rights as an Englishman. They were also subject to banishment from England, and were usually deported to Barbados or Jamaica where Quaker colonies were subsequently developed. William apparently escaped serious harm to himself or his possessions during this time, while he was living and working in the midst of the Quaker community of London.

As if the sufferings from religious persecution were not enough, a natural disaster, the plague, struck London in April 1665, affecting everyone who lived in London. It killed a peak total of 10,000 Londoners in one week in August 1665, but had subsided by January 1665/6.[20]

It is uncertain if William remained in London during the epidemic, or if he traveled back to Birlingham to stay with his family in that safer rural setting. He certainly learned about the high risk of disease that could exist in a crowded city. Thomas and Esther personally felt the impact of the plague, for some of the men who worked for them contracted the disease, and their servant, Elizabeth, died of the disease on September 14, 1665.[21]

CHAPTER 4

Marriage to Sarah Kempe 1665/6

In February 1665/6, one month after the plague subsided, William Biddle, aged 32, and Sarah (Smith) Kempe, a widow aged 27, married each other in a Quaker wedding ceremony at the Friends Meetinghouse on Westbury Street, Spitalfield, London.[1]

Westbury Street was also known as Quaker Street because of the unusually large number of Friends who resided in that area. The Westbury Meetinghouse, also sometimes referred to as the Wheeler Street Meetinghouse, was a public meetinghouse of the Friends that was particularly abused during the years of religious persecution. It was also a common site for weddings of Friends in the 1660s. Thomas Stokes and Mary Bernard were married there on December 30, 1668, and another friend of William and Sarah's, Henry Salter, had married widow Hannah Stringer there on August 3, 1666.[2] Both couples would remain associated with William and Sarah in future years.

The wedding certificate indicates that among the Friends present as witnesses to the ceremony were Thomas Biddle the cordwainer, William's previous apprentice master, Thomas Taylor, presumably the husband of William's sister Jane and James Wasse, chirurgeon, of London, who would be involved later with matters concerning West Jersey.[3]

William's wife, Sarah (Smith) Kempe had been baptized February 11, 1637/8 in the parish of St. Botolph, Bishopsgate, London, a daughter of John and Anne (Wright) Smith. She had an older sister, Frances, who was baptized on December 5, 1626 and married Edward Bigley in 1649. John Smith, Sarah's father, was a member of the Cooks' Company of London, a trade that qualified one to prepare and sell cooked foods, such as keepers of inns, restaurants and victual houses. Sarah's mother died in 1644. Her father remarried, to Elizabeth Ellis in 1646, but he died in 1647, leaving Sarah, aged nine, under the care of her stepmother. Sarah may have lived with the Ellis family until she married.[4]

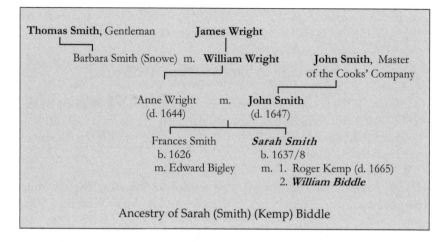

Thomas Smith, Gentleman   James Wright

Barbara Smith (Snowe) m. William Wright   John Smith, Master
                                                  of the Cooks' Company

Anne Wright   m.   John Smith
(d. 1644)   (d. 1647)

Frances Smith   *Sarah Smith*
b. 1626   b. 1637/8
m. Edward Bigley   m. 1. Roger Kemp (d. 1665)
                          2. *William Biddle*

Ancestry of Sarah (Smith) (Kemp) Biddle

Wright of Marbury, Cheshire. Her maternal grandmother was Barbara Smith, daughter of Thomas Smith of Henley-on-Thames, County Oxford, Gentleman.[5]

Sarah apparently inherited the majority of her parent's estates. This would have included perhaps several hundred pounds of currency and two houses: a smaller one near Bishopsgate Street (within the City of London) and a larger one on Bishopsgate Street Without (the same street as it extended beyond the City walls). The latter was perhaps the site of an inn operated by her father, John Smith.[6]

At age eighteen, on November 24, 1656, Sarah had married Roger Kempe, weaver, a man who was probably then about sixty years of age. The marriage was a civil ceremony, in the manner of the Puritans. Presumably both parties to the marriage were religious non-conformists at that time. Roger Kemp died April 12, 1665, before the onset of the plague. He died intestate (without a will) and Sarah Kemp administered the estate.[7]

When Sarah Kempe became a Quaker is unknown, but it may have been before the death of her first husband. While there are no Kempe family members known to have lived in Northampton, a Sarah Kemp was imprisoned in that town in 1663 for attending a meeting of Quakers at the home of Daniel Wills.[8] Sarah may have joined the Friends and she may have been an active and traveling member before her marriage to William.

The couple resided on Bishopsgate Street Without after the wedding, presumably in the larger of the two homes owned by Sarah. This home was between the Spittle, the hospital on Bishopsgate Street, and White Gate Alley (Widegate Street), sites that are about half a mile apart. The home was apparently among the more luxurious on the street, as it was found to have six hearths on the Hearth Tax Roll of 1668.[9] Undoubtedly it was larger than needed by William and Sarah, so there were probably additional uses for the dwelling, such as lodgings for travelers, offices for businesses, or shops for trades.

Sarah had entered this marriage at age twenty-seven, an orphan, a widow, and financially secure by her inheritances. Now that she had become a Quaker, her possessions were subject to seizure by the authorities. In an attempt to at least partially protect her possessions, Sarah left the house registered in her previous name, Sarah Kempe.[10]

On Sunday, September 2, 1666 the Great Fire of London began, completing its destruction by September 7, 1666. The home of Sarah and William was spared, for the fire did not extend beyond the city wall at Bishopsgate Street.

Thomas and Esther were less fortunate, and their home and many possessions were lost to the fire.[11] They moved their residence across the Thames to the parish of St. Mary Magdalen, in Bermondsey, Southwark, Surrey. Joseph, Edward and John Biddle lived nearby.

The Friends' main Meetinghouse, the Bull and Mouth Meetinghouse at Aldersgate, was lost in the fire. An alternate site for a meetinghouse was immediately sought and the site chosen was the old Devonshire Manor house on Bishopsgate Street, very near to the home of William and Sarah Biddle. All of the most important business of the religion was now to be conducted from that new meetinghouse. William and Sarah began to attend meetings for worship at Devonshire Meetinghouse.

CHAPTER 5

Strengthening Quakerism, Family, Inheritance, Planning for a Quaker Province in America 1666-1676

Until this time the growth of the Quaker movement was still very dependent upon the Publishers of the Truth, the traveling Quaker ministers. There were unconnected meetings for worship throughout England and beyond, with very little central organization to the religion. There was the Two Weeks Meeting of London, from which emanated most of the decisions on policy for the Friends, but there was a need for a system that would link the scattered congregations. There had also been several episodes of internal disagreement that had weakened the religion. The loss of meetinghouses in the Great Fire of London, and the destruction of meetinghouses by the persecuting civil authorities had further weakened Quakerism.

Simultaneously though, the religious movement was strengthened by the continuing convincement of Englishmen, urban and rural, not only of the lower classes, but also some from the propertied and professional classes. The spirit of those who were already convinced and practicing Quakerism, their industriousness and their ability to stand by their principles and beliefs, was an example that encouraged the convincement of others. It also earned Quakerism the respect and understanding of many other people in England. The result was that while the Society of Friends was continuing to grow in strength and numbers, a more formal degree of organization had to be developed to allow it to grow properly.

George Fox had recognized this need. In 1667 he called for the formation of "Monthly Meetings," groups of Friends who would gather at regular intervals for worship and for business. Instead of offering a central board of leadership, Fox left most of the power and decision-making to these local meetings.[1] Locations where Friends gathered regularly for worship became designated as Monthly Meetings. Many of these meetings were founded throughout England, both in cities and in rural areas. Each of the Friends gifted with the ability to be ministers, including the remaining Publishers of the Truth, became associated with one of these Monthly Meetings. Because of this closer association of the ministers with a particular group, there was much less traveling ministry.

Regular business meetings were also established in the monthly meetings to oversee the needs of Friends in each jurisdiction. The business meetings were held in a meeting for worship and they addressed the needs of the poor, the persecuted, the widowed, the orphaned and any others of their members in need of their help. These meetings created a sense of discipline in the membership, encouraging Friends to stay by the "Truth."

In London, five Monthly Meetings were established and the Two Weeks Meeting was continued. The latter group continued its prestigious role as the guardian of the religion.[2] It was attended irregularly by all of those persons in leadership positions in the religion. Devonshire House became one of the five London monthly meetings and George Whithead became its principal minister.

An even greater degree of organization was needed and in 1667 George Fox established Quarterly Meetings[3] in each shire or county to tie together the numerous monthly meetings located throughout England. They were attended by a few appointed representatives from each of the monthly meetings as well as by others who would be appropriate to the business of the meetings. The quarterly meetings were designed to be attended by the most "seasoned and weighty" Friends who would understand the religious tenets and the business needs of the Religious Society of Friends and who would apply themselves to the advancement of the movement and the preservation of its ideals.

Whenever possible, general meetings were held and attended by Friends from all of England and beyond. The first Yearly Meeting called for worship and business was held in London in 1668.[4] This Yearly Meeting was attended by representatives appointed by the Quarterly Meetings and others whose presence was needed to complete the business of the meeting. These "representative" Yearly Meetings were designed to have a limited attendance, for the Conventicle Act would not allow a large congregation of Friends without fear of arrest.

In spite of the creation of this formal organization, there was not a single committee of leadership. The composition of the monthly, quarterly and yearly meetings would vary with each meeting. This practice allowed the development of a new, informed generation of participating leaders, especially in rural areas, and gave all Friends an equal opportunity. Such Friends as Thomas Ollive, Daniel Wills, Samuel Jennings, John Kinsey, George Hutcheson, Mahlon Stacy and many others were able to find expression of their ideas and a meaningful involvement in the religion despite the fact that they did not live in London. The associations of Friends from all over England in these meetings led to a strengthening of the informal communication channels that had evolved among Friends.

The decisions reached in these meetings were agreed upon by consensus, or if necessary by the "sense of the meeting," with those not in favor of the decision agreeing not to "stand in the way" of others. Those who attended the meetings could discuss each matter with the understanding that there was complete freedom of discussion and debate, but the decision must abide by the "Truth" of the religion and Christianity, and it must consider and respect the needs and rights of all of those who would be affected by the decision. Besides practicing democracy in their religious meetings for worship, the Quakers had developed a system of representative democracy in their business meetings.

After their marriage in 1665/6 William and Sarah had taken up residence in the large home owned by Sarah on Bishopsgate Street Without, in a neighborhood heavily populated by Quakers and located near the Devonshire House Monthly Meeting, the site of most of the important business of the Quakers. William and Sarah had switched their attendance from the Westbury Monthly Meeting to the Devonshire House Monthly Meeting for both worship and business meetings.

In this location William and Sarah were in association with the principal Quaker merchants, shopkeepers, tradesmen and bankers or goldsmiths of London. Living in this center of Quakerism, they undoubtedly learned quickly about each new idea and thought that developed as the religion continued to grow. William is known to have attended one session of the prestigious Two Weeks Meeting,[5] and if the records had been preserved, it might be proven that he attended other sessions as well.

It was in this environment, which allowed the expression of new ideas created by the Quakers, that individuals like William Meade, a Quaker minister, could, with the help of such attorneys as Thomas Rudyard and Ellis Hooks, train himself well enough in the laws of England to be able to successfully defend himself with William Penn in court in later years.[6]

Sarah gave birth to the first child of the marriage in the summer of 1667, but this child, Sarah, died of teething on August 9, 1667. A second child, Elizabeth, was born on June 25, 1668. But while Sarah was pregnant with their third child, Elizabeth died of the griping on September 16, 1669. The third child, William Biddle, Jr., was born on December 4, 1669. His birth was followed by that of John on December 27, 1670 and then by Joseph on February 6, 1672.[7]

In the spring of 1672 Edward Biddle of Birlingham, William's father, died. His will, drawn up on December 9, 1670, was proved on May 11, 1672. It had been signed by only his mark, but it was witnessed by the signature of his wife, Penelope, who was named as sole executrix. As expected, Edward's real estate holdings were left to his oldest son, Thomas.

Penelope would retain one-half of his estate during her lifetime, but upon her death her half of the estate, plus the bed and coffer which had belonged to Edward's brother Thomas, would be passed on to the eldest son, Thomas. William's legacy was only ten shillings, and William Jr., received two of his grandfather's best lambs.[8]

Edward in his will left William's siblings Jane, Joseph and Edmund, only ten shillings each; these children, like William, had undoubtedly been provided for through apprenticeships or, in Jane's case, a gift at the time of marriage. Another daughter, Mary, not mentioned in the will, was apparently deceased at that time. Daughter Elizabeth (Biddle) Stone was to receive ten pounds upon the death of her husband, and Thomas Stone, Edward's oldest grandson, was left five pounds to pay for an apprenticeship upon his thirteenth birthday. Richard the youngest son, by then twenty-five years old, received ten pounds from his father. He died sometime before 1684 leaving behind a widow, a daughter, Jane and a son whose name is not known.[9]

Intolerance of non-conformist religions continued in England with no sign of relief. The Conventicle Act had been renewed and strengthened by Parliament in 1670. The Westbury Meetinghouse, where William and Sarah had been married, continued to receive abuse from the persecutors. On November 13, 1670, 41 persons were taken from that meetinghouse and placed in Newgate Prison. Among those arrested were Henry Wills, Henry Salter, John Budd, John Day and Samuel Coles, all friends of William and Sarah.[10] The following month two Friends, Francis Collins and Percivale Towle, were fined for attending meetings for worship at the Ratcliffe Meetinghouse.[11]

By 1672 persecution of Quakers by the civil authorities for meeting together for worship had lessened. The Friends took advantage of this pause in religious persecution and held a Yearly Meeting which included a General Meeting for Worship in London, on May 29 and 30, 1672. The Meeting was held at the Devonshire House, London, attracting many rural Friends to London, and affording the London Friends the opportunity to meet with the rural leaders. At this Yearly Meeting a great deal of concern was expressed for those Friends overseas. A collection was made to assist those Friends, and Edward Man and Thomas Gibson of Bishopsgate Street, merchants, were appointed to see that the needed support was shipped to these distant Friends.[12]

The interest in Friends overseas had been reawakened by George Fox. The traveling ministers had successfully carried the message of Quakerism to America where scattered communities of Quakers had been formed. Barbados and Jamaica had become the homes of some of those Quakers banished from England under persecution. Other convinced Friends lived in Bermuda. George Fox felt the need to bring better order to these scattered Quaker communities. He commenced his trip from England on August 11, 1671.[13] When in Barbados he was first confronted with the problem of enslaving Negroes. He commented to those Quakers involved in slavery that he hoped that they would consider those persons enslaved as really being indentured, and that they would be given their freedom after a period of time.[14]

When the visit to Barbados and Jamaica was completed, George Fox traveled to Maryland where he met with Friends in their General Meeting. He then traveled northwards through the American territories through New Jersey and New York to Rhode Island, visiting the Quaker communities on the way.

Fox passed through the territory known as Nova Caesaria a second time on his return trip to Maryland, through the territory under the proprietary ownership of Sir George Carteret and John, Lord Berkeley. He found the Quaker settlement at Middletown, led by Richard Hartshorne, brother of Hugh Hartshorne of Devonshire House Monthly Meeting in London. Nearby was Shrewsbury, another Quaker community inhabited by a small number of Quakers including the families of Richard and Abigail Lippincott and Eliakim and Lydia Wardell. He found that the first Friends Meetinghouse in New Jersey was under construction in Shrewsbury.

As George Fox and his party traveled further through the Berkeley portion of New Jersey, they noted that this territory was still uninhabited except for the Indians. It was still almost entirely in its original wilderness state. This was not unexpected, for John, Lord Berkeley, a land soldier, probably had neither the resources or skills to settle this undeveloped part of New Jersey. Only a few Dutch and Swedes had shown an interest in settling any part of this territory.[15]

George Fox continued his journey back to Maryland and after a short trip to Virginia and the Carolina territory he returned to Maryland and departed for England. When he arrived there on June 28, 1673, he was too late to attend the Yearly Meeting of Friends held in London May 20 and 21, 1673. At these meetings the subject of Friends overseas was again discussed, and it was decided to print and send books to Friends of England, Wales, Scotland, Ireland and overseas. Only books that were approved by the "censorship committee" of the meeting would be sent.[17]

Upon his return to England, and before he was imprisoned again for expressing his religious beliefs, George Fox was able to meet with some of the Quaker leaders, particularly William Penn. During the meetings, Fox's observations regarding the Quaker activities in America and the wilderness state of the territory he had visited rekindled the idea of developing a Quaker settlement there. William Penn already had some knowledge of the land in that region, for he had been accompanied by Josiah Coale on a carriage ride from Bristol to London in December 1667.[18] Coale would have told Penn of his efforts to purchase lands from the Susquehanna Indians that had inspired others to develop a Quaker settlement in 1660. The idea of developing a new Quaker territory and government had existed since 1659 and the concept was rapidly becoming a feasible project. However, any real excitement about such a plan had to be suppressed when the Dutch recaptured New Amsterdam on August 1, 1673.

William and Sarah were probably aware of the possibility of the development of a new Quaker settlement and would have shared in the excitement that it must have created among Friends. However, their concentration on the matter was disrupted by the serious illness of John, aged two, who died on September 27, 1673 of smallpox.[19]

During this time the Quakers of London were subjected to additional forms of religious injustice and persecution. The Church of England needed funds to rebuild London churches that had been destroyed by the Great Fire. Church officials, with the agreement of the civil authorities, assessed all persons of each neighborhood to raise funds to rebuild the churches and to support priests for them. All were taxed, including the Quakers and other so-called Non-Conformists who did not attend Anglican services.

Friends of London refused to pay this unjust tax. Constables, backed by the magistrates, allowed the church officials or their agents to enter the homes of the Quakers to confiscate their possessions. These valuables were then taken to the local alehouses and auctioned off for the amount of the church assessment. Many times the possessions taken were of greater value than the assessment and were sold for less than their real market value. If money in excess of the church tax was obtained, it was seldom returned to the Quaker owner.[20]

No matter how well organized the Quaker movement was, the Quakers of London were now subject to this additional threat of loss of property. Little could be done except to record the injustices, which they did through Meetings for Sufferings that they held weekly, usually at Devonshire House. These records of atrocities were presented to the civil authorities whenever the opportunity arose.

On February 9, 1673/4 the English and the Dutch settled their differences over their American colonies with the Treaty of Westminster, placing the ownership of what became New York and New Jersey back in the hands of the English Crown. Even before the English ownership or proprietary rights could be reaffirmed, Edward Byllynge discovered that John, Lord Berkeley wanted to sell his interests in the New Jersey territory. Byllynge, in trouble financially, allied himself with another Quaker, John Fenwick, and the Berkeley rights were bought by Fenwick from Berkeley, for Edward Byllynge, for £1000. The indenture was signed on March 18, 1673/4.

In seizing this opportunity, Byllynge and Fenwick had begun the process of establishing title to this large territory where the Quakers could settle, relatively free from religious persecution. Moreover, at least in the mind of Edward Byllynge, this was a place where new ideas concerning reforms in government might be able to be practiced.

Undoubtedly this furthering of the developing Quaker dream was discussed by all English Quakers when Yearly Meeting was held in London on June 10, 1674.[21] There were many problems involved in the Friends' claim to ownership of the Berkeley part of New Jersey, but now plans could begin.

During this time the Biddle home on Bishopsgate Street Without was again disrupted by tragedy. In the spring of 1674, Joseph, only fourteen months old, contracted measles and died on April 8, 1674. He was buried with his siblings at Chequer Alley, a Friends burial ground.[22] Of William and Sarah's five children, only William Jr. (now a little over four years of age), remained alive. Though the parents continued their activities in both business and religion, they now understood only too well the problems of living in the crowded city.

During this period William and Sarah worshipped with Friends of their area at the Devonshire House Monthly Meeting. Devonshire House was spared from the most vehement abuse by persecutors, making it possible for most Quakers of that area to worship there on First Day. It is not certain why, but the government did allow many of the most important meetings of the Quakers to take place. Perhaps it was because there were activities by other religions and business interests occurring simultaneously in the same manor house.[23]

Realizing the importance of education to their children, the Devonshire Monthly Meeting established a school for the children of "poor" Friends, a non "Latin" school, where the basic educational needs of all of the children of Friends could be met.[24]

Another event which aided the Quakers in establishing their claim to the New Jersey land occurred when Charles II, on June 29, 1674, reconfirmed by an indenture his grant of the lands to his brother James, Duke of York. On July 29,1674 James, Duke of York reconfirmed the grant of the Cartaret portion of the New Jersey territory, but he did not reconfirm the title of John, Lord Berkeley in the original indenture. At this time the unofficial boundary between the portions of the New Jersey territory was a line between Barnegat Bay on the Atlantic Ocean and the mouth of the Pennsauken Creek on the Delaware River.[25] This new division line significantly reduced the amount of land in the Berkeley portion of New Jersey. This boundary would have to be addressed by the Quakers with Carteret.

The claim to title was clouded further by the fact that Edward Byllynge and John Fenwick became involved in a bitter disagreement over who owned the rights to the land, if their claim could be proven. Byllynge was already deeply in debt — a debt he claimed was due to the expensive habits of his wife, but which probably reflected as well his own free-spending.[26] Many of his debts may have been owed to other Quakers, and those that were not purchased by the Quakers to protect Byllynge and his claim to the proprietary rights to the New Jersey territory.

These Quaker creditors became increasingly worried about the status of the claim to the New Jersey territory. In order to settle the dispute between the two Quaker claimants, William Penn was requested to arbitrate the differences between Byllynge and Fenwick. He was able to help them reach an agreement.

The Tripartite Agreement, an indenture, was signed February 10, 1674/5. By that agreement, the territorial rights were divided into one hundred shares and John Fenwick settled for ownership of ten of these shares and a payment from Byllynge of £400. The money for this payment was raised by William Penn and two others, Nicholas Lucas and Gawen Lawrie, who, with Penn, were appointed as trustees for the interests of Edward Byllynge. Thus began a trusteeship that was to continue until Byllynge's financial affairs were restored to proper order.[27]

It is very likely that during this time William and Sarah, along with other Quakers, became creditors of Edward Byllynge and felt that their loan would entitle them to part of the ownership of the rights of the territory, if the title could be cleared. Acting as a group, Quakers proceeded to make their dream of a Quaker settlement in America become a reality.

Undoubtedly ideas were more completely formulated during the Yearly Meeting of Friends held at Devonshire House, London, on June 4, 1675.[28] It was then and afterwards that John Fenwick, believing that he had clear title to one-tenth of the land, began to sell parcels of it to Quakers at the rate of £5 per 1,000 acres. By July it was apparent that Fenwick was also in financial difficulty. He signed an indenture July 17, 1675, mortgaging his remaining interests in the New Jersey territory to John Edridge of

Middlesex, who was also a member of the Devonshire House Monthly Meeting, and Edmund Warner of London.[29]

John Fenwick did not understand the overall plan to develop a constitution for the territory for the protection of the settlers, nor did he seem to fully understand that his title might be in question if the claim to the land was not strengthened. He arranged for the transportation of settlers to the new land and he settled a colony there at Salem, in the southern portion of the territory, on November 23, 1675.[30] Fenwick continued to sell lands even after his arrival in Salem. Richard Lippincott from Shrewsbury, many miles to the north, apparently traveled to Salem to purchase 1,000 acres from Fenwick on August 16, 1676.[31]

In all it was estimated that John Fenwick had sold as much as 150,000 acres of his land.[32] Since this property was located safely within the territory that had been assigned originally to John, Lord Berkeley, it was unlikely that Sir George Carteret would try to dispute these purchasers' rights to that land in the Salem Colony.

In the meantime the civil authorities in England had decided to reinforce the Conventicle Acts, creating a problem that Quakers needed to discuss and, if possible, bring under control. On October 18, 1675 a meeting was held to address this issue. Among other actions and decisions taken at the meeting, free legal counsel and training were offered to all Friends by Thomas Rudyard and Ellis Hooks, thus furthering the efforts of the Quakers to become well versed in English law.[33]

In the spring of 1676 another meeting was held with representatives from all of the Quarterly Meetings. Thomas Ollive came to London for this meeting as a representative from Northamptonshire. The sufferings of Friends were presented to representatives of the Crown as a result of this meeting,[34] but persecution for religious principals continued. This was very likely a topic discussed at the Yearly Meeting for Friends held in London on May 17, 1676.[35]

The members of the Byllynge trusteeship in London continued to attend to their duties skillfully. Under the leadership of William Penn, steps were taken to perfect the title to the New Jersey territory. On June 19, 1676 the trustees purchased John Fenwick's mortgage from Edridge and Warner for £205.[36] Then, holding all of the rights originally in the possession of John, Lord Berkeley, they set out to negotiate with Sir George Carteret for a suitable division line between the two portions of the New Jersey territory.

On July 1, 1676 the Quintipartite Agreement was written and signed by all parties. Cleverly, this agreement made a diagonal boundary line across the New Jersey territory, necessarily including some of the territory that James, Duke of York had regranted to Sir George Carteret, and in this way legitimatizing the Berkeley grant. The boundary, which was to run from the east side of Little Egg Harbor to the point on the Delaware River at latitude 41 degrees 40 minutes, would give over one-half of the land mass to the newly-formed West New Jersey territory.[37]

The division established a territory with good farmlands and good forests, having both mountains and access to the sea. Moreover, it provided the opportunity to control shipping up the Delaware River. The agreement did more to improve the claim of the territory than had been thought possible. This clever set of negotiations must be credited to William Penn, who engineered the Quaker claim into this favorable position.

The way was now clear for the development of a claim to the governing rights to the territory. The entire Quaker dream for a province included the development of a system of government, a system in which the people would have a chance to govern themselves and to determine their own destinies.

CHAPTER 6

The Concessions and Agreements of West New Jersey

The establishment of a settlement of Friends in America was not the most important goal of the religious Quakers. They were interested in founding an area that would be self governing and in which major reforms in government could be introduced. From this unlikely group — non-conformist in religion, dress, speech and thought — ideas on reform in government that incorporated the concept of democracy were taking shape.

Quaker leaders including George Fox, Edward Byllynge and William Penn had written and spoken about reforms in both government and in the English judicial system. Their ideas had been expressed in London at a time when a search for new ideas was prevalent among the intelligentsia there. Those meeting with the Royal Society in London, including John Locke, were striving to find new systems; even these academic leaders may have added thoughts and encouragement to the Quaker plan. Now it was time to establish an experimental government that included these reforms so that they could demonstrate to their critics that their ideas could succeed.

By August 6, 1676 a constitution was written: "The Concessions and Agreements of the Proprietors, Freeholders and Inhabitants of the Province of West New Jersey in America."[1] The document represented an attempt to establish a government in which the power resided with the people,[2] and which provided a unique framework for a truly representative democracy. The government that was established under this constitution in West New Jersey would also provide its citizens with a guide for economic and social democracy.

It is uncertain who the actual author of the Concessions and Agreements was. The ideas and the style represented contributions by many people with differing backgrounds and skills. The principal author is thought to be that person most intimately involved in the formation of the province, and the first signer of the constitution, Edward Byllynge. His pamphlet, *A Mite of Affection*, published in 1659, contains many features in common with the Concessions and Agreements.[3] Ideas of the enlightened George Fox and William Penn, especially concerning the judicial system, are also found in the Concessions and Agreements. But the constitution and the plan to use it were clearly the practical result of the Quaker experience with persecution in England.

The Concessions and Agreements first divided the entire land mass of West Jersey into ten parts which were to represent "ten tribes of men." This procedure was similar to the division of Athens by Cleisthenes in about 500 B.C., when Greek democracy was formed. It is uncertain if the Greek experience in democracy is the source of this division into Tenths, or whether it had another basis.[4]

Even before the known date of the writing of the Concession and Agreements the proprietary shares and the rights of the province had been divided into one hundred shares by the Byllynge trustees on February 10, 1674/5. Continuing in very orderly fashion, the constitution required that each political subdivision, (each Tenth) would represent ten proprietary shares. All of the Tenths were to be surveyed and laid out after the native Indians were sufficiently informed of the plans of the settlers, and only after the lands had been purchased from the Indians.

When elections were held, a freeholder or a proprietor would be elected from each propriety in each Tenth, guaranteeing each Tenth ten representatives on the one hundred seat General Assembly of the province. In this way elected representation in the General Assembly would be evenly distributed geographically, preventing any one area of the province from dominating the others.[5]

This method of distribution introduced an additional new concept: the ownership of proprietary interests by one hundred or more persons, instead of a select group of people or a single individual. This concept of multiple small ownership of proprietary rights was never found acceptable by the English governing authorities, for it destroyed the traditional concept of proprietary government.

From the year of settlement, 1677, to March 25, 1680, the government was to be run by commissioners appointed by the trustees in England. The people of the province were to elect their own assemblymen on March 25, 1680, the first day of the year under the Julian calendar. The electorate consisted of all male inhabitants, freeholders and proprietors of the province. There would be no property or religious qualifications for the electorate as there were in England. Those elected must be drawn from the male freeholders or proprietors.

The elections would be held annually, by secret ballot. After the General Assembly was elected by the electorate in each propriety in each Tenth and convened, then the Assembly would elect the commissioners for the province. The Assembly would also elect the treasurer and the register, who was the keeper of the seal. The electorate of the proprieties and the Tenths would continue to elect their own justices and constables.

The commissioners elected by the General Assembly were to be "ten honest and able men," who would carry on the affairs of the province during adjournments of the Assembly. But all significant actions of these commissioners had to be referred back to the General Assembly for final vote. The commissioners were judges in the courts and were also responsible for regulating and laying out the lands of the province. As a result of the Quakers' strong reaction against the authoritarian system of government in England, there was initially no provision in the Concessions and Agreements for a single leader or governor in the planned structure of government. The power rested entirely in the elected General Assembly.[6] This was not an unusual situation in the formation of new democratic governments. When the first constitution of New Jersey was formed after the Revolutionary War, the Governor was given very little power.[7]

In the General Assembly all debates were to be held in private sessions, but votes were to be taken in public and the voting record of each member kept, in order that an elected public official might be held responsible to the electorate. The Assembly was presided over by a Chairman that the assemblymen elected from among themselves. The Chairman was to certify a quorum of fifty percent at each meeting, and to guarantee freedom of speech for each Assemblyman.

Elected representatives to the General Assembly were expected to represent the interests of their electors. And each assemblyman was to be paid one shilling per day during the sessions of the General Assembly, so that they would be known to be working for the people. All taxes were to be approved by the Assembly. All appeals of the courts were to come to the Assembly. The Assembly was to make all laws or changes in the laws for the province, providing that those laws did not violate the fundamentals of the Concessions and Agreements of the province, and provided that the laws were not contradictory to the laws of England. If an assemblyman offered or gave a "favor" to an elector, he was considered ineligible to sit on the Assembly or to hold any other office of public trust in the province for a period of seven years.[8]

The Concessions and Agreements guaranteed a number of rights to the individuals living in the province. The most important of these was, of course, freedom of conscience on matters concerning religion for all people, not just the Quakers. There was to be no religious persecution, such as that experienced by Quakers in Massachusetts. The churches were considered to be public houses, and were free from duty or taxes. All people were guaranteed freedom of access on all waterways leading from the ocean to any part of the province, a guarantee also granted to

Englishmen from the Magna Carta. And, freedom of access on all roadways in the province was also guaranteed.

To protect the property rights of the people, all surveys and property transactions as well as wills and inventories of estates were to be carefully registered and recorded. Property transactions, including those involving proprietary rights, were also to be recorded in duplicate in England. If a person had property legally surveyed and registered as his land and held it for seven years, then the land would no longer be subject to review or resurvey. There was no custom of common land, so each person was expected to provide pastureland for his own cattle, and no one could claim land because his cattle had made a habit of grazing on any particular site.[9]

No arrests were to be made without a summons that defined the charges and allowed reasonable time for a response. By application of these laws there were to be no searches of property without warrants. No person was to be deprived of life, liberty, or property without a trial by jury, and the accused had the opportunity to object to jurors chosen to hear their case. No person would be required to pay an attorney, for all people could plead their own causes if they so desired. No fees were to be paid to the keepers of the jail by any prisoner. The Concessions and Agreements were to be displayed to the public so that the people of the province would be fully aware of the laws of the land.[10] All courts were to be open to the public so that all persons in the province would be free from oppression and slavery.

Persons elected to positions of public trust were required to "subscribe" their names in a book indicating their intent to carry out their public duties responsibly. The subscription required that all people would be treated justly and equally. If an official did not act properly, penalties were applied, such as divestiture from office for his lifetime. Oaths based on religious sacraments were not required as they had been in England.[11]

Courts were established, and there were always to be three elected judges or justices on the bench. This avoided the unfairness experienced in England when single appointed justices had been able to make prejudiced or biased judgments. Every court had a jury of "twelve men of the neighborhood."[12] The jury was given the dominant role in the courtroom, an idea undoubtedly contributed by William Penn after his experience in the Penn-Meade trial of 1670, by which the role of the jury in the English courtroom was significantly altered.[13] Any person prosecuting another for any reason other than murder, treason, or felony could forgive the defendant before or after the court acted. If a trial involved an Indian as a plaintiff or defendant, the jury was to consist of six Indians and six men of the neighborhood.[14]

The criminal code of the province was in part dictated by the Concessions and Agreements. Burglary was to be punished by two-fold restitution. If offenders were unable to make restitution, they could be made to work to pay off the amount. There was no imprisonment for debt. Proof in all criminal and civil matters was to be by "averment" (affirmation) by at least two honest persons. The only capital crimes were murder and treason. The sentence and the manner of execution for those convicted of capital crimes had to be decided by the General Assembly. Any person found to bear false witness in the courtroom was dealt with severely, subjected to the sentence that would have been given to the individual against whom they had tried to bear false witness. This was clearly a reaction to the many false informers who had preyed on the Quakers in England.[15]

The democratic system of government developed by Quakers in the Concessions and Agreements was not a totally new creation. Rather, it was perhaps in part a rediscovery of an idea that was 2,100 years old and tried before in Greece. Those involved in its creation recognized that in many ways the governing and judicial systems of England were the most socially advanced and just systems available in the world to that time. In producing this constitution, they included what they considered the strengths of the English form of government, creating a new system which modified these strengths, made logical extensions and reforms to them, and added new ideas of their own.

"The Concessions and Agreements of the Proprietors, Freeholders and Inhabitants of West New Jersey in America" was the first "Quaker Experiment in Democracy," and the first "holy experiment" of the Quakers. It represented a strong, persuasive, pacifistic protest against the unjust features of the English governing and judicial systems. However, it was framed in a very positive and progressive manner. The Quakers created it and they intended to try to live by it to demonstrate to the world that it was a workable system.

When compared to the charters and constitutions of the other American colonies, including the "Frame of Government of Pennsylvania" created by William Penn five years later, The Concessions and Agreements of West New Jersey was more liberal, more inclusive of new ideas, and more fundamentally protective of individuals rights. It was a true attempt to establish a government "of the people, by the people, and for the people."

The Concessions and Agreements was never meant to be a governing document that would protect the rights of Quakers alone. It was designed for the protection and participation of all inhabitants of the West Jersey Province. West Jersey was not created as a theocracy. No other constitutional document was created again that was so comprehensive in defining individuals' rights until the creation of the Bill of Rights of the Constitution of the United States one hundred years later.

It was necessary to take this constitution to West Jersey as soon as possible, for due to the impatience of John Fenwick, other Friends were already settled in the Salem Colony. Though the land that they had settled upon was unlikely to be disputed as being part of the John, Lord Berkeley, territory, the local Governor of the Crown, Edmond Andros, in New York, had not recognized the right of the Salem settlers to govern themselves. They were therefore placed under the jurisdiction of the court of the Crown located across the Delaware River at Upland.

Upon completion of the Concessions and Agreements of West New Jersey, those Quakers in England most familiar with the formation and the meaning of the document signed it in London in August of 1676. Thirty-one Friends signed the first page of the document, including Edward Byllynge, the first signer, and the Byllynge trustees, William Penn, Gawen Lawrie and Nicholas Lucas. Thomas Rudyard, the attorney, was also one of the early signers. Daniel Wills, Thomas Ollive and William Biddle, who were committed to the project and apparently very familiar with all of the details, were the fifth, sixth and eighth signers of the constitution. Others who would be associated with them in the West Jersey Province also committed themselves to the experiment with their signatures at that time, including Percivale Towle, Thomas Budd, Samuel Jennings, Francis Collins, William Royden, William Emley, William Peachee, Thomas Lambert, Mahlon Stacy, Benjamin Scott, Thomas Hooton, Robert Stacy and Henry Stacy.[16]

On August 18, 1676 the Byllynge trustees commissioned three persons to inspect the lands for the future West Jersey settlement, planned for the following spring. Those commissioned were: Dr. James Wasse of London, Richard Guy, then of the Salem Colony in West Jersey, but originally of Stepney Parish, Middlesex, England, and Richard Hartshorne of Middletown, East Jersey, brother of Hugh Hartshorne of Devonshire House Monthly Meeting. Dr. Wasse was to be sent to West Jersey with supplies and with the copy of the Concessions and Agreements to familiarize the Salem settlers with its features and to encourage them to sign it too. William Haige was to arrange for the transportation of Dr. Wasse and the supplies in the ship of Samuel Groome.[17] Thus, definite plans for the settlement of West New Jersey under the new Concessions and Agreements of West New Jersey were well under way by mid-August of 1676, well before the first official Quaker settlers set sail from England to the new province.

CHAPTER 7

Promoting, Marketing and Settling
the West Jersey Province

From their vantage point in the midst of the Quaker community in London, William and Sarah must have been involved in the plans for the West Jersey Province. They were probably already creditors of Edward Byllynge or of the Byllynge trustees. They knew those Friends chosen as Settlement Commissioners. Richard Guy lived in nearby Stepney Parish,[1] Dr. James Wasse had attended their wedding,[2] and Richard Hartshorne was the brother of Hugh Hartshorne who attended meetings for worship with them at the Devonshire House Monthly Meeting.[3]

Information received by the Byllynge trustees from the commissioners would have been shared with all of the members of William and Sarah's Monthly Meeting. The plan of the trustees was to settle the land as far as possible up the Delaware River, so that the Shrewsbury and Middletown settlements of Friends would be within easy traveling distance.[4] However, settling a community that far above the mouth of the Pennsauken Creek would test the validity of the claim to the land defined by the division line between East and West New Jersey in the Quintiparte Agreement.

Promotional literature was initially prepared by the creditors of Edward Byllynge; later it was clarified and expanded by the Byllynge trustees. Documents distributed to Friends described the land and its potential for making a good living by farming or by trade. It was proposed to divide the territory into one hundred proprieties. The ninety shares in the possession of the Byllynge trustees were offered first to Quakers for purchase. The promotional efforts implied that the proprietary rights would include not only the land rights, but also the governing rights to the territory. It was emphasized that the Quakers should not immigrate to West Jersey simply to escape religious persecution.[5]

The Concessions and Agreements included enticements in the form of land grants to be given to people who decided to settle the new land early in its development. If a person was not able to buy proprietary rights, but had the approval of one of the proprietors and wanted to emigrate before April 1, 1677, he would be given seventy acres of land for himself, and an additional seventy acres of land for each able man servant and fifty acres of land for each weaker man servant or female over the age of fourteen. After the term of an indentured servant was completed, he or she was to be granted fifty acres of land for their own use.

In this way, the less wealthy Friends had a chance, from the earliest days of the planning of the settlement, to gain ownership of a fair portion of the territory for their labor. Under the Concessions and Agreements these granted lands were allowed to be attached by a "quitrent," in the manner of rural England, amounting to one penny per acre for town land and one halfpenny per acre for other land, payable to the proprietor who originally owned the land. However, the use of quitrents never was implemented in West Jersey.

The offer of land grants to early settlers was to continue for three years until April 1, 1679, with decreasing amounts of land offered and increasing amounts of quitrents charged in each year.[6] It was quite usual to offer an enticement to those who were willing to settle a wilderness territory. This system of land grants and incentives would place the ownership of the land in the hands of many, thereby increasing the number of freeholders in the province and guaranteeing that in three years' time there would be a large enough electorate to participate in the system of government specified in the Concessions and Agreements.

The inclusion in the Concessions and Agreements of the provision to continue the quitrent system in this province was probably the idea of more aristocratic and propertied Friends like William Penn and Edward Byllynge. The quitrent was in fact a vestige of feudalism in rural England, where land-owners for many more years continued to have their land and wealth subjected to this system of taxation. William Penn eventually charged quitrents on all of his proprietary lands in Pennsylvania.

At the time of the drafting of the Concessions and Agreements those Friends who would be the most intricately involved with the actual distribution of the land probably made no objection to the inclusion of these quitrent provisions. Many of them from farming backgrounds in rural England however, like William Biddle, viewed quitrents as a suppressive force that had been detrimental to their parents and grandparents. Therefore, when given the chance, the West Jersey Land Commissioners and proprietors eliminated the practice of attaching quitrents to their land sale transactions. In this manner the Quaker leaders involved in the settlement of the province added another unique feature to the Quaker experiment in democracy: they established the practice of all land transactions being completed in fee simple.

Next, the Byllynge trustees had to struggle with the financial aspects of the settlement of the province. They had agreed to oversee the chaos of the financial affairs of Edward Byllynge. They controlled the ninety proprietary shares that had been assigned to him, and they also controlled John Fenwick's ten shares, having purchased the mortgage that he made with Edridge and Warner. The actual status of these latter ten shares was too confusing for them to try to sell any interests related to them until more accounting work could be done. The trustees had to concentrate first on the Byllynge shares.

The trustees had incurred additional expenses against the account of Edward Byllynge. They had raised £400 to pay off John Fenwick, and £205 to purchase the Edridge-Warner mortgage. They had incurred further debt in the cost of preparing promotional materials and in transporting Dr. James Wasse to America and also for the supplies that they sent with him. They had to provide funds for the purchase of lands from the Indians and to pay for surveying portions of the territory. Presumably they had raised these funds from Friends by promising them proprietary shares and rights yet to be released from the account of Edward Byllynge.

In the fall of 1676 the Byllynge trustees decided to set the price of one proprietary share at £350. If they were successful in selling all of the ninety shares, they would be able to raise £31,500. Since the exact size of Edward Byllynge's debt is not known, it is uncertain how much money needed to raised before the trustees would be able to consider his affairs in order so that they could dismiss themselves. They began to release proprietary shares in August of 1676 and continued until September 27, 1683 when they turned over the remaining interests to Edward Byllynge, his debt presumably settled.[7] The trustees had released £10,500 worth of proprietary shares and rights by then for money owed to them by Byllynge, so it is likely that his debt was approximately that amount.[8]

Through the initial sales of full proprietary shares by the trustees, and the secondary sales of fractions of shares by these original West Jersey proprietors, there were more than one hundred and forty five proprietors of the province by February 14, 1687/88.[9]

The process of dividing up the proprietary rights to the land, which began with the Tripartite Agreement, was carried on by the Byllynge trustees and continued to be permitted under the Concessions and Agreements. The process, which totally changed the English concept of proprietary ownership — allowing land ownership in fee simple for many people with meager estates — was an important step towards economic democracy.

The trustees began to sell and assign proprietary shares and rights as early as August of 1676. The first transaction was made with William Haige by lease and release agreements of August 29 and 30, 1676, for one proprietary share.[10] Presumably the transaction was made in lieu of money to reimburse him for the expenses he had incurred in sending Dr. James Wasse to America with money and supplies.

The next transaction was with Thomas Hooton by agreements of lease and release of November 5 and 6, 1676, for one full proprietary share in satisfaction of the £350 owed to Thomas Hooton by Edward Byllynge.[11]

The next transactions involving the proprietary shares took place on January 22 and 23, 1676/7, at the offices of Thomas Rudyard in London where several Friends gathered to settle accounts with the Byllynge trustees. William Biddle was present with his friends Thomas Ollive, haberdasher from Willingborough in the County of Northampton, and Daniel Wills, practitioner in chemistry from Northampton. Together they received a full proprietary share, the agreement stating that the value of the share was £400, representing £133.6s.8p. that Edward Byllynge owed each of them. The indenture was witnessed by Harbert Springett (brother-in-law of William Penn), Benjamin Griffith, Thomas Rudyard, Thomas Boynett and Joseph Burley.[12] A later indenture dated April 4, 1677 modified the ownership of that proprietary share, specifying that William Biddle owned a "moiety" (half) of the share, and Thomas Ollive and Daniel Wills each owned one-quarter of the share.[13]

On January 22 and 23, 1676/7, other transactions took place in Thomas Rudyard's office. Thomas Ollive and Daniel Wills were granted an additional share together, each of them owning one-half, for £175 owed to them by Edward Byllynge.[14] Another share was released at the same time to six Friends in equal parts. The group, all from London, were Richard Mew, Percivale Towle and Nicholas Bell, all of Ratcliffe, Peter Hailes and Thomas Martin of Limehouse, and Richard Clayton of Bishopsgate Street.[15]

Between February 27, 1676/7 and March 2, 1676/7 nineteen more proprietary shares of the West Jersey Province were released by the trustees, each with a value of £350. By the time of the sailing of the first settlers on the ship *Kent* in the spring of 1677 approximately forty shares had been released by the trustees.[16] These included the ten shares assigned to John Fenwick, and an additional ten released to five Friends of Yorkshire: Joseph Helmsley, Thomas Pearson, George Hutcheson, Mahlon Stacy and Thomas Hutchinson, for a value of £3500 owed to them by Edward Byllynge.[17]

It is uncertain why the share released to William Biddle and his friends Thomas Ollive and Daniel Wills on January 23, 1676/7 was valued at £400, higher than any other share. It is interesting to speculate that this may have occurred as the result of a transaction two years prior to that time, on February 10, 1674/5, when a debt for exactly that amount was contracted by the Tripartite Agreement to buy out John Fenwick. It is possible that William, Thomas and Daniel may have agreed to pay for that transaction if it counted as their payment for a full proprietary share when the shares became available.

Any plan that William may have had of traveling to the West New Jersey Province was interrupted when Sarah, who had become pregnant again, had problems at the time of delivery. The infant died on January 29, 1676/7, only one hour old.[18]

On March 3, 1676/7 a final copy of the Concessions and Agreements was presented to Quakers living in England, and the signing of the document took place that day.[19] On March 4, 1676/7 George Fox addressed an epistle to Quakers in England who were the prospective first settlers of the West Jersey Province. In his message Fox recognized the commitment that these settlers had made to the Quaker experiment to guarantee its success. He encouraged them to remain loyal to their faith and their religious principles, "for the many eyes of other governments of Colonies will be upon you; yea, the Indians too see how you order your lives and conversations. And therefore let your lives and words and conversations be as becomes the Gospel." [20]

George Fox, with these words, set the tone and the spirit for the West Jersey Quaker experiment in democracy. Surely many Friends worshipped both silently and vocally with this subject on their minds when the Yearly Meeting of Friends was held the next day, March 5, 1676/7, in London at the rebuilt Bull and Mouth Meetinghouse.[21] Friends from all over England who were interested in playing a role in finalizing the plans for the transportation of settlers to West Jersey were gathered at those meetings.

In early April, 1677 William Biddle was again in contact with other investors in the proprietary shares of the West Jersey Province. On April 1, 1677, he purchased a one-quarter proprietary share from Joseph Helmsley and Thomas Pearson, two of the Yorkshire proprietors. This fraction of a share was purchased for £37.10s.[22] On April 4, 1677 William had the indenture of January 23, 1676/7 clarified before Daniel Wills and Thomas Ollive departed England.[23] By then Sarah and William had invested £237.10s. in proprietary shares of the West Jersey Province thus showing their resolve to participate in the venture. However, when it came time for the first settlers to depart from England for America, they were not yet prepared to go.

The ship *Kent* sailed from England in the spring of 1677 as scheduled, with 230 Quaker passengers, many of them known to William and Sarah including Thomas Ollive and his wife and Daniel Wills and his children. Those remaining in England and London would learn only slowly, by letters carried by returning ships, of the experiences of these first settlers. The Byllynge trustees had appointed eight of the passengers as commissioners as called for by the Concessions and Agreements. These included Thomas Ollive, Daniel Wills, John Kinsey, John Penford, Joseph Helmsley, Robert Stacy, Benjamin Scott and Thomas Foulke. Richard Guy of the Salem Colony was also appointed as a commissioner.[24] The commissioners were to lay out the lands and to govern until March 25, 1680 when the first elections were to be held in the province.

The commissioners on the *Kent* were aware of the difficulties that John Fenwick had previously encountered with Edmond Andros, Governor of the Crown, representing James, Duke of York. They also knew that their title to the rights to the territory was not perfect, for the Duke of York had not confirmed the sale to the Quakers. They showed good judgment and diplomacy by stopping at Sandy Hook, near Shrewsbury, East Jersey before completing their voyage to their new homeland. From this landing place they presented themselves and their plans to Governor Andros in New York. The governor had received no acknowledgment of their rights from England, but he allowed the appointed commissioners of the trustees to serve as his magistrates in their new settlement. However, he insisted that the court of their settlement be subservient to the court of the Crown at New Castle on the western bank of the Delaware River.[25]

The commissioners returned to the *Kent* and continued on to New Castle, where they were surprised by orders received there from Governor Andros. A five percent import tax had been imposed on the possessions of each of the settlers — a particular example of injustice against the Quakers as it was unusual for Englishmen to be taxed upon entering an English Colony, and especially unusual to be taxed on their personal possessions. Though the tax was unexpected and caused great concern among the early Quaker settlers, it was later used as an example of the unjustness of the governing authorities of England, thus helping the Quakers in their attempt to gain a stronger claim to the title of the West Jersey territory.

With the import tax paid, the settlers, with their remaining possessions, disembarked from the *Kent* on August 16, 1677, on the east bank of the Delaware River at Raccoon Creek. Though they had already received considerable information and advice about the West Jersey lands, it was not until they had spent several weeks inspecting the terrain themselves that they were prepared to decide where their town should be settled. A site was chosen far enough up the river to be within easy reach of the East Jersey settlements of Friends, as desired by the Byllynge trustees.

The leaders of the First and Second Tenths decided to form their town for both Tenths together, on a tract of land on the western shore of the Assiscunk Creek, located at the down-river end of Mattinunk Island in the Delaware River. After considerable debate, the town was called Burlington.

The town lands were actually an island as the tract was surrounded by a stream that entered the river on western side of the land and connected with the Assiscunk Creek, which bordered the tract on its eastern border all the way back to the river.

The settlers brought their possessions from the ship to Burlington Island. They began to identify places where they could make temporary shelters that would see them through the upcoming winter. The sails of the ship were used as tents, and some people found banks of the streams where they created caves to live in. The carpenters among them immediately set out to make log cabins. They also learned from the Swedes how to make a wooden frame, weave clapboards around it, and then seal it with clay to keep out the cold air. Collectively, they found many ways to get settled in their new town. Under a tent made of sails they were able to have their First Day Meeting for Worship for the first time without threat of persecution.

Beginning in September and October 1677 the commissioners, aided by the other settlers and the Swedes and the Dutch who already lived in the territory, began purchasing the lands of the upper four Tenths from the Indians. Four purchases of land were made, for territory that encompassed the land from the Assinpink Creek at the falls of the Delaware River to Oldman's Creek, extending inland to the headwaters of the boundary streams. The lower tract did not interfere with the lands of the Salem Colony of John Fenwick.[26]

Immediately after that business was accomplished, the First and Second Tenths boundaries were defined. Richard Noble, surveyor from the Salem Colony, laid out the center street of the town of Burlington from the river inland to the stream that surrounded the island town. This street, High Street, was to serve as the dividing line between the two upper Tenths. The lands of the First Tenth were to extend from High Street up the Delaware River to the mouth of the Assinpink Creek. The lands of the Second Tenth were to extend down the Delaware River to the mouth of the Pennsaukin Creek.

Richard Noble, assisted by the settlers who had been encouraged to come to the province by Daniel Wills and Thomas Ollive, such as William Matlack and George Elkinton, began to lay out the streets of the town. Broad Street, was formed perpendicular to High Street through the center of town, extending from the western bank of the Assiscunk Creek to the meadowlands along the stream that surrounded the town on its western edge. Another street, variously referred to as Second Street, Pearl Street, or River Street, was laid out along the Delaware River bank, perpendicular to High Street, bordering the south end of the waterlots on the river. Two other streets were laid out on the east side of High Street and three streets were laid out on the western side of High Street, all parallel to this principal street of the town of Burlington.[27]

As defined by the Concessions and Agreements, each Tenth had to be owned initially by ten specific proprietary shares, or holders of the rights to those shares. The ten proprietary shares representing the First Tenth were those associated with the Yorkshire proprietors Joseph Helmsley, Thomas Pearson, George Hutcheson, Thomas Hutchinson and Mahlon Stacy. These proprietors had sold numerous fractions of their shares to other Quakers to encourage them to emigrate to the province.

The division of the lands of the First Tenth in the town of Burlington was overseen by Joseph Helmsley, Thomas Foulke and Robert Stacy (Mahlon's brother) during the earliest days of the settlement of the territory. The Yorkshire portion of the town was laid out in ten lots of land, each containing about eighteen acres, and each lot representing a full propriety of town land. Each town lot was further divided into smaller parcels representing the amount of land that would be assigned to the owner of a fraction of a share, the size of the parcel or town lot being proportional to the size of the fraction of the share. Further land was to be assigned along the waterfront, waterlots also proportional in width to the size of the fraction of the proprietary share owned by each individual.[28]

William and Sarah were assigned a three-acre parcel of land on the south side of Broad Street, on the east side of High Street, which represented part of the land that they were entitled to by their purchase of a one-quarter proprietary share in the First Tenth from Helmsley and Pearson.[29]

The London side of the town of Burlington was divided evenly between the ten proprietary shares represented by Thomas Budd, Thomas Hooton, Daniel Wills, John Penford, John Ridges (represented by Abraham Man), Thomas Ollive, John Kinsey (represented after his death by Benjamin Scott who owned one-third of that propriety), William Peachee, John Smith and Richard Mew. Each propriety was assigned three parcels of land in the town itself and one tract of land in the "townbound" lands, immediately outside of the streams that surrounded the town.

The parcels were assigned by drawing lots. The first tract was nine acres which fronted on the west side of High Street and ran back parallel to the river to the eastern edge of Third or Backmost Street, as it was sometimes called.

The second tract was a lot of approximately nine acres that fronted on the Delaware River and extended from the low-water line on the river southward to the stream that surrounded the island. These lots were divided from the land that extended from the western side of Third Street to the mouth of the boundary stream on the western side of the town.

The third tract was a waterlot which was divided from the lands situated north of Pearl Street and ran to the low-water mark on the Delaware River, land that extended from the west side of High Street to the east side of Third Street. Each propriety received approximately two hundred feet of waterlot land.

The fourth tract assigned to these London proprietors consisted of sixty four-acre lots of townbound land, each fronting on the Delaware River and extending inland to the south. The tracts lay between a great swamp at the mouth of the stream that bounded the western edge of the town and the mouth of the Rancocas Creek (Northampton River).[30]

Each of these townbound lots was large enough to allow the settlers to begin to raise the livestock, grains and other foods needed by the rest of the inhabitants of the West Jersey Province. William and Sarah did not have any portion of these parcels of land assigned to them, but as owners of a one-half proprietary share in the London or Second Tenth, they would eventually be able to claim their portion of these town and townbound lands.

Once these divisions in the town and the townbound lands had been made, each of the settlers could set out to construct shelters for protection in the oncoming winter. Perhaps the most popular shelter was a simple log cabin, constructed from the trees on the lot. That fall, numerous temporary shelters were hurriedly built throughout the town

As the group of Quaker settlers strengthened their hold on the new land, they encountered the original residents of the territory, the Dutch and the Swedes. But more important than their encounters with the Europeans were their encounters with the Indians. Peter Jergoe and Henry Jacobs, who had been settled there for some time, were able to interpret for the settlers until they became familiar with the language of the Indians. They knew that they had to learn the Indians' language in order to work toward establishing a good relationship with these natives of America.

As they completed their shelters and grew more confident that their relationship with the Indians would be friendly, the settlers began to explore the more remote lands of the province so that the commissioners would be able to divide these rural lands fairly. They were able to use the many Indian trails for their exploration, highways in the wilderness that had existed for centuries. These passageways of the Indians allowed them to travel easily to the East Jersey settlements of Shrewsbury and Middletown, southward to the Salem Colony of John Fenwick, northward to the falls of the Delaware River, southward to the Third and the Fourth Tenths, and even eastward to the ocean at Little Egg Harbor where the Indians visited yearly to fish.[31]

To facilitate their access to these trails, the settlers extended the streets of the town to the boundary stream in both the Yorkshire and London halves of the town. They then constructed the Yorkshire Bridge to connect with the trails that would lead to the north and east of the town and the London Bridge which allowed them to proceed to the trails to the Rancocas Creek and southwards. Realizing that the waterways were actually the most efficient highways, they also began to construct their own boats and canoes.

Although they had organized themselves well in their new settlement, it was the fall season and they had limited supplies to see them through the winter months. They were dependent upon the Friends of East Jersey and Salem, as well as the Dutch and Swedes, for the grain and livestock that they needed then for food, and would need for planting and propagating in their first spring. The area was abundant with wildlife which provided a valuable source of food for the settlers during that first winter and in the years that followed.

Perhaps the biggest surprise to these newcomers was the fact that the Indians, having had contact with the prior settlers and explorers from Europe, understood that their own tranquil world and ways were changing. A sense of cooperation was easily accomplished with the natives and the Indians shared their corn and grain with the settlers. They showed them their ways of hunting and fishing, which were more efficient than the European methods. The Indians would frequently bring game or fish that they had killed or caught to sell to the less-experienced settlers.

In the spring, after their first winter in the wilderness of the West Jersey Province, the Burlington settlers began to distribute and assign additional townbound lands to those settlers who had either purchased them by buying fractions of a proprietary share or earned them, by the provisions of the Concessions and Agreements, by coming to the province early in its development. As additional ships arrived, other settlers joined them to accept additional homestead lands. During the first spring in the province homes were built and farms were established in the townbound lands of Burlington. Homesteads were developed by many, including William Peachee and William Heulings, on lots fronting on the Delaware River and by Samuel Lovett and others on an inland lot.

One of the important accomplishments of this second year of the settlement was to establish adequate supplies of grain and livestock to make the community self-sufficient. During this year they discovered that there were clay and shell deposits sufficient for brickmaking and the manufacture of mortar and plaster. Though they had not been able to construct sawmills, they were developing plans to do so. With these resources and with the skills of the settlers who were trained in the building trades, they were able to build several houses in the town of Burlington in the second year that were almost as fine as the homes that they had left in England. The logs were hand-hewn, but the parts requiring milling came from England, shipped to them by the Quaker merchants of London. Houses of this quality were constructed on the lots of Thomas Ollive, Daniel Wills, Thomas Hooton and Thomas Budd, all on the west side of High Street. Budd also constructed a malt house and a brew house on his property to supply beverage to the settlers.

It was during this second year of the settlement that the upper two Tenths were able to establish a great deal of independence. Burlington was similar to many rural towns of England. Many of the settlers lived in the town or close to it. The agricultural lands that supported the townspeople were nearby. In these first two years few if any of the new English settlers lived far from the principal town of the province. The Friends of West Jersey were still not entirely certain of the safety of the wilderness, nor were they completely convinced of the stability or permanency of their apparently good relationship with the Indians.

Although all of their interactions with the Indians had seemed friendly to that time, the commissioners realized that the Indians were vulnerable to the effects of alcohol, and that they were experiencing a great incidence of illness including death from smallpox. Several times during these early years the Quakers met with the Indian Chiefs in formal sessions in the center of Burlington, presumably at the intersection of Broad and High Streets. Platforms were constructed for the Friends to be seated on one side and the Indian chiefs facing them on the other side. Accounts of these meetings were conveyed by Friends to their peers, especially by Thomas Budd who was particularly sensitive to the plight of the Indians.[32] The concern of the Friends for the welfare of the Indians resulted in long-lasting positive and trusting relationships between the natives and the new settlers.

By the winter of 1678/9 the Quaker settlers knew that they were ready to claim the larger tracts of land at a greater distance from the town. They knew that they could live safely even near the Indian villages. The economic success of individual settlers and of the West Jersey Province was dependent upon making these more rural lands productive so that trade with other colonies and communities overseas could be established.

The way was clear now to proceed with the next phase of the development of the West New Jersey Province. This accomplishment was probably most appreciated by Mahlon Stacy, who with other settlers from Yorkshire arrived on the ship *Shield* in December 1678. He and others with him were able to proceed directly to the falls on the Delaware River and to build their homes in that location. They immediately began to clear acreage for cultivation, having no need to waste valuable time or money developing temporary quarters in the capitol town of Burlington even though there were lands assigned to them in the town.

It had been decided by the commissioners that the lands would be made available by dividends, a number of acres related to a whole share or a fraction of a share owned by a proprietor. By March 19, 1678/9, the commissioners had decided that the first portion of the first dividend for all proprietary shares of West Jersey would be for 3,200 acres for a full share. On that date the surveys by Richard Hancock of the lands along both shores of the Northampton River (Rancocas Creek) were recorded. Sixteen hundred acres of these lands were surveyed to William and Sarah Biddle on the eastern shore of the Northampton River. The land was located between the tracts of land of Daniel Wills to the south and Thomas Ollive to the north.[33] Recognizing the safety of the rural lands of the province, Wills and Ollive moved to those tracts of land in the spring to develop their homesteads, as did other settlers. The majority of the work force of the West Jersey Province was absent from the town of Burlington that spring while they developed houses, outbuildings and mills on these rural homesteads.

Not all of the original commissioners continued to serve the settlement. After the initial purchase of lands from the Indians and after the laying out of the town of Burlington, Joseph Helmsley and John Penford returned to England. John Kinsey decided to settle his family across the river at Shackamaxon in Pennsylvania. Kinsey died in October of 1677 and was buried in Burlington at the burial ground located at that time at the southeast corner of Broad and Wood Streets in the London portion of the town.[34] Benjamin Scott took over the responsibility of overseeing the interests of the Kinsey proprietary share. He owned one third of it by then, and Dr. Robert Dimsdale and Thomas Budd each purchased another one-third of that share. Scott left the province to go to Barbados in 1678, and after looking after his properties there, he returned to England on the ship *Expedition* on March 31, 1679.[35] Robert Stacy, another of the original commissioners, was joined by his brother, Mahlon Stacy, in December of 1678, but Robert stayed in Burlington attending to his tannery. William Emley and Thomas Foulke helped Mahlon Stacy settle the rural lands of the First Tenth. Thomas Foulke, having spent the first two winters in a cabin on the east side of High Street, moved to Crosswicks Creek in 1678/9 to settle his family and his homestead in that location. Daniel Wills and Thomas Ollive, Commissioners from the Second Tenth, went to the

Northampton River to develop their rural homes, but Thomas Budd remained in Burlington in his comfortable home on the southwest corner of High and Pearl Streets.

Unfortunately, very few records survive for this period of government of the West Jersey Province up to the spring of 1680. Apparently Edmond Andros, Governor of the Crown living in New York, exercised little direct interference with the attempt of the Quakers to govern themselves. Although he had made their court subservient to the court of the Crown at New Castle, on the western bank of the Delaware River, it appears that the Upland Court was called on to judge on only one matter during these early years.[36]

Land was claimed by survey against the proprietary rights by individuals entitled to the lands by their ownership of the rights and by the constitution, the Concessions and Agreements. Few if any deeds of sale were recorded however. Since the validity of the claim of the governing rights and land rights remained uncertain, those who invested in the proprietary rights and spent money on improvements were taking a risk, for they might eventually lose their investment. Those Quaker settlers who did invest and inhabit the land knew that English law favored those who were in actual possession of property. They believed that their efforts to settle the land and to establish their homesteads might eventually strengthen their claim to the property.

Although the Concessions and Agreements did not specify that the province was to be settled only by Quakers, the fact was that there were few non-Quakers among the early settlers. The one major exception to this was Thomas Revell, who immigrated to Burlington with Mahlon Stacy on the *Shield* in December 1678. Revell moved to a house at the falls near Mahlon Stacy's homestead, and he lived there for several years before moving to Burlington, where he became an important member of the West Jersey Province. He was a scrivener or scribe, an essential skill to have brought to the province. He was a signer of the Concessions and Agreements, indicating his understanding of the Quaker experiment in democracy. He later served as the registrar of the province and as a clerk and recorder for most of its civil institutions for many years.

During the first two and a half years the Quaker settlers enjoyed the peace and prosperity of the West Jersey Province. They prepared themselves for the beginning of their self-government, due to take place after the general elections scheduled for March 25, 1680. Friends were allowed to worship without experiencing any persecution from agents of the Crown. Friends from other American colonies soon learned that their prospects might be better in West Jersey than in their own colonies. For

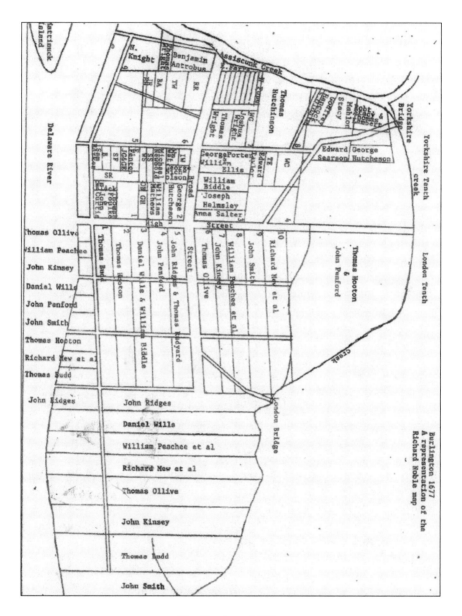

Burlington, 1677.
A representation of the Richard Noble map.

example, Freedom Lippincott, son of Abigail and Richard Lippincott from Shrewsbury, East Jersey, moved to Burlington in hopes of greater opportunity. He stayed after he married Mary Curtis, who was a relative of the wife of John Woolston Sr., and of Judie Ollive, wife of Thomas Ollive.[37] Later he was joined by his brother, Restore Lippincott, who married and settled in West Jersey. Richard Guy and his wife Bridget also moved to the First Tenth from their original home in the Salem Colony. Numerous other Friends from New York and Rhode Island, in particular, were beginning to pay attention to the success of the West Jersey Province as its immediate goals for development were accomplished.

The Concessions and Agreements had called for elections to be held on March 25, 1680. Thomas Budd was placed in charge of administering this requirement of the constitution. He had notices distributed to all of the residents of the province advising them to sign the Concessions and Agreements and then participate in the first election for commissioners of the province. The elections were held and the commissioners elected, but Thomas Budd was subsequently arrested by Governor Andros for inciting the people. The governor did, however, allow five of the eight elected commissioners to act as magistrates under his own commission. Thomas Ollive, Daniel Wills, William Emley, Mahlon Stacy and Robert Stacy served in this capacity as the first elected and then appointed officials of the West Jersey Province.[38]

Those Friends in London who had been closely involved in the planning of the West Jersey settlement and government were keeping informed of events in the province. They were still under the threat of religious persecution. The experience of the West Jersey Province represented their hope, for they could not foresee an end to the persecution of the English church and governing authorities. They received many accounts of the life and events in the province, not only from those traveling back to England, but also from letters written by settlers of the new province.

Although the London Friends, including William and Sarah Biddle, were still at great risk of fine or arrest, they admired the fortitude of their colleagues who had committed themselves to settling the wilderness and to establishing the planned Quaker experiment in democracy in America.

Quakers were settled peacefully in West New Jersey, claiming and developing their lands without objection. They were beginning to establish their governing rights and were hopeful that they would soon have their judicial rights. They were able to practice their religion without interference. They were on the verge of realizing their dream.

CHAPTER 8

London 1676/7 to 1681

For Quakers like William and Sarah who remained in London, religious persecution intensified. Their leaders met at the chambers of Ellis Hooks on June 12, 1677 with Samuel Jennings, another Friend who was interested in the West Jersey Province.[1] In this meeting and in others held that year, the Quakers discussed the fact that the governing authorities had begun to use a new weapon against them, enforcement of the Act of Recusancy. Under this act a person could be fined £20 for not attending Anglican church services for one month. Although the Act was originally intended to catch Roman Catholics who might still be worshipping in that faith, it was now being applied to the Quakers, making it impossible for some people of limited means to continue to live in England while following their religious beliefs.[2]

When their friends Henry and Anna Salter decided to emigrate to John Fenwick's Salem Colony later in 1677, William and Sarah took the opportunity to send a letter with them to Daniel Wills, asking him his personal opinion of the new land.[3] The Salters arrived on the Delaware River in November of 1677.[4] They settled at Salem, where they had purchased one of the largest parcels of land that Fenwick had sold to any individual —a 10,000-acre tract in the region of the Cohansey River and Alloways Creek, purchased for the meager price of £50.[5] The letter from William and Sarah was delivered as promised to Daniel Wills, but Wills did not immediately respond. Instead of a written response, he asked Joseph Helmsley to visit William and Sarah in London upon his return to that city and to give to them a first-hand description of the new land.[6]

When he arrived in London, Helmsley was pleased to tell William and Sarah about his experiences in the West Jersey Province. He had studied the lands and had assisted in the first purchase from the Indians. He was able to describe the appearance and the habits of the Indians and the richness of the land. He told them about the division of the town of Burlington, and that land that had been set aside for them there. He knew the Yorkshire Tenth best, and he further described the lands as one traveled up the Delaware River on the Indian trails, by the islands in the Delaware River, to the falls on the river. It is possible that Joseph Helmsley's description of the lands influenced William and Sarah in their eventual selection of a site for their own homestead. During that same visit Helmsley probably gave them a first-hand account of the import tax and the limitations imposed on the settlers and their planned government by Governor Andros, but he would have confirmed the satisfied status of the settlers in their first months in the province and that the Quaker settlers were freely practicing their religion without any restriction by the governor.

During the years 1678 and 1679 there was an even stronger revival of the use of the laws enacted to suppress non-conformist religions in England. Undoubtedly these injustices were discussed by the Quakers when their Yearly Meeting was held at Devonshire House on June 22 to 24, 1678.[7]

In the fall of that year the situation worsened acutely because of the Titus Oates Plot, which was thought to be a plan to assassinate King Charles II. By this time James, Duke of York, was a declared Roman Catholic, and he had been removed from his position as head of the Admiralty. He was believed to have been involved in the plot, and was exiled for awhile to Scotland. Struggling with the rumor that Louis XIV had secretly agreed to send an allowance to Charles II in return for continued toleration of Roman Catholics in England, Parliament was concerned about the threats to the national Church of England and began to discuss plans for choosing a different successor to the English throne.

These events led to a renewal of the enforcement of the acts against non-conformist religions. Fines and imprisonments of Quakers under the Act of Recusancy and the Conventicle Acts increased. However, perhaps because Catholics were the focus of government concern, the Friends of the Devonshire Monthly Meeting were able to continue their religious and business activities without serious interruption.

Happiness again entered the home of William and Sarah Biddle, on Bishopsgate Street Without, when on December 23, 1678 a daughter, Sarah, was born. With her older brother William, Jr., then nine years old, she would live to maturity.[8] The elation of the parents over the birth of this daughter strengthened their resolve to remain involved in the West Jersey plan.

William and Sarah completed a purchase for an additional one-sixth of a proprietary share of the province from Elizabeth Bell, the wife of Nicholas Bell, mariner of Ratcliffe, who was absent from London at that time. The indenture, dated December 29 and 30, 1678, was witnessed by Percivale Towle.[9]

By agreements of lease and release dated October 6 and 7, 1679, William and Sarah sold this one-sixth proprietary share to Robert Chinton.[10] This was the only time that they sold proprietary rights. Nicholas Bell signed an additional indenture of confirmation on December 31,

1679.[11] Probably William and Sarah had purchased this one-sixth proprietary share to give Bell, the mariner, additional funds to support one of his merchant ventures; his indenture was witnessed by William Satterthwaite,[12] a person known to be a friend of William and Sarah.

Perhaps it was at the Yearly Meeting of Friends held at Devonshire House June 10 and 11, 1679[13] that William and Sarah had an opportunity to discuss West Jersey affairs further with Benjamin Scott, who had recently returned from there and from Barbados, where he had seen Joseph Biddle, William's younger brother.[14]

Scott gave them a first hand account of the events of the settling of West Jersey. He could accurately describe the quality of the houses being built in Burlington, and the lots and the divisions of the town, particularly the location of the High Street lot reserved for them.[15] Since their daughter, Sarah, was only a baby, they were not yet ready to emigrate, although they were becoming increasingly convinced that they should join Friends in the new land.

The Quakers in West New Jersey continued to complain about the import tax imposed on them. The Byllynge trustees, with Edward Byllynge and other involved Quakers, petitioned James, Duke of York, through his secretary, Sir John Werden, to have the import tax removed. Sir John Werden brought the matter to the Duke's attention on September 29, 1679, at the same time raising the question of the right of the Quakers to govern themselves in West Jersey. The Duke of York was now in a precarious situation because of the Titus Oates plot and Parliament's discussions about finding an alternate successor to the throne. James had been approached about the governing rights also by Robert Barclay, one of the prominent Quaker leaders of Scotland, who had been requested by George Fox and William Penn to use his influence with him. The efforts paid off, and James, Duke of York, agreed to submit the questions to Sir William Jones, the recently-retired Attorney General of England.

The efforts of those Quakers who went to West Jersey to settle the land, to establish their own government and to take legal title (or at least possession of the territory) had strengthened the Quakers' claim to the territory. Now they needed those Quakers in England to help them get the guarantee of their governing rights, for the first elections were to be held in just six months on March 25, 1680.

In the spring of 1680 the letter that William and Sarah had long awaited from Daniel Wills arrived in London. Wills wrote from Burlington January 6, 1679/80, confirming the excellence of the land and his general satisfaction with the province. He stated,

... let every Man write according to his Judgment; and this is Mine, concerning this country: I do really believe it is as good a Country, as any Man need to dwell in; and it is much better than I expected every way. For land I will assure thee, here is as good by the Judgment of Men, as any in England.

He further counseled William and Sarah, "and if you have a stop within yourselves, let not any thing farther you until the way clears to your full satisfaction." [16]

William Penn, with his obligation as a trustee of the affairs of Edward Byllynge, had kept himself financially uninvolved in the affairs of the West Jersey Province. From his vantage point as a trustee, as a Quaker, as a guardian of the interests of the less wealthy Quakers who had undertaken the full economic burden of the development of West Jersey, and as a member of the ruling class of England, Penn learned from his experiences with the West Jersey plan that there was great potential in the colonization of America. King Charles II owed the Penn family £16,000, in particular William's father, Admiral Penn, now deceased, for his accomplishments on the seas for the English crown. Understanding that the financial resources of Charles II might not be great enough to satisfy the debt, and perhaps realizing that there might be economic advantages both to himself and to the Quakers, William Penn petitioned King Charles II in June 1680 for a grant of land that would take in the remaining wilderness territory on the western bank of the Delaware River in lieu of the money owed to the family. From his role as a trustee he understood that this action might help to protect Quaker interests in West Jersey. By submitting his petition at that time, while Sir William Jones was considering the questions posed to him by the Quakers, Penn forced the Crown and the colonial authorities to concentrate their attention on this region of America.

The Quakers of London and elsewhere in England learned of William Penn's plan, and of his possible development of another colony in America when they met in London on June 1, 1680 for their Yearly Meeting, held again at Devonshire House on Bishopsgate Street.[17]

It was also about this time that Samuel Jennings, an owner of one-quarter of a proprietary share, and deeply interested in the West Jersey plan of the Quakers, immigrated to West Jersey. His wife was a first cousin of Thomas Ollive. Jennings had participated in some of the meetings of importance in London and, as would be proven later, he was known and trusted by William Penn. The Jennings arrived in West Jersey in September 1680,[18] the year that the Concessions and Agreements became the law for the province.

On July 23, 1680 Sir William Jones presented his opinion on The West Jersey questions to James, Duke of York. He felt that the Duke could not legally demand customs or any other duty from the inhabitants of the province. He further stated that the land rights and the governing rights belonged in the hands of the proprietors of West Jersey. The Duke indicated to the Quakers that he would accept this opinion and that a second grant would be forthcoming. These concessions were major victories for the Quaker settlers.

By August 1680 the Byllynge trustees had assigned approximately fifty proprietary shares of West Jersey to individual Quakers or groups of Quakers, either for money owed to them by Edward Byllynge, or for money paid to the trustees for Byllynge's account. By this time more than £2,300 in cash had been received over and above the amount attached by his debts, and which therefore rightfully belonged to Byllynge.[19] The Byllynge trustees, continuing to believe that both governing rights and the proprietary land rights would both be given to the Quakers who purchased these rights, began to negotiate with the Duke of York's attorneys. They hoped that with the proven skill and influence of William Penn on their side, they would be able to have these governing rights given to this group of committed Quakers. It was felt that it might cost more money to obtain this kind of agreement,[20] but any payments to the Duke of York had to be handled discreetly because the sentiment of Parliament and of the average Englishman was not favorable toward him.

It was at this point that the carefully followed plan of the Byllynge trustees went awry. Edward Byllynge, perhaps learning that the powerful William Penn was showing a great deal of interest in the land adjacent to the West Jersey territory, may have been afraid that he would be left without any further ability to participate in the Quaker experiment in democracy. He may have feared that all he had contributed would be taken over by Penn. Certainly the relationship between these two men changed at this time. Byllynge knew that over half of the proprietary shares in the province had been granted to others. If he was excluded from any role in the government of the province, with only a minority of the proprietary interests in his possession, he would have little ability to profit from these residual shares after the trusteeship dissolved. On the other hand, if he alone owned the governing rights he would be able to protect himself financially in the future.

On August 6, 1680 Edward Byllynge presented a document to James, Duke of York, in which, "for and in consideration of the competent sum of lawful English money unto his said royal highness in hand paid" [21] James, Duke of York, signed the document without even the review of his attorneys giving the governing rights of West New Jersey to Byllynge.[22] Edward Byllynge had gained access to enough money to purchase the governing rights of the territory. He probably did this in part by borrowing an additional £2,000 from his son-in-law Benjamin Bartlett, for soon after that time Bartlett received five full proprietary shares for that amount that Edward Byllynge owed him.[23]

The Quakers of West New Jersey did not learn about the status of the governing rights then, but they did learn quickly about the news of the cessation of the import tax. When Samuel Jennings passed the New Castle customs point on about September 1, 1680, no import tax was demanded of him.[24]

Edward Byllynge, apparently trying to calm down any understandable irritation of the trustees and other Quakers towards him, promised to be a benevolent governor. He and the trustees realized that a deputy governor had to be assigned to the province, and apparently Byllynge took the suggestion of the trustees, for he sent the Commission of Deputy Governor to Samuel Jennings, whom he had never met.[25] Jennings decided not to mention his commission to the settlers immediately.

Although they may well have held elections on May 25, 1680 as prescribed by the Concessions and Agreements, apparently no meeting of the General Assembly was convened. However, the settlers were feeling more confidence in themselves and their ability to operate the province on their own. In September 1680, under Deputy Governor Samuel Jennings, they began to keep record of their land transactions in the Book of the Province. Thomas Revell, non-Quaker, had apparently been elected Registrar of the province by then, for he recorded each of the indentures.[26]

On February 7, 1680/1, William Biddle, attending the prestigious meeting of the Two Weeks Meeting of London with many of the important London Quakers, had the opportunity to meet Isaac Marriott before Marriott departed for Burlington, West Jersey. Isaac presented himself to that meeting that day to receive a certificate of removal (which would introduce him to the Friends of Burlington and would assure them that he was clear to marry); he intended to marry the sister of the wife of Samuel Jennings, Joyce Ollive, another first cousin of Thomas Ollive. Among others attending this meeting with William were Thomas Rudyard, the attorney for the Byllynge trustees and the person who would later become the first Deputy Governor of East Jersey; James Claypoole, who would head the Free Trade Society later founded in Pennsylvania; John Edridge, who had been the owner of one-half of the mortgage that John Fenwick held on the Salem Colony; and John Stokes, brother of Thomas Stokes,

<u>1680</u>

From the Mens Meeting in London the 7th day of the 12th month 1680/1

To our Friends & Brethren at Burlington in the Collinie of New Jersey in America or else where.

These may satisfie whome it doth or may Concerne that Isaac Marriott of Holborne in London Joyner the son of Richard Marriott of Wappingham in Northampton Shire Husbandman deceased declared unto us his Intentions of Marriage with Joyce Ollive Daughter [of] Richard Ollive deceased & Sister to Samuel Jennings Wife and being now in New Jersey aforesd he desired he desired [*sic*] a Certificate from this meeting; (he producing a Certifficate to this meeting from his Mother signifieing her consent) & after Enquiry made we doe not finde but that he is Clear from all other Women Concerning Mariage & that as far as we know, he is of an honest Conversation as becomes the Truth he makes profession, & soe we know nothing by him that may hinder or obstruct his proceeding but that in the fear of the Lord & with the consent of Friends there he may proceed to the Accomplishing his intended mariage soe with the Salutation of our dear Love to you in the unchangeable Truth of our God we rest and remaine your Friends & Brethren.

John Stokes	Tho. Scott
Isaac Jenings	Wm. Townsend
Tho. Hollinesworth	Tho. Rudyard
John Strongfellow	Wm. Mackett
John Eldridge	Fran: Camfield
Geo. Watt	John Elson
John Staples	James Claypoole
Charles Bathurst	Edward Man
John Edge	William Biddle
Rich: Whitpaine	Fran[ci]s Plumstead

Opposite page (transcription above):

Certificate of Removal
of Isaac Marriot 7th 12 month (February) 1680/1.

— from the Two Weeks Men's Meeting in London, copied from microfilm at the Friends Historical Library at Swarthmore College. The original records are in London.

1680

13

From the Mens Meeting in London the 7th day of ye 11th mo: 16[80]
To Our Friends & Brethren at Burlington in the Collonie of
New Jersey in America or elswhere.

These may Satiffie whome it doth or may Concerne yt Isaac
Marriott of Holborne in London Joyner & Son of Richard
Marriott of Wappingham in Northampton Shire Husbandman
deceased, declared onto vs his Intentions of Marriage w Joyce
Ollive Daughter Richard Ollive deceased & Sister to Samuell
Jonings Wife and being now in New Jersey aforesd he desired
he desired a Certificate from this meeting: (he producing a
Certificate to this meeting from his Mother Signifieing her
Consent) & after Enquiry made we doe not finde but that
he is Cleare from all other Women Concerning Mariage & that
as far as we know, he is of an honest Conversation as become
the Truth he makes profession of soe we know nothing by him
that may hinder or obstruct his proceedings but that in the feare
of ye Lord & advice & Consent of ffriends there he may proceed to the
Accomplishing his intended Mariage soe with ye Salutation of or
deare love to you in the unchaingeable Truth of or God wee rest
and remaine yor ffriends & Brethren.

John Stokes
Isaac Jonings
Tho: Hollingsworth
John Strongfellow
John Edridge
Geo: Watt
John Stuploe
Charles Bathurst
John Edge
Rich: Whitpaine

Tho: Scott
Wm Townsend
Tho: Rudyard
Wm Mackett
ffran: Camfield
John Elson
James Claypoole
Edward Man
William Biddle
ffrans Plumstead

previously of Devonshire House Monthly Meeting and now a resident of West New Jersey, having been a passenger on the *Kent* in 1677.[27]

On March 4, 1680/1, William Penn received his patent for the territory of Pennsylvania. On April 14, 1681, Penn, not wanting to be in conflict of interest, resigned from the Byllynge trusteeship. He complained to James, Duke of York, that the islands in the Delaware River were not included in his grant of the Pennsylvania territory. By June of 1681, Penn had requested that the Duke grant to him the territory around New Castle to include the islands in the river at that location.[28]

John Werden, and possibly others, felt that Penn was "very intent on his own interests in those parts." [29] Having been granted the rights to these new territories, William Penn did go on to demonstrate his intent to own or control more of the rights in the region in general. He eventually purchased the rights to twelve of the one-hundred proprietary shares of the West Jersey Province, and one twenty-fourth of the proprietary rights of the East Jersey Province. It is uncertain if he made these purchases to further protect his interests in Pennsylvania, or to further aid the West Jersey settlers, or possibly to attempt to annex these other territories to Pennsylvania.

On April 10, 1681, William Penn commissioned his cousin, William Markham, as deputy governor of Pennsylvania. Markham arrived in Pennsylvania by August 3, 1681, when he chose commissioners for Pennsylvania and reorganized the Pennsylvania Courts.[30] Penn put the plan for developing Pennsylvania into effect promptly. Burlington in West Jersey would no longer be the only port of trade on the Delaware River. West New Jersey, now populated by more than 1,400 people, would now have to compete with Pennsylvania for additional settlers and trade.

:

CHAPTER 9

Emigration to West New Jersey — Summer 1681

Those Friends residing in London and elsewhere in England were still living under religious persecution. William Penn and others had tried to help by using their influence with members of Parliament, but these efforts had failed. In 1681 there was no hope that religious persecution would end in England for many years. The representatives of the Church of England were still entering the homes of Quakers who had not paid tithes, and confiscating their possessions. The civil authorities continued to use the Act of Recusancy and the Conventicle Acts against the Quakers. The authorities were threatening also to disrupt the burial grounds that the Quakers had established.[1]

By the spring of 1681, William Biddle, now 47 years old, and Sarah, now 43, faced the probability that they would never have full control of their civil rights if they stayed in England. They understood the Quaker experiment in democracy which was being implemented in West New Jersey and they knew that their friends and associates there were experiencing the many freedoms that they all had hoped for. Leaving London for the New World was now an even more attractive idea to them.

For the most part they were quite comfortable in their home on Bishopsgate Street Without. William, Jr., now 11 years old, was probably attending the Friends School held at Devonshire House. Their daughter, Sarah was two and a half years old. However, her parents realized that many dangers to their health remained if the family continued to live in the crowded city.

William had gained many skills during his years in London through his association with the many industrious people in the Quaker community. He had learned from tradesmen and merchants how to market and ship goods overseas, and it appears that he had shipped goods to West New Jersey with the goods of other Quaker merchants on the ship *Success* in September 1678. The clerk recording the shipment referred to him as William Biddulph, a name more familiar in London. Other men shipping goods on the same vessel included Edward Man, Hugh Hartshorne and William Crouch, all people known to have associated with William Biddle through the Devonshire House Monthly Meeting.[2]

An international bank, perhaps the first of its kind, was established at Devonshire House.[3] Through his friends who were associated with that institution, William had the opportunity to learn how to invest money as well as how to finance merchant endeavors. Perhaps even more important for him was the opportunity to become familiar with English law under the tutelage of Thomas Rudyard, Ellis Hooks and others skilled in law who lived in his community. William was already totally familiar with the Concessions and Agreements. If he decided to settle in the new territory where this constitution was to be used, he would be prepared to defend it.

William and Sarah had been gradually making plans to leave London. They had invested a portion of their money in the proprietary rights to the new West New Jersey territory in anticipation of an eventual move there. They owned three-quarters of a proprietary share. It was estimated that each full proprietary share would eventually be worth in excess of 20,000 acres in the province.[4] William and Sarah were very close to making their final decision to transport their family and their possessions to West New Jersey.

It was probably at the Yearly Meeting of Friends held on May 24, 1681 at Devonshire House[5] that they learned that the ship *Thomas and Anne* would be departing for the West Jersey Province from the Thames that summer. This 100-ton ship, though older than most, was considered quite safe.[6] It was even easier for William and Sarah to make their decision when they discovered that a number of their friends would be making the passage on the same ship including Benjamin Scott, who was returning there with his entire family. To dispel any doubts that he might have had about the ship, William may have visited it while it was docked at Gravesend in July of 1681, taking on cargo and passengers. He found that the Scott family had already boarded the ship, for Margaret, Benjamin's wife, was pregnant; their daughter Elizabeth was born on board the ship on July 7, 1681, before they set sail. The delivery was attended by widow and midwife Bridget Bingham, who was traveling with her son James. Also in attendance at the birth were the ship's doctor, Robert Dimsdale, and his wife, Mary.[7]

William must have discussed the lands of the province with Dr. Dimsdale during the passage, for after they arrived in the territory, having inspected the lands together, William agreed to sell 500 acres on the Northampton River to the doctor. Dr. Robert Dimsdale and his wife later returned to England where they maintained their residence at Bishop's Stortford, Hertfordshire,[8] not far from London. He may have served as ship's doctor on other vessels that brought Quakers to the new lands as it is known that he returned again to the West Jersey Province at the time of William Penn's first visit to Pennsylvania.

By August 3, 1681, William and Sarah had apparently made the decision to move their family to West New Jersey. At the Monthly Meeting held at Devonshire House on that date they received their certificate of removal from the meeting, enabling them to join the new Quaker community in Burlington. The certificate showed that they intended to take a servant with them to the province, Mary Parnell of Northampton, daughter of the deceased John Parnell of that town. The certificate given to them also verified that Mary was single and clear to marry, information that would be useful to the Friends of Burlington should she wish to become engaged to marry there.[9]

The Biddles were wished farewell by their many friends of the Monthly Meeting that day, many of whom would continue to play a vital role in Quaker activities in London and in Pennsylvania in the future. George Whitehead, the most prominent spiritual leader of the Monthly Meeting, became the leader of the Quaker religious movement after the death of George Fox.

Having paid their passage of £5 for each adult, ten shillings for each child, and forty shillings per ton for the cargo they wished to transport with them,[10] they loaded themselves and their freight on the *Thomas and Anne* on August 3, 1681 while the ship was docked on the Thames. They said farewell to their relatives, Edmund Biddle, of Clement Danes, Westminster, probably William's younger brother,[11] and Thomas and Esther Biddle and their son Benjamin, at the ship's side that day. William and William, Jr., had probably made one final trip back to Birlingham that summer to say farewell to the family and friends who still lived in his home town — it was very likely that they would never see these people again.

It was comforting to know that they had friends and relatives in London who would oversee the sale of their houses and ensure that the funds were transferred to them in the new land.

There was no reason to look back. They had given long and careful consideration to the decision to participate in the first Quaker experiment in democracy, just beginning in West New Jersey.

That same day, August 3, 1681, William is shown in records written in London to have sold by indenture 300 acres of land along the Rancocas Creek in West Jersey to one Richard Baynum for £20, part of the 1,600-acre tract that had been surveyed to William by the commissioners.[12] The deed, not signed by either William or Sarah or witnessed by anyone known to have been associated with them, was drawn up on a day when the family must have been extremely busy with the details of boarding the ship. It was prepared in a manner much different in language and style from other deeds pertaining to land sales in the province.

These rights were purchased years later from the widow of Richard Baynum by William Penn. No land along the Rancocas Creek had been reserved for it, so this led to a disagreement between William Biddle and William Penn twenty years after the alleged indenture was created. Penn and James Logan discussed the indenture several times in their letters to each other.[13] It is not known if the matter ever was resolved. However, the indenture found its way into the possession of the heirs of William Biddle.[14]

The ship *Thomas and Anne*, with Thomas Singleton as Master, departed from its dock on the River Thames in mid-August, 1681.[15] The number of passengers on board is uncertain, for the original passenger list has not survived. The names of some of them, however, are known from other existing records. Besides William and Sarah Biddle, their two children and their servant, Mary Parnell, there were Benjamin Scott and his wife Margaret and their five children: John, Margaret, Martin, Bridget and the newborn Elizabeth. The widow Bridget Bingham was there with her son James.[16] Elias Farre and his wife, close friends of Henry Stacy who was then in West New Jersey, also took passage on that ship.[17]

Francis Collins, a widower, took his children with him to Burlington on this trip: Joseph, Sarah (who later became the second wife of Dr. Robert Dimsdale), Priscilla, Margaret, Elizabeth and Rebecca.[18] Two daughters of Thomas Curtis of Northampton were on board, Sarah and Elizabeth, each indentured for four years: Sarah to Benjamin Scott[19] and Elizabeth to Elias Farre.[20] Sarah Curtis would later become the wife of Peter Harvey,[21] and Elizabeth would marry James Atkinson.[22]

Other passengers included Dr. Robert Dimsdale and his wife, Mary, Thomas Crandall, Edward Ellis and John Essington. Edward Man, an important Quaker merchant of Bishopsgate Street, shipped goods to West New Jersey on the *Thomas and Anne*.[23] The trip was undoubtedly made more comfortable because of the composition of the group of passengers. There were plenty of servant girls to look after the small children, so the adults were able to enjoy their own time together. Even the smallest children developed a sense of togetherness from this experience and remained faithfully in touch with each other for the rest of their lives.

Though some records indicate that the *Thomas and Anne* was to go to New York,[24] other notes suggest that it went directly to West New Jersey.[25] The ship was loaded entirely for West New Jersey with cargo and passengers, so it is unlikely that it put into New York on the way. As did many of the ships that transported Quakers to America, it stopped at Barbados for supplies and food, giving the passengers a chance to see Friends who had been sent there from England years earlier. This was particularly advantageous for Benjamin Scott, who had property there that needed his attention.[26] William Biddle wanted to visit Joseph Biddle, then a resident of St. Michael's, Barbados. This Joseph Biddle was probably William's younger brother. He was a Quaker, for he had been fined twice for failure to bear arms,[27] and he signed a letter to the Meeting for Sufferings in London along with other Barbados Quakers on October 28, 1680.[28] Records indicate, in fact, that William Biddle, two children, a servant and three slaves were in Barbados about 1680.[29]

The passengers, including William, purchased slaves while in Barbados. Despite the words of George Fox against slavery, the plantations of Barbados were dependent upon an economy of slavery. The island served as the source for many of the slaves who eventually lived in West New Jersey. By the Concessions and Agreements the settlers were required to have one able-bodied servant for each one hundred acres that they claimed, as a means of insuring that the land would be properly developed.

The *Thomas and Anne* arrived on the Delaware River, en route to Burlington, in October, 1681. It must have stopped at the customs point at New Castle as required, but the stop would have been brief and there were no taxes. There was undoubtedly also a stop at Upland (Chester) to land some passengers, including John Essington.

It was not until the ship reached the mouth of the Northampton River (Rancocas Creek) that signs of life were visible on the West Jersey side of the river. First was the farmstead of William Heulings, followed by the nursery lands and the house and barns of William Peachee, and then the barns and pastureland of William Brightwen. Nearer the town there was smoke coming from the chimney of the home of Thomas Potts and then from the cabins of William Brightwen and John Long on Wood Street.

The *Thomas and Anne* came to its anchorage at the foot of High Street, where several more buildings and homes could be seen by the newcomers. Happy to have reached their destination, they eagerly searched the shore for familiar faces among the crowd that had gathered to welcome them. After more than a month of traveling, if any of the passengers were disappointed in the sparsely-settled appearance of the town that lay before them, compared to the sophisticated city left behind, their feelings were quickly relieved. Before them lay a town only recently carved out of the wilderness, dressed in fall finery provided by the leaves of maple and oak trees.

Only the area of the landing place and High Street beyond it were cleared enough for them to view the town; the rest was hidden by the forest. The home of Seth Smith, shared with Thomas Foulke when he was in town, was on the east side of High Street. On the west side of the street, two hundred feet down-river, sat the taverns of John Hollinshead and John

Cripps, with Pothouse Alley separating them.[30] Up High Street one could see the home of Thomas Budd on the corner of High and Pearl Streets.

The residents of Burlington escorted the newcomers up High Street, towards their new temporary home. Along their route were the houses of Thomas Budd and the nearby malt house and brew house that he had constructed on his property. Then there was the house of Thomas Gardiner on the portion of the Thomas Hooton lot that had been assigned to Henry Stacy. The next lot was William Biddle's High Street lot, the one-half propriety that he owned in the London portion of the town.

On the other half of the lot were the home and the cooper shop of James Wills, whose father, Daniel Wills, with John Antrum was building another house on the western side of the second portion of the nine-acre lot. The remainder of the street was clear of houses until the southwest corner of High and Broad Streets where one came upon the nine-acre lot of Thomas Ollive with his log cabin and his town house. The Ollive town house was to be home for William and Sarah Biddle until they could claim their own land and build a homestead.[31] Thomas Ollive and his family were by now living in their more rural homestead on the Rancocas Creek.

Their temporary new home was conveniently located in the exact center of the town near the marketplace. William knew from his conversation in London with his friend Joseph Helmsley that he also owned the third lot eastward from High Street, on the south side of Broad Street in the Yorkshire half of the town. William had carried all of these sites in his thoughts and imagination for a long time, and now that he was seeing them for the first time his dreams were becoming reality.

William had arrived too late to participate in the first Yearly Meeting of Friends, which had been held in August at the home of Thomas Gardiner in Burlington.[32] Elections had already been held as prescribed by the Concessions and Agreements, but the General Assembly did not plan to meet until November. William would be able to attend those sessions but he would not yet be able to qualify as an elected representative to the General Assembly.

With the arrival of William Biddle, Elias Farre and Benjamin Scott, Samuel Jennings could at last discuss the changes that had been made by Edward Byllynge when he took over the governing rights. The fact that there was a Governor and that Samuel was the appointed deputy governor had not been announced to the Quakers of West New Jersey. When the General Assembly met, these three newcomers who knew Byllynge could bring the intentions of the Governor and the fact that a new provision for a governor had to be added into the Concessions and Agreements.[33] These three could support his plan and could share with the group their belief that

Edward Byllynge did eventually plan to immigrate to West New Jersey, and that he would govern them benevolently.

William may have told the leaders of the town about another of Edward Byllynge's interests. During the early conversations. Byllynge had expressed concern about regulation of the sale of manufactured items, and he had discussed this problem in his treatise, *A Mite of Affection*, written in 1659.[34] The Concessions and Agreements did not address this issue. When the General Assembly met in November, it established a committee to oversee the regulation of weights and measures for the province. William Biddle, even though he was not an elected member of the Assembly, was appointed as a member of that committee, his first public duty in his new home.[35]

Opposite page (transcription below):

To the Meeting of Friends in West Jersey Greeting

These are to certifie all friends and others concerned that whereas William Biddle of Bishopgate Street London shoemaker and Sarah his wife with there servant Mary Parnell daughter of John Parnell of Northampton deceased being now intended to transport themselves into West Jersey who so far as we know or understand have behaved themselves soberly and honestly as becomes Truth and Righteousness and that the said Mary Parnell so far as we can understand is cleare from all engagements in relation to marriage to which the dear love in Truth we subscribe your friends and brethren Dated at our monthly meeting the 3rd day of the 6th month 1681   Devonshire House

William Crouch	Michael Russell	Thomas Choakely
Theodore Eclesten	William Phillips	Caleb Pusey
William Machett	Francis Plumstead	Thomas Hollingworth
Clement Plumstead	Isack [?] Jenings	James Hoday
Rec[hard] Whitpayne	George Greene	Anne Whitehead
William Ingram	John Ellis	Mary Whitpayne
Edward Man	Isack Jenings	Mary Wooley
Hugh Hartshorne	Thomas Miller	Grace Bachus
John Paulling	Gilbert Mace	Mary Plumstead
Abraham Godderance	George Whitehead	Elizabeth Bignall
	John Pike	
	Walter Thallis	

Certificate of Removal for William and Sarah Biddle and their servant Mary Parnell from Devonshire House Meeting, London to West Jersey, 3rd 6th month (August) 1681.

—copied from microfilm of the Chesterfield Monthly Meeting miscellaneous records at the Friends Historical Library, Swarthmore College

CHAPTER 10

Burlington, West New Jersey — 1681

During these early days in Burlington, Sarah and William soon became familiar with the settlement and the people living in and around the city. There were 31 houses, inns and log cabins in town. Many of the couple's old friends lived outside of town, so they could travel by horseback to visit them and to observe how they had built their homesteads.

Perhaps the most startling new experience was the presence of the Indians around them and among them. The Indians had been exposed to Europeans for about eighty years, so most of them had adopted apparel like the settlers. The Indian language was difficult to master, but some of the early settlers like Thomas Budd and Thomas Gardiner Jr. had developed a serious interest in the Indians and were able to interpret for the others.

The Quakers and the Indians established a peaceful relationship despite the cultural difference between the two groups. The Indian population had been significantly reduced by diseases caught easily from the Europeans — measles, smallpox and tuberculosis — to which they had no prior exposure and therefore no immunity. Their native means of treating illness with roots and herbs were not particularly successful, but the medical treatments used by the Quakers were not always very successful either.

The Indians sold corn, beans and fruits to the Quakers, as well as wild turkey, fish and deer that they had killed. This made daily life relatively easy for the Quakers, by the time that the Biddles arrived in town.

On the First Day of Quaker Worship in Burlington the Biddles learned what it felt like to worship with their friends in peace, without the threat of persecution. They had long been looking forward to participation in the activities of the Burlington Monthly Meeting. The meeting for worship that day was held in the home of Thomas Gardiner, but sometimes the meetings were held at the homes of John Woolston or Thomas Budd.

William and Sarah were fortunate compared to many of their shipmates, for they were able to settle into relatively luxurious accommodations. Most new inhabitants of the province had to find shelter by camping out until they could construct a simple log cabin. There were several cabins available to newcomers to Burlington, but the home of Thomas Ollive was one of the finest that had been built in the province to that time. In London, the Biddles' home had been near the center of Quaker activities and they may have shared it with Quakers who visited the city from rural England. Now they occupied a home belonging to Thomas Ollive that was in the center of the Quaker activities of West New Jersey.

William and Sarah were living in Ollive's home August 7, 1682, when the Burlington Monthly Meeting appointed a committee to meet there at eight o'clock in the morning later in the month to attend to a matter of business for the meeting.[1] On September 27, 1682 Thomas Ollive sold the home, along with an adjacent three-acre lot he had bought from John Kinsey Jr., for £10. The indenture of sale stated that William and Sarah Biddle were living in the house, and that the lot on which it was built contained one acre and included a log cabin where Robert Hudson, the carpenter, lived. The entire property was sold to Oliver Hooton of Barbados (son of Thomas Hooton of Burlington and Philadelphia) for £84.[2] Oliver Hooton died shortly after that time, before he could take possession, but his estate did not sell the property for many years. It is likely, therefore, that William and Sarah continued to live there until they finished building their own home in 1684.

The house was durable, for it was eventually sold by Oliver Hooton's estate to Thomas Kendall, bricklayer, in 1693,[3] and then by Kendall to Edward Hunloke in 1700.[4] It still stands at 406 High Street in Burlington.

The leaders of the government of the province came together in Burlington on November 25, 1681 for the General Assembly Meeting. Sarah and William already had an understanding of the governing affairs of the province and they were particularly pleased to see that the courts of the province were now being held under the authority of the governing rights of the province. The justices were people they knew well, including Robert Stacy, Thomas Ollive, Samuel Jennings, Thomas Budd, John Thompson, Thomas Lambert, Mahlon Stacy, Richard Guy and Edward Bradway. No longer were they subjected to the whims of the single magistrates of London, for now at least three justices always sat on the bench of the court, and the jury, according to the provisions of the Concessions and Agreements, was predominant in the decision process in the courtroom.[5]

While only a small portion of the province had been settled, that had been accomplished rapidly, especially considering that there was no powerful wealthy force behind the settlement. It had been done largely because of the energy and the monies that the settlers had collectively put into the project. Burlington had considerable undeveloped land left in town, but many of the settlers had already moved out into the rural lands of the upper two Tenths. The development of these farmsteads was proceeding nicely, giving the province more economic strength than would be apparent to an observer measuring the success of the settlement by the degree of building in Burlington.

The lands of the Third Tenth had been purchased from the Indians and were now being distributed to the proprietors of record for the ten proprieties of the Tenth. The elected General Assembly was just now holding its first meetings. The offices of Governor and deputy governor would be added to the system of government as required by Edward Byllynge, the owner of the governing rights. A Governor's Council and the group of Land Commissioners were formed and functioning. Officers of the province had been elected. Daniel Leeds was the surveyor for the province. William Emley was the sheriff of the territory which now reached from the Assinpink Creek, near the falls on the Delaware River, to Oldmans Creek, many miles down river from Burlington. Thomas Revell had been elected as registrar of the province,[6] but his talents were to be shared with Pennsylvania, for Governor Markham had requested that Revell also be clerk of the Pennsylvania court established at Upland.[7]

On the eve of the first meeting of the General Assembly, William and Sarah realized that the Quaker dream, which had taken twenty years to develop, was now a reality. They knew that there was much more to be done and they hoped to share in preserving this world of new rights and freedoms for future generations.

The elected government of the West Jersey Province, as specified by the Concessions and Agreements, began to function when the first General Assembly met on November 21 through 28, 1681, attended by the assemblymen who had been elected in the spring of that year in each populated Tenth.

The first business of the Assembly was to amend the constitution. The amendment, introduced by Samuel Jennings, called for and defined the role of a governor. As everyone had by now learned, Edward Byllynge had been awarded the governing rights to the province, and he had commissioned Samuel Jennings as his deputy governor. Jennings proposed that the role of the Governor be subservient to the will of the General Assembly and the commissioners, who were elected annually by the General Assembly and would serve as the Governor's Council. The General Assembly would thus continue as the dominant body in the government.[8]

The General Assembly accepted the amendment. If Edward Byllynge had been consulted, he might have had difficulty accepting all of the features of the amendment, for it created a weak governorship for the province. But Jennings had assured them that the change was made in the spirit of the Concessions and Agreements that Byllynge had been so instrumental in forming.

The General Assembly reenacted many of the provisions of the Concessions and Agreements, confirming its commitment to this document. The most important new act of the session was the passage of an act of taxation. The tax, to "defray the public debt and the charges of the province," was to raise £200 for the province, £20 from each Tenth. The tax was levied on the proprietors, freeholders and inhabitants of the province according to the assets of each individual. Its enactment showed that the resident proprietors recognized that they were unable to fund the heavy economic burden of the development of the province alone. This burden was placed upon all those who settled in the province or who benefited from its creation and development.[9] In addition the deputy governor and the Land Commissioners of the province administered the land transactions without the use of quitrents.

The act of taxation system limited the economic liability of several people who had invested in the proprietary rights of West Jersey. The rights of those proprietors who remained in England, not taking action on their land rights, were protected, and they were not liable for the economic burden involved in the development of the province. These non-resident proprietors included George Greene, Michael Russell, Anthony Bellers and William Crouch, all Quakers of London.

For resident proprietors like William Biddle, further economic liability would take the form of taxation on assets, including lands that they had claimed for themselves. Because there were no quitrents, they would not receive any future income from lands they had sold or distributed from their proprietary rights, but those lands were not counted as their assets. This practice was in contrast to that of William Penn in Pennsylvania, who continued to collect quitrents on property that he sold or transferred from his proprietary rights.

The non-proprietor inhabitant of the province now knew that he could work to earn his ownership of land, but he also knew that when he became a landowner he would be expected to contribute his share to the maintenance of the province. It was now clear to those who settled in West New Jersey that they would be economically responsible for the public good.

The Act for the Regulation of Weights and Measures was passed on November 25, 1681, and as mentioned previously, William was a member of this committee appointed by the General Assembly.[10]. Within two years at least two other acts were passed, defining and regulating the manufacture of bricks and the process for tanning. These acts confirmed that the first Quaker legislators were concerned about safeguarding the rights of the consumers of the province.

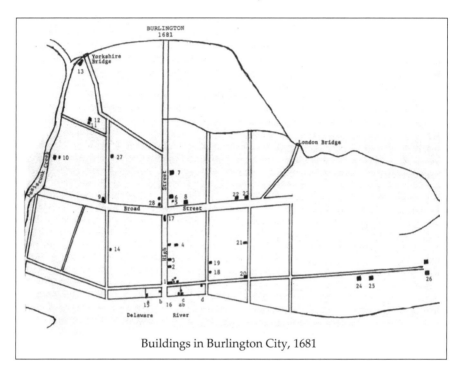

Buildings in Burlington City, 1681

1. Thomas Budd's House, malt house, brew house, bolting house and stable
2. Thomas Hooton's house
3. Thomas Gardiner's house
4. James Wills' house and cooper shop
5. Thomas Ollive's log cabin occupied by carpenter Robert Hudson
6. Thomas Ollive's townhouse
7. John Cripps' townhouse
8. John Woolston's townhouse
9. Thomas Wright's townhouse
10. Joseph Pope's house and barns
11. Samuel Oldale's house on Pudding Lane
12. Robert Stacy's house bought from Godfrey Hancock
13. Robert Stacy's tanhouse
14. Jon Eldridge's cabin
15. a. George and Mary (Cooper) Bartholomew's cabin
    b. Seth Smith and Benjamin Wheate's house
16. a. John Hollinshead's Inn
    b. John Cripps's Inn
    c. John Cripps's log cabin on Potters Alley
    d. Bernard Devonish's house
17. Marketplace
18. William Brightwin's log cabin
19. John Long's house
20. Jonathan Beere's house
21. John Antrum and Daniel Wills's townhouse

22. Townhouse of mariner Peter Bosse
23. Thomas Eves's townhouse
24. Thomas Pott's house in Ollive Town
25. Thomas Ollive's waterlot and house
26. William Brightwin's pastures and barns
27. William Cooper's lot, cabin and blacksmith shop
28. Anna Salter's lot and log cabins

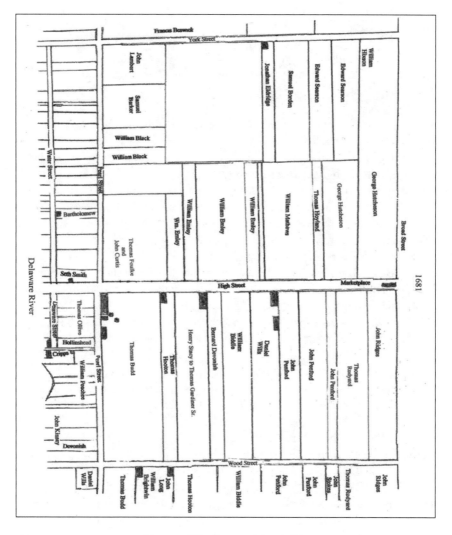

Center of Burlington City, 1681.

On December 5, 1681, Deputy Governor Samuel Jennings with some of his Council, including Thomas Ollive, Daniel Wills, Thomas Gardiner, Thomas Budd, Benjamin Scott, Thomas Lambert, Robert Stacy and Mahlon Stacy, acting as the first Land Commissioners of the province, issued new rules and regulations for distributing lands from proprietary shares. Until that time lands distributed were usually in large single tracts, such as the 1,600-acre tract assigned to William Biddle on the Northampton River (Rancocas Creek). William had already decided to sell 500 acres of that tract to Dr. Dimsdale and another 300 acres of it apparently had been sold to Richard Baynum in London. William would sell off or trade other smaller portions of that tract in the future until all of it had been distributed from his possession.

By the new rules, all new land claims had to be settled within six months of establishment of title, or the claim would no longer be valid. The commissioners specified that the initial dividend in land for those owning proprietary rights would be a first portion of a first dividend of 3,200 acres per proprietary share. It was promised that a second portion of this first proprietary land dividend would be made, representing 2,000 more acres per proprietary share, to be distributed when enough people had settled in the province to create a demand for the land. Four hundred acres were allotted per proprietary share within the town bounds of Burlington. In the town itself, town lots and wharf lots were to be distributed to the proprietors who held proprietary rights in the Yorkshire and London Tenths. The sizes of the lots were to be determined by the amount of the proprietary share owned by the individual.[11]

Other rules issued by the commissioners allowed for no more than five hundred acres to be settled in any one tract by any one person, proprietor or inhabitant. No more than forty perches (660 feet) per one hundred acres could be claimed on a navigable stream, and no person could claim land on both sides of a navigable stream. The commissioners thus prevented any obstruction of access to waterways, a right guaranteed to the settlers by the Concessions and Agreements.

In later actions taken by the Land Commissioners, the rules for the number of persons needed to settle a tract of land were altered. Previously, by the Concessions and Agreements, one able-bodied man was needed for each one hundred acres. The commissioners were now willing to allow as few as two able-bodied persons to settle a tract of land that could be as much as five hundred acres. This change in the provisions of the Concessions and Agreements meant that people could more easily establish plantations and homesteads and most importantly, it meant that there would be fewer servants and slaves needed to accomplish the settlement of the province.[12]

The gradual allotment of land rights by dividends allowed for an orderly settlement of the province. Although the Concessions and Agreements and the rules and regulations of the Land Commissioners did not require the lands of the province to be settled by Quakers only, other rules allowed that to happen. In the First and Second Tenths, all of the proprietary rights were owned by Quakers, and the rules of distribution required that in order to gain title to land, one had to get the prior approval of the Quaker leaders. The result was that the lands of the first two Tenths were almost exclusively settled by Quakers.

On the same day that the Land Commissioners first met, December 5, 1681, the Burlington Monthly Meeting also met to discuss its business. William was present, and that day he was assigned to a committee that included Thomas Budd and Benjamin Scott, formed to look into a concern that the Monthly Meeting had about an intention of Daniel Wills.[13]

On December 8, 1681, William and Sarah had the opportunity to participate in one of the pleasurable social activities of the town. That day they attended the marriage of Thomas Barton to Ann Borton. It was a wedding held in the manner of the Friends, with the bride and groom taking each other in marriage before their friends under the care of the Burlington Monthly Meeting.[14] William and Sarah were among the guests who signed the marriage certificate as witnesses, according to Friends' customary practice.

CHAPTER 11

Surveying and Claiming Land 1681-1682

There was some degree of urgency for William and Sarah to decide where they would claim their lands and build their homestead. Most of the earlier settlers had claimed land on the Delaware River and navigable streams, giving them access to overland and waterway transportation routes. The amount of prime land remaining unclaimed on the river, in particular, was limited. Also, the fast-approaching winter would make it difficult to explore the available land.

William had the description of the lands in the upper Two Tenths in his mind when he arrived in the province, having learned about it from Joseph Helmsley and Benjamin Scott. Now he had to make his decision about choosing land based on his own observations. The experience of living in the town of Burlington was good, for it put him in touch with the others who had previously made their decisions, thus saving him some traveling to examine all the tracts of land. The records of land already claimed allowed him to see what lands were still available. He had the added advantage of the experience of the early settlers, which taught him that he could safely plan to establish a large homestead and farming lands at a distance from Burlington, despite the wilderness and the Indians.

William revisited the lands along the Northampton River (Rancocus Creek) several times, but found that the 1,600-acre tract of land that had been assigned to him at that location was not suitable for the type of homestead that he had in mind.

Thomas Ollive had chosen the best location along the Northampton River and Mill Creek, where he had constructed a mill for the farmers of the area. Thomas Eves and John Roberts were already living on farms at this location. Freedom Lippincott, whose wife was related to Thomas Ollive's wife, was planning to claim land near the Ollive homestead. John Woolston had also claimed some of the land of the Ollive tract and was negotiating the sale of some of it to Thomas French.

Upstream from this tract of 1,600 acres Daniel Wills had settled with his family. Some of those people who traveled to the province with Daniel from England had also decided to settle in that area of the Northampton River. Wills claimed his land along another small stream that flowed into the Northampton River, and he was able to establish a small mill there for his own use. William Evans, Thomas Harding, John Borton, John Paine, George Elkinton and Thomas Stokes all had established their homes in the area. William knew on his first visit that it was too crowded on the Rancocas Creek to satisfy his own plans for his settlement. He decided that it would be best to sell off the remainder of this tract in small portions to these neighbors and others who would eventually want to expand their holdings in that location. For his own homestead, he would concentrate on finding another less crowded site.

William began to explore the lands of the First Tenth, northeast along the Delaware River up to the falls of the river, far above Burlington, where Mahlon Stacy, Thomas Lambert, William Emley, Joshua and Thomas Wright and John Lambert had developed their homesteads. He also looked at lands to the southeast, near the Indian village of Oneanickon where Michael Newbold and others had settled their families on lands that originated with the proprietary rights of George Hutcheson. This land was attractive, having been partially cleared and very fertile for farming, but William felt that it was set back too far from the Delaware River, the best route of transportation.

In his explorations William noted that there was no real center of development between Burlington and the falls. He found the property he wanted midway between the two locations, on the land adjacent to Seppasink Island on the Delaware River, about six miles above Burlington.

With the proprietary rights that he held, William was entitled to claim 800 acres in the First Tenth for the one-quarter share he had purchased from Pearson and Helmsley, and 1,600 acres in the Second Tenth for his one-half proprietary share. He was restricted by the fact that his friends had committed him to a 1,600-acre tract on the Rancocas Creek that he did not want, and by the recent rules of the General Assembly and their Land Commissioners. Now, when he claimed land, he was limited to 500 acres in any one tract, and he had to settle that land within six months or he would lose title to it. He retained the right to claim 300 acres of land in the townbounds of Burlington as well as numerous town lots and wharf lots for his three-quarters of a proprietary share.

The first official survey and claim of land in West Jersey by William and Sarah was an unusual one. It showed that they may have been aware of the desire of William Penn to control the Delaware River. Or perhaps they understood, as did Penn, that the islands in the Delaware River were not clearly owned by either Pennsylvania or West Jersey. If the ownership to the islands was not established, trade and safety on the river would not be guaranteed to the inhabitants of either territory.

Regardless of their intent, on December 17, 1681 a survey was recorded to William and Sarah for Seppasink Island, in the Delaware River,[1] a claim that created a disagreement between William Penn and William and Sarah Biddle that lasted the rest of their lives. William Penn understood Sarah's role in managing the Biddles' finances, for when he wrote to his secretary James Logan years later, he referred to the fact that Sarah had claimed the island of 278 acres, after she had bargained with the Indians for it, and after she had been warned not to do so by friends in West Jersey and by Governor Markham of Pennsylvania.[2] Sarah may have known that Penn's agents were beginning to negotiate with the Indians for the first land purchase from the natives, and that this tract would include Seppasink Island. He would soon select that area for his rural home in Pennsylvania, to be called Pennsbury, on the west bank of the Delaware River just to the west of that island.

William and Sarah had decided to claim the land on the east bank of the river adjacent to Seppasink Island for their homestead. They needed the certainty of ownership of the island to protect their land, and Sarah's claim had insured their rights as well as the rights of the West Jersey Province in the river. The deed for Seppasink Island was made official when William had it recorded in books of the province by Thomas Revell, registrar of the province, on December 17, 1681.

On December 20, 1681 William made a joint claim of land with his friend Benjamin Scott. They had surveyed, claimed and recorded a tract of land of 635 acres on the Delaware River between Burlington and the mouth of the Rancocus Creek, between the homesteads of William Peachee and William Heulings. Only 135 acres of this tract of land belonged to William Biddle.[3] This site might have been chosen because it could serve as a docking site for vessels if they established shipping trade with Barbados or other locations.

On January 10, 1681/2 Thomas Revell, registrar, recorded the next survey in the Books of the Province:

> Surveyed then more for William Biddle one parcel of land Abutting on yᵉ maine River of Dellaware against Sepasinke Island beginning at yᵉ mouth of a small Creek which bounds yᵉ land of William Beard, runns thento by yᵉ River Sixty five chains to a black oake for a corner then into the woods south and be east southerly Seventy seven chains to a black oake for a second corner, Then to East Sixty four chains to a white oake for a corner, thento north and by east to a black oake marked in a swamp att the head of a small runn of water and by yᵉ said runn descends to yᵉ creek and corner first aforesaid, surveyed for five hundred acres.[4]

Sixty years had gone by before that this property was resurveyed by more experienced surveyors with more sophisticated equipment. It was discovered then that the boundaries described by the survey actually contained 881 acres.[5]

This so-called 500-acre tract of land was to be the future homestead for William and Sarah and their family. It was a location remarkably similar to the rural Birlingham home site in England where William had been raised. They appropriately named their new homestead "Mount Hope." Although the area was less settled than other locations they had seen, there were several families already living nearby. By then, in 1681/2, their neighbors included John Snowden, William Beard, Anthony Woodhouse, William Black, Robert Murfin and John Hooton.

To complete the legal requirement to settle the land within six months, it is quite possible that the Biddles built a simple log cabin with a basement. It was constructed on one of the hills on the property, set back only a short way from the river. This house would be used by those hired by William to begin the work that was necessary to turn this wilderness tract of land into a comfortable, productive homestead. Some of the slaves brought from Barbados may have lived there with the carpenters and the men assigned to clear the lands after the title was established. The foundation of such a house of unknown origin that still exists on the original tract may be the site of this first home on the property.

William made an additional survey and claim of land at nearby Springhill, further back from the river in the area that later became Mansfield Township. This survey consisted of 322 acres and it included one hundred acres that was considered a town lot at Springhill.[6] William later sold the tract to John Underhill, who moved to West Jersey with several other Quaker families from Oyster Bay, Long Island, in the New York territory.[7]

There were numerous reasons why the Biddles chose the Mount Hope site six miles up the Delaware River from Burlington for their homestead. William was already familiar with the advantages of living on a river from his experience growing up in Birlingham and later in London. He could travel overland by the Indian trails which passed by Mount Hope, but the river gave him a second way to transport his farm products to Burlington and beyond. The land was good for farming, but it would also afford him an easy route to some of the most arable land in the province, near Oneanickon, the Indian village where Indians had farmed for centuries.

It would be possible to establish his own mill at this site, a choice that William would not have had if he had built on the original site chosen for him at the Rancocas Creek. At Mount Hope he had chosen high ground, safe from flooding, and well drained, making the chance of contamination of well water very unlikely. By deciding not to live in the town of Burlington they would no longer be subjected to the diseases that accompanied city living, diseases that they had experienced with severe consequences in London.

Mount Hope was to prove a very healthy environment, for William and Sarah outlived almost all of their peers in West Jersey.

They must have perceived the need for a stronger Quaker settlement at the location midway between Burlington and the falls, and nearer to the East Jersey communities of Middletown and Shrewsbury. Over time their home became a center of Quaker religious life, and it served as the place where Quaker business of the upper two Tenths was conducted. They were joined in this location by other Quaker families who played important leadership roles in the province. Among these were Percivale Towle, Samuel Andrews, William Satterthwaite, and at the Crosswicks Creek settlement, Francis Davenport and the Foulkes and Bunting families.

William, with his familiarity with the Quaker experiment in democracy, had emigrated from London to participate in the government and the judicial system created by this dream. As an owner of a significant portion of proprietary shares and rights, he would be considered for an elected role in the governments and the courts. If he had joined his associates in the congested area of the Second Tenth not all of them would be able to participate in the structure of the new government. By settling in a different location within the province, in the less populated First Tenth, William was better guaranteed of election to the General Assembly.

The area where Mount Hope was located was favored by the Indians too, and by settling there, William and Sarah could establish good relationships with them. For the rest of their lives Indians continued to live with them at their homestead.

The lands of the homestead were ideal for farming and for raising farm animals, but Seppasink Island offered another advantage not found at any other location. The island could serve as a safe pastureland for their livestock and salt hay grew there abundantly, providing a natural source of hay for their oxen, cows and horses, making it possible to use more of their land on the mainland for crops for consumption and trade.

CHAPTER 12

The Story of the Seppasink Island Controversy

Seppasink Island was and remains a 278-acre island located in the Delaware River between Pennsylvania and New Jersey. The fact that William and Sarah Biddle claimed Seppasink first under their proprietary land rights shows that they understood not only the value of the tiny land mass, but that there was a need to establish a clear title of ownership to the island. William Penn was trying to make the same claim for the island with his Pennsylvania proprietary rights.

The issue at stake was not simply a matter of determining which individual, William Biddle or William Penn, or which territory, West Jersey or Pennsylvania, established title. In fact, these islands did not clearly belong to any one person or territory and they were therefore potentially available to be claimed by anyone. Such a claim by a third party not associated with the interest of Pennsylvania or West New Jersey could jeopardize trade and safety on the river for both territories, West Jersey and Pennsylvania, thus endangering the ability to successfully settle both Quaker territories. The settlers of the two territories, including William and Sarah Biddle and William Penn, could not have known how complicated the issue of the ownership of the islands was then or prior to that time.

Starting in 1624 the Dutch had settled a fortified town on the larger island of Mattinuck Island, in the river off the future site of the town of Burlington.[1] Later in 1625 the Dutch seat of government in the territory was placed on that island,[2] but this fortified capitol was abandoned in late 1626 in favor of New Amsterdam which later became New York.[3]

On February 15, 1667/8 Peter Alrick received a patent from Governor Nichols, the English Governor of the Crown stationed at New York City, for Mattinuck Island and for the "island to the north" (Seppasink Island) where there was a small stream on the mainland near the island suitable for building a mill.[4] When the Dutch reclaimed the territory on August 1, 1673, Peter Alrick's patent ended. It was not restored when the English reclaimed the territory with the Treaty of Westminster on February 9, 1673/4.

Following this change of title to the territory, Edmund Andros was commissioned Governor for the territory by James, Duke of York, representing the Crown of England. On November 5, 1675 Andros purchased lands from the Indians on the western shore of the Delaware

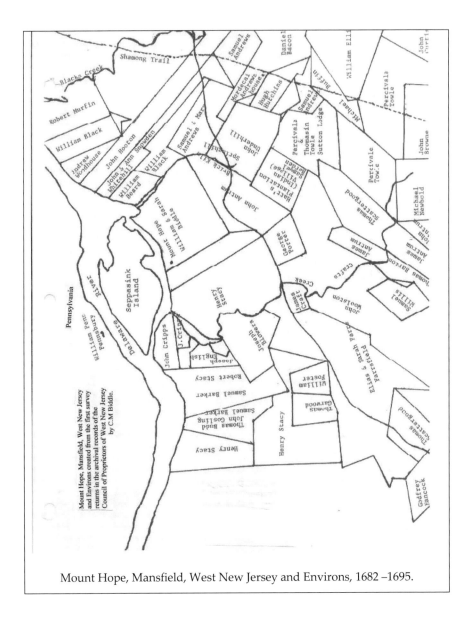

Mount Hope, Mansfield, West New Jersey and Environs, 1682 –1695.

River, to include all of the islands in the river nine miles above and below the falls of the river.[5] Later, on November 18, 1678, Captain Cantwell, representing Governor Andros, made more purchases of land on the western shore of the Delaware River, including all of the islands in the river, except Peter Alrick's Island, Mattinuck Island.[6] Robert Stacy, one of the original West Jersey Commissioners accepted by Governor Andros, had been placed in charge of Mattinuck by Governor Andros on November 14, 1678.[7] The Quaker settlers of Burlington had been given the use of the island by Governor Andros almost from the time of their arrival in the province.

The August 6, 1680 grant by James, Duke of York, to Edward Byllynge and the trustees for the Byllynge interests refers back to the grants of 1664 which stated that the territory of New Jersey was bounded by the Delaware River on the west. This 1680 grant did not mention specifically the islands in the Delaware River, but it did generally state that all islands were included in the West Jersey bounds. A broader interpretation of this statement might have been sufficient to support the West Jersey rights to the island, particularly since no other documents assigned the ownership to any other party or government.

William Penn believed that these islands in the Delaware River belonged to his Pennsylvania territory, but they had not been mentioned in his patent from Charles II dated March 4, 1680/1. Before they left London, William and Sarah, along with the entire group of Quakers interested in West Jersey, were familiar with the Penn's interest in these islands, and they knew that Penn had sent an inquiry to Sir John Werden, the Duke of York's secretary, concerning the islands. Werden replied to William Penn on July 16, 1681, stating that the islands were not clearly his.[8] Two months earlier, on May 12, 1681, Werden had sent a note to Governor Andros in New York in which he stated that the Pennsylvania boundary was the Delaware River on the east, but he expressed some uncertainty over the bounds of the West Jersey territory, suggesting that even the attorneys were unclear on this matter and it would take careful study of the grants to reach a decision.[9] Obviously William and Sarah were aware of this controversy, as evidenced by their claim for the island made so quickly and decisively, and their action aided the claim of the West Jersey Province.

It was during these early months in the West Jersey Province that Sarah, as later mentioned by James Logan, bargained with the Indians for the ownership of Seppasink Island. She was timely in her actions, for starting in April of 1682, Governor Markham of Pennsylvania, representing William Penn, also started bargaining with the Indians of Pennsylvania for the purchase of land in the Pennsylvania territory, to include the islands named Mattinuck, Seppasink and Orecktons in the Delaware River. This treaty was completed and signed by July 15, 1682.[10]

To counter this action by William Penn, Robert Stacy gave Mattinuck Island to the town of Burlington on September 27, 1682,[11] with the stipulation that the income from the island was to be used to support a school for the children of the town of Burlington and the children of the First and Second Tenths of the province. This gift was acknowledged and the income was dedicated for that purpose by an act of the General Assembly on September 27, 1682. At this time it became clear that both Mattinuck and Seppasink Islands were claimed legally by persons with West Jersey proprietary rights, under the system of government legally conducted in the West Jersey Province.

On June 11, 1683 William Penn, then visiting Pennsylvania and still interested in the islands, appointed Christopher Taylor, Thomas Holmes and Thomas Wynne of Pennsylvania to meet with Samuel Jennings, Governor of West Jersey, and his Council to discuss the rights to the river islands.[12] Thomas Budd, John Gosling, Mark Newbie and Henry Stacy, all commissioners at that time, were involved in the discussions held on June 16, 1683. In the communication that they received, written on June 20, 1683 by William Penn, it was apparent that no decision had been reached in these initial talks.[13] At the meeting of the West Jersey General Assembly held in Burlington September 5 through 8, 1683, it was requested that the Governor and "as many of his council as he shall think fit" should join with William Welch, Samuel Willis and William Peachee to continue "treating" with the commissioners from Pennsylvania and Governor Penn over the rights of the river and the river islands.[14] These three were apparently chosen by another authority, perhaps the Burlington Monthly Meeting, but more likely the town of Burlington.

William Penn had stated in his communication of June 11, 1683 that in his opinion the "propriety of the river" belonged to him, and that the West Jersey claim did not go beyond the low-water mark on the Delaware River, the traditional boundary for lands along tide waters in England.[15]

William Penn had been granted the Delaware territory on November 21, 1682. The grant specifically included the islands within a twelve-mile radius of New Castle, but the provisions of this grant were completely separate from the provisions of the patent for the Pennsylvania territory made earlier.[16] The fact that Penn might be anxious to annex some of the territory of West Jersey to his Pennsylvania was probably understood by Friends of London and West Jersey. This was noted by Sir John Werden when he wrote to Governor Dongan in New York on March 10, 1683/4 stating that the Commissioners of Trade in London were unanimous in their opinion that no lands beyond the bounds of East and West New

Jersey should be separated from his government, which included the lands of New York and New Jersey, and that he should do all that he could to prevent uniting any part of either Jersey with Mr. Penn, "Mr. Penn being very intent on his interests in those parts." [17]

There were apparently a number of discussions by representatives of government and perhaps of the Monthly Meetings of the Quakers in both Pennsylvania and West New Jersey to try to settle this issue by negotiation and possibly by arbitration.[18] The conditions requested by William Penn in his letter of June 11, 1683, were that if all of the islands were returned to him, then he would return one-half of Mattinuck Island to the town of Burlington for the public good.[19] This condition was not accepted. Other letters written later suggest that Penn tried to negotiate with William and Sarah Biddle for Seppasink Island, offering to give one half of the island to them for their lifetime, then one-half of the island to their children for their lifetimes, and finally upon their deaths the island would become entirely the property of William Penn.[20] This offer of negotiation was not accepted either.

William and Sarah went on to enjoy their ownership of the island by farming it, harvesting the hay and using it as pastureland for their livestock. This certainly would have been a scene that aggravated William Penn as he viewed the island from his Pennsbury estate on his second visit to Pennsylvania from 1699 to 1701.

It was during this visit that Governor Penn and the West Jersey officials again met to discuss the islands in the river. On June 26, 1700 it was noted at the meeting of the Council of Proprietors of West Jersey that officials from Pennsylvania had stopped some of the residents of West Jersey from cutting reeds from one of the islands in the Delaware River.[21] The council discussed the matter, asking by what authority the Pennsylvania officials had acted. They wondered if William Penn thought that he had ownership to "even the bottom of the river."

A committee was formed consisting of Governor Andrew Hamilton and Proprietor Councilmen Samuel Jennings and Thomas Thackera and they were instructed to meet with officials from Pennsylvania to obtain an explanation. The actual decisions reached in this meeting are unknown, but from indirect sources, and by the later letters of William Penn, it appears probable that the ownership of the islands was to be decided by the location of each island relative to the deeper channel of the river.[22] Seppasink Island and Mattinuck Island were separated from Pennsylvania by the deeper channel, so they would have remained in the possession of the West Jersey Proprietors. Seppasink Island also remained in the possession of William and Sarah Biddle. When a later disagreement arose between them and William Penn over the rights and the legitimacy of the indenture with Richard Baynum concerning a 300-acre tract of land purchased on the Rancocus Creek on August 3, 1681, William Penn threatened to renew his claim to Seppasink Island if he did not soon obtain payment for the value of the Baynum indenture that he had purchased. The issue apparently was never settled during the lives of William Penn or William and Sarah Biddle.

There had always been a small risk that someone could claim the islands of the Delaware River and set up a separate province between the two Quaker territories. Such an action would seriously restrict the ability of either territory to use the river as a trade route. Twice such a claim was actually attempted. A former deputy governor of Pennsylvania, Captain Charles Gookin, placed a claim for the islands and the rights of the river before the Lords of Trade in England, but the proposal was not accepted.[23] Also, shortly before the Revolutionary War, a Lord Rochford attempted to obtain a grant to some of the islands in the Delaware River, but this claim was denied by the Crown of England.[24]

The issue of which territory owned the islands in the Delaware River was not settled until after the Revolutionary War. In 1783 a joint commission was established by the states of New Jersey and Pennsylvania. On May 27, 1783 in New Jersey and on September 20, 1783 in Pennsylvania these commissioners signed the final agreement. Each state was to have access and concurrent jurisdiction upon the water. The islands, the dry land in the river, were each to belong to the state that had dry land nearest to it.[25] Thus Seppasink Island and Mattinuck Island officially became part of New Jersey. William and Sarah Biddle's claim, made more than one hundred years before, was finally validated.

The Indians, the Lenni Lenape, were the most successful negotiators in this process. They had certainly not understood the English concept of land ownership or boundaries. They sold some of their lands more than one time which was not discouraged.[26] As a result they sold the islands in the Delaware River at least four times between 1675 and 1682, twice to the representatives of the Crown, once to William and Sarah, and once to the agents of William Penn.

CHAPTER 13

Burlington 1682 – 1684
with Samuel Jennings as Deputy Governor

Although it had been five years since the first Quaker settlers founded the town of Burlington, the physical construction of the town had proceeded more slowly than anticipated by the early West Jersey leaders. By the time that William and Sarah arrived there were in excess of fourteen hundred people living in the province, but most of these residents claimed land and built their homesteads outside of the town.

The collective efforts of these rural settlers had, however, provided for the needs of the other inhabitants of the province. William Peachee established a nursery which supplied the townspeople and the farmers with fruit trees for their orchards. William Brightwen, butcher, not only kept the bull for breeding the cows of the settlers, he also kept stocks of animals of many species which served as food for the settlers or as stock for newly-arriving farmers. The clay deposits in the town were protected and used by the inhabitants until the lands were claimed, and later developed as brick-yards for the building of houses. Robert Stacy established a tannery near the junction of the Assiscunk Creek and the creek that bordered the town, the London Ditch. James Wills, cooper, made the barrels in which farm products could be shipped to overseas markets. William Cooper and Samuel Willis, blacksmiths, saw to the shoeing of the horses and producing ironware for the settlers.

Grain mills were established by Thomas Ollive at Mill Creek and by Mahlon Stacy at the falls of the Delaware River, in addition to some built at other locations. Saw mills were established to prepare lumber to build the houses of the region. Carpenters, including Robert Hudson and Richard Fenimore, built houses with the lumber prepared by the sawmills. Joiners, such as Isaac Marriott, did finer work with the lumber, including furniture-making. All kinds of alcoholic beverages were available to the settlers. Thomas Budd built a malt house and brew house on his town lot, and probably these were operated by John White, maltster, assisted by Benjamin Wheate.

If there was any commodity that they did not have but needed, inhabitants of the province could get it from London. Thomas Ollive had encouraged Peter Bosse, mariner, to settle in Burlington, and other mariners, such as Robert Hopper and Samuel Groome would regularly cross the Atlantic Ocean to bring new settlers and supplies to the province.

Several farm communities were developed throughout the province. At the falls of the Delaware River Mahlon Stacy led the development, accompanied by John and Thomas Lambert, William Emley, Thomas Wright and Joshua Wright with his son-in-law Peter Fretwell. Stacy had even constructed a unique tidal mill, a mill that worked both directions with the tide, that was to benefit all of the farmers of the area.

Thomas Foulke and Robert Murfin were the first settlers along Crosswicks Creek. The lands near the Indian village of Oneanickon were settled by Michael Newbold and his family. The Rancocas Creek development had been directed by Daniel Wills and Thomas Ollive. Samuel Coles had settled the more distant lands between the branches of the Pennsauken Creek, well inland from the river, and he was joined by William Matlack in this location. The area around the Newton Creek was settled by the Irish Quakers, and they were joined by Henry Stacy and Francis Collins. At Redbank, the sons of Thomas Gardiner and Daniel Wills, Thomas Gardiner Jr. and John Wills, had established their homesteads.

The town of Burlington had been slowed in its development by the fact that many new residents of the province preferred to settle themselves in the rural lands. Many Quakers also favored the attraction of Pennsylvania as it was now being advertised and encouraged for settlement by William Penn. The majority of the town lots of Burlington, as defined by the survey and the maps of Richard Noble, were slow to be developed. The houses that had been built were widely separated, and they were often surrounded by overgrown lots that had neither been sold by the proprietors who owned them, nor built upon by the persons who owned them.

Along the Assiscunk Creek, and along the London Ditch, the stream that surrounded the town, there were swamps, as drainage ditches had not yet been constructed by the townspeople. These wetlands served as the homes for snakes and turtles, and as breeding grounds for the most dreaded living creatures of the province, the mosquitoes. In the spring of the year when it was wet, and after each rainstorm, the dirt streets of the town were almost unusable. The roads had been constructed simply, for travel by foot or on horseback and for driving livestock down them. They were not intended for stages or carriages, for it would be many years before any of these vehicles were used in the province. Streets and bridges were further worn out by the livestock of the residents, for not uncommonly hogs would get loose and wallow in the puddles in the streets. This happened often enough that the leaders had to invoke the practice of earmarking domestic animals to make the owners of the hogs responsible for controlling them.

Each inhabitant was finally required to register his earmark with the clerk of the court.

Realizing that the town was not being built up as rapidly as they thought it should be, and feeling the growing competition from Pennsylvania, the leaders of the province changed the rules about claiming and settling lands along the Burlington waterfront. Originally each proprietary shareholder of the Yorkshire Tenth would be allowed approximately 250 feet of waterfront lots located in ten separate blocks. The owners of a proprietary share in the London Tenth were each allowed a block of about 180 feet of waterlots. Now the General Assembly decided that if a person claimed a waterlot and did not build upon it within eight months of establishing title, he would lose the title to that land. No longer was it necessary to claim waterlots on the basis of the proprietary right from which it was purchased. Each person who purchased the rights to a waterlot could claim a lot on any location along the waterfront that had been previously unclaimed.[1] This action relieved the restrictions of the previous rules and eventually led to stimulation of the growth of the town waterfront.

William and Sarah Biddle lived in the town of Burlington for the first two years of their residence in the West Jersey Province. During this time several of the inhabitants of Burlington left, but a number of persons arrived and settled, including people who were important to the further growth and versatility of the community. James Hill, cordwainer (shoemaker), settled in the town. He built his home on the west side of High Street on land that he purchased from William. Thomas Gladwin did the same. As a blacksmith he took the place of Samuel Willis, who moved out of town, and William Cooper, who moved himself with his family to Pyne Point in the Third Tenth.

Richard Basnett took over the operation of, and then the ownership of John Hollinshead's Inn on the river front. John Cripps and Thomas Potts continued their eating establishments, and eventually Henry Grubb built an inn on the north side of Pearl Street, on the west side of High Street across Pearl Street from the house of Thomas Budd. William Myers and his family arrived in Burlington to take up residence in the house built by John Antrum on the land of Daniel Wills. As a butcher he eventually took over the business of William Brightwen, who moved to Philadelphia. William Myers established a slaughterhouse on the river front in the Yorkshire half of the town. William Budd, brewer, joined his brother Thomas in Burlington. He was helped in his trade by Nathaniel Ible, and later he was joined by his brother, John Budd. Daniel England, mariner, also established himself in the town.

Christopher Wetherill, tailor, purchased land from George Hutcheson and built his home on the east side of High Street, near the northeast corner of High and Broad Streets, the marketplace area of the town. Anthony Morris, merchant, constructed his home and business on the east side of High Street, near the town wharf. He contributed significantly to the development of the town before he moved to Philadelphia. Doctor Robert Dimsdale came back to the province from England, and with Daniel Wills served as the medical practitioners for the province in its earliest days.

In 1682 William and Sarah, with their two children, servant and slaves were living temporarily in Burlington. The most important task for William, after he had claimed the land for their homestead, Mount Hope, was to prepare the land for planting of the crops that would eventually feed them and to arrange for building the necessary houses and barns on the property. Immediately William moved the two male slaves and other newly-hired servants to the property to manage the propagation of his recently purchased livestock there. These workers were also responsible for starting to clear the land for the planting.

While they were still living in Burlington, that town began the practice of having its main Fair Days on the first day of May and the first day of November yearly, as officially directed by the General Assembly in 1681.[2] Those who resided in the town could frequently gather to trade information and ideas with one another, but on the Fair Days all people of the province stopped whatever they were doing and came to town. Burlington was supported by the trading activities of several of its inhabitants who had remained in touch with the Quakers of London, Barbados and Jamaica. They developed markets for the farm products of the province and regularly imported finished goods from England. At each spring fair the farmers could get the supplies that they needed including seed, livestock and young fruit trees. At the fall fair they would cart the products of their farms back to town for sale or exportation. If their profit was great enough they would be able to purchase or trade for goods from England or for products of the tradesmen in town. Even if the season had not been profitable, it was a pleasant time, and a time to renew acquaintances with people not seen for many months.

Meanwhile, in London, Edward Byllynge, realizing that he had angered his fellow Quakers by taking away their governing rights to the province, he wanted them to like him so he began to take steps to appease the Friends. On November 10, 1681, it was announced in all of the Monthly Meetings of England that he was donating 10,000 acres of his lands in West New Jersey to needy Friends who wanted to move to the province, but did not have the money to buy land there. They were offered between 50 and 100 acres each if they went to West Jersey and became resident there.[3] In his announcement Byllynge stated that he too intended to go to the new land, confirming the information that William Biddle, Elias Farre and Benjamin Scott gave Samuel Jennings and presumably other residents of the province. Byllynge obviously hoped that this action would increase the rate of settlement of the province and that it would change the attitude of the Quakers back in his favor.[4]

A number of families took advantage of this offer, including Roger Park of Northumberland[5] and Richard Haines and his family of Oxfordshire, who received his deed April 21, 1682, the day he and his family boarded ship for West New Jersey.[6] Samuel Burroughs of Wilton[7] and John Brewster of Northumberland[8] also accepted the offer. However, not enough of the Quakers took advantage of this gift to use up the full 10,000 acres offered by Byllynge, and because there still many unclaimed acres, he was not, therefore, totally successful in his endeavor.

William Penn, in England, with others, continued to work on the plan to protect the claims of the proprietors of West New Jersey to their territory. On February 2, 1681/2 Penn and eleven other affluent people of England and Scotland purchased the proprietary rights to the East Jersey territory from the widow of Sir George Cartaret.[9] These twelve investors immediately sold half of their interests to twelve additional investors to form a group of twenty-four proprietors for East Jersey.[10] James, Duke of York, had no trouble in accepting this limited group of people that he could easily identify as proprietors, and he issued a new grant to them on March 14, 1682/3.[11] There were many Quakers among this group who were known to William Biddle, including Gawen Lawrie, Hugh Hartshorne, Clement Plumstead, Thomas Rudyard and Edward Byllynge. They elected the respected Robert Barclay, a Quaker from Scotland, as the Governor of their province. Within the year Thomas Rudyard, attorney for the Friends of London, was made deputy governor of the province,[12] and he and his family came to East New Jersey.

In West New Jersey elections were held in the Tenths in April 1682, and the assemblymen for the province were elected. The General Assembly met from May 2 through 6, 1682. William Biddle was elected by the Assembly as a member of the Governor's Council and as a Land Commissioner.[13] As a member of the Governor's Council he had the added responsibility of being a justice of the courts of the province, but it is quite possible that he had also been independently elected as a judge by one of the Tenths, for on April 17, 1682, before the General Assembly met, William Biddle and Thomas Gardiner as justices at the Burlington Court, acknowledged an indenture of John Murfin to James Pharoe.[14] Non-assemblymen Elias Farre and Benjamin Scott were also elected to commissioner positions by the Assembly at that session. They all signed the Subscription of Office as called for by the Concessions and Agreements on May 8, 1682.[15]

There were thirty-three elected assemblymen present at the General Assembly meeting, and Thomas Ollive, the most experienced resident proprietor, was elected Speaker of the House.[16] At this meeting it was decided that each Tenth would be allowed to sell 500 acres to raise additional monies for the public good. At the rate of £10 per one hundred acres, this could have raised £500 for the province. However, all of the Tenths were not settled, so the amount realized was considerably less.

This action by the Assembly was the first in which the general assets of the proprietors of the land of the West New Jersey Province were used to offset the public debt. Apparently the tax that had been enacted in November of 1681 had not been sufficient to meet the public needs of the province. It was also decided at these meetings that the court of the province would be held in two locations, at Burlington and at Salem.[17]

The schedule for the Quarter Court Sessions was made for Burlington on the eighth of May, the eighth of August, the third of November and the twentieth of February each year. Presumably the first session of the Quarter Court was held on May 8, 1682 in Burlington, but the records are not clear enough to tell if it met or which judges were in attendance. The same Assembly changed the Fair dates for Burlington to May tenth and eleventh and November first and second yearly.[18]

The social life and religious life of the residents of West Jersey were intertwined. Outside of Burlington, Quaker Meetings for Worship were held at the falls of the Delaware River, near the Assinpink Creek, at the home of Thomas Harding near the Rancocas Creek, at Newton Creek, and at the home of Samuel Nicholson in the Salem Colony. The residents of Burlington and those who attended these other meetings worshiped on first day and on fifth day weekly. Since almost all of the inhabitants of the town were Quakers, nearly the entire community met at the home of Thomas Gardiner each first day. On the first second day of each month the Burlington Monthly Meeting also held its meeting for business at the home of Thomas Gardiner.

While William and Sarah resided temporarily in Burlington, awaiting the completion of their homestead at Mount Hope, they attended and actively participated in the worship and business of the Burlington Monthly Meeting. At the business meeting held August 7, 1682 a committee was appointed, to meet at the home of William Biddle, to settle by arbitration a disagreement that had arisen between two Friends.[19] The Monthly Meeting had previously requested that Friends arbitrate their differences, rather than settle them in court. William was frequently asked to serve as an arbitrator in disputes during his life in West Jersey. In his personal affairs, William almost always submitted differences that he had with others to arbitration, indicating his firm belief in the ability of this process to settle most issues.

The second Yearly Meeting of Friends was held in Burlington on September 6, 1682.[20] Friends were accustomed to traveling great distances to meetings such as this. Friends arrived in Burlington from Virginia, Maryland, New York, East Jersey and the newly-formed Pennsylvania. It was an important time for Friends to meet new Friends, or to renew their past friendships. For Mary Parnell, William and Sarah's servant, it was a particularly exciting time. She and William Wood, who was originally from New York, became engaged to marry.

The commissioners of the province were requested to attend the Quarter Court Session held in Burlington on August 8 and 9, 1682. The record does not reveal who attended, but it is assumed that William Biddle was there, for he had recently been elected to this responsibility. That day the courts recognized that the bridges that had been constructed over the streams surrounding Burlington, the Yorkshire Bridge and the London Bridge, were in poor repair. Thomas Budd and Thomas Gardiner were directed to see to the needed repairs. The court also directed that the town's first public building be constructed, a log cabin prison. Also, the price of a quart of ale or beer was set at no more that two pence, and Henry Grubb and Benjamin Wheate were appointed ale tasters for the jurisdiction.[21]

When court met again at Burlington on September 26, 1682, William Biddle was seated on the bench.[22] He was joined that day by Samuel Jennings, Thomas Ollive, Robert Stacy, John Chaffen, Thomas Budd, John Cripps and Benjamin Scott.

That day was a busy one for the leaders of the province, for not only did the court meet, but another session of the General Assembly began, a session that would last through September 28, 1682. Perhaps because of the claim of Seppasink Island by William and Sarah, but maybe for other reasons, the town residents had become acutely aware of William Penn's desire to own the islands in the Delaware River. The West Jersey residents undoubtedly knew that Penn was due to arrive in Pennsylvania in the next month. The General Assembly accepted Robert Stacy's gift to Burlington of Mattinuck Island in the river, and the income from it to maintain schools, a gift intended to strengthen West Jersey's claim to ownership of the Island.[23]

The General Assembly also gave permission to the town of Burlington to appoint people to regulate several town matters — presumably the first time that the town was given permission to appoint or elect its own government.[24] A town committee would be better able to protect the interests of Burlington and to direct the further development of the capital city of the province.

Mary Parnell and William Wood presented their intention of marriage to the Burlington Monthly Meeting in September and October, it being the custom of Friends to present their intentions two times to the overseeing meeting. The overseers of the meeting had the information provided by the Certificate of Removal given to Sarah and William by the Devonshire Monthly Meeting just prior to their departure from London, a document that stated the clearness of Mary Parnell to marry (*illustrated on page 70*). The Burlington Monthly Meeting gave its approval and William and Sarah released Mary from service. She married William Wood on October 8, 1682. The newlyweds left their home in Burlington and went to Marbleton, New York, where they remained for a year and where their first child, Anne, was born. They then moved to Hopewell, West New Jersey, and from there to a farm that they developed near Oneanickon. They stayed in close association with William and Sarah for the rest of their lives.[25]

The Quaker practice of holding the business meetings of the men and the women Friends separately had begun in England before the settlers came to West Jersey. It was continued in the province. When women had a concern they would present it to the Men's Monthly Meeting for discussion and final approval. Sarah participated in the Women's Monthly Meeting in Burlington with her neighbors and friends. The women had begun to worry about how they might keep the province protected from those who were not conducting their lives by ethical standards. In particular they were concerned about the behavior of non-Quaker servants who had come to Burlington who were not behaving properly and were not being overseen well by their employers. The women presented this concern to the Burlington Monthly Meeting on November 6, 1682:

> Dear Friends we having a sense upon us concerning the matter that is there being many Friends that bring servants over with them and have no occasion for them when they come here so we desire if you so meet that no servants be disposed of till our monthly meeting be satisfied that Truth may not suffer by parting with them to such as do not posses the same Truth with us.

Sarah Biddle	Frances Taylor
Eliz Hooton	Ann Jennings
Hellen Skeen	Jane Atkinson
Ann Butcher	Susan Budd
Susan Brightwen	Judith Noble
Mary Crips	Anne Peachee
Frances Antrum	

And this is the concensus [*sic*] of the whole meeting.[26]

The Concessions and Agreements had called for a province that would be open to all persons. All proprietors, freeholders and inhabitants were to benefit from the freedoms and rights of the governing system. The women Friends accurately expressed the sentiment and worry of the Quakers of West Jersey in their concern. In England the people had been overseen by a very strong, central religious authority. In West New Jersey the Friends were that authority. Besides overseeing the protection of the institution of marriage, identifying and aiding the poor, the orphaned and the widowed, they were concerned that all inhabitants of the province should be controlled by or control themselves in the manner of Christians. There was no other authority except the General Assembly and the courts to help them with this concern.

Thomas Budd and Deputy Governor Samuel Jennings strongly favored the settlement of only Quakers in the upper two Tenths. They would not let large tracts of land fall into the hands of non-resident proprietors. They prevented even Edward Byllynge, the Governor, from claiming large tracts of lands in these upper Tenths. It was feared that a non-caring non-resident, even though a Quaker, might try to profit from the sale of the lands. There were no efforts to develop industries that would require the importation of laborers who might not be Quakers, despite the probability that they themselves, the resident proprietor leaders of the province, might profit handsomely from such endeavors. The Province of West Jersey was forced to develop as a rural, peaceful homogeneous Quaker community, unrealistically protected, at least temporarily, from outside influences and authority, including the largest fear, the return of religious persecution.

It must have been of great interest to Samuel Jennings, Thomas Budd and the other leaders of West Jersey to watch William Penn encourage the development of Pennsylvania. Industry was encouraged to settle there. Many people from differing religious backgrounds settled there, but the majority of the earliest settlers were Quakers. They remained in control of the government because of the ownership of the proprietorship by William Penn, but also because of the design of the governing system. Quakerism in Pennsylvania was to undergo a fairer test in a melting pot environment than it would receive in West New Jersey.

At this same the meeting of the Burlington Monthly Meeting held November 6, 1682, William was asked to serve on a committee that was formed to meet with a carpenter, Walter Pumphary, concerning the building of a meetinghouse for their use.[27] This carpenter, with Richard Fenimore, bricklayer, had constructed a number of the homes in and near Burlington. Apparently no agreement could be reached with Pumphary, for the contract was later made with Francis Collins.

The General Assembly of Western New Jersey next met May 2 through 15, 1683, with thirty-seven members in attendance. Thomas Ollive was re-elected Speaker of the House. William was elected an Assemblyman from the First Tenth in the spring elections, and the General Assembly reelected him a commissioner on the Governor's Council, which made him a Justice again, and he was appointed this time as a Land Commissioner.[28]

The Assembly passed regulations in this session requiring each Tenth to maintain its own roads. Brick manufacturing and the tanning process were also regulated by acts of the Assembly. The rules for taking up land in the province were simplified. Now a first settlement could be by one person, and a second claim of land could be settled by any two able-bodied people. For those who owned large fractions or full proprietary shares in the province, this meant that they could claim and settle more lands without having to procure more slaves or contract with more servants. Those who wanted to claim building lots in Burlington were required to build on the lots within six months, or they would lose their rights to the land. The need for public buildings was acknowledged and the contracts for building a courthouse and a market house were awarded to Thomas Budd and Francis Collins, who were to be paid 1,000 acres of unappropriated land in the province. In this action the Assembly had decided to use the land assets of the proprietors to meet public needs. The legislative body in this session also decided on the election days for the Tenths. Elections thereafter were to be held on April 14th in the First Tenth and on April 10th in the Second Tenth.[29]

During these meetings of the General Assembly the ownership of the governing rights by Edward Byllynge was first seriously contested. William Penn, on his first visit to Pennsylvania, from October 27, 1682 to August 30, 1684, had quietly begun to communicate with John Fenwick in the Salem Colony to try to work out the differences that remained between Fenwick and the leaders who had formed the constitution and the settlement of the West Jersey Province at Burlington. Just before the General Assembly sessions were to adjourn, in May 1683, late at night in a thunderstorm, Penn and Fenwick arrived in Burlington to present themselves to the Assembly and to discuss the controversy of the ownership of the governing rights of the province. Heated discussion ensued, some of it directed against Edward Byllynge. Penn, as a past trustee of the Byllynge interests in West Jersey, presumably thought that those who purchased shares of propriety in the province had also purchased governing rights. Undoubtedly he was angered by the actions of Edward Byllynge.

Thomas Mathews, Edward Byllynge's land agent in West Jersey, was later to confirm in a letter written to George Fox on June 11, 1683, that

Penn and Fenwick had slandered Byllynge at those meetings, at a time when he was not present to defend himself. Mathews suggested that only Thomas Gardiner and William Biddle showed moderation in the discussion. In that letter he also confirmed that Thomas Budd and Samuel Jennings had acted against Byllynge by not letting Mathews settle tracts of land in the Second Tenth for him.[30] They finally suggested that the Byllynge lands could be settled in one place, in the largely undeveloped Third Tenth, which would keep his influence in the province away from the area inhabited by the majority of the Quakers who had already settled in West Jersey.

This interference by William Penn in the affairs of the West Jersey Province led to several actions that helped to unite the inhabitants of the province and to define the status of the governing rights. John Fenwick now more clearly understood the overall purpose and plan of those who authored and accepted the Concessions and Agreements of the West Jersey Province. He ended the estrangement of the Salem Colony from the Burlington settlement by officially joining his interests with those of the government at Burlington.[31] A general meeting of the inhabitants of the province was called, and through a series of queries many of the provisions of, as well as the body of the Concessions and Agreements were reconfirmed as the basis of the government of the West Jersey Province. In an unprecedented move, the inhabitants of West Jersey held an election for governor among themselves, electing Samuel Jennings and bypassing any recognition of Edward Byllynge as Governor of the West Jersey Province.[32]

During that same session the General Assembly removed an assemblyman and commissioner, John Skene, from office, but the reason for the removal is not shown in the existing records.[33] Skene, a Scotsman and a Quaker, had been aided by Edward Byllynge when he was down on his luck in England. Byllynge had supplied him with land and encouraged his emigration to West Jersey.[34] The inhabitants of the province had recognized John Skene's abilities, for they elected him to these offices. By the rules of the Concessions and Agreements he could not have been divested of office merely because he was an ally of Edward Byllynge; there must have been more to the story that was not recorded.

The General Assembly, for the purpose of supporting the ownership of the governing rights by the proprietors, appointed a committee of fourteen assemblymen, including William Biddle and his associates Thomas Ollive, William Emley, John Gosling, James Nevill, Mahlon Stacy, Henry Stacy, Daniel Wills, Thomas Budd, Richard Guy, Francis Collins, Thomas Lambert, Mark Newbie and William Peachee. The committee was instructed to send letters to eight London Friends including George Fox and three others known personally by William Biddle, namely Charles

Bathurst, George Whitehead and William Crouch. The letters were to stress the points that supported the claim of the proprietors, other than those of Edward Byllynge, to the ownership of the governing rights of the province.[35]

Later that year Penn purchased from John Fenwick the ten proprietary shares given to Fenwick in 1674/5. An indenture of March 23, 1683/4 officially placed the remaining unappropriated landrights in these ten shares in the possession of William Penn.[36] John Fenwick had sold about 150,000 acres of the land rights from those shares prior to the sale.[37]

Later Penn would gain possession of two additional full proprietary shares. One of these was the share of William Haige, the first share that had been released by the Byllynge trustees.[38] The other one was the share owned by Daniel Waite, for which William Biddle had been the attorney.[39] Thus, William Penn became the owner of twelve percent of the proprietary rights of West New Jersey and one twenty-fourth of the proprietary rights of East New Jersey. With these interests he could justify playing a role in the governments of both New Jersey Provinces, if necessary, to protect the interests of Pennsylvania.

The General Assembly sessions ended on May 15, 1683. The newly elected officers of the province, including William Biddle, signed the Subscription of the Office.[40] The governmental and judicial systems of the West New Jersey Province were beginning to function as the Quakers in England planned.

William had been present on the bench of the court on December 19, 1682 and on February 20, 1682/3 with other justices, Governor Samuel Jennings, Robert Stacy, John Chaffen, Elias Farre, Mahlon Stacy, Thomas Budd and John Cripps.[41] He had attended in the colder months of the year, but the attendance records do not reveal that he attended the courts held that year in the warmer, productive months of May, June and August. By then he had turned his attention to the development and construction of his homestead, Mount Hope. There were carpenters, bricklayers and masons to oversee, as well as the clearing of fields and planting of crops on his 500 acres.

Though William was not in attendance during this time, the courts did meet, and they carried out the directives of the General Assembly. Overseers for the highways were appointed. John Shinn and John Woolston were selected for the First Tenth. John Cripps, Thomas Mathews, Benjamin Scott and Daniel Wills were chosen for the Second Tenth. Richard Fenimore and Francis Collins were appointed as overseers for the size of bricks. Benjamin Wheate, James Hill, Jonathan Eldridge and Thomas Farnsworth were chosen to oversee the tanning process, the weights and measures and as ale tasters.[42] A special court was held on May 26, 1683 to make assessments for the highways.[43] In each court session many cases were withdrawn, suggesting that the Friends involved may have settled the issues outside the courtroom by arbitration.

William Biddle, as one of the parties involved in the claim to the ownership of Seppasink Island, appropriately refrained from participating in the discussions that were called for by William Penn in his letter of June 11, 1683.[44] These meetings between officials from Pennsylvania and West New Jersey concerned the ownership of the islands in the Delaware River. It must have been disconcerting for William Penn to see the farming activity of William and Sarah on Seppasink Island, planting, building shelters upon it and raising some of their livestock there.

The Yearly Meeting of Friends was held again in Burlington on September 4, 1683 at the home of Thomas Budd.[45] Again Friends came from all over the colonies. William Penn was present along with many other Friends of Pennsylvania. At least temporary harmony was restored among Friends as they focused their attention on matters concerning their Quaker religion.

On the next day, September 5, 1683, another session of the General Assembly began, a session that was to last through September 8, 1683 although all of the Assemblymen had to take time away from their farm chores to attend. Perhaps it was the spirit of the Yearly Meeting that carried over to the Assembly meeting, for the legislative body, now remembering that Edward Byllynge had stated that he might move to the West New Jersey Province, encouraged his emigration by setting aside a four-acre lot in the town of Burlington for his use.[46] Shortly after that time the Governor and the commissioners appointed a special commission to oversee the surveying and laying out of a town, Billingport, to be located at the mouth of the Mantua Creek, down river from the lands already settled.[47]

The Assembly also passed an act that better protected the security of the residents of the province. The act required that all persons who came into the province must have certificates that verified their character and their claims. In another act the Assembly restated the rule that no person could purchase land from the Indians without the permission of the Governor and the Land Commissioners.[48]

The Assembly also called for a registration of the residents of the province, which amounted to a first census. The inhabitants were to list the name of the ship that had brought them to the province, the date of their arrival and names of the members of their family who were with them and of each of the servants who came with them. This list, apparently available when the first history of West New Jersey was written in 1765, has since been lost.

This session of the Assembly also appointed a special committee consisting of the Governor and as many of his council as he saw fit, along with William Welch, Samuel Willis and William Peachee. The latter three may have represented the newly-formed town committee of Burlington. The committee was to meet with some of the officials of Pennsylvania to discuss the ownership of the islands in the Delaware River and other issues that needed to be worked out by the authorities of the two territories.[49]

On September 27, 1683, in London, by a release indenture, the Byllynge trusteeship ended. The unsold shares of propriety were turned over to Edward Byllynge by the remaining trustees, Nicholas Lucas and Gawen Lawrie.[50] The exact number of shares owned outright by Byllynge at that time is not known, but these shares were the only ones recognized as being associated with the governing rights. Now that the affairs of Edward Byllynge were in order and he was acting on his own behalf, it would be even more difficult to take these governing rights away from him.

William and Sarah Biddle had worked very hard through the spring, summer and fall seasons to prepare their homestead for their permanent occupancy. In the spring of the year their livestock had produced their first young. They had planted their first acreage in corn and other grains. Now in the fall of the year the crops had been harvested and the workmen had nearly completed their house. They had spent many days living at the site and less time in Burlington. Now it was time for the fall Fair Days in Burlington and since most of the more difficult work was completed, they would be able to return to the town and stay there for several weeks. They now knew exactly what they needed to purchase at the fair to see them through the winter months at Mount Hope.

The public activities of the province were now conveniently arranged, for the Quarter Court session was held on November 3, 1683. William sat on the bench that day with his associate Governor Samuel Jennings and fellow justices Thomas Budd, John Gosling, Thomas Ollive, William Emley, Elias Farre and Mahlon Stacy.[51] The court session was brief, for the General Assembly also started its first session that day.

While he was spending so much time at Mount Hope, William continued to explore the area to familiarize himself with the remaining unclaimed lands nearby. He had decided to give up the 322-acre survey at nearby Springhill. When he was contacted by John Underhill from Oyster Bay, Long Island, William made a verbal arrangement to sell this choice piece of property to him.[52]

Samuel Andrews also came down from Oyster Bay, and he too made a verbal land contract with William for his land.[53] Others from New York would later do business with William since they knew that he had proprietary rights to many acres.

On November 8, 1683 William went to the office of Thomas Revell, Registrar of the province, to see that the survey was properly recorded for the Underhill land, a 500-acre tract that included the 322 acres previously surveyed to William. It is apparent from the recorded survey that Samuel Andrews' land was already identified and defined by that date, for one of the borders of the Underhill land is in common with one of the survey lines of the Andrews property, even though the survey would not be recorded for several more months and the deed verifying the sale of the land by William to Samuel was not recorded for another five years.[54] William had made some kind of verbal land contract arrangement with Samuel to encourage him to settle in the neighborhood.

These settlers had undoubtedly already started to build their homes and to farm the land. They had to have a good start on the development of their homesteads, as did William, for the winter months were coming on and little could be done to develop the homesteads further until spring.

The General Assembly met on November 3, 1683, and the sessions continued until November 8, 1683. A committee was appointed by the Assembly to develop a position paper that could be presented to Friends in London in support of the resident proprietors' claim to the ownership of the governing rights to their province. The committee included William Biddle and Thomas Ollive, John Gosling, Mahlon Stacy, William Emley, Thomas Budd, Daniel Wills, George Hutcheson, Robert Stacy and Governor Samuel Jennings.[55] The points that were made by the committee were undoubtedly those expressed later by Thomas Budd and Samuel Jennings in their written statement prepared February 28, 1683/4.[56] The position paper pointed out the sequence of events that had led to their claim to the rights, crediting Edward Byllynge with a large role in the development of the province.

The Assembly also expanded the list of persons who should receive letters from them asking for their support in London. The list now included James Martin, a London minister and a brother of Thomas Martin who had purchased his one-sixth proprietary right the day William received his first West Jersey rights in London. Also included was Henry Stacy, who had left the province and returned to his family in Spitalfield, London. Before he left, Henry Stacy had purchased some lands near Seppasink Island, including seven and one-half acres that he purchased from William Biddle from the Mount Hope tract.[57] It may have been the intention of Henry

Stacy to build a mill there, but, he died shortly after returning to England. It is possible that William may have built a mill on the site anyway, or the property may have merely served as a part of the wharf that he developed on the riverbank. Years later the property came into the possession of Thomas Potts,[58] who was a mill expert in the province.

The Assembly in those sessions also voted to replace the vacancies among the commissioners. John Hollinshead and Richard Basnett became commissioners in the place of John Chaffen and the divested John Skene; Henry Wood and Robert Zane of the Third Tenth replaced Henry Stacy and Mark Newbie, the first banker of the province who was now disabled and possibly deceased.[59]

The resident proprietors' claim to the ownership of the governing rights to their province was further weakened when King Charles II issued a patent to them on November 15, 1683. The patent informed the residents of West New Jersey that the Crown recognized Edward Byllynge as the Governor of the West New Jersey Province.[60] This did not deter the resident proprietors from their plan to try to remove the governing rights from Byllynge's possession.

Following these fall meetings in Burlington William and Sarah moved most of their possessions to the new Mount Hope home. There is no evidence that they stayed in Burlington that winter, but they are not known to have officially moved to Mount Hope until April 7, 1684.[61] The homestead was sufficiently finished to allow them to occupy the house. Their investment in that location was so great by then that it required their direct supervision.

They were probably aided by hired or indentured farm workers, under the supervision of William, who had been well prepared by his father as a youth at Birlingham for this rural life. The warmth of the newly-constructed home was particularly increased when Friends of that area gathered at Mount Hope to worship together in the manner of the Friends for Meeting for Worship.

William returned to Burlington again on February 24, 1683/4 when he served as a Land Commissioner, along with Francis Collins and John Gosling, in acknowledging an indenture between Mathew Allen and Hannah Kimball.[62] He may have been there also returned again on March 3, 1683/4 with Sarah for the Burlington Monthly Meeting. Certificates of travel were issued to Thomas Budd and Samuel Jennings at that meeting, as they prepared to travel back to London to present their case to Friends there regarding their claims to the governing rights to the province.[63]

William was also in Burlington for the General Assembly meetings that were called into session on March 29, 1684 and continued through April 5,

1684. The legislative body made a significant decision, to send Samuel Jennings and Thomas Budd to London to officially represent their claims.[64] George Hutcheson agreed to accompany them at his own expense.

It was recognized that this trip would be expensive and the finances of the province were not in good order. Samuel Jennings, the popularly elected Governor, was not as financially secure as some of the other resident proprietors. A method to pay for the trip had to be devised.

Under the tutelage of William Penn, the Assembly developed a system of bonding, which immediately raised £100 for Jennings' use in London. In addition the Assembly established another £100 line of credit for his use if he needed it while they bonded others too, all backed by the decision to purchase 3,000 acres from the Indians from the lands above the falls of the Delaware River. The bonds would be secured by the money received from the sale of these lands, or those holding the bonds, issued at interest, would be able to claim the lands for themselves if the tract could not be sold.[65]

Since this method introduced the possibility that the Assembly might have to sell the land to those who were not Quakers, they had wisely located the tract in an area far from the region that was already settled by the Quakers of West New Jersey. In implementing this system of bonding, the Assembly and William Penn demonstrated that the original intention of the Quaker residents of the province to tax themselves, to be financially independent of the proprietors, and to leave the proprietors free from the financial burden of the public debt of the province, had been temporarily abandoned. The resident proprietors were fully aware of these actions of the Assembly.

In another act of this General Assembly, it was decided to cooperate with Pennsylvania in matters concerning criminal offenders. If persons convicted of crimes in Pennsylvania were found in West Jersey, having escaped before their punishments had been carried out, those persons were to be subject to the same penalty to which they had been sentenced in that neighboring territory.[66] This may be the first act of reciprocity between two neighboring jurisdictions in America. It probably resulted from the meeting between the officials of both territories that had been forced by the interests of William Penn in the islands in the Delaware River.

At the end of this session the Assembly elected Thomas Ollive as deputy governor, to serve in the absence of Samuel Jennings while he was in London.[67] Thomas Ollive had been the Speaker of the House for each of the sessions of the Assembly held to that time and he had been a leader of the province since its founding.

At the Burlington Monthly Meeting held April 7, 1684 it became apparent that William and Sarah and their family had permanently moved to their home at Mount Hope. The Monthly Meeting gave permission for First Day Meetings for Worship to be held at their home, "beginning the next First Day, and it is left to Friends there to consider whether to continue it or not." [68]

William now began to sell some of the land that he did not need for his personal use. The price of land in the upper two Tenths was £10 per 100 acres. A deed was recorded by Thomas Revell on the books of the province on May 10, 1684, indicating that William Biddle of Mount Hope had sold a 100-acre tract located on the Pennsauken Creek to Thomas Williams, tanner of Burlington, for the price of £10. [69]

CHAPTER 14

The Homestead, Mount Hope, Mansfield, West Jersey

After carefully examining the several tracts of land that they had claimed, William and Sarah decided that the features of the 500-acre tract on the Delaware River near Seppasink Island made that land the best for the development of their homestead. A wide bluff extended along the river, high and safe from flooding, overlooking a major portion of the island. Further inland were numerous flat areas suitable for cultivation. There were ample virgin woodlands composed of white and black oak, chestnut, hickory, gum and maple trees.

Perhaps the most important feature of the land was the huge meadow on the side of the property furthest from the river, a meadow that was high enough to be usable year round as pastureland, and low enough to remain moist for the growth of the natural grasses that could be harvested several times each year. Wildlife was abundant on the Mount Hope tract, and migratory birds rested in the coves between the mainland and the island. The fish in the river could be caught more easily in the shallow channel between the two properties, except for the shad, which were in the deeper channels of the river in the spring. Deer, grouse and turkeys could be hunted on the island as well as on the dry uplands.

The large bluff along the river was chosen as the site on which the house would be built. The location was near the edge of the bluff on the down-river end, at the beginning of an indentation where a small stream entered the river. Boats could be docked easily at this location, safe from the tides and storms. Nearby was the stream which could be used for bathing in the warmer months of the year. A mill might be built on the stream for processing the grains grown on the farm. The dam required for the mill would create a pond that would be naturally stocked with fish, turtles and wild fowl, and in addition would serve as a source of ice in the winter months.

Having claimed the Mount Hope tract and Seppasink Island in the winter of 1681/2, William protected the family's rights to the land by settling two of his bondsmen and other indentured or hired servants on the tracts the following spring. He purchased the needed pairs of livestock to begin to propagate animals that they would need for labor and food. The slaves and servants looked after the livestock and began to clear the lands that were to be cultivated. The sites for the family gardens and orchards

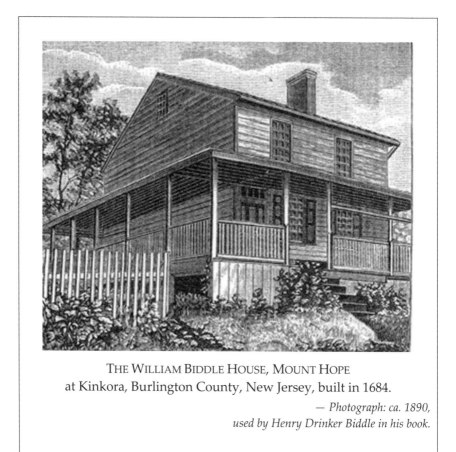

THE WILLIAM BIDDLE HOUSE, MOUNT HOPE
at Kinkora, Burlington County, New Jersey, built in 1684.

— Photograph: ca. 1890,
used by Henry Drinker Biddle in his book.

were prepared and planted. As was the custom of the time, a plain cabin was built on one of the hills further back from the river, a cabin that served as shelter for the farm laborers and the builders. The cabin, with a cellar carved into the hillside and lined with river rock mortared together, was constructed above the ground with logs cut from the woods of the tract. A simpler shelter was constructed on the island for the protection of the animals and those workers who stayed with them. During this first spring it was possible to clear and plant as much as twenty-five acres in corn, and then to harvest as much as 1,400 bushels of this grain[1] which would be exported with the crops of the established settler, Mahlon Stacy. It was necessary to make the farmlands productive as soon as possible, for this was the family's only source of income.

William did not have the experience to build the house that he wanted to have at Mount Hope. He had in mind a plan for the home, but he needed the help of others more skilled in building. The house that he wanted was more complex in design than the other homes that were being built on the farms of the province. He had to be ready to start construction by the spring of 1683 if there was to a chance of moving in by the fall or winter of that year.

Many journeymen and their apprentices or laborers were involved in the construction of the house. Clay for bricks, material for mortar, logs for boards, beams and shingles, rocks and glass were needed to construct the home. Bricks were being made in Burlington, but since the bricks of this house do not meet the specifications in size legislated by the General Assembly, it is very likely that William had the bricks for his home made from clay that was found near the building site, clay that is still present in that location and is ideal for the manufacture of bricks. Shells, soil and animal dander were easy to collect for the production of mortar and plaster. Trees were felled, and though the huge logs for the foundation could be hewn into shape and positioned at the site, it is uncertain if the lumber for the frame of the house, the sills, the clapboards and the shingles was sawed at the site, or transported from a more distant sawmill. Anticipating the need for glass, William had brought a chest of glass panes with him from London for use in his new home. By the spring of 1683 all of the materials were accumulated and ready for the builders to use to construct the house.

To build such a house many journeymen were needed. William employed sawyers, carpenters, masons, bricklayers and joiners to complete the task, plus the help of many laborers besides the slaves. William knew some of the men skilled in the building trade who resided in the province. A number of them purchased their own homelands from him shortly after the completion of the Mount Hope home. Though the deeds indicate that they paid William for these lands, it may have been that the payment was received in the form of work on the Biddles' new home.

It is not certain if William served as his own contractor for the project or whether he relied on a master builder to oversee the job. There were many men in the province who could have done it. There is no evidence which builders were involved. His neighbor, Samuel Andrews, had constructed the Friends Meetinghouse in Oyster Bay, Long Island before he left that place.[2] He lived almost next door to the building site and he was constructing his own home at the same time, so it is logical to speculate that he may have been the contractor.

The basement of the house was excavated into the bluff and the walls of the cellar were formed by mortared river rock, with the wall being extended to three feet above ground level. The rocks were so well-secured

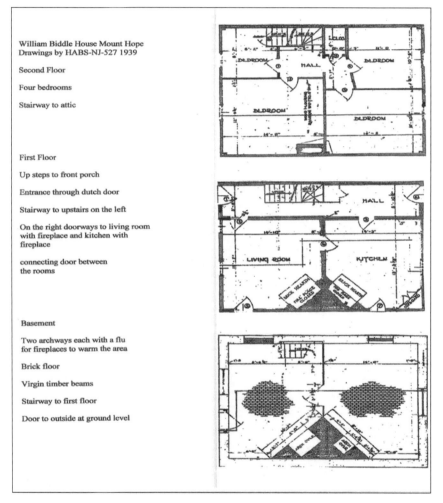

Floor Plan of Mount Hope.

and the bluff so well-drained that the basement was waterproof once it was in place. The house was further supported by large hand-hewn timbers, approximately twelve inches square, placed on top of the river rock walls. The frame was attached to the foundation by the tenons of virgin oak three by sixes secured in the mortises of the foundation timbers by wooden pegs. The footings for the chimney were made of the imperfect homemade bricks, but they were strong. They were made in the form of arches so that the chimney, which carried four flues, would not crumble. Two fireplaces were made in the basement inside the arches so that the space there would be kept warm and dry. A doorway led from the outside into the basement, and a stairway on the inside led from the basement to the floor above. The basement floor was lined with brick, adding to the comfort of the area, which was approximately twenty-eight by nineteen feet, divided into two rooms. This may have been the sleeping quarters for some of the servants and slaves.

As construction proceeded it became possible to enter the first floor of the house from a door from the porch on the front of the house, the formal entrance, on the side away from the river, or by a door from the lean-to positioned on the upriver side of the house, a door that led into the kitchen. Entering through the formal first-floor door — a two-part dutch door — they came into a hallway that revealed the stairway from the basement and another stairway that led to the second floor of the house. The two main rooms of the first floor opened from that hallway, first the front room or living room, and further along, the back room, the kitchen and dining room. The fireplaces in these two rooms were positioned diagonally in the common corner between the rooms on the outside wall of the house. These first floor rooms were of nearly equal size had a connecting door between them. Although for family use usually, the rooms were perfectly suited for the needs of the Friends of the area as meeting rooms for the women and men Quakers for worship and business. The stairway to the second floor led to four bedrooms: a larger bedroom and three smaller bedrooms, one for each of the children and an extra bedroom for guests or for a live-in tutor or companion. A third stairway led to the attic, a space that could be used for storage or for additional sleeping quarters.

The house was constructed so that it would be dry and warm, and resistant to the river winds. The virgin timber frame was filled in with bricks for insulation and additional support. The bricks and frame were covered on the outside by clapboard and on the inside by plaster. Windows, made with the glass that William had brought from England, were positioned on all sides of the house to allow a view in all directions and cross-ventilation for relief, when possible, on hot summer days.[4]

When the house was completed it was obvious that it had been named appropriately as Mount Hope. Perched atop the bluff, where all visitors had to travel up hill to reach it, it appeared lonely by itself until it was occupied and surrounded by the necessary buildings and gardens of the homestead. It was constructed so well that it remained standing until 2008 atop that bluff overlooking the river and the island.

By the time the house was ready for occupancy, the surrounding buildings and necessities were all in place. A lane had been laid out from the house to the Indian trail that led from Burlington to Shrewsbury and to the falls on the Delaware River. A barn, a work shed and a barnyard were built conveniently near to the house. A garden of several acres was laid out to provide produce for the family and their staff. An orchard of several acres, started from stock that William had obtained from William Peachee's nursery, would provide the family with apples, peaches and pears. The garden and the orchard were both fenced in to protect the crops from both domestic and wild animals.

In the barnyard were oxen, milk cows, sheep which were needed for their wool and as food, and hogs. William also had one brood mare and three town horses by then.

The farm family that had evolved may have been different than the one William and Sarah had in mind as they contemplated their move to the West Jersey Province from London years before. They needed farm workers to help them maintain the homestead and to be productive on the farm. They hired and possibly indentured Quaker planters, husbandmen and yeomen who had limited resources and needed jobs to help them get started in the new country. Mount Hope served as a means of employment for these people until they could earn enough money to start on their own. William, as a proprietor, could provide them with land when they were ready to pay for it or had earned it. Several times land was divided from his proprietary rights for individuals who had apparently reached this point of independence through his employ. These farm workers oversaw the care of the animals and supervised the work of the slaves, giving William the freedom he needed to attend to his duties as a commissioner, a judge, an assemblyman and a Quaker leader

These farm workers probably lived in the simple log cabin that was initially constructed on the property. They were aided in their work by the two male slaves. One of these Negro slaves may have married an Indian woman who came to live with him at Mount Hope to help Sarah in the house.

Perhaps the most important new member of the family was Indoweys, an Indian who took up residence at Mount Hope and became known as "William Biddle's Indian." [5] Apparently William and Indoweys spent a great deal of time with each other. When William Sr. and William Jr. wanted to travel in the province on their exploring trips, Indoweys could accompany them, revealing to them the most prized places of the Indians, and the most valuable tracts of land in the province. If they came upon other natives, Indoweys could interpret for them. He could hunt wild game much more efficiently than they could for themselves. He knew how to kill the predator animals like the wolves, thus helping them to protect their livestock. He was invaluable to the Mount Hope family.

Why Indians took up residence with some families who settled in West Jersey is uncertain. Perhaps they realized that their world was changing, and that it would never return to the one that they had known before. They also learned that the settlers, especially the Quakers, would treat them well. Having seen the ways of the Europeans even before the Quakers arrived, some of the Indians had adopted the dress of the white men. The relationship between Indoweys and William was obviously honest and understood by others, for although no Indians were allowed to purchase liquor in the province, when Indoweys went on an errand for William to Burlington he was allowed to purchase rum for his master without being questioned by other residents of the Tenth.[6]

For William the move to Mount Hope meant that he had to commute frequently the six miles to Burlington to attend to his civil duties. They would have had a boat for the trips, for the river was the easiest route to the town if weather permitted. The channel inside Seppasink and Mattinuck Islands helped to protect them from the weather on cloudy and windy days, but the water highway could be used only if the tide was right. Their alternate route was the Indian trail, which was positioned far enough back from the river to permit fording the streams on horseback. When he had to stay overnight in Burlington, William may have occasionally lodged at the inn of either Henry Grubb or Richard Basnett, or stayed at the home of friends.

Though Mount Hope was located in a remote area, it was frequently visited by settlers passing by on land or on the river from the falls or from the community that was developing at Crosswicks Creek, as they made their way to Burlington. It became the habit of the Quakers of the immediate neighborhood to worship at Mount Hope on First Days, permission having been received for this from the Burlington Monthly Meeting.[7] In those early years at Mount Hope, the Biddles were joined by the families of Samuel Andrews, the Beards, the Snowdens, John Hooton, the Harveys, the Bordens, the Blacks and the Towles, among others, in worship on First Days. Beginning two years later, when the Burlington Quarterly Meetings were held at Mount Hope, all of the Quaker leaders of the upper Tenths would visit the house.

Though they had taken a risk by investing all of their assets in this venture, William and Sarah were now as financially well-off as they had been before they emigrated. Moreover, they were now wealthier than most of the Quakers who immigrated to the West Jersey Province. William had been able to protect and increase their assets and income through improvements made on the lands that they claimed and settled. He had realized financial gains by buying good land early on and selling some of it for a profit. They had been able to estimate what it would cost to settle in

West Jersey from documents written to help market the territory.[8] They were within their budget up to this point, but they realized that their future depended upon their ability to sell their excess land, and to keep their own lands productive.

The composition of their farm family was different than they may have envisioned, and the homestead setting may not have been to their liking in every detail, but, compared to their life in London, they were quite comfortable and appreciative of their new homeland. They could see out the window of their home across the island and across the river to where William Penn was beginning to construct his home, Pennsbury. Despite the differences that they had with him, William and Sarah Biddle must have felt pleased to know that William Penn, the chief proprietor of Pennsylvania, would situate his rural homestead directly across the river from the site that they had chosen for themselves.

The dutch door entrance of Mount Hope.

— *Photograph 1939, HABS-NJ-527*

CHAPTER 15

Thomas Ollive, Deputy Governor
April 5, 1684 – November 3, 1685

Although the elected governor of the province, Samuel Jennings, along with Thomas Budd and George Hutcheson, had gone to London, the business of the province continued under the leadership of Thomas Ollive as Deputy Governor. Elections were held in each Tenth in April, as called for by the Constitution and the General Assembly. William was returned by election to the General Assembly from the First Tenth, and when the Assembly met he was nominated and reelected to the position of commissioner on the Governor's Council, which carried with it the added duties of being a judge. He was again elected a Land Commissioner.[1]

By then Dr. Robert Dimsdale had returned and become a resident of the province and was able to assist Dr. Daniel Wills with the medical needs of the residents. Dr. Dimsdale purchased one-third of the proprietary share that had originated with the deceased John Kinsey, and, even though the 500-acre tract along the Rancocas Creek that he bought from William Biddle was recorded as being surveyed to him on October 13, 1682,[2] he gave up this survey and instead claimed lands and built his home in the Second Tenth, further up the north branch of the Rancocas Creek.[3] Dr. Dimsdale was also elected to the General Assembly and by that body as a commissioner at the sessions held May 12 through 14, 1684.[4]

Perhaps the most important action of this General Assembly was that of setting a new direction for taxation by deciding to tax the property owned by residents in West New Jersey. The residents had previously been ordered by law to record their deeds. Now the tax rate was set at 5 shillings per 100 acres for those lands held "certain," and 2 shillings, 6 pence per 100 acres for unimproved land.[5] It was hoped that all of the residents would register their lands, and that the current extent of settlement in the province would make this tax sufficient to cover its expenses. If the tax was sufficient, then the unappropriated lands of the proprietors would no longer be needed to pay for the debts of the public and the residents of West Jersey would have gained autonomy. This would help their case as it was being presented in London.

In other actions, the Assembly directed that each Tenth should elect its own overseer of highways, a tax assessor and a tax collector. Again, public registration was requested for all residents of the province.[6]

In the courts held in Burlington, the deputy governor and the justices attempted to enforce registration by the residents of the province. The problem Tenths were the Third Tenth and below, where population was sparse and there was more absentee ownership. A number of the Swedish settlers and their heirs were settled there too. The justices on the bench on June 3, 1684 and June 17, 1684 included William Biddle, along with Thomas Ollive, Robert Stacy, Elias Farre, Robert Dimsdale, Daniel Wills, Robert Turner, Thomas Gardiner and Francis Collins. Besides the Swedes, other large landholders of that area were Henry Stacy, Robert Turner, Francis Collins and Samuel Carpenter. Some of the lands that had been sold for the public account by Samuel Jennings and Thomas Budd were also included.[7] In order for the tax to be successful it would have to be raised from more than just the First and Second Tenths.

At one of the court sessions William came to the aid of John Newman, carpenter, who had been convicted of breaching the peace and causing harm to another person. William loaned Newman money to pay the fine and court costs, indicating that William had some interest in the welfare of this carpenter —, perhaps he had helped to build his home. In addition, during that session William was asked to be one of the arbitrators in a dispute between two of the inhabitants of the province.[8]

The court also let the residents of the province know that they were serious about the responsibility that had been assigned to them for maintaining the roads. John Borton was fined 20 shillings for not performing his share of work on the roads in the Second Tenth.[9]

On June 24, 1684, the inhabitants of the First Tenth held a meeting to elect the officials directed by the General Assembly and to see to the proper registration of the lands of that Tenth. William registered 500 acres unimproved, which meant that his tax bill for the year was 12 shillings, 6 pence. The 500-acre tracts of land that he had promised to John Underhill and Samuel Andrews were both listed as lands held certain (settled upon), and each was taxed £1.5s. John Hooton and Percivale Towle were elected as tax assessor and tax collector for the area around Mount Hope.[10]

Despite the issue over ownership of the governing rights, William and Sarah remained confident in the stability of the West Jersey government. They had exercised most of the unappropriated land rights to which they were entitled by then. Since it was not likely that any more would be issued soon, they decided to purchase more proprietary shares which would immediately give them rights to claim or sell more land.

On August 9, 1684 they completed the purchase of an additional one-quarter proprietary share from Joseph Helmsley of Yorkshire, England, for £48.15s. The deed was witnessed by William Ellis, then a resident of

Tunstall, Holdernesse, County of York, England.[11] Later, Ellis would move to West Jersey and become a neighbor, taking up land near Mount Hope.

On August 22, 1684 William and Sarah completed a purchase of an additional one-sixth proprietary share in West Jersey from Samuel Clay, a merchant of London, for £45.[12] With these two purchases William would be eligible for another 1,333.33 acres of unappropriated land, enough to cover the verbal contracts that he had made with Underhill and Andrews.

The latter deed and purchase were overseen and witnessed in London by Edward Biddle, probably William's younger brother.[13] Edward had thoughts about moving to Pennsylvania, apparently, for he had purchased a 500-acre tract in Pennsylvania with the other first purchasers of land in that territory.[14] However, he never completed these plans.

Although William could spend most of his time at Mount Hope supervising the farming, he had to return often to Burlington for his civic duties. As the government of the province matured, the schedule of meeting dates was set for the convenience of the rural residents.

On August 8, 1684 William attended the Quarter Court in Burlington. He was joined on the bench that day by Thomas Ollive, Robert Stacy, Daniel Wills and Francis Davenport. At that session it was stated to the residents that no one was to fell trees on land that had not been taken up (claimed, surveyed, or settled), it being recognized by the court that these unappropriated lands were really the reserve lands of the Proprietors.[15]

During the first week in September the Yearly Meeting of Friends was held again in Burlington and the entire Biddle family went to Burlington to worship and socialize with other Friends of the region. By now there were many Quakers who had emigrated to Philadelphia and Pennsylvania. After discussion a decision was made that the Yearly Meetings should, after that time, be held on alternate years in Philadelphia and Burlington, a practice that lasted until 1760.[16]

William had to return to Burlington for a special session of the Burlington Court on September 16, 1684. The principal reason for holding the court was to settle a dispute over a debt between two parties, but while they were there the justices issued a Letter of Administration to Hannah Newbie, widow and executrix of the deceased Mark Newbie.[17] Newbie had been essentially the first banker of the territory. He had come to the province realizing better than others monetary confusion involved in exchange rates between currencies. He had brought a large supply of coins with him from his native Ireland — known as Patrick's Pence — and had placed a great number of these coins into circulation in the province. The Assembly allowed this to happen, and even officially recognized it with the stipulation that no one was obliged to accept more than five shillings worth of Newbie's half-pence in payment from any other person. In the absence of any other form of banking, Mark Newbie stood behind the coins and offered to redeem them on demand.[18] His attempt to simplify the coinage of the province ended with his death. The action of the court allowed his wife to administer his estate and presumably to redeem all of the coins.

William had the chance to spend most of the next six weeks at Mount Hope overseeing the harvest. By now there were in excess of seventy-five acres of land in cultivation. Arrangements to ship corn and grain to Barbados and Jamaica and other ports had to be made in conjunction with the other farmers of the First Tenth.

On November 1, 1684 William and his family returned to Burlington for the fall Fair Days. William saw to recording the deed of sale of 150 acres of the Rancocas Creek land to William Evans, carpenter, that day, and he received £15 for the transaction.[19]

Following the Fair Days, on November 3, 1684, the Quarter Court was held,[20] followed by a meeting of the General Assembly. Awaiting word from London on the governing rights, the General Assembly decided that no new actions should be taken, so they adjourned.[21] The deputy governor, the commissioners and the assemblymen had no way of knowing that an arbitration panel of twelve Friends, including George Fox, had met in London eight times by then to discuss governing rights in the province and they had reached a decision.

On October 15, 1684 eight members of the panel signed a decision, agreeing that the West New Jersey governing rights belonged to Edward Byllynge.[22] William Biddle knew at least four of these signers personally: George Whitehead, William Crouch, Charles Bathurst and Richard Whitpaine. The others, whom he knew at least by reputation, included James Parker, Charles Marshall, Thomas Hart and William Shewin. The committee had the chance to meet and hear the arguments of Samuel Jennings, Thomas Budd and George Hutcheson, as well as the points made by Edward Byllynge himself and William Penn, who had returned to London by then. Meetings continued to be held after October 15 to try to settle the differences between Friends.[23]

Samuel Jennings and Thomas Budd, still feeling wronged by the judgment, tried to take the matter further to the courts of Westminster. It was not until late September, 1685, that the matter was finally concluded.[24] When the result of the arbitration was finally made known to the inhabitants and resident proprietors of West Jersey, they realized that they would never have the full governing rights they had hoped for. William knew the men who had made the decision, and, continuing to trust that his friend Edward Byllynge would govern honestly and justly, he remained fully invested in the proprietary rights and shares of the West Jersey Province.

On November 18, 1684 William returned to Burlington to sit on the bench of the court for a special session so that people of the province could register their deeds. He was accompanied by Thomas Ollive, Daniel Wills and Elias Farre.[25] An indenture of John Renshawe was acknowledged by William Biddle and Daniel Wills.[26] While in town William visited Thomas Revell and saw to the recording of a deed of sale of 500 acres to his neighbor John Underhill at Springhill for £50.[27]

During the remaining winter months William made several more trips to Burlington to attend to matters of the court. He was in court on November 29, 1684 to acknowledge an indenture of John Antrum to William Myers.[28] On December 11, 12 and 16, 1684 he was on the bench to hear a case concerning the disposition of the goods of a ship that had run aground. There were many issues involved in that case, which was heard before the usual jury, issues that involved a knowledge of the laws of the province concerning burglary as well as knowledge of maritime law. William was chosen to participate in an arbitration panel to settle part of the dispute.[29]

The long winter months were interrupted again by another trip to Burlington on January 6, 1684/5, when he and Thomas Gardiner acknowledged an indenture for John Ogborne and Joseph Blowers.[30] On January 26, 1684/5 William returned to Burlington to participate in a special session of the court to hear a case concerning an unpaid debt.[31] Apparently the winter weather prevented William's return to Burlington for the Quarter Court session held on February 20, 1684/5 (32).

Events in England were to continue to have a serious effect on the Province of West Jersey. King Charles II died before Parliament could resolve the issue of who would be the best successor to the throne. James, Duke of York, was crowned King James II of England. He had been in exile, but James II knew intimately the plans of all of the colonies. With the advice of the Lords of Trade, he soon sent his trusted representative, Edmond Andros, back to America as the Governor of the Dominion of New England, a coalition of all of the territories north of New York. In addition he questioned the need to continue the tax-free ports in East and West Jersey.[33] It was vital for the Quakers in London and in West Jersey to work peacefully with this new king, for their most important need was to persuade him to repeal the laws of religious persecution.

The Burlington Monthly Meeting continued to make plans to build a meetinghouse that would be more suitable for holding the Yearly Meetings. They were feeling the pressure of the rapidly developing Friends' community of Philadelphia and they might have feared the loss of holding Yearly Meetings in Burlington. They requested pledges of funds from the membership for the construction. William pledged £3 to the building project on March 2, 1684/5.[34]

On April 9, 1685 the Land Commissioners issued a warrant for 100 acres of unappropriated land to William Biddle, land that was apparently owed to or earned by James Silver, planter, probably for work that he did for William at the Mount Hope homestead. No deed of sale is found, so it is assumed that the agreement settled a work contract or an indenture that existed between the two parties.[35]

William Biddle attended to his civil duties at the Quarter Court session on May 8, 1685 in Burlington. An especially difficult decision faced the jury and the bench that day. Two defendants came before the court charged with the same crime. One pleaded not guilty and the other pleaded guilty. The jury found the party who pleaded not guilty to the crime to be guilty, thus proving that he had lied to the court. The accomplice was fined heavily, but the defendant who lied to the court was sentenced to thirty lashes with the whip on the naked upper body. The bench included William with Thomas Ollive, Robert Stacy, Elias Farre, Robert Dimsdale, Thomas Gardiner and Daniel Wills.[36] These Quaker judges believed a man's word was what made the entire governmental, judicial and economic system of their world work. Despite the fact that this must have been a difficult sentence for these Quakers to administer, they knew that lying required a severe penalty, for its tolerance would destroy all that they stood for and were trying to do in this new land.

William returned to Burlington with the rest of his family on May 10, 1685 for the spring Fair Days. Sarah and her daughter Sarah, now six years old, would have been especially happy to get together with their friends in town after spending the long winter at the rural Mount Hope. That day William saw to it that Thomas Revell recorded the sale of 200 acres of land to John Newman, carpenter, located along the Assiscunk Creek next to the property of John Butcher. William was paid £20 for the tract.[37]

While in Burlington, William and Sarah learned from George Hutcheson the current state of affairs in London. He had returned from London and notified the residents of the province that they did not and would not own the governing rights. Of even more concern was the news he brought of the continued religious persecution of Quakers by the authorities in London. It had been such a long time since they had lived under that threat that Hutcheson's news must have seemed even more horrible to them. He was able to confirm the fact that shortly after William and Sarah left London, their meeting, the Devonshire House Monthly Meeting, had become a target for the persecutors. George Whitehead had been fined three times in 1682 for preaching, each time losing £20 or more in money or goods. William Crouch had also lost considerable goods to fines, as had William Kent, Richard Whitpaine and Francis Plumstead.[38]

The worst atrocity occurred on April 1, 1683 when troops entered Devonshire House during a Meeting for Worship and struck several of the worshipping Quakers on the head. John Sparefield had managed to get home that day, but he died of his head injuries fourteen days later.[39]

Other Quakers, including George Keith, were in jail for refusing to take an oath, along with John Reading from the Peel Monthly Meeting and Thomas Thackera. The courts were filled with Quakers taken before the magistrates for refusing to obey the Conventicle Acts or the Act of Recusancy, or for failure to pay Church of England tithes.[40]

Upon hearing the news from George Hutcheson, William and Sarah could be thankful that they and their children no longer were experiencing this unjust persecution. They had to wonder how long it would continue in England, and whether they would be able to keep religious persecution from happening in their West Jersey Province.

The General Assembly meetings began May 12, 1685 and lasted through the next day. William had returned as an Assemblyman, elected from the First Tenth. The Assembly reelected him to the position of commissioner, so he would continue to serve as a member of the Governor's Council, as a Land Commissioner and as a Judge. The legislative body, now fully aware that they could expect that Edward Byllynge would exercise his rights as Governor soon, continued the same tax rates on the lands that they had implemented the previous year, and then they adjourned.[41]

The Biddle family returned to Mount Hope, more solemn than they had been before they left it, concerned certainly about the news of the governing rights, but particularly worried about the plight of their friends in London. They saw to the planting of their cleared acreage, and William set out to explore more lands and to better define the properties to which he deserved title in the town of Burlington, including the waterlots and town lots that he could claim on his London and Yorkshire proprietary shares.

He would have had an opportunity to do this when he visited Burlington on June 1, 1685 to attend to duties of the Burlington Court. William and other members of the court confirmed the validity of an indenture of Thomas Ollive to John Woolston, allowing it to be recorded in the land records of West New Jersey.[42] The next day at the court Martin Holt made a complaint against William Biddle, but the records are not specific as to the problem.[43] On July 5, 1685 William was back in town to have surveyed and recorded to himself a 500-acre tract at Oneanickon, next to the land that had been claimed by William and Mary (Parnell) Wood and near land of the Newbold family.[44] He was planning to develop another farm in that location.

William continued to attend to matters concerning his real estate throughout that summer. On July 25, 1685, by an indenture signed and sealed before Abraham Senior and Thomas Revell, he sold 100 acres in the Second Tenth to Walter Pumphary, carpenter, for £8.,[45] On August 4, 1685 he sold to James Hill of Burlington a choice townlot that had forty feet of frontage on the west side of High Street and went through to Wood Street where it had fifty feet of frontage.[46]

William missed the Quarter Court session held August 8, 1685 when the rules for the earmarks for identifying livestock owned by each inhabitant of the province were published.[47]

He had to attend the next court session for he was summoned to it by the complaint of Thomas French over some boundaries of the lands along the Rancocas Creek. On September 4, 1685 Thomas French and William agreed to submit their differences over the property to arbitrators, and if they could not agree, then to an "umpire" for final decision.[48] This action resulted in the two parties swapping some parcels of land.[49] It had become apparent to William on his first inspection of the land in that location that it would be impossible for him to ever claim a clear title to his full 1,600-acre tract.

At this same court, while he was still on the bench, William was a witness to evidence presented concerning a couple who had abused their children. The family was summoned to appear before the next court session.[50]

On September 5, 1685 the first Yearly Meeting of Friends was held at the Meetinghouse in Philadelphia.[51] William and his family were undoubtedly pleased to have the chance to visit the city and to see the many Friends from the region who came to the gathering, among them some from London whom they had not seen for several years. Each year more Quakers were emigrating to Pennsylvania and Philadelphia was developing rapidly. Their West Jersey friends, Samuel Carpenter, Anthony Morris, Robert Turner, Robert Stacy, and upon their return from England, Thomas Budd and Thomas Hooton, moved to Philadelphia.

On October 5, 1685 William Pankhurst (Pancoast) was asked by the Burlington Monthly Meeting to visit with William Biddle to see if he would supply the glass from his glass chest to glaze the proposed new meetinghouse, this gift to be in addition to the pledge of £3 that William and Sarah had already made to the project.[52] William had come to the province with enough glass to glaze several homes if he had the opportunity to build them.

The customary date for the Quarter Court to meet was November 3, 1685. At that session the newly-appointed deputy governor of Edward Byllynge, John Skene, took over the government and the courts. Skene, the previously divested commissioner, Scotsman and Quaker, having received his commission from Edward Byllynge, read his commission as deputy governor to the court that day and dismissed the magistrates from the bench.[53] The justices, led by the former deputy governor, Thomas Ollive, left the bench. Skene called for the court to reconvene at ten o'clock the next morning, but since he had dismissed all of the elected magistrates, no court was held on that day and time. This new state of affairs posed a serious concern for the leadership of West New Jersey, including William Biddle and his peers.

CHAPTER 16

Edward Byllynge, Governor,
John Skene, Deputy Governor
November 3, 1685 - January 16, 1686/7

In the past when the certainty of the ownership of the governing rights was clouded, the residents of the West New Jersey Province, principally the resident proprietors, had assumed that the right to govern themselves was theirs and they exercised that right according to the rules of their constitution, the Concessions and Agreements.

Now that the arbitration panel of Friends in London had made its decision in favor of the rights of Edward Byllynge, the West New Jersey Proprietors faced the fact that they no longer had even a possible chance of owning the governing rights to the province. Edward Byllynge, a Quaker, had been instrumental in forming the rules of their society with them but now he had used his wealth and social position to change their plans and rights to his benefit. They could not be sure of his future intentions and how they would be affected.

Byllynge had replaced Samuel Jennings with John Skene as deputy governor of the West New Jersey government. The resident proprietors had dismissed Skene from other responsibilities in the past, and they did not trust him now. It is not clear whether Byllynge knew that the residents of the province would not want this man as their deputy governor.[1]

It is uncertain if Skene had instructions from Governor Byllynge to hold new elections, or if the residents took it upon themselves to reelect their representatives again that fall. Whatever the reason, the elections demonstrated their intention to govern themselves and may have prevented John Skene from appointing his own government and judicial officials. Elections were held in each of the Tenths, and fifty Assemblymen were returned to the General Assembly held in Burlington on November 25, 1685. This included ten representatives from each of the upper four Tenths and ten from the Salem Colony. Thomas Ollive was again elected as the Speaker of the House. Byllynge's appointment of Skene had aroused the interest of the entire population of the province.[2].

The Assembly reelected their officers that fall too. William was reelected a commissioner and thus he was again a member of the

Governor's Council and one of the Land Commissioners, and he served as an ex-officio judge of the province.[3]

The General Assembly meeting was brief. Edward Byllynge had made several requests of the Assembly through his deputy governor, John Skene, and he had forwarded a new Charter and Bills for the Assembly's approval. He requested that proxy voting be allowed and that John Skene, Andrew Robeson, George Hutcheson, Richard Lawrence, John Cripps and Thomas Mathews be allowed to vote by proxy for the twenty-two shares owned by Byllynge and his son-in-law, Benjamin Bartlett. The Assembly, in the conservative manner of the Quakers, took these matters into consideration. The Assembly did not intend to make any decisions at that session. They referred the requests for further study to a committee that consisted of William Biddle, Thomas Ollive, William Emley, George Hutcheson, Robert Stacy, Samuel Jennings, James Budd, Robert Dimsdale, Robert Turner, Thomas Thackera, Francis Davenport, Andrew Robeson and James Nevill.

The Assembly then set the tax rate for the following year at five shillings per one hundred acres for lands "certain," and three shillings per one hundred acres for unimproved, "uncertain," lands. They then adjourned to the next scheduled meeting date, May 12, 1686,[4] giving the committee ample time to deliberate over Edward Byllynge's requests with regard to the governing of the province.

The courts had not met since John Skene had dismissed the justices from the bench, but now that there were elected justices again, the court sessions resumed on December 15, 1685. Deputy Governor Skene was on the bench,[5] and the courts throughout his tenure were attended in almost every session by William Biddle accompanied by James Budd, George Hutcheson and Thomas Gardiner, and less frequently by the other trusted Quaker leaders, Richard Guy, Elias Farre and Francis Davenport. These elected justices were intent upon protecting the rules of the Concessions and Agreements. They saw to it that the need for at least three justices on the bench was preserved. And they continued the other practices of the judicial system, including requiring two-fold restitution for burglary and allowing "exception" to jurors by defendants (allowing defendants to reject potential members of the jury).

About the same time that William and Sarah moved to their new home, Mount Hope, a number of other Quakers settled in that general region of the First Tenth. The largest community developed at Crosswicks Creek where the Buntings had settled, joining Thomas Foulke and Francis Davenport. There were enough Quakers in these more remote parts of the First Tenth to make it possible to start another regular meeting for worship and business. The Quakers from the falls on the Delaware River, Oneanickon, Crosswicks and the Mansfield area began to meet together at unofficial monthly meetings beginning on October 2, 1684. The business meetings were held at the home of Francis Davenport at the Crosswicks Creek since he was the leader of Friends of the area. It was decided that the business meetings would meet the first Fifth Day of each month at the tenth hour of the morning at that location.[6] William and Sarah joined area Friends in these business meetings, but they continued to worship on First Days at Mount Hope with their closest neighbors.

On January 7, 1685/6 William was asked by the Friends of the area to participate in an arbitration panel with William Emley, Francis Davenport and Mahlon Stacy to decide a difference over ownership of land between Thomas Scholey and Isaac Horner, who had recently arrived from Long Island.[7] The matter was apparently decided in favor of Thomas Scholey, for on January 20, 1685/6 William sold 100 acres in the Second Tenth along Assiscunk Creek to Isaac Horner for £10. This indenture was witnessed for William by Charles Woolverton and William Deane, husbandmen, who lived in that neighborhood.[8]

That winter and spring William was busy not only directing the further improvement of his farmlands, but traveling several times to Burlington on civic and personal business. He attended the court January 1, 1685/6, February 20 and 22, 1685/6 and March 26, 1686.[9] At the February court sessions hearings were conducted over the problems that James Budd was having in establishing his pottery in Burlington. It was also recognized that James Harrison was having difficulty procuring bricks that he needed, perhaps for the construction of Pennsbury, where he was the agent for William Penn.[10]

William Biddle also continued to manage the land in Burlington to which he had rights through his purchase of proprietary shares. On March 1, 1685/6 he sold 50 acres in the First Tenth to John Calowe, wheelwright, along with a waterlot in the town of Burlington. He received £14 for this sale, indicating that the waterlot was of considerable value, probably because it was on the northwest corner of Pearl and York Streets.[11] This lot eventually would become the site of the inn of Abraham Senior and then the home of Joseph White.

On April 14, 1686 William sold another 500 acres to the newly-arrived John Rodman, from Rhode Island. He received £50 for this land, which was located on the south side of the Rancocas Creek, in the Second Tenth, next to the lands of Thomas Hooton and John Hollinshead.[12]. Thomas Rodman, brother of John, would later settle another tract adjoining his brother. The township of Chester and then the town of Moorestown were later founded on these lands.

On May 19, 1686 William, Mahlon Stacy and George Hutcheson witnessed the sale of a one-fourth proprietary share to mariner Robert Hopper.[13] On May 20, 1686 William and Sarah received a one-fourth proprietary share from Thomas Hutchinson for £80.6s. "to the said William Biddle due and owing." The indenture was witnessed by Alice Hutchinson and the Quaker minister James Martin, and acknowledged before justices George Hutcheson and James Budd.[14] With this additional proprietary interest William would immediately be entitled to an additional 800 acres of rural lands and more town lands.

On April 1, 1686 the Chesterfield Monthly Meeting, as the group of Quakers who had begun to meet in the First Tenth came to be known, asked Sarah and her neighbor, Mary Andrews, to visit with Bridget Guy, wife of Richard Guy, who lived just down river from Mount Hope, to ask if they would take in the daughters of the deceased John Browne. John Horner had overseen the affairs of the deceased, and he had reported the facts concerning the estate and the orphaned daughters to the Monthly Meeting.[15]

Friends in West New Jersey were now better organized. They had begun to oversee the affairs of the residents of the neighborhood, a role they had been used to in England when fortunes of a Friend or his family suddenly changed because of fines, imprisonment, injury, or illness. In England families received such protection through their parishes, and in New England the towns had assumed that responsibility. Here in the wilderness, however, there were no other institutions or authorities, governmental or religious, to offer support and it was vital that the Friends help each other

The entire Biddle family visited Burlington on May 10 and 11, 1686 for the spring Fair Days, joining many of the inhabitants of the Upper Two Tenths. At this gathering everyone would have learned that King James II had announced an amnesty for the Quakers for their offences against the Conventicle Acts and the Act of Recusancy. He issued his mandate March 15, 1685/6,[16] approximately one year after he had ascended the throne.

It was not a quarantee of complete religious toleration but it reduced the intensity of the persecution. Numerous Quakers who had been imprisoned were released. Many Quakers who were being prosecuted in the courts were released by this mandate, including Edward Biddle, Alexander Parker, William Macket and Clement Plumstead,[17] all of whom were known to William and Sarah.

At this time, through his communication with Quakers who were traveling back and forth from London to West New Jersey, William received news of his family in England. Edward Biddle, his brother, had a wife Anne and children Edward and Mary.[18] They had decided not to immigrate to their lands in Pennsylvania, now that the opportunity for Quakers to live a normal life in London had improved.

William also learned that since the death of his mentor Thomas Biddle, from pneumonia on January 7, 1682,[19] his wife Esther had barely managed for herself. She remained as a leader among the women of the Friends, but she was largely dependent upon the monthly meeting for her maintenance.[20] Esther's son Benjamin was still in close association with William's brother Edward, living in Westminster.[21]

In addition William learned that his oldest brother, Thomas, had died in March 1684/5, leaving the family home to his wife Mary for her lifetime.[22] They had had no children. His sister, Elizabeth (Biddle) Stone, was well and living in Kinnersly Green, in the Parish of Severn Stoke. His sister Jane and her husband Thomas Taylor were also well. The children of his deceased brother Richard were in good health. Richard's daughter Jane was being cared for by the widow of her uncle Thomas, and his son was living with his mother.[23]

Following the fun of the spring Fair Days, the Quarter Court met in Burlington on May 12, 1686 with William on the bench. He was accompanied by Deputy Governor John Skene, George Hutcheson who had been elected or appointed as president of the court, Elias Farre, Andrew Robeson, Thomas Gardiner, James Budd, Richard Guy, Mahlon Stacy, Richard Lawrence, George Deacon, Francis Davenport and Francis Collins. This was a true Provincial Court, for the judges present represented all of the four populated Tenths and the Salem Colony.[24]

The court, the judges and the juries heard that the London Bridge, the bridge over the stream in the London portion of Burlington, needed repairs again. They also heard cases concerning the theft of hogs, abuse of the elected constable and attempted rape. The rapist was found guilty, and they had to apply the punishment of whipping: thirty-nine lashes of the whip from the cart's tail, over a period of three hours on the morning of the following day.[25]

These staunch Quaker judges had learned early in the Quaker experiment in democracy that no matter how carefully they tried to create a perfect Christian world, there were still those among them who would wrong others. It was necessary to maintain a system of justice that protected the rights of the innocent, and the judges continued to insist that their government be conducted in a democratic manner. The people continued to elect their own government, constables, tax and court officials.

Late in the day of May 12, 1686 the General Assembly reconvened in Burlington with fifty Assemblymen present. The meetings lasted through May 15, 1686.[26] Every room in the inns of Burlington and the spare bedrooms of the residents of the town and its environs must have been filled with these legislators. The presence of all these elected officials showed the residents of the province that their democracy was working.

The members of the committee appointed to study the Charter and Bills and other requests of Edward Byllynge, a committee that included William Biddle, were allowed time to meet and to finalize their report to the Assembly. The committee recommended that the voting proxies could be allowed, but that no more than one proxy should be allowed for each proprietor, and the proxy should be a person who was "an occupant and resident of and upon such proprietors land within the Province." This suggestion of the committee essentially eliminated the list of proxies that Edward Byllynge had offered, even though they had accepted his proxy request. It limited his power in the Assembly to that of every other proprietor, even though he was the Governor of the province. In addition, the committee did not agree with the Charter and Bills submitted by Byllynge. They reasoned that it was "not so proper to have the Governor at so great a distance to make Concessions for the Constitutions of this Province, which is best understood by such as are present upon the place," and they further objected because they felt that if "the governor may make void those Concessions at first made by himself and the whole body of proprietors, he may with more ease make void these now sent, if he please." [27]

The Assembly voted unanimously to back the report of the committee, turning down the modifications that Edward Byllynge had tried to make in the government. The elected Assembly was back in control. They further requested that a letter be sent to Edward Byllynge asking him to empower his deputy governor to confirm laws that the Assembly and the deputy governor felt necessary to enact for the good of the province. If Edward Byllynge approved their request, the residents of West New Jersey would essentially have regained their power to govern themselves. They further challenged Deputy Governor John Skene for appointing rangers to take up stray animals for the benefit of the Governor, and they appointed their own rangers for this purpose. They also objected to the fact that Skene had not accepted Thomas Revell, their elected recorder, as clerk and registrar for the province. The Assembly renominated and reelected non-Quaker Thomas

Revell to those positions and, by this action, they announced to Edward Byllynge that it was their right to nominate and appoint the officers of the state and trust for the province.[28]

The committee appointed to study the recommendations and requests of Edward Byllynge had prepared and delivered an excellent defense of the rights of the residents of the province. They had set the tone of the Assembly which went on to defend these rights — rights that all of the Quaker proprietors, including Edward Byllynge and the trustees, had agreed to many years before that time. In this way they defended their right to retain the liberties that they were establishing in the West New Jersey Province. It was a sign that they would be stronger in defending their rights in the future.

With this done, the Assembly began to attend to the business of the province. The Third and Fourth Tenths were now adequately populated and needed their own government and courts. The Assembly agreed that those two Tenths should now be a separate jurisdiction from the First and Second Tenths. A court was established that would alternate between Redbank and Newton.[29] This would make the work of Deputy Governor John Skene more difficult, for if he meant to oversee the courts of the province, he would have to travel considerable distances. The Assembly also agreed to pay the deputy governor £50 annually.[30]

In this session the Assembly also recognized that the roads of the province had to be improved and new roads had to be established. They directed that the road from Burlington to Salem be laid out and they appointed several persons to supervise the task. They appointed William Emley, George Hutcheson and William Biddle as surveyors, responsible for developing a new road from Burlington north to the falls on the Delaware River. Mathew Watson was to assist them and to establish a ferry over one of the streams that the road had to cross. The road was to be marked by May 23, 1686, and made "passable for cattle and travelers" before October 10, 1686. If the job was not done, the surveyors would be fined £50. They were empowered to insist that the inhabitants of the Tenths involved either participate in the construction of the roads or pay someone else for doing their share of the work.[31]

The Assembly also discussed the proposed surveying of the division line between the East and West Jersey Provinces, a line that had been defined by the Quintipartite Agreement of July 1, 1676. A group of West New Jersey proprietors had brought the matter to the attention of the General Assembly. The Assembly agreed to the proposal that was made and suggested that the group visit the site where the survey line was to start and report their findings at its next meeting, to be held November 3, 1686.[32] Apparently the proprietors Thomas Ollive, Mahlon Stacy, Samuel Jennings, George Hutcheson, Thomas Lambert and Joseph Pope were already actively involved in this issue. They were communicating with Gawen Lawrie, the ex-Byllynge trustee, who was now deputy governor of East New Jersey, under the Governorship of Robert Barclay, who was still in Great Britain.[33]

The East New Jersey proprietors had established a Board of Proprietors on August 1, 1684 and that board began to oversee the land affairs of East Jersey on April 9, 1685.[34] The West New Jersey proprietors had not separated their land business from the government and the judicial system of the province. The Land Commissioners, created by the Concessions and Agreements, oversaw the land warrants, the surveys and transactions involving claims or sales of land. There had been no good reason to change the system, but now that they did not officially own the governing rights they had to begin considering ways to separate the affairs of the proprietors from the government of the province.

Soon, however, they would wish that they had taken the affairs of the proprietors out of the hands of the General Assembly and the commissioners earlier, for on June 30, 1686 the Governors of the three territories, John Skene of West New Jersey, Gawen Lawrie of East New Jersey and Thomas Dongan of the New York territory met in New York to discuss the boundary lines between those three regions.[35] The West New Jersey proprietors realized then that although their land rights were still in their possession, others were discussing the boundaries of their lands. Certainly this was an unacceptable situation.

Upon the adjournment of the General Assembly, William Biddle returned to Mount Hope and his family to see to the business of completing spring planting. He made arrangements with George Hutcheson and William Emley for laying out the road from Burlington to the Falls that would pass right through the Mount Hope property. They marked the roadway by the prescribed date, May 23, 1686. Then they began to inform the inhabitants of the First Tenth of their obligation to complete the road work. A schedule was set to allow for its completion by October 10, 1686.

William had several opportunities that summer to use the new road bed as the work progressed, for he returned to Burlington on June 9, 1686, apparently to see to matters for the Burlington Court. As justices, William Biddle, Richard Guy and Mahlon Stacy acknowledged an indenture between Robert Wade and Deputy Governor John Skene.[36] It was probably that same day that the Land Commissioners met, for William was issued a warrant for 500 acres of unappropriated lands of the province.[37]

He returned to Burlington on August 9, 1686 to attend the session of the Quarter Court. He was joined on the bench by Deputy Governor John Skene, George Hutcheson, James Budd, Elias Farre, Thomas Gardiner and Francis Davenport. Christopher Snowden served as Attorney General for the King at this court session. The judges and jury reached a verdict of not guilty in the case of the suspicious cause of death of a slave. They also sentenced a women to one half-hour in the pillory with a sign to be placed on the pillory signifying in capital letters that she was "A false perjured infamous women." [38]

William Biddle Jr. had a chance to leave his duties on the farm on August 12, 1686 when he went to Burlington to attend the wedding of Elizabeth Browne to Thomas Knight.[39] It was at weddings such as this that Quaker youth had their best opportunities to socialize.

On September 2, 1686 the Chesterfield Monthly Meeting requested that William Biddle and Mahlon Stacy be their appointed representatives to the Yearly Meeting of Friends to be held in Burlington.[40] William went to Burlington earlier than the meeting date, probably to help make preparations for the Yearly Meeting, but also to take care of personal business. On September 6, 1686 he sold 100 acres of land to Joseph Ambler from Philadelphia for £9. Witnesses to the indenture included John Langford and recorder Thomas Revell and Justice Francis Davenport acknowledged the document.[41] However, it was not until the next day, September 7, 1686, that the Land Commissioners met to issue the warrant for the 100 acres to William that made the sale official.[42]

In addition to their Monthly Meetings for business and worship, Friends had established the practice of holding General Meetings which would be attended by Friends from more than one Monthly Meeting. It was at a General Meeting held at Salem, West New Jersey, the 11th of the 2nd month 1682, that it was ordered that a Quarterly Meeting be held on the second day of the fourth month 1682 at Burlington. It was also ordered that a Quarterly Meeting be held at Salem on the third second day of the ninth month 1682. Though no records of the minutes of these meetings have been found, it is assumed that they took place and were the beginning of the Burlington Quarterly Meeting. Except for a minute indicating that Friends of Shrewsbury would belong to Burlington General and Quarterly Meetings there is no evidence that any more than these two meetings were held.[43]

The official meeting date for the Yearly Meeting of Friends was September 8, 1686. Quakers from all over the region converged on Burlington, taxing the facilities of the town and its environs to accommodate them. At this Yearly Meeting consideration was given to the formal establishment of a Burlington Quarterly Meeting.

The Yearly Meeting recognized that the home of William Biddle was near the center of the developed areas of the upper two Tenths. They requested that a Quarterly Meeting be established at Mount Hope, to be held at the tenth hour of the morning on the last Second day (Monday) of the ninth (November), twelfth (February), third (May) and sixth (August) months of the year.[44] The Quarterly Meetings of the Religious Society of Friends were business meetings, held in a meeting for worship to be attended by those "weighty and seasoned" Friends who best understood the matters of the religion, as had been suggested by George Fox.

By this assignment of the Yearly Meeting, Mount Hope became the center of business for the Quakers in the First and Second Tenths of the West New Jersey Province. The Quarterly Meetings were for both men and women, although they met separately as was the custom among Friends. The women met in the kitchen-dining room and the men met in the sitting room on the first floor of the home. The Chesterfield and Burlington Monthly Meetings and other meetings for worship in the area appointed members to attend the Quarterly Meetings and the meetings were attended by any other Friends who might be necessary to help complete the business at hand. These meetings carried on the business of the Yearly Meetings between sessions, and those who attended them were usually Friends who were also involved in the civic affairs of the province. From that time on it was not unusual for the business of the Friends and the business of the West New Jersey Province to be discussed simultaneously at Mount Hope.

William was back in Burlington two days later, on September 10, 1686, for a special session of the Burlington Court. He sat on the bench with fellow justices Deputy Governor John Skene, George Hutcheson, Mahlon Stacy and Elias Farre. Several cases of debt were brought against Richard Basnett successfully, but they were peacefully satisfied by the defendant. The court learned that Thomas Pearson had not settled his affairs with Edward Byllynge. George Hutcheson, another of the Yorkshire proprietors, was also asked to account for monies and to see that they be paid to Edward Byllynge.[45]

William continued to return to Burlington almost weekly. On September 13, 1686 he received a warrant for 50 acres from the Land Commissioners, an amount that suggested it may have been meant for a person who had been indentured to or worked for him.[46] On September 20, 1686 William acknowledged an indenture between Elias Farre, executor of the deceased Henry Stacy and Robert Hudson, carpenter, for 150 acres along the Rancocas Creek, situated in the tract of 1,600 acres that had originally been assigned to William Biddle by survey. Either Elias Farre, the executor, or Henry Stacy, before he returned to England, must have made an arrangement by sale or land trade with William in order for that indenture to have been valid.[47] Undoubtedly Robert Hudson had earned the land by his labor in building one of Henry Stacy's houses in Burlington, probably the last house that Stacy had built on his waterlot west of High Street.

In October William was busy with the harvest of the crops on the farm. He had been successful in clearing more land than others in the area. He had also probably started to clear the 500-acre tract that he had claimed at Oneanickon, next to the land of William Wood, where he had already started to develop a farm with a house and barns. His success was noted even by William Penn, in a letter discussing the state of affairs at Pennsbury with James Harrison, his agent there, the fall of 1686. He mentioned that he "hoped that Harrison had been as successful as William Biddle who had 150 acres planted in corn." [48]

William knew that if he was to be successful financially he had to make his lands productive, and he had to sell crops and excess lands that he did not need for himself. At the rates that were being paid for corn, if his 150 acres did produce well, he might expect a return of £800 if the crop could be sold.[49] However, expenses of growing, shipping and labor would greatly offset this profit.

William did go on to claim more lands against his proprietary rights. It was probably on October 6, 1686 that the Land Commissioners met again. That day they released another warrant for 300 acres to William that was apparently part of the land that he traded with Anna Salter for some of her proprietary rights.[50] It may have been that same day that the Land Commissioners approved a survey for William for 270 acres next to lands of Hannaniah Gauntt, John Skene, Charles Read, John Browne, John Day, Samuel Barker, Peter Harvey and Daniel Leeds.[51]

William Biddle and his family returned to Burlington again on November 1st and 2nd, 1686 for the fall Fair Days. He stayed for the Quarter Court held on November 3, 1686 and was accompanied on the bench by Deputy Governor John Skene, James Budd, Francis Davenport, Thomas Gardiner, Richard Guy, William Emley and Elias Farre.[52] Apparently no General Assembly was held at that time, and once the court was adjourned William was able to return to Mount Hope. However, he returned to Burlington on November 8, 10 and 11, 1686 to attend to other matters of the Burlington Court.[53]

On November 29, 1686 the first Burlington Quarterly Meeting of the Religious Society of Friends was held at Mount Hope. There are no attendance records for the women's meeting, but they must have met. The men's meeting was attended by Thomas Budd, John Borton, Thomas Barton and William Peachee from the Burlington Monthly Meeting. It is uncertain who attended from the Chesterfield Meeting. No important business was documented as having been done at that session. They may have discussed the business of the next meeting, including Thomas Budd's concern that no attempts had been made to convince the Indians of the virtues of Christianity.[54] To satisfy this concern, at the next session of the Burlington Quarterly Meeting, held on February 22, 1686/7, they made preparations for Thomas Budd and Robert Stacy to meet with the Indians to discuss religion.[55]

It was the custom of the Friends of England and of West New Jersey to establish burial grounds for their deceased. Such sites had been established in association with most of the meeting places of the Friends in the province. At the Chesterfield Monthly Meeting held January 6, 1686/7, the meeting requested that William Biddle, John Snowden, William Black and John Hooton find a suitable burying ground for Friends of the Mount Hope area.[56] The committee reported back to the Chesterfield Monthly Meeting on February 3, 1686/7 that they had chosen a site. It was a two-acre tract on lands occupied by Samuel Andrews, lands that he had agreed to purchase from William Biddle, but for which no indenture had been recorded. Samuel Andrews made out a deed to William and the others of the committee for the land.[57]

It has been difficult to determine the exact site of this burial ground. The lands of Samuel Andrews and some of the lands of Percivale Towle were adjacent to each other. The Towle plantation was sold to the Gibbs family eventually, and some of the Gibbs land became the lands of the Mansfield Preparative Meeting of Friends. The burial ground may well be the same as that of the current Mansfield Preparative Meeting. The burial site is less than two miles from the Mount Hope home, and the burial ground would have been overseen by William the rest of his life. A few years later the Quakers removed all of the markers from their gravesites at the request of the Yearly Meeting, so no markers are found for those years.

William kept the burial ground deed in his possession for the Chesterfield Monthly Meeting to be sure that the claim for the land could be proven. He probably remembered vividly that the authorities of London had tried to disrupt the burial ground of the Friends in that city. This plot was probably the site where Samuel and Mary Andrews had buried their daughter Hannah, who died November 7, 1686. Others later interred at that site included Jacob Andrews, son of Samuel and Mary, deceased December 1, 1689; John Hooton, deceased November 7, 1688; John Horner, deceased by April 27, 1689; Samuel Andrews, deceased September 19, 1693; and Mary Andrews deceased in the mid-1690s; among other Friends who died in those early years.[58]

Meanwhile, further matters concerning the West New Jersey Province, the ownership of its governing rights, and the boundary lines of the West New Jersey Province were being discussed by others who lived both inside and outside of the province.

Edward Byllynge as the chief proprietor and Governor of the West New Jersey Province had received what was left of his proprietary shares from the remaining trustees by September 26, 1683 and he had proceeded to mortgage and sell some of his shares. The main person he dealt with was the non-Quaker Dr. Daniel Coxe. He mortgaged a share of the proprietary rights of the province to Dr. Coxe in 1683 and lost it by forfeiture to Dr. Coxe.[59] This was the first share released to a non-Quaker. Dr. Coxe, a wealthy physician of London and a physician to the King's Court, was aware of the plans of the Quakers in the colonies, and through his relationship with Edward Byllynge he expanded his investment in the West and East New Jersey Provinces. Dr. Coxe lived on Aldersgate Street and attended the church of St. Botolph. This part of London was near the center of the activity of the Friends, so he was known to many of the Quakers. Edward Byllynge sold more proprietary interests to Dr. Daniel Coxe in 1685,[60] and in 1686,[61] including all of his interests in the East New Jersey Province.[62]

Meanwhile the division line between East and West New Jersey became a concern to Edward Byllynge and he decided that it should be better defined. Discussions were begun with Robert Barclay, Governor of East New Jersey and agreed to settle the line by arbitration. On January 8, 1686/7 Deputy Governor John Skene of West New Jersey met with Gawen Lawrie, Deputy Governor of East New Jersey. The two, accompanied by William Emley, surveyor of West New Jersey, and Joseph Reid, surveyor of East New Jersey, received the decision of the arbitration panel.[63] It is uncertain whether the decision was subject to review by the proprietors who had been sent to examine the points of the proposed line by the General Assembly.[64] The decision of the arbitrators was accepted and the negotiations were bonded: the party who broke the agreement was to pay £5000.[65] This decision paved the way for the survey of the line by George Keith, who by then had left London and was residing in Shrewsbury, East New Jersey.

It is uncertain whether the residents of West New Jersey knew that Edward Byllynge was ill, but he died of phthisis (consumption, later known as tuberculosis) on January 16, 1686/7.[66] Although he may have told his Quaker friends that he wanted to have his son-in-law Benjamin Bartlett take over the governorship of the West Jersey Province if he died,[67] this did not happen.

Edward Byllynge's family did not fully understand the significance of the West New Jersey experiment in democracy. Dr. Daniel Coxe purchased their interests in the province, including the governing rights. The residents of West Jersey would hear about the death of Byllynge several months later from their remaining friends and relatives in London.

The governing rights to the province had passed out of the hands of the Quakers.

CHAPTER 17

Dr. Daniel Coxe, Governor
February 26, 1686/7 – August 18, 1688

The Quakers of West New Jersey remained determined to continue their "Quaker experiment in democracy." Despite the supposed loss of their governing rights to Edward Byllynge, they had managed to regain control of the government and the courts of the province. Although John Skene had apparently been instructed to exert more power over them by Edward Byllynge, he had been thwarted in this by the politically astute Quaker residents. The resident proprietors knew the problems of the province best, and they continued to make decisions that would benefit the further development of the territory. They had managed to keep the influence of Byllynge to a minimum.

During these years the Quakers of West New Jersey faced the competition for settlers from the developing province adjacent to them in Pennsylvania. They had lost and would continue to lose several of their most important leaders and citizens to Pennsylvania including Robert Stacy, Thomas Budd, Anthony Morris, Samuel Carpenter, Thomas Hooton and William Brightwen. In later years even Samuel Jennings, perhaps the most important spiritual and political leader of West New Jersey, would spend three years living in Pennsylvania, working for William Penn.

To combat this competition for settlers from Philadelphia, the West New Jersey settlers had adopted new rules for claiming and settling lands. Unlike Pennsylvania West New Jersey had originated and retained a policy of not charging quitrents. They also took steps to encourage the building of homes and businesses in the town of Burlington to make it more liveable. The settlement of Pennsylvania by William Penn may have slowed the immigration of new Quaker families into West New Jersey, but it did not stop the influx of new residents entirely. A steady stream of new settlers continues to arrive bringing new talents, skills and trades to the province, and they created a need for the sale of more lands in the upper two Tenths.

Through the careful sale of fractions of proprietary shares and land to other emigrating Quakers, they encourages claiming and settling of the more rural lands of the First and Second Tenths. Numerous families had moved to the upper Tenths of the West New Jersey Province from Long Island, including Samuel Andrews, the Horners, the John Feake family and the John Underhills. Freedom Lippincott had moved from Shrewsbury, East New Jersey, and he was later joined by his brother, Restore. From the Quaker community of Rhode Island the merchants Arthur Cooke, Walter Clarke and James Newberry had invested in the lands of the Second Tenth. Thomas and John Rodman had moved there from Rhode Island too., Hannaniah Gauntt moved to the First Tenth from Massachusetts. Even William and Mary (Parnell) Wood returned from New York.

Families continued to immigrate to West New Jersey from England bringing with them new and important skills for a growing community. Francis Davenport, milliner, and John and Samuel Bunting, masons, all from Derbyshire, came to Burlington and then settled themselves at Crosswicks Creek with Thomas Foulkes and the Robert Murfins. William and James Budd, brewers, and John Budd, upholsterer, joined their brother, Thomas Budd, in the province. Robert Hopper, mariner, claimed lands from the partial proprietary share he had purchased from George Hutcheson. Hopper's expertise allowed the farmers and tradesmen of the province to more easily export their products to other lands. Others who participated in the further settlement and development of Burlington included James Hill, cordwainer, James Marshall, merchant, Thomas Gladwin, blacksmith, Richard Basnett, innkeeper, William Myers, butcher, Christopher Wetherill, tailor, William Hunt, carpenter, Charles Read, tailor, Samuel Furnis, saddler, Thomas Raper, whitesmith, James Sherwin, butcher, Symon Charles, surveyor and Doctor Robert Dimsdale. Settlers on the rural lands included the John Day family, John Crosby, millwright, William Ellis from York, Daniel Bacon, grocer, James, William and Joseph Satterthwaite and the family of Richard Haines, husbandman, who died on the voyage across the Atlantic Ocean, on the way to the new land.

These new Quaker inhabitants of West New Jersey and many others, helped to strengthen the grip of the Quaker leaders and proprietors of the upper two Tenths on the right to rule themselves. They would soon need this extra support to help them defend their liberties and rights, now that the governing rights to the province had fallen into the hands of a non-Quaker, Dr. Daniel Coxe.

The West New Jersey Quakers were tested when they had to accept another non-Quaker, Edward Hunloke, an Anglican, into their community. Hunloke moved to Burlington and purchased land from Thomas Bowman on the east side of the Assiscunk Creek.[1] Hunloke became the second non-Quaker of importance to live in the town. The first, Thomas Revell, continued to be a respected and an important member of the community as the registrar of the province. On February 21, 1686/7 Edward Hunloke was chosen by the court to sit on the grand jury at the Quarter Court session. He was surrounded by Quaker jurors, and adjacent to the bench of Quaker justices, including William Biddle.[2] He was accepted into their community in a leadership role, but probably on their terms. It was important that he learn about their plan of government and their means of conducting the business of the court as soon as possible.

On February 26, 1686/7, in London, Dr. Daniel Coxe completed his initial purchase of the interests of the Byllynge heirs in the proprietary rights of the West New Jersey Province.[3] Coxe knew the plans of the Quaker settlers of West New Jersey. He had counseled with William Penn and other Friends of London before he had purchased the rights. Penn either did not have the opportunity to buy those proprietary rights, or was not interested in owning them. By then he had experienced over five years as chief proprietor of Pennsylvania, and he may have realized that the expense of ownership of the proprietary rights did not stop with the purchase of the rights. The settlers of Pennsylvania had continued to expect support from him, but they were not willing to give up much in return. Even the quitrents had proven hard to collect.

When Penn purchased the proprietary rights of John Fenwick to the West New Jersey Province, he accomplished what he had set out to do there. That purchase enabled him to protect trade on the Delaware River for the merchants of New Castle (Delaware) and Pennsylvania. The Quakers of West New Jersey and of England owned the overwhelming majority of the one hundred proprietary shares and rights of West Jersey. Despite this, Dr. Daniel Coxe had purchased that portion of the shares and rights associated with the governing rights, as determined by the grant of James, Duke of York, in 1680, and the arbitration decision of the London Friends in 1684. The resident proprietors could expect that the ownership of these proprietary rights and governing rights by Dr. Coxe would lead to a change in the province. They had begun to prepare again for the preservation of their Quaker experiment in democracy.

Unexpectedly very little change took place in the running of the government or the courts during the first eight months of the Coxe governorship. Since no written orders or changes were received by the officials in charge, John Skene continued in his role as deputy governor. The court sessions, the elections in each Tenth, and the General Assembly continued as scheduled.

Resuming the business of the territory, William Biddle attended the Quarter Court session of February 21, 1686/7, when he met Edward Hunloke. That day in court the bench had to decide on sentences for a kleptomaniac and for a person who falsely defamed another resident of the Second Tenth. The burglar was sentenced to make four-fold restitution for his crime. The gossiper was sentenced to stand in the pillory.[4]

Following that session of the court, William did not serve as a jurist again for more than one year. It is uncertain if this is because he was not elected to do so, or if he was occupied with other matters for the resident proprietors. He may have chosen to devote full time to his expanding land interests.

On April 7, 1687 William, leaving the supervision of the farms to William Jr., traveled to Burlington to visit with John Langford, the brother-in-law of Edward Hunloke. He sold a 500-acre tract to Langford that day for £54.[5] That land came into the possession of Edward Hunloke to satisfy a debt owed to him by Langford.

William probably also had a chance to discuss the affairs of the province with his Quaker friends in the town of Burlington. The elections for the Tenths were to be held shortly, and the matters of the land rights and the boundary line with the East New Jersey Province had to be settled.

On April 21, 1687 a meeting was called by Deputy Governor Skene and his Council. The meeting took place at the home of John Cripps in Burlington. Three East Jersey representatives wanted to discuss the boundary line between the two provinces. They requested that the Surveyor General of West Jersey meet with the Surveyor General of East Jersey at Little Egg Harbor to select the starting point for the survey line between the two provinces.[6]

Even though the government officials were playing a role in the decisions, there was not a consensus among the proprietors on the decision reached by the Barclay-Byllynge arbitration committee concerning the position of the boundary line and the bonding of the decision for £5,000 to which William Emley had consented. It was becoming more obvious that the resident proprietors of West New Jersey must organize themselves to protect their land rights, and that they had to begin to find a way to separate the land rights from the government rights.

At this phase of the negotiations there was no way to prevent George Keith, then the surveyor from East New Jersey, from surveying the boundary line between the two provinces. Keith began the survey at the proper point at Little Egg Harbor, as called for by the Quintipartite Agreement of July 1, 1676. However, he mistakenly surveyed the line too far westward in its course, as he discovered when he reached the Dobie Plantation on the southern branch of the Raritan River, sixty-two miles down the line of survey.[7] He ceased surveying at that place, but the damage had been done. He had made a mistake that would be very difficult for the East and West Jersey proprietors to correct.

The spring Fair Days brought relief from the challenges of the winter months for everyone. Despite the fact that Sarah Biddle tried to make the weekly shopping trips to the Burlington marketplace on days when weather would permit, there were many weeks when she could not get there, for the cold and the rain made it an unpleasant trip by boat or by horseback. There were some weeks when even William preferred not to make the trip, and on those occasions he sent the servants or the Indian, Indoweys, to the town to obtain the necessary items.

Sarah, concerned about each member of her family, had experienced a difficult winter. William Jr., then seventeen years old, was interested in making accomplishments of his own. His father placed him in charge of the tracts of farmland distant from Mount Hope, at Oneanickon and Mount Pleasant, promising him that at least some of the profit from those ventures would be his some day. Sarah worried, however, for when he spent many days and nights at Oneanickon, near the main Indian encampment, she was concerned for his safety. She was comforted by the fact that the William Wood family and the Newbold family were living nearby.

Sarah was also having a difficult time trying to keep her daughter productive and occupied. Sarah Jr.'s most frequent playmate, Hannah Andrews, twelve years old, the daughter of neighbors Mary and Samuel Andrews, had died that past November.[8]

On the spring Fair Days, May 10, 11 and 12, 1687, residents of the province would meet and catch up on what happened over the winter months. Freedom Lippincott's wife Mary arrived carrying her new baby, Thomas, who had been born under the supervision of the midwife of their neighborhood, Grace Hollinshead, with Judy Ollive, Hannah Eves and Jane French in attendance.[9] Suzannah Furnis was nursing her infant, Benjamin, who had been born in Burlington in March, with midwife Elizabeth Gardiner in attendance, assisted by Rachell Marshall, Mary Gladwin and Elizabeth Ible.[10] At the Assiscunk Creek settlement Frances Antrum had given birth to her son Thomas the preceding November with Anne Pancoast, midwife, in attendance, assisted by Ann and Ester Butcher.[11]

Each neighborhood had the capability of supporting birthing in homes, and only infrequently did they need to summon Dr. Robert Dimsdale to help with a delivery. These rugged pioneer women helped each other as the number of first-generation Americans in the West New Jersey territory increased.

During the Fair Days, on May 12, 1687, the Quarter Court session was held, but William did not attend even though he was still in town. At this court some of the younger Quakers, perhaps encouraged by Quaker elders, decided to make trouble for the non-Quaker, Edward Hunloke. James Hill, James Satterthwaite, James Wills and Richard Haines brought evidence against Edward Hunloke for breaking the rule of selling liquor to the Indians. Hunloke admitted his guilt and paid the fine.[12] He learned that day that these resident Quakers intended to continue the constitution and the judicial system that they had brought to West New Jersey. Hunloke passed the test. The relationship between him and the Quakers continued to improve and strengthen. He evidently understood the important governmental ideals of the Quakers and in time he helped them to accomplish their goals.

Later that same day the elected General Assembly met in Burlington,[13] probably at the inn of Richard Basnett. This was an extremely important meeting for the Quakers of the province, for a number of decisions had to be reached that day by the legislative body, decisions that would change the manner of doing business in the court and in land affairs in the province. As usual, justices were elected by the Assembly, but now, since there were more qualified people who could be judges living in the town, they began to appoint more of these local people to the Burlington Court.

The job of a justice had become more burdensome. There were Quarter Court sessions and there were weekly courts held in the town for petty matters. The new justices who appeared on the bench after that Assembly Meeting were James Marshall, Richard Basnett, William Myers and Edward Hunloke, all of whom lived in Burlington. They were intermittently supervised by the more senior Quakers Elias Farre, Richard Guy, Daniel Wills and William Emley, who would see to it that the rules of the court, created by the Concessions and Agreements, were preserved.[14]

The Assembly again faced the problem of who should have final responsibility for the debts of the province. In 1682 they had taxed residents according to their ability to pay. In 1684 they had begun to base the tax on the lands held by the residents of the province. Now that the governing rights were out of their control and out of the control of the Quakers, a more traditional decision was made. Faced with a public debt of £1,250, the legislative body turned the responsibility for this debt over to the resident proprietors. They felt that the "stocks of the people of the province were small," and they could not bear the expense. It was decided that the resident proprietors should accept the responsibility of this public debt, and that they should meet to solve the problem after the adjournment of the General Assembly. In an important companion decision, the Assembly felt that the resident proprietors, not the General Assembly, should take care of the management of the unclaimed lands of the province.[15]

It was further recognized in this Assembly that James Budd should be compensated for his efforts in traveling to England on behalf of the resident proprietors and the province as the liaison between them and Governor Daniel Coxe. Budd had also accomplished business with Dr. Coxe that was beneficial to himself, convincing him, in partnership with Benjamin Bartlett, to buy his interests in a pottery business that he had attempted to establish in Burlington.[16] Recognizing the value of Budd's services, the Assembly ignored any personal gains he had made and resolved that the resident proprietors should reward him with acreage to be taken from their stocks of unclaimed land of the province.[17]

During this session of the General Assembly the resident proprietors had successfully carried out their plan to separate the management of the unappropriated lands of the province from the governing system of the territory. The proprietors, not the General Assembly, would be responsible for backing public debt and for assigning unappropriated lands to new owners. The courts would play a role only in settling property disputes. Governor Coxe, or his representative, had to deal with the resident proprietors to receive his own land rights. In addition, they had placed the financial responsibility of the public debt of the province back onto the proprietors of the territory. Even though this would penalize those who were proprietors, it might have a sobering influence on the new governor, Dr. Coxe, who may have owned as many as twenty-two shares of the proprietary rights of the province. If this economic reality proved over-burdensome for the governor, perhaps he would relinquish some of his rights to the province to others, perhaps even to the existing proprietors and to some of the Friends in London.

On May 25, 1687, the first general meeting of the resident proprietors took place in Burlington. Fifty-nine resident proprietors were present, including William Biddle. The group recognized that their asset was their unappropriated land and they agreed to back the debt of the province with 15,000 acres of land, valued at £8 per 100 acres. The tract was to be purchased from the Indians from the land between the Crosswicks Creek and the Assinpink Creek, above the falls of the Delaware River. They arranged to assign the entire debt to one of their members, Thomas Budd, who accepted the debt in exchange for the land.[18]

To try to raise the £1,250, the group taxed each proprietary share the amount of £12.10s.½d. a tax that applied to the resident proprietors and a tax that was meant to pertain to the London proprietors as well. The amount to be raised by each proprietary share was to be paid by May 20, 1688. If it was not received by then, Thomas Budd would receive the land instead. The agreement was signed by all of the resident proprietors present, including William Biddle,[19] who by that time owned 1.413 proprietary shares and rights more than any other resident proprietor. As a result of this action of the resident proprietors, William and Sarah now owed £17.14s. as their part of the debt.

Thomas Budd moved quickly in identifying the land that he wanted to claim. He purchased the land from the Indians and had it surveyed by June 4, 1687.[20]

To be successful economically in West New Jersey, William and Sarah knew that they had to sell lands, but even more important, they had to make the lands that they claimed for themselves productive. They had committed significant funds to the development of the farm lands at Oneanickon so that these lands would be under cultivation. Their son, William Jr., was overseeing this venture.

The summer of 1687 was difficult for everyone. There was a severe drought that brought near-starvation conditions to the developing West New Jersey Province. Friends from New England came to their rescue by shipping a load of grain to them late in the summer.[21] William certainly would have experienced financial losses that season. The crops under cultivation at Oneanickon had been lost. It is possible that he was able to save some of the crops grown at Mount Hope by having the farm laborers irrigate the crops with water from the river.

Fortunately for William and Sarah their homestead had such abundant natural resources that they were able to survive the drought better than many others. Fish from the river and forage from the island and great meadow allowed them to save their livestock from starvation.

William, possibly with Sarah, traveled to Burlington on Tuesday, August 2, 1687. That day they sold 150 acres of prime farmland to Charles Read, tailor, of Burlington for £18. John Woolston Sr. and Joseph Satterthwaite were on hand to witness the indenture, which was acknowledged before justices Daniel Wills and Andrew Robeson.[22] The cash or credit that they received from that transaction would have been very useful in such hard times.

William returned to Burlington the following Monday for a second meeting of the group of resident proprietors. It is probable that the Land

Commissioners had met on the days of the Quarter Court, and now the resident proprietors had adopted the same meeting schedule. The main business that day was to complete the action directed by the General Assembly for James Budd. They deeded 1,000 acres to James Budd for land to be purchased from the Indians along the Rancocas Creek beyond the line of the prior Indian purchase.[23] James Budd had continued to travel to England to deal with Governor Coxe and he was so successful that eventually Dr. Coxe asked him to be one of his land agents in the province.[24]

Despite the drought, the Burlington Quarterly Meeting of Friends met at Mount Hope on August 29, 1687. In addition to William and Sarah, who hosted the men and women meetings, other attendees were Thomas Butcher, John Woolston, William Brightwen, Thomas Barton, Percivale Towle, Francis Davenport, Samuel Jennings, Samuel Andrews and Thomas Ollive. The meeting began the practice of appointing members to attend the Yearly Meeting of Friends. Ollive, Jennings, Davenport and Andrews were asked to attend the upcoming Yearly Meeting,[25] which was to be held in Philadelphia on September 7, 1687, but only Thomas Ollive and Samuel Jennings attended.[26] Apparently the severity of the drought prevented the more distant Friends from traveling to the city.

When the residents of the First and Second Tenths came together for the fall Fair Days in Burlington on November 1 and 2, 1687, they probably had already received the letter that Governor Coxe had written to them on September 5, 1687. This long awaited communication from the wealthy, non-Quaker governor addressed his thoughts on administering the business of the province. Dr. Coxe indicated that he had been in communication with William Penn and other Quaker leaders of London. He indicated that he was certain that his governing rights were as strong as those of William Penn's in Pennsylvania. Since he was a physician to the King's Court in London he would have known what was being said about these rights in that setting, so he was fairly well assured of his rights to govern the province. It was apparent to the resident proprietors that Governor Coxe did have a good understanding of the carefully constructed plans of the Quakers of West New Jersey. He guaranteed them that they could continue their freedom of conscience on matters of religion. He agreed to continue their court system with trials by jury and the right of the defendant to object to specific jurors. Beyond these points he felt that the government might have to be chartered again to conform to English law, "the best in the world." But he did not then or later send any new charter or bills.[27] He must have realized that the Concessions and Agreements did conform to that standard.

Dr. Coxe continued the appointment of John Skene as deputy governor for the province. He also formally inquired if the residents would like him to appoint the officers of the province, or if they preferred to continue to elect their own officers. As an East New Jersey proprietor, Dr. Coxe already understood the problems of the boundary dispute between the two provinces. He also knew that the West New Jersey Province was being deprived of land by the Barclay-Byllynge boundary agreement and by the Keith Line.[28]

Despite the misery and the financial reverses that the residents of the province were experiencing from the drought, and despite the concern and uncertainty of the role and attitude of Governor Coxe toward them, their spirits were now lifted by the good news that he sent. Their emissary to him, James Budd, and the Friends of London, perhaps even Edward Byllynge before his death, had prepared the wealthy physician well for his role as Governor of this Quaker Province. He was willing to continue their system of government, their courts and the individual liberties that they had tried so hard to protect in their society. In addition, it was quite possible that he would take their side in the boundary dispute with East New Jersey. They needed an ally in this matter, for the very powerful Scottish and English proprietors were difficult for them to confront. William and the other resident proprietors must have been optimistic about the news they had received from the new Governor of their province.

The day following the fair, November 3, 1687, more warrants for land were issued against proprietary rights. It is uncertain if the entire group of resident proprietors came together again that day, or if a sub-committee, or even the Land Commissioners, met to accomplish the task. Presumably William Biddle was involved, for that day he received a warrant for 150 acres of land. He immediately made a verbal land contract (a mortgage) with James Sherwin for this land. The tract was surveyed on the south side of the Rancocas Creek and Sherwin built his homestead there, but the deed for this transaction was not recorded for another nine years.[29]

William returned to Mount Hope that day elated by the prospect of finding solutions to the problems that he had been concerned about for the past months. With their 1.413 proprietary shares, the Biddles were more heavily invested in the West New Jersey Province than their peers. However, since more land dividends had not been issued to existing proprietary shares, William and Sarah could not claim more land, or sell more land, unless they bought more fractions of proprietary shares. Now, with Governor Coxe also interested in claiming land, it was very likely that a way would be found to issue more land rights to each proprietor for the shares already owned. In addition to this probable new declaration of a land dividend, William prepared to gain the rights to new unappropriated lands by negotiating with Anna Salter for a purchase of her 2/12ths proprietary share.

The event that the resident proprietors were waiting for occurred on February 8, 1687/8. Adlord Bowde had been sent to the province by Governor Coxe as his principal land agent. Bowde requested a meeting with Deputy Governor John Skene and his Council to ask for the assignment to his employer of the full first dividend rights to the twelve shares that Dr. Coxe had in his possession at that time. The group met in the inn of Henry Grubb in Burlington. John Skene, realizing that he and his Council did not have the right to speak for the resident proprietors and to grant the request of the Governor, proposed that another meeting be held of the resident proprietors to make the decision.[30]

A meeting of as many of the resident proprietors as could be gathered was held February 13, 1687/8 in Burlington. They determined that on the basis of the fact that Governor Coxe would be encouraging the emigration of many people to the province to carry on the economic ventures of whaling, sales of natural resources and the development of new industries, there was good reason to distribute the full first land dividend. This meant that each full proprietary share would receive 5,200 acres of unappropriated land. They had already distributed 3,200 acres per proprietary share for this first dividend, so an additional 2,000 acres would issued per proprietary share, or a proportionate amount of land for fractions of shares. This would complete the distribution of the first land dividend for the proprietary shares of the West New Jersey Province. Those who had already received the first portion rights for that dividend, such as William and Sarah, would now be entitled to an additional 2,000 acres per share. For Dr. Coxe, his agent Adlord Bowde would be able to pay the Indians for the land and claim 5,200 acres for each of his twelve proprietary shares.[31]

The group agreed to issue a warrant to Dr. Coxe for 62,400 acres, representing the full 5,200 acres per proprietary share for the twelve shares that he claimed at that time. A warrant was issued to Andrew Robeson, Surveyor General, with the instructions for him to survey the land to Dr. Coxe in one or two tracts in each of two locations, the first above the falls of the Delaware and the second in the lower Tenths between the Cohansey and Bearegate Rivers. But the land had to be purchased from the Indians.[32]

With this decision, the resident proprietors had declared the residual to the first dividend to their own proprietary rights. The agreement reached between the two parties also meant that the Governor had sanctioned the right of the proprietors to limit the claims of the unappropriated lands in the first four Tenths to those forty proprieties, ten in each Tenth, which were already associated with ownership of lands in those Tenths. William would be able to claim his 2,820 acres of additional lands in the populated First and Second Tenths, while Governor Coxe would claim lands in more remote areas of the territory. This was a continuation of the original concept of the method of land distribution put into effect by the Concessions and Agreements. The Quaker resident proprietors had protected their right to control the settlement of the unclaimed lands of the four upper Tenths with the exception of the vast acreage above the falls of the Delaware River.

The resident proprietors did not adjourn after completing their business with Adlord Bowde. They knew that they had to organize themselves to protect their rights in the future. When they met in a group of sixty or more, there was no possibility that they could efficiently accomplish their business. Undoubtedly, most of them stayed in the town or at least in the environs of Burlington that night. There must have been an interesting amount of political jostling that went on in the inns of Burlington that evening to prepare for the events of the next day.

On the next morning, February 14, 1687/8, they met again. It was at this meeting that they decided to create a smaller representative group of proprietors called a Council. They would be responsible for conducting the business of the proprietors, including further distributions of the unclaimed acres associated with the proprietary shares.

Elections were held in a manner not previously experienced in West New Jersey. The political jurisdictions were changed. The first two Tenths were now considered as a county, Burlington County, and the areas of the Third and Fourth Tenths were now combined into a territory referred to as Gloucester County. The division of their territory into counties, comparable to the shires of England, was a more traditional and comfortable means of subdividing the province for these Englishmen.

They held the elections by county and they elected eleven members to the newly created Council of Proprietors of West New Jersey. Six men were elected from Burlington County: William Biddle, Samuel Jennings, Thomas Ollive, Elias Farre, Mahlon Stacy and Francis Davenport. Five men were elected from Gloucester County: Andrew Robeson, the Surveyor General, William Royden, John Reading, William Cooper and John Wills.[33]

With the formation of the Council of Proprietors of West New Jersey the resident proprietors had essentially taken the affairs of unclaimed land management out of the hands of the government of the province. They were now organized enough to confront the Board of Proprietors of East New Jersey about the boundary dispute if they felt it was necessary.

The rules of the new organization were established. Voting for membership was to take place on the traditional election days of the counties. For Burlington County this was to be April 10th annually. A resident proprietor would be able to vote for the officers in his county if he owned even a fraction of a share. Each member of the council was to be paid two shillings per day for his work with the council.[34] In this way it was implied, as it had been stated by the Concessions and Agreements concerning the payment of Assemblymen, that the members of the council were to protect the interests of all of the proprietors of West New Jersey, not just their own interests. The charter members of the council were all resident proprietors who already had considerable experience with the land affairs of the province. William Biddle, as the largest holder of proprietary shares and rights among the resident proprietors in Burlington County, was qualified and prepared for this position through his experience as a land commissioner and a judge.

Later that month, on February 27, 1687/8, the Burlington Quarterly Meeting of women and men of the Society of Friends met as scheduled at Mount Hope. The attendance records are incomplete, but joining William and Sarah that day were at least Thomas Barton, Percivale Towle, Thomas Ollive and Samuel Bunting. although there had only been five meetings of the group to that time held at Mount Hope, William had records in his possession that were felt to be important enough to be bound into a book. He turned these records over to Samuel Bunting who was directed by the meeting to see that they were bound.[35] These notes may have been the minutes of the unofficial Quarterly Meetings that took place in Burlington, prior to the meeting being established at Mount Hope.

The Surveyor General and the Council of Proprietors of West Jersey wasted no time in laying out the lands directed to be surveyed by the meeting of February 13, 1687/8 with Adlord Bowde. Now that the decision had been made, they did not want to take a chance that any other political event would interfere with the opportunity afforded by that meeting. The first purchase of land from the Indians was made as early as March 30, 1688 on the lands above the falls. That day William Biddle Jr. and Thomas Budd, with John Wills as interpreter, and accompanied by Henry Greenland and Thomas Bowman, visited the Indians above the falls and signed the agreement of sale for the first portion of the lands that were purchased on the rights of Dr. Coxe in that location.[36] The second purchase of lands from the Indians above the falls was completed by April 9, 1688.[37]

Andrew Robeson supervised the purchasing and signing of the agreements with the Indians for the lands in the Lower Tenths on April 30, 1688,[38] and June 24, 1688.[39] However, he went beyond the recorded understanding in these purchases. Approximately 300,000 acres were purchased and surveyed at that time. This was enough land to cover the entire first dividend of 5,200 acres for all of the proprietary shares that Dr. Coxe might ever claim, perhaps as many as twenty-two shares, which would require 114,400 acres. In addition, a second dividend of 5000 acres per proprietary share for his interests would require another 110,000 acres. This purchase was for even more land than needed for Dr. Coxe. It is possible that they had agreed to prepare the way for the second land dividend in the meeting of February 13, 1687/8. Or, the Council of Proprietors may have worked out this plan with Governor Coxe, for it is apparent that his funds were used to pay the Indians for the land. All of these arrangements had to have been made prior to April 1, 1688, the date from which the interest charges for the land claims were to start. Undoubtedly the council had directed Andrew Robeson to take this action with the full knowledge of Dr. Coxe, for both parties were to benefit from a second dividend of land being declared for the proprietary shares.[40]

The business and government of the province continued under the rules of the Concessions and Agreements. Elections were held in April in the counties. Not only were the local officials elected, but the resident proprietors elected their new Council that month. Elias Farre and John Willis were not continued as Council of Proprietor members and the total number of Council members may have been reduced to nine. It is uncertain if new justices were elected, for the same ones that had been on the bench since the last election continued to serve in the courtroom.[41] It is not certain, either, if new assemblymen were elected, for the General Assembly may not have met after the spring Fair Days in Burlington that year; at least, a meeting was not recorded.

The Quarter Court session was held May 12, 1688 as scheduled. The constables that had been elected in several townships were presented to the court for approval. Daniel Leeds was to be the constable for the Birch Creek area, Thomas Foulke for Chesterfield, John Wilsford for Nottingham, and the court, still having control over the very lowest Tenth, the Cape May area, appointed Samuel Mathews as the constable for that region.[42]

At this session of the court it became the practice of the Grand Jury to identify the problems of the province and for the jury and the bench of the court to direct corrective actions. It was recognized that Francis Collins had not completed the public assembly hall, even though he had been under contract to do so since 1683. He was directed to finish the hall by June 15th of that spring under penalty of £50 if he failed to do so. The citizens were directed to repair and establish new bridges in the province. Specifically, the Yorkshire Bridge and the bridge over the Assiscunk Creek at Godfrey Hancock's needed repair. A common pound, a fenced yard, was to be established in Burlington to accommodate the swine that were running free in the town.[43]

It is likely that William remained a justice during this one-year interval that he did not sit on the bench of the court. He may have been so busy with personal matters and with the business of the proprietors that he was not able attend to that civic duty. Whatever the reason for not being there before that time, he did reappear as a justice when the Quarter Court met again on August 8, 1688. By then there were very important reasons for his attendance.[44]

Now that he had received permission to claim more lands under his proprietary rights, William began to sell more lands and to record the lands that he had previously promised to others. He was now entitled to an additional 2,820 acres from the second portion of the first land dividend for his 1.413 proprietary shares. In addition, if the Council of Proprietors had agreed upon a second dividend of 5,000 acres per proprietary share, as suggested by the actions of their Surveyor General, William and Sarah were entitled to an additional 7,080 acres of unappropriated lands in the West Jersey Province.

On April 10, 1688, Election Day, William was in Burlington not only to vote, but also to record the sale of a 100 acre tract to Hance Monseur of Senaminsinck (Cinnaminson), for which he received £10.[45] On June 10, 1688, he sold 150 acres of rural land and a town wharf lot to James Satterthwaite for £23. The rural acreage was located next to the land of Robert Dimsdale, above the forks of the Rancocas Creek. Thomas Revell, still in Burlington, served as a witness when the indenture was acknowledged before justices Edward Hunloke and Richard Basnett.[46]

On July 10, 1688, now that he had the rights to the acreage, William recorded the sale of 600 acres to his neighbor, Samuel Andrews. The Andrews family had occupied that land since the fall of 1683. William was paid £63 for the tract.[47] He had land rights remaining to protect the acreage that he had claimed for himself and had begun to improve. He continued negotiations with Anna Salter for her 2/12ths proprietary share when he saw her on August 8, 1688, when she and her son John Salter presented an indenture to the Burlington court that justices William Biddle and Edward Hunloke acknowledged.[48] In the transaction that William made with Anna, he had agreed to give Anna Salter and her son 500 acres for their use then, if he could have the 2/12ths proprietary share for all of its rights beyond the first dividend issued to the proprietors. Some of those 500 acres of land were already identified and settled. Samuel Nichols and Robert Stiles each owned and had settled on 100-acre tracts on the Pennsauken Creek.[49] Perhaps even the transaction with Peter Long that was completed that day was on lands that William had supplied to Anna.

The resident proprietors may have known that their rights to manage their affairs, including their land affairs, might still be at risk in the future. They had fortunately made all of the decisions necessary to allow them to proceed with the further distribution of some of the unappropriated lands of the province just in time.

Unknown to them, on April 7, 1688, King James II issued orders to Governor Edmund Andros of the Dominion of New England to take over the governorship of New York and both provinces of New Jersey.[50] King James II had usurped the governing rights of Governor Coxe. He had given the rights away to Edward Byllynge and now he took them back from Dr. Coxe. The East New Jersey proprietors, a group which included Dr. Coxe, had surrendered their governing rights to the Crown.[51] It is uncertain if this action was taken by Dr. Coxe in London, or possibly by some of the London proprietors of West New Jersey. Certainly the resident proprietors of West New Jersey had not given their permission to the proprietors of London for any such action. Although it would take time for the change in government to take effect, the West New Jersey proprietors now had to prepare to face a new governing authority as they tried to continue the individual liberties and rights of the society that they were creating in the new world. William Biddle returned to the bench of the Quarter Court in Burlington on August 8, 1688 to prepare for the new regime.[52]

CHAPTER 18

Sir Edmond Andros,
Governor of the Dominion of New England
under King James II of England
August 18, 1688 – April 18, 1689

On Saturday, August 18, 1688, the tranquility of Burlington County was broken by the arrival of Sir Edmond Andros.[1] The Governor and his Council reached the town by horseback, traveling through the province from East New Jersey on the rough roads of the territory. Their presence was obvious to the settlers along the trails of what had so recently been wilderness — the men and horses created enough noise to shatter the usual quiet of the countryside. Anyone who went to the roadside to look was surprised to see the governor accompanied by his colorful redcoat guards blowing their trumpets to announce their arrival.

The Governor's party crossed the Yorkshire Bridge into Burlington City and made its way to the town center, the intersection of Broad and High Streets, and the site of the markethouse, the assembly hall, the newly completed courthouse and the simple log prison. Residents and visitors made their way to the meeting place. The young came out of curiosity, but the elders knew that it was their duty to appear before the new Governor. The only invitation that they would receive was the call of the trumpet. And they feared the changes to come.

Without delay, Sir Andros read his commission from James II and proclaimed himself Governor of the Territory. He introduced his secretary, Edward Randolph, and the members of his council who were with him. Governor Andros did not want to stay in this remote territory any longer than necessary to conduct his official business. He could see that the infrastructure of the territory was primitive. The roads and bridges were barely sufficient to allow passage for his group. The jail facility was entirely inadequate. He and Edward Randolph observed that West New Jersey was sparsely settled by simple country folk and that not one military man was to be found in the territory.[2]

Governor Andros probably knew John Skene, the then-deputy governor of the territory. He may have recognized those Quakers with whom he had negotiated before when they came to the area in 1677, including Thomas Ollive, Daniel Wills, William Emley and Robert Stacy.

Edward Randolph, Secretary to Governor Andros, attended to most of the details of organizing the new government of the province. He met with John Skene and relieved him of his position as deputy governor, although he did continue to use him as his agent in West New Jersey. He made Skene responsible for carrying out the programs and changes that Governor Andros and King James II wanted to install in the government of the province.[3]

One of the main reasons for the King to take over the provincial government was the fact that the ports of the province had been duty free. Although it was not conspicuous, the residents of West New Jersey had been carrying on a significant and growing trade with other ports. Now steps would be taken to tax imports and exports. The most serious problem for the resident Quakers, however, was the loss of their ability to govern themselves. There would no longer be elections for a General Assembly, or for a Governor's Council. All justices were now to be appointed by the Crown. The West New Jersey inhabitants had no guarantees that they would be able to continue the liberties in the courts or in their religious lives to which they had become accustomed.

Edward Randolph announced that the Governor would continue the current justices in office But they offered commissions to the magistrates, which would have to pay a fee to John Skene in order to retain their positions. The Quaker justices objected to this reversion to the ways of old England, but they could not prevent the change. They soon adopted the philosophy of James Nevill of Salem, who was one of William Penn's agents in the province, who observed that "it is part of a wise man not onely to see that which is before his eyes, But to forsee things to come." [4]

William Biddle had prepared for the change by returning to the bench of the Burlington Quarter Court ten days before that time. He and many of the other Quaker justices purchased their commissions and continued to sit on the benches of the courts of the counties and the province. In this way they had the opportunity to continue the court system that they had instituted under the Concessions and Agreements. It was fortunate that they had already removed the responsibility of land distribution from the government of the province. However, they would have to test the new system to see if Governor Andros was going to object to their authority to administer the land rights.

They did not know what restrictions might be placed on their religious lives by the new government. They knew that Andros and Randolph were not pleased with the state of their public buildings and roadways. They could anticipate that the tax burden on the residents would increase significantly to pay for more substantial public improvements. William and his Quaker peers realized that the Quaker experiment in democracy might be seriously challenged by the new action of King James II. They had to decide how they could preserve as much as possible of their original plan.

On August 27, 1688 the Burlington Quarterly Meeting of the Religious Society of Friends met at Mount Hope, attended by the "weighty and seasoned" Quakers of the province, there to oversee the business of their religion. They appointed some of their members, including William Biddle, to be their representatives at the Yearly Meeting.[5] This business meeting at rural Mount Hope was the first opportunity that the Quaker leaders had to discuss in private the actions of Governor Andros. In this setting they could safely begin to try to develop a strategy to preserve their liberties and rights.

On September 5, 1688 the Yearly Meeting of Friends was held in Burlington. Friends came from all over the West New Jersey territory, from East New Jersey, from Pennsylvania and from throughout the east coast settlements. William attended as an appointed representative from the Burlington Quarterly Meeting with his friends Percivale Towle, John Day, Richard Guy, William Watson and John Wilsford. Thomas Budd represented the Philadelphia Monthly Meeting. John Hampton and George Keith attended as appointed representatives from the Shrewsbury Monthly Meeting. Christopher White represented the Salem Meeting and others joined them from other monthly meetings of the region to discuss the business of the Religious Society of Friends.[6] During the days of the Yearly Meeting the town of Burlington and its suburbs were bustling. The annual event provided a brief break in farm chores before the harvest season. It was an important time for all of the urban and rural Quakers to take time off and concentrate on their religion. It has been reported that as many as fifteen hundred Friends might have attended such an important annual gathering.

The West New Jersey resident proprietors among the gathered Quakers undoubtedly took this opportunity to discuss with George Keith the status of the boundary line between East and West New Jersey. No apparent means of correcting the errant line was reached by those who actually lived in the provinces. Soon after this meeting, George Keith removed from East

Jersey to Philadelphia, where he became headmaster of the first Quaker school established there at the direction of William Penn.[7]

Perhaps the most important subject discussed by the Quakers during these Yearly Meeting sessions was the concern brought to the meetings by the Quakers of Germantown in Pennsylvania. They felt that a policy should be established to abolish slavery. Friends were generally familiar with the position of George Fox on the subject, a policy that he had established when he had been confronted by slavery while visiting in Barbados in 1671. He had stated that he hoped Friends would consider their contracts with their slaves as indentures, and that these servants would be given their freedom after a specified period of time.

Fox's suggested policy had not been generally adopted by the Friends of the region. In these discussions the group recognized that they could not resolve the problem at that time. They concluded in their minutes that "it was adjudgement not to be so proper for this meeting to give a positive judgment in this case It having so general a relation to many other parts and therefore at present they forebear it." [8] They realized that slavery was wrong, but it had become so integrated into the economy of the developing territories that it was impossible for them to agree to end it abruptly. The discussion of the subject that day was the beginning of the dialogue that would eventually lead to the antislavery policy of the Yearly Meeting of Friends decades later.

In London that same day (September 5, 1688) the previous Governors of East and West New Jersey, Robert Barclay and Dr. Daniel Coxe, came to a compromise agreement concerning the boundary line between the two provinces. They agreed that the line struck by George Keith should remain in its entirety as far as the Dobie Plantation on the south branch of the Rariton River. They recognized that the extension of this line would deprive the West New Jersey proprietors of many acres of land, so they defined a semicircular tract north of the end of the Keith Line to be assigned to West New Jersey to compensate them for their loss. The new line extended northeast from the end of the Keith Line to a series of identifiable natural boundaries. The first of these was a point on the north branch of the Rariton River. From there the line ran northward to a point on the Passaic River and then to the Pequannock River which it followed to its most northern point. If it had not reached latitude 41 degrees by then, it was to run in a straight line northward to that latitude.[9]

The two men agreed to submit their agreement to the East and West New Jersey proprietors for their approval. For the remainder of William

Biddle's lifetime, this boundary line was the one agreed to by both proprietary groups. Years later when disagreement over the boundary between the two provinces reoccurred, other solutions were sought.[10]

The Quaker residents of the area had, with the completion of the Yearly Meeting of Friends, successfully conducted the business of their religion and held meetings for worship without challenge by the agents of Governor Andros. It was apparent that their religious rights were to remain intact. Now it was time for them to test the authority of the newly-formed Council of Proprietors of West New Jersey with regard to control over land rights.

The day after the Yearly Meeting, September 6, 1688, a meeting of the resident proprietors of West New Jersey was held, taking advantage of the fact that there were many proprietors in town with a keen interest in the proprietary rights of the province. It was agreed that day to change the quorum of the Council of Proprietors of West New Jersey from six to five. It is uncertain if the proprietors also elected another Council then, but they apparently continued a membership of eleven, even though there were at that time only nine members on the council. They also set the meeting schedule for the council to at least once a quarter, the day after the Quarter Court session. This was either the same, or close to the schedule that the Land Commissioners had set for themselves.[11]

Later that same day, the Council of Proprietors met with other interested proprietors. At that meeting it was acknowledged that a 300,000-acre purchase of land had been made from the Indians with the knowledge of Governor Coxe, for he had supplied the money to make the purchase. This was enough land to allow declaration of a second dividend of 5,000 acres per share for the land rights of the proprietary shares. It was agreed that the purchase price for the lands would have to be paid to Dr. Coxe before Andrew Robeson, the Surveyor General, would be able to lay out the lands for a proprietor or his designee. For Dr. Coxe's lands above the falls the cost was twenty five shillings for one thousand acres and for his lands in the lower counties the cost was twelve shillings and six pence for one thousand acres. The resident proprietors were allowed to settle the debt over time, but interest on the purchase was to begin April 1, 1688.

Apparently all of the arrangements to purchase the lands from the Indians and to disburse them had been made prior to April 7, 1688. The interest established for ownership of lands above the falls was two shilling and six pence, or ten percent per annum, for 1,000 acres. It was even more, eighteen pence per annum, or twelve percent per annum, for 1,000 acres in the lower counties.[12] The resident proprietors gladly agreed to these exorbitant interest rates charged by Dr. Coxe because they wanted to declare the second land dividend against their proprietary shares in order to start claiming and selling tracts of land again. They had many unclaimed tracts of land remaining in the populated areas and could satisfy their land rights without need to claim any of the land Dr. Coxe had purchased from the Indians.

For William Biddle the declaration of a second land dividend would mean that he would be entitled to an additional 7,050 acres of land. By then he had completed the verbal transaction with Anna Salter and John Salter to purchase their 2/12ths proprietary share.[13] When this purchase was officially recorded as complete, William and Sarah had ownership of 1.58 proprietary shares and rights in Burlington County and would be entitled to an additional 833.33 acres of unappropriated lands in the second proprietary land dividend.

To further test the ability of a resident to sell land, William returned to Burlington on September 12, 1688 with William Satterthwaite to arrange the recording of the deed between them. Satterthwaite had purchased a 100-acre tract from William for £10.[14] The land was near the Mount Hope homestead and the two families remained in close association with each other for several generations.

Thomas Ollive, president of the Council of Proprietors of West New Jersey, assembled the council in Burlington on September 18, 1688. In addition to Ollive the council members at that time were William Biddle, Andrew Robeson, Samuel Jennings, Francis Davenport, Mahlon Stacy, William Roydon, William Cooper and John Reading. There was much more work to be done to protect the interests of the proprietors. It was decided at that meeting that Samuel Jennings would review all deeds and issue warrants for the council for Burlington County, a responsibility with which he was familiar having overseen this duty as Governor in past years. John Reading was to do the same for Gloucester County. The rules for claiming land were restated and remained similar to the rules established by the Land Commissioners in past years. Again it was made clear that no person could purchase lands from the Indians without permission of the council. Surveys for each land claim had to be returned to the council for approval before the claim would be considered valid.[15]

The actions of the Council of Proprietors of West New Jersey did not go unnoticed by the governing administration. By October of 1688 Edward Randolph, Secretary to Governor Andros, had instructed John Skene to have all of the records of the province surrendered to him. Skene then requested that Thomas Revell, clerk of Burlington County, and John Reading, clerk of Gloucester County, turn their records over to him. The Council of Proprietors met from October 10 through 12, 1688 to consider this action. They had to agree to turn the province's records over to John Skene but they requested records relating to land matters remain in their possession. Fortunately Skene lived among them so that the documents, including the property records, that were placed in his possession remained in the West New Jersey Province and the Proprietors were able to get a receipt from him.[16] Without those land records it would have been almost impossible to conduct the business of distributing more land.

The Burlington Quarter Court met again on Tuesday, November 6, 1688. The schedule for Quarter Courts had been changed by the new government. Now they were to be held on the first Tuesday of November, February, May and August. William Biddle was on the bench that day with James Marshall, William Myers, Richard Basnett, William Emley and Daniel Wills, with John Skene and non-Quaker Edward Hunloke.[17] These justices, the majority of whom were Quakers, were to stay on the bench for the duration of the Andros governorship, continuing to protect the features of the West New Jersey court system that had been initiated by the Concessions and Agreements.

In this session the court attended to a number of deficiencies apparently pointed out by Governor Andros and Edward Randolph. Numerous roads and bridges were ordered to be repaired. It was directed that a good prison be built in the town, and a "pinfold" for stray animals was to be constructed. Innkeepers as well as all owners of alehouses and ordinaries were to turn in their old licenses. New licenses were issued to Henry Grubb, Abraham Senior, Peter Jennings and Christopher Snowden. The court further divided the county into constabularies of Nottingham, Chesterfield, Mansfield, Wellingborough, Northampton, Evesham, Springfield and Chester. Each district was assigned or allowed to elect constables and overseers of the highways with the approval of the court.[18]

During these fall months William Biddle continued to sell land against his first dividend proprietary rights. He sold 50 acres to John Feake of Long Island on November 10, 1688 for £5.[19] He sold an additional 75 acres within the town bounds of Burlington to Samuel Furnis, saddler of Burlington, on December 10, 1688 for £15.[20]

On December 11, 1688 an event occurred in England that would once more change the lives and prospects of the West New Jersey residents.

King James II was quietly dethroned and his daughter Mary and her husband, William of Orange, became Queen Mary and King William III.[21] There was no immediate change in the status of the government of the Dominion of New England or of the West New Jersey Province, but it was reasonable to expect that Governor Andros who was disliked by the inhabitants through out America had served King James II for many years, would be recalled to England. The West Jersey inhabitants needed to anticipate working toward a favorable change in the future.

During the winter months of 1688/9 there were numerous business matters that required William's attention concerning the Council of Proprietors, the courts, and the Religious Society of Friends. Despite the fact that February was one of the coldest month of the year, William attended the session of the Quarter Court and the Court of Common Pleas held in Burlington on February 5 and 6, 1688/9.[22]

At this session of the Quarter Court the residents of Burlington gave recognition to the newest settler in their town, John Tatham, Esquire. In past years, Tatham had been associated with the Quakers of London, where he was known as John Gray.[23] In 1684 he had become a proprietor of West New Jersey by his purchase of a one-quarter proprietary share from the London Quaker leader, Benjamin Antrobus.[24] He had subsequently changed his name and moved to Pennsylvania, where he remained in association with the Friends. When he returned to England Dr. Robert Dimsdale had requested that John Tatham he be among those who were to look after his affairs in West Jersey.[25]

John Tatham, a non-Quaker, who was the attorney and agent for Dr. Coxe moved to Burlington, where he claimed a fifteen-acre tract of land within the town from the rights of George Hutcheson, Thomas Hutchinson, Thomas Wright, Benjamin Antrobus and Freedom Lippincott.[26] The tract was set apart on the northeast corner of the town fronting on the Pearl Street and on the lane by the Assiscunk Creek. Tatham built his mansion house on that land and surrounded it with the necessary outbuildings. Luxurious gardens and orchards filled the tract and the land was fenced, creating a compound that was isolated and private, separated from the rest of the town. This town home site rapidly became more elegant than any of the other homes in town. Tatham had ample access to the river as well for he claimed a 100-foot water lot on the most northeast corner of the river front of the town.[27]

On Tuesday, February 5, 1688/9 John Tatham was introduced to the ways of the Quaker justices of the town when he was placed on the grand jury. William Biddle, John Skene, Edward Hunloke, James Marshall, Daniel Wills and William Myers were the justices on the bench. Routine matters of the court were attended to, including the temporary removal of a license to sell liquor of Christopher Snowden. The roadway to the Northampton River (Rancocas Creek) was directed to be built to the land of Robert Hudson. John Wills was licensed to keep a ferry at that location to allow travelers to cross the stream to Wills' land and the connecting roadway to Pennsauken. Constables identified for the townships included James Satterthwaite and Joseph Adams for Burlington, Robert Pearson for Nottingham, Robert Wilson for Chesterfield, John Roberts for Chester, John Browne for Mansfield, Daniel Leeds for Springfield, Freedom Lippincott for Wellingborrow, John Hilliard for Northampton and George Smith for Eversham.[28]

That winter the Council of Proprietors received a notice of the Barclay-Coxe Agreement on the boundary line between the two Provinces. William returned to Burlington for another meeting of the council on February 14 through 15, 1688/9. The advantages and disadvantages of the agreement were discussed by the group and it was decided to call together the entire body of resident proprietors to endorse the agreement. The council also restated some of the rules that had been issued previously for taking up lands. They reemphasized that no proprietor could claim lands not previously purchased from the Indians. They expanded a proprietors rights by allowing each proprietor to take up land on rights anywhere in the province and in any amount to which they were entitled to, so long as the land had been purchased from the Indians.[29] This change replaced the original method of associating each proprietary share with a particular Tenth. The lands purchased by Dr. Coxe from the Indians could now be claimed more easily by any proprietor.

While in Burlington for the meetings William supervised the recording of the indenture by which he sold 100 acres of unappropriated land rights to Anthony Woodward, husbandman, for £12.[30]

One week later, on February 22, 1688/9, all of the resident proprietors of West New Jersey gathered in Burlington to discuss the Barclay-Coxe boundary agreement. Although they wanted to attach certain qualifications to the agreement, they decided to notify Dr. Coxe of these conditions separately and to ratify his agreement. Fifty-eight resident proprietors signed the document led by John Tatham as an attorney for Dr. Coxe. The agreement would be sent back to London for final approval by Dr. Coxe and the West New Jersey proprietors who lived there [31]

William stayed in town for the meeting of the Council of Proprietors of West New Jersey on February 22, 23, 1688/9. The members again discussed the rules for taking up land. The first request for issuance of a warrant for lands of the second dividend was presented to them. They approved that request, issuing a warrant to James Read, the husband of widow Smith, the wife of the deceased John Smith who had been one of the original ten London proprietors who had moved to Delaware.[32] From that time on, the council was able to continue to issue warrants related to this second dividend. William Ellis was another of the early recipients of such a warrant.[33]

William was able to return to his homestead Mount Hope where he worshipped with his family and neighbors on First Day February 24, 1688/9. The next meeting of the Burlington Quarterly Meeting of the Religious Society of Friends was held there on February 25, 1688/9.[34] Although no business record concerning the affairs of the religion was kept, the Friends did have the opportunity to discuss the options available in their efforts to retain the powers of the courts and government established under the Concessions and Agreements. They had not given up their dreams of a unique social and political system, their Quaker experiment in democracy.

On March 1, 1688/9, a meeting of resident proprietors was held in Gloucester. This meeting served as a ratification and confirmation of a previous election and changes in the composition of the council. The general meeting of the resident proprietors held in Burlington on February 22, 1688/9 had probably recommended that the council consist of only nine members. The new Council membership would change when when on April 10 and 13, 1689 it elected new members. John Tatham and George Hutcheson with William Biddle, Thomas Ollive and Samuel Jennings as trustees from Burlington County, and Thomas Gardiner Jr. with William Roydon, John Reading and Andrew Robeson as trustees from Gloucester County.[35]

Despite the fact that it was time for the rural resident proprietors to prepare for the planting of their crops, President Thomas Ollive called for additional meetings of the Council of Proprietors even before the newly designated Council had begun to function. They met in Burlington on March 25 and 26, 1689.[36] William returned to Burlington for the meetings.

By this time the resident proprietors had learned about the change in the monarchy in England. They needed to begin to take steps to protect their interests and to reestablish their authority in the West New Jersey

Province. On the first day of the meetings, William Biddle and William Roydon were requested to go to John Skene to demand the return of the records of the province. The council apparently suggested to Skene that if they could not repossess the records they would allow him to keep them in the province as long as he gave them easy access to them when they were needed.[37]

The council, knowing now that James II was no longer King, spent the night in town and reconvened the next morning. They probably worked late into the night composing a letter to Dr. Coxe — the most likely person to take over the position of Governor — in which they tried to explain their hopes and aspirations for the future. The letter was signed for the council by Thomas Ollive, William Roydon, Andrew Robeson, Samuel Jennings, John Reading and William Biddle.[38]

It was fortunate that William Jr. was now old enough to oversee spring preparation of the farmlands for William had to leave his homestead again when another meeting of the Council of Proprietors was called on April 11, 1689.

He attended the meeting in Burlington that day and was joined by a sufficient number of members of the newly-elected Council to make a quorum. Present with William Biddle were John Tatham, Thomas Ollive, George Hutcheson and Samuel Jennings.[39] It was apparent to the leaders of the Proprietors of West New Jersey that a change in the governorship was likely, making it even more important that they communicate with Dr. Coxe but they needed to be in touch also with the other West New Jersey Proprietors in London.

The group agreed that William Biddle and George Hutcheson should write a more comprehensive letter to Dr. Coxe, reminding him of their reasons for establishing the West New Jersey Province and their desire to continue their presence there. They needed to describe the problems that had confronted them as well as their indebtedness and what they had done to control the public debt. Dr. Coxe must be advised of the conditions that they felt should be placed on the boundary agreement they had already approved at his request. William and George prepared the letter, which cleverly explained the position of the resident proprietors and subtly suggested to Dr. Coxe that he, as a proprietor of both East and West New Jersey, could probably solve many of their problems by claiming land properly with his dual proprietary rights. They further explained how, by using his influence with Benjamin Bartlett, he could aid them in returning to their business of distributing the lands of the province. In addition they learned John Skene would not release the records in part because of his loyalty to Bartlett.[40]

To emphasize their point further they prepared a second letter to Dr. Coxe. They intended to send the letters and their signed agreement on the boundary line to Dr. Coxe through Thomas Budd, who by then was a resident of Philadelphia but who remained deeply involved financially in the affairs of West New Jersey. Copies of the letters were preserved in the minutes of the Council of Proprietors of West New Jersey, and the originals were posted to London. All parties in West New Jersey hoped that their excellent working relationship with Dr. Coxe could be reestablished, and that he would be able to reclaim his role as Governor of the Province.[41]

One week after the letters were sent from Burlington, on April 18, 1689, a surprising event took place in Boston. The people there, upon learning of the fall of King James II, gathered and arrested the Royal Governor Edmond Andros and members of his council who were living among them. The governor and his party were placed on a ship and sent back to England shortly thereafter.[42] By June 1, 1689 Deputy Governor Francis Nicholson of New York had quietly departed for England by his own volition.[43] With this action in Boston, the Dominion of New England was abolished and its Governor was no longer present to govern the West New Jersey Province. For the first time in many years the people of New Jersey were not under the direct control of any agent from England or the Crown.

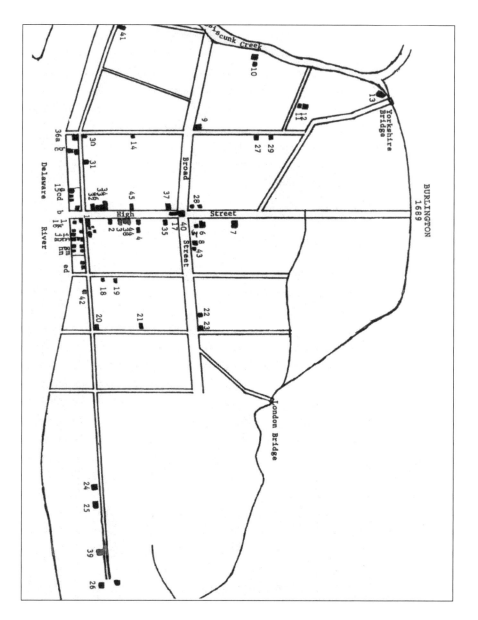

Burlington, 1689.

Buildings in Burlington City 1689

1. Thomas Budd's house, malt house, brew house, bolting house and stable
2. Richard Love's house
3. Thomas Gardiner's house
4. James Wills' house and cooper shop
5. Oliver Hooton's log cabin
6. Oliver Hooton's townhouse
7. John Cripps' heirs townhouse
8. George Huthcheson's townhouse
9. Townhouse of mariner Robert Hopper
10. Joseph Pope's house and barns
11. John Smith's house on Pudding Lane
12. Peter Fretwell's house bought from Robert Stacy
13. Peter Fretwell's tanhouse
14. Thomas Lambert's townhouse
15. a. Robert Wade's waterlot and cabin
    b. Seth Smith's and Benjamin Wheate's house
    c. James Martin's and Percivale Towle's bakehouse
    d. Percivale Towle's townhouse
16. a. Henry Stacy's heirs' house
    b. Lawrence and Virgin (Cripps) Morris's house
    c. Lawrence and Virgin (Cripps) Morris's log cabin
    d. Bernard Devonish's house
    e. Mary (Budd) (Gosling) Collins' house
    f. Rebecca Decou's home bought from brewer Nathaniel Ible
    g. James White's house
    h. Lawrence Morris's house bought from Henry Stacy's heirs
    i. Richard Basnett's Brickhouse
    j. Basnett's Brewhouse
    k. Thomas Ollive's lot; house leased by Charles Read for home and tailor shop
    l. Henry Grubb's Inn
    m. Daniel Coxe's house on pottery lot
    n. Daniel Coxe's pottery
17. Marketplace
18. William Brightwin's log cabin
19. John Long's house
20. House of carpenter James Barrett
21. William Myers' house
22. Townhouse of mariner Peter Bosse
23. Thomas Eves' townhouse
24. Thomas Pott's house in Ollive Town
25. Joan and John Dewsbury's house
26. William Brightwin's pastures and barns
27. William Cooper's lot and cabin
28. Anna Salter's lot and log cabins
29. John Butcher's townhouse
30. Thomas Revell's townhouse
31. William Crue's house and potters shop
32. James Marshall's house
33. Thomas Raper's Whitesmith shop
34. Thomas Raper's house
35. Friends Meetinghouse and burial ground
36. a. John Calowe's house, site of Abraham Senior's inn
    b. Samuel Barker's townhouse
    c. William Myers' butcher shop and slaughterhouse
37. Christopher Wetherill's house and tailorshop
38. James Hill's house and cordwainer shop
39. Martin Holt's house
40. Courthouse
41. John Tatham's house and lot
42. James Satterthwaite's house
43. George Huthcheson's second townhouse
44. Thomas Gladwin's house and blacksmith shop
45. Samuel Furnis's house and saddle shop
46. James Marshall's house and general store

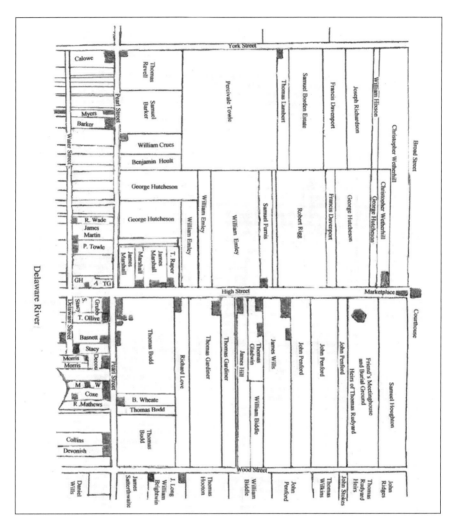

Center of Burlington City, 1689.

CHAPTER 19

Dr. Daniel Coxe Governor
April 11, 1689 to March 1, 1691/2

The West New Jersey Quaker resident proprietors had done all that they could to try to reestablish their government. Now they could only wait to see what would happen in London. A period of uncertainty settled over the province. It was critical for them to return to the form of government that they had enjoyed before the takeover of King James II. They needed to continue their judicial system and their legislative assemblies but if the Crown should take exception to their efforts they might be subject to a charge of treason. While they sought a means of continuing their Quaker experiment in democracy, it was necessary for them to continue as much of their personal and public lives as they could, and to initiate actions that would at least protect, if not strengthen, their interests and investments in the province.

Although he was in the midst of overseeing the preparation of his farmlands for the coming growing season, William, with his family, took a day off from chores to travel to Burlington to shop and attend to business. Knowing that they would have a number of parcels with them on the return trip, they took the boat down the river and tied up at the wharf lot of Richard Basnett, located just to the west of the town landing at the foot of High Street.

William first stopped to visit Thomas Gladwin, the blacksmith, to see if they could complete business that they had agreed to some time before that day. William had allowed Thomas Gladwin to use one of his lots on the west side of High Street to build his home and business. William may have received ground rent for the land. Thomas's business was prospering, in part because he had established it in a location that was very convenient for the townspeople. That day, April 23, 1689, Thomas agreed to pay William Biddle £6.11s for the lot. The two men, accompanied by Thomas's children, Mary and William, walked to the home and office of Thomas Revell at the corner of York and River Streets and had the deed recorded. The lot was 58½ feet wide and reached back to the west from High Street to one-half the way to Wood Street by the same width. It was located between the lots of James Hill, cordwainer (shoemaker) on the north, land that had also been sold by William, and James Wills, cooper (barrel maker), on the south. The indenture was witnesses by yeoman Thomas Harding and surveyor Symon Charles.[1]

With that business concluded, William went on to other matters he wanted to attend to that day. He stopped at the slaughterhouse of William Myers, butcher, on the river side of River Street. William Myers agreed to purchase a pair of oxen from William Biddle for £11, and William Biddle agreed to purchase a butchered fat hog from Myers for £1.13s. The transfer of the goods would be carried out for them by Daniel Leeds.[2]

A few days later tragedy struck the Mount Hope neighborhood. John Horner, who lived just up-river from Mount Hope, died. William, with others from the Chesterfield Monthly Meeting, including Francis Davenport, Samuel Andrews, Percivale Towle, William Watson, John Snowden and Isaac Horner went to the John Horner home April 27, 1689 to take inventory of the estate and to make the initial arrangements for the care of his orphaned children.[3] It is uncertain to whose home the children were taken, but at the Chesterfield Monthly Meeting held May 2, 1689 the affairs of John Horner were discussed. William, with Francis Davenport, Samuel Andrews and John Snowden were directed to oversee the care of those children.[4]

John Horner had been present at the Burlington Quarterly Meeting held at Mount Hope the preceding February. It was necessary that the Friends of the area look after each other at times of family crisis. A means of protecting the interests of the settlers through the Monthly Meetings of Friends and through the provincial court system had been established. At that time the status of the court systems was uncertain, so the affairs of John Horner would not be presented to the court until later.

It was decided that the courts would continue to meet according to the schedule imposed on the province by the Andros government. The only person with permission to carry on business for that regime was John Skene so he called for the Quarter Court and the Court of Pleas to meet in Burlington on May 7 and 8, 1689 under his direction. He was accompanied on the bench by Edward Hunloke, Daniel Wills, James Marshall, Richard Basnett and William Emley. The bench proceeded to conduct business under the rules of the Concessions and Agreements and under English law as had been done before that time.[5]

William was absent from those sessions of the court, and this was probably when he traveled to Little Egg Harbor to claim land for the protection of the boundary line of the province. It was important to complete this business before the next meeting of the Council of Proprietors of West New Jersey. William, with Samuel Jennings and Daniel Leeds, probably accompanied by William Jr. and others who knew the language of the Indians, traveled the Indian trails on horseback to the seaside at Little Egg Harbor where the Indians migrated yearly to be able to harvest shellfish .Daniel Leeds completed two surveys, one for Samuel Jennings of 533 acres which included the Indian fishing wharf,[6] and another on adjacent land of 500 acres for William Biddle.[7] These lands were sufficiently close to the point of origin of the Keith Line to protect the interests of the West New Jersey proprietors. While the men were there they would have seen that the inlet was wide enough to eventually establish a shipping port in that location. If that could be done, many miles of travel for ships could be saved in transporting their farm products to Barbados and Jamaica.

This was the first trip by Quaker settlers to that area to claim lands. William would travel to this location many times in the future, for he developed a familiarity with the area and would lay claim to more lands in that location. A few years later Henry Jacobs (Faulkenburg) from Burlington located his homestead in that region by the Coast.[8] He was joined by Mordecai Andrews and Edward Andrews[9] the sons of Samuel Andrews, and by about 1700 they would be joined by John Brown[10] and others from the Shrewsbury community who developed a settlement of their own. The early settlers of Burlington County recognized the attraction of brief visits to this coastal region, a habit that had been established by the natives of the land before their time. When the community of Little Egg Harbor was more established, and after a Meeting for Worship was formed there, the Friends of Burlington County developed the practice of having a yearly retreat there. In the late 1680s this area was still in its untouched natural wilderness state.

The spring Fair Days for Burlington were held on May 10 and 11, 1689, but it is uncertain whether the General Assembly met, as it should have done on the following day. The legislative body could not act legally on matters for the province for it had been dismissed by the Andros government. Elections continued to be held in each constabulary, for at least the minor offices, so it is likely that these determined Quakers continued to elect their assemblymen also. If they did meet, it was informally. No trace of records from such clandestine legislative gatherings remain if they were recorded to tell the tale or to give cause for a charge of treason against the Quaker leaders of the province. The practice of witnessing indentures in the presence of those who had been justices was continued. On May 11, 1689, an indenture of Joseph Adams was witnessed by William Biddle with Edward Hunloke and Thomas Revell.[11]

It was permissible for the Council of Proprietors of West New Jersey to meet, for the acquisition and distribution of the land of the province for this function had been separated from the government, and the Crown had never objected. The council did meet on May 13 and 14, 1689, and William attended the gathering. The group remained under the presidency of Thomas Ollive. They discussed surveying more lands, and their willingness to receive more claims of land from the resident proprietors was made known. Rates for surveying lands were reset at 8 shillings for the first 100 acres of a tract, and 2 shillings, 6 pence for each additional 100 acres in the same tract.[12] William paid Daniel Leeds 18 shillings for the survey that he had just completed for him. William and Samuel Jennings reported to the council that the surveys that had been done at Little Egg Harbor to protect the interests of the group. The survey map and the descriptions that they presented to the council were approved, and the tracts of land were officially recorded as being in their possession that day.[13]

Following the Burlington Quarterly Meeting of the Religious Society of Friends held at Mount Hope in late May, 1689, William set out to expand his own farmlands. He had Daniel Leeds resurvey the lands in Springfield, near Oneanickon, and this resurvey officially gave him title to a tract of 270 acres adjacent to the 230-acre tract he previously had claimed.[14] In addition, he had surveyed to himself an additional 323 acres adjoining the 500-acre farm located next to William Wood at Oneanickon.[15] He had already built a dwelling house and barns on the latter farm, and William Jr. was living at that location overseeing the development of that land.

When the Council of Proprietors met again on July 25, 1689, in Burlington, they officially approved these additions to William's land holdings. Now fully recovered from the losses that he had incurred in the year of the drought, William, with his son, pursued their plan to expand their acreage under cultivation so that they could export the products of the farm. This was the best means available to them for increasing their monetary wealth.

In the summer months of 1689 the Quakers of West New Jersey learned from Friends in London that on May 24, 1689 King William III and Queen Mary had allowed the passage by Parliament of an Act of Toleration[16] thus ending over thirty years of religious persecution for the Quakers. No longer would the provisions of the Conventicle Acts or the Act of Recusancy be used against their friends and families in England. The Quakers who had immigrated to the West New Jersey Province now knew that they did not have to fear the return of religious persecution in England

and they had reason to believe that their worship in West New Jersey would also proceed without persecution or interference by the Crown. The Act of Toleration did not apply to everyone in England. It did not include Roman Catholics and the Quakers would still be unable to hold public office, because those who agreed to take public positions, elected or appointed, were required to take an oath of office that was based on the sacraments of the Church of England. Friends in London had worked for the development of an alternate oath of office for the Quakers but that had not yet been approved. King William III in alliance with his native Holland, had set out on a campaign of war against the Catholic King Louis XIV of France. He probably allowed the Act of Parliament because he needed all of the support that he could get for his developing war plans.

The deep involvement of the Crown in the war with the French distracted its attention from the affairs of the West New Jersey Province. The Quaker leaders of the province soon realized this, and with a little more assurance from Dr. Daniel Coxe, they were ready to resume their own courts and government. Anticipating that the Crown would request them to support the war effort financially, the pacifist Quakers began to prepare themselves for the situation.

The Burlington Quarterly Meeting was held at Mount Hope on the fourth second day of August, 1689. The men and women who met recognized that the Chesterfield Meeting had reached the point in its development where it should now be declared an official Monthly Meeting, and agreed to that new status. Also, the group appointed members to represent them at the Yearly Meeting of the Religious Society of Friends soon to be held in Philadelphia. William Biddle with Percivale Towle, Thomas Lambert, John Willsford, John Shinn and William Watson were selected to attend the meetings as representatives of the Burlington Quarterly Meeting.[17]

On September 1, 1689, William was able to take his family to Philadelphia to join with the many other Quakers of the region at their Yearly Meeting. Philadelphia was rapidly developing into a modern city. It was quite evident that the Friends of London had concentrated their economic resources on the Pennsylvania territory instead of supporting the entire region that included West New Jersey. William and Sarah saw some of those friends who had left them, including Elizabeth and Thomas Hooton and Sarah Budd, wife of Thomas Budd, who may have been in London still, attending to the business of the Council of Proprietors. Both families had left their homes on High Street in Burlington and moved to the more sophisticated environment of the burgeoning Philadelphia of William Penn.

Friends undoubtedly expressed concern at these meetings over the aggressive war efforts of William III. They had to begin to plan for how to deal with whatever attempts the King might make to have them support his activities. The Friends of Philadelphia were not very sympathetic with the problems that West New Jersey was having over governing rights to that territory. The Friends of Pennsylvania were protected by their governor, William Penn, and they did not have to struggle to exert their political ideals except with Penn himself.

Upon completion of the harvest of the farmlands, the Mount Hope family again joined the other families of the region at the fall Fair Days in Burlington, November 1 and 2, 1689. William and Sarah were able to meet some of the newest arrivals to the town, among them the William Righton family who had moved there from their home in Bermuda. John Gardiner, son of Thomas Gardiner Sr., had married Sarah Righton, the daughter of William Righton.[18]

During the Fair Days, William was also able to make arrangements to sell another 100-acre tract along the Northampton River (Rancocas Creek) to Thomas Harding for £14. He was pleased to find that land values were beginning to appreciate. The indenture of sale was recorded several days later, on November 11, 1689.[19]

Normally the Quarter Court would meet in Burlington on November 3, 1689, but under the unofficial leadership of John Skene, the residual representative of the Andros Government, the court schedule was in disarray. Many sessions were abbreviated or postponed during that time, and that November no session of the court was held. The province clearly needed to have its governing authority and leadership reestablished.

All through this period of uncertainty the Council of Proprietors of West New Jersey continued to meet. They convened on November 4, 1689 in Burlington under the chairmanship of their president, Thomas Ollive. The council discussed the possibility of making more purchases of land from the Indians in order to be able to make more land available to the proprietors.[20]

On December 22, 1689, a special meeting of the Council of Proprietors of West New Jersey was hurriedly called. William was not able to attend but he learned the content of the meeting from his peers shortly after that time. A packet of papers had been received from Dr. Coxe and the Council agreed to call another meeting for February 15, 1689/90 to further discuss the matters he presented.[21]

When that meeting was held, William was in attendance. It was learned that Dr. Coxe had followed some of the suggestions made to him in the letters from the West New Jersey proprietors in April 1689. Dr. Coxe had purchased the land of Thomas Budd, but for a lower price of £900.[22] He had settled some of his own lands along the provincial boundary line in that same location,[23] guaranteeing the West New Jersey resident proprietors that at least that portion of the boundary line would be stable. He demonstrated that he was in touch with their friends in London, for the signed Coxe-Barclay Agreement now included the signatures of not only Dr. Coxe and Benjamin Bartlett, but also London Friends John Bellers and Robert Squibb and others known personally to William, including Dr. James Wasse and William Crouch.[24]

The material that they received did not convince them that Dr. Coxe would be able to reestablish all of the governing rights he had before the takeover by King James II. It is unclear if Dr. Coxe's letters expressed his expectations of the council, or if he had instructed his attorney, John Tatham, who was then a member of the council, to communicate his expectations for him.

Even the Council of Proprietors could not continue to escape the uncertainty of the time, for during this meeting objections over the way it did business were received from proprietors outside the council. Apparently some felt that Council members were paying too much attention to their own personal affairs and not enough to the affairs of proprietors who were not on the council. Following this accusation the entire Council resigned, calling for another election to be held to reconstitute the body.[25]

A last piece of business was not completed. A letter had been received from the Board of Proprietors of East New Jersey questioning the boundary line between the provinces. The council, as it resigned, referred this matter to a meeting of the "general assembly." [26] It is uncertain if this meant that the matter was to be placed back into the hands of the General Assembly of the Province, which would next meet in May 1690 — if at all —, or if it was to be referred to a meeting of the entire group of resident proprietors who would have to convene to reelect the Council of Proprietors of West New Jersey.

The council members may have felt that their signing the Coxe-Barclay agreement and the establishment of ownership of lands, particularly by Dr. Coxe along the partition line, was enough of an answer to the East New

Jersey Board. The fact that the letter went unanswered would be used by the East New Jersey proprietors in later years when they wanted to reposition the boundary line more to their advantage.[27]

Despite the fact that there were no assurances as to their right to govern themselves or to hold court, the traditional West New Jersey leaders realized that the judicial system had to be reconvened on a regular basis. On May 12, 1690, the Burlington Quarter Court met to reestablish its authority.[28] It adjourned to June 3, 1690, when it began to function again. William Biddle was again on the bench with John Skene, Edward Hunloke, James Marshall, Daniel Wills Sr., Richard Basnett and William Myers.[29] After the court session of August 6, 1690, John Skene retired from public life. He was probably in poor health because he died shortly thereafter.[30] The other justices involved in reestablishing the court, along with Thomas Lambert, Mahlon Stacy and William Emley, would continue to see that it met regularly and conducted its business under the rules established by the Concessions and Agreements, which was consistent with English Law.

Friends of the Chesterfield Monthly Meeting decided at their meeting of July 3, 1690 to alternate the site of their First Day Meetings for Worship. A meetinghouse had not been constructed and Friends had to travel long distances to gather on First Days. They decided to authorize private homes as sites of worship, including the homes of Francis Davenport in Crosswicks, Mahlon Stacy at the falls of the Delaware River, Thomas Lambert, Robert Murfin, Edward Rockhill and William and Sarah Biddle at Mount Hope in Mansfield.[31] By this schedule First Day Meeting for Worship would be held at Mount Hope at least one First Day each month for the Chesterfield Monthly Meeting. This confirmed the authorization given by the Burlington Monthly Meeting in 1684 to hold First day Meetings for Worship at Mount Hope. William and Sarah were pleased to continue to use their home as a place for worship and to conduct the business of Friends of West New Jersey.

William attended the Quarter Court sessions at Burlington held August 6 through 9, 1690 as one of the justices. The main business of the court was to hear the actions that John Tatham, attorney for Dr. Daniel Coxe, brought against some of the doctor's employees who were living at Cape May.[32]

Friends again gathered at Mt. Hope on August 25, 1690 for the Burlington Quarterly Meeting. William, with Robert Young, Percivale Towle and William Watson were appointed to attend the upcoming Yearly Meeting of Friends in Burlington on September 10, 1690.[33]

It had long been recognized that the region needed a printer. Friends at the Yearly Meeting agreed to support William Bradford as the official printer for their printing needs. Bradford, a Quaker printer, had been trying to support himself in Philadelphia. He was known to the Quakers for he was the son-in-law of Andrew Sowle the main printer for the Friends in London.[34] The Yearly Meeting decided that they would import six books of Quaker literature from London per year and they would pay Bradford to produce two hundred copies of each of these works which would then be sold to the Monthly and Quarterly Meetings of the region. In this way they would be able to support William Bradford well enough so that he need not seek work from others.[35]

For this level of support the Quaker leaders expected to be able to censor all of the printings of William Bradford, a practice that had been common in London when they were last there even when religious persecution was rampant. In taking this action it was clear that the Quakers of Pennsylvania and West and East New Jersey had completely misunderstood the meaning of freedom of the press as it had been championed by John Milton years before in England. Moreoover, they had lost touch with the feeling of the times in England where even in September 1690, the idea of freedom of the press was finally gaining acceptance.[36]

A printer like William Bradford clearly understood that fact. Just five years after this contract was made with Bradford, a law was passed in England to guarantee freedom of the press.[37] West New Jersey Quakers had not included this freedom among the liberal guarantees of their constitution, the Concessions and Agreements. The charters of Pennsylvania had not been so inclusive as to recognize this freedom either.

The Quakers had always been under the threat of religious persecution, and although they had used censorship themselves, it had been used to try to protect their membership from undesirable influence in printed materials, not to threaten the rights of others. They had been threatened by the official censorship of the press as applied by Parliament and the Crown. They did not understand that it was not their right to use this weapon, even if it was to be used to protect their own religious interests. Overlooking this freedom in their own governments and constitutions was a critical omission, and it would hamper their cause and bring criticism of them in the future.

Much to the dismay of the elders of the Friends attending the Yearly Meeting, even the fundamentals of Quakerism were being subjected to examination in the provinces at that time. The most important business placed before the assembly was the concern of George Keith. Keith seemed to be a solid convert to Quakerism, having spent at least five months in prison while in England for not taking an oath of the Crown. After he finished his business in East New Jersey, including partial completion of the survey between the East and West Jersey Provinces, he moved to Philadelphia at the urging of William Penn, who recognized his great intellect. Keith became the headmaster for the first Friends School of the City.[38]

Instead of devoting himself to the job as headmaster for which he was hired, Keith entered a period of introspection and examination of Quakerism. He came to the conclusion that the religion should have a creed, a firmer standard to guide it, a clearer definition of its own beliefs in relationship to standard Christian tenets. His presentation to the Yearly Meeting began a debate and struggle which led to a schism in the Quakers of the region. Keith would continue to express his opinions, many of which were the opposite of those of George Fox, the founder of the religion.[39]

This schism led to the formation of a group of Quakers called Christian Quakers, or "Keithians," separate from the traditional body of the religion. Among the converts were Thomas Budd and Daniel Leeds, each of whom had been important to the development of the West New Jersey Province. Eventually even George Hutcheson, the very active Yorkshire proprietor, would join them. Early in the movement, the printer William Bradford took the side of George Keith.

Quakerism was severely threatened by George Keith. His thoughts ignored some of the most important tenets of the teachings of George Fox, but the Quaker founder had died on January 13, 1690/1[40] and thus his views could not be heard. In response to criticisms, the traditional Quaker leaders prepared a stricter code of discipline for the membership, causing the Keithian movement to become more insular.

For William it must have been disheartening to see such confrontation, but he and Sarah had committed themselves to the religion and its traditional ways and it was their intention to continue as loyal Quakers.

While in Burlington that October William had decided to claim additional land in the town against his proprietary rights. Symon Charles, surveyor, laid out a three-acre tract for William on the south side of Broad Street, next to the Assiscunk Creek. The survey was recorded by the Council of Proprietors and was recorded in the survey book of Daniel Leeds.[41] Later, an additional survey expanded the lot at that site to six acres.[42] This gave William a convenient and sheltered landing for his boat in the City of Burlington.

The Council of Proprietors of West New Jersey had not met since their mass resignation in February 1689/90. Apparently a meeting of the resident proprietors had been held to elect a new council, for the council met again on October 13, 1690.[43] Thomas Ollive continued as its president. John Tatham, the non-Quaker attorney of Dr. Coxe, was no longer on the council and Samuel Jennings had decided to take a position in Pennsylvania as an employee of William Penn, so he too was no longer a member of the body. In Pennsylvania, Jennings, once the Governor of West New Jersey, conducted business for William Penn, including trips through the countryside to collect quitrents from those who occupied Penn's land.[44]

In reorganizing, the council created a new category of person to attend their meetings, an attorney for each involved county. Apparently it had been decided that some of the business conducted by the council prior to that time had not been in the best interests of all of the resident proprietors. Now each county had its own attorney sitting with the council to insure that the interests of the general resident proprietors of that county were considered in any council deliberations.[45]

William returned to Burlington in the first few days of November. The Council of Proprietors of West Jersey met on November 1, 1690, the same day that the fall Fair Days in Burlington began. William attended the meeting as a member of the council.[46] During that time he received a warrant for 50 acres of unappropriated land which he had assigned to William Nichols, husbandman, probably for services performed by Nichols at Mount Hope.[47] At the end of the meetings and the Fair, William remained in town to sit on the Bench of the Burlington Quarter Court held on November 3 and 4, 1690.[48]

The next three seasons of the year were relatively uneventful. No challenges to the rights of the West New Jersey settlers were made by Governor Coxe or by the English Crown. The meetings of the institutions of West New Jersey continued. The courts, the Friends Meetings for Business and Worship, and the Council of Proprietors of West New Jersey continued to meet and do business. Only the General Assembly either did not meet, or if it did, it not keep minutes of its meetings. William missed some of the court sessions in early 1691, but he participated in the meetings of the Council of Proprietors and the Burlington Quarterly Meetings which continued to be held in his home, Mount Hope. On February 5, 1690/1, the Chesterfield Monthly Meeting placed William Biddle in charge of the funds for the relief of the poor,[49] and by August 8, 1691 William had resumed his place on the bench of the Burlington Quarter Court.[50]

On August 18, 1691, William and Sarah sold 50 acres to William Deane, husbandman, for £5. This tract was the first land owned by William Deane in the area that would later become known as New Hanover, near the Oneanickon lands of William Biddle and William Wood.[51] Eventually Deane acquired a farm of 624 acres in that location.[52] He was the son-in-law of Robert Hopper, mariner, who in turn was the son-in-law of Thomas Wright and had purchased and lived in the house that Wright had built in Burlington at the corner of Broad and York Streets in 1682.[53]

It is of interest that the indenture between William and William Deane was witnessed by William Biddle Jr. and Thomas Biddle, a cousin of William Biddle. This was the first record of this Thomas Biddle in West New Jersey, and the specific relationship between him and William has never been discovered. Thomas is mentioned as a cousin later in the will of William Biddle, so it is recognized that he was a relative. He was known as a person familiar with boats and waterways and he became a ferryman and associated with mariners from other shores. On August 18, 1691 he is found to be in the company of his cousin William and other farm people of the Mansfield area to officially witness an indenture.

In September 1691 the Yearly Meeting of the Religious Society of Friends was held in Philadelphia.[54] Sarah attended as an appointed representative of the Burlington Quarterly Meeting.[55] The Women's Yearly Meeting was apparently more organized now and its business was recorded at this session. Sarah attended with her neighbor Mary Andrews who was also representing Burlington Quarterly Meeting. They joined with prominent Quaker women from other areas such as Abigail Lippincott from Shrewsbury, Hannah Carpenter from Philadelphia and Ann Dilworth, Elizabeth Key, Alice Wood, Jane Biles and Lydia Wade.[56]

The greatest concern during the sessions of the Yearly Meeting was the continued expression of anti-Quaker sentiment by George Keith. The Keithian movement was increasing in influence in both Philadelphia and West New Jersey.

The fall months of 1691 were calm and routine as far as civil matters in the West New Jersey Province were concerned. On September 21, 1691, an indenture was completed that made William and his friend, Percivale Towle, attorneys for Joseph Helmsley, the Yorkshire proprietor, for his rights in a 1/6th proprietary share of the province and 1,000 acres in Salem that he had purchased from John Fenwick.[57] The early days of November were spent in

Burlington at the fall Fair, and the Council of Proprietors again met on November 3, 1691 with William in attendance.[58]

That same day the Quarter Court session was held requiring William to be back on the bench.[59] By November 5, 1691 it was apparent that Friends of the Chesterfield Monthly Meeting realized that the courts were again reliable. They agreed to present the affairs of the estate of the deceased John Horner to the Burlington Court and they appointed a committee, which included William Biddle, to accomplish the settling of the estate.[60] On December 4, 1691, William, with Francis Davenport, was appointed a guardian of the children of the deceased John Horner.[61]

On November 10, 1691 William finally completed a business arrangement that he had started in 1688. An indenture was completed and signed that day by the executors of the estate of Anna Salter, completing a transaction that William had started with Anna prior to her death. This indenture confirmed that William had traded 500 acres of land rights to Anna Salter in exchange for her 2/12ths proprietary share in West Jersey, not to include the first dividend rights.[62] Undoubtedly, before her death Anna had already sold the land William had traded to her, judging by the amount of land sold by her in the Second Tenth, especially along the Pennsauken Creek. However, an official indenture confirming the arrangement with William had not been completed prior to her death. Anna's husband, Henry Salter had predeceased her, and her son, John, had died just before she did, in November 1688.[63] The trustees of Anna's estate judged that the disposition of the estate should include an indenture to William Biddle for the proprietary rights so that the intention of Anna and her son would be on record.

On November 10, 1691, with the completion of this indenture William and Sarah had completed the last transaction that they would make for proprietary rights to the Province of West New Jersey. They now owned 1.58 proprietary shares of the province, more than any other resident proprietor at that time. They were entitled to 7,332 acres of unappropriated rural lands for these rights under the first dividend, and 7,900 acres of unappropriated rural lands under the second dividend of the proprietors' council. As of that date they had sold 6,090 acres of these rural lands to others and had kept 2,736 acres for their own use. In Burlington they had sold two town lots on High Street, two waterlots, and 75 acres of townbound lands. They had spent approximately £411.11s. for their proprietary rights, and they had received about £450 for their land sales to that time. Thus, in 1691, ten years after they arrived in the West New Jersey

Province, William and Sarah had recovered the amount of money that they had invested in the province, at least in expenses for proprietary rights. They had in reserve their own developed lands, their homestead, and many residual and future land rights. After ten years they could now begin to make a profit from their investment.

When the Byllynge trustees decided to settle the West New Jersey Province, they had written to Richard Hartshorne in East New Jersey to tell him of the settlement and the fact that the main town of the West New Jersey Province (later to be called Burlington) would be established far enough up the Delaware River to be accessible to the East New Jersey Quaker settlements of Shrewsbury and Middletown. Communication between the Quakers of the two provinces did occur. Two of the children of Richard and Abigail Lippincott from Shrewsbury, Freedom and Restore, married and settled near Burlington, beginning a long line of Lippincotts in the province.

The road to the East New Jersey Quaker settlements passed very near the Mount Hope homestead of William and Sarah. Their son William Jr. began to court a girl from Shrewsbury and on December 13, 1691, William Biddle Jr. was married to Lydia Wardell in the Shrewbury Meetinghouse.[64]

Lydia's parents, Eliakim and Lydia (Perkins) Wardell, had come to Shrewsbury from Hampton, New Hampshire (then still part of Massachusetts). Her mother was the daughter of Isaac Perkins, who had settled in that location in about 1639.[65] Eliakim's father, Thomas Wardell (originally Wardell), was born in the parish of Alford, Lincolnshire, England, and came to the Massachusetts Bay in 1634 with his wife Elizabeth. After a few years in Boston, where Eliakim was baptized 23 November 1634, they were dismissed to the church "at the Falls of Paschataqua," now Exeter, New Hampshire, where Thomas was an innkeeper.[66]

Lydia Perkins married Eliakim Wardell at Hampton, New Hampshire, on October 17, 1659. They became Quakers in New England at the time when persecution of Quakers there was most severe. Lydia apparently was so upset with the persecution that in protest she reportedly walked into a steeplehouse church service unclothed, as a "naked sign." She was punished for her action by whipping.[67]

Under continuing pressures of religious persecution, Lydia and Eliakim left New England and came to Shrewsbury, East New Jersey, settling there in 1667.[68] They were some of the few settlers of Shrewsbury in 1672 when

George Fox visited the community and later wrote that their Meetinghouse was under construction.

Following their wedding, William Jr. and Lydia moved to some of William Biddle's property, probably the 823-acre farm next to William Wood and the Newbold family near the Indian encampment of Oneanickon. Between 1692 and 1707 they had seven children.

Dr. Daniel Coxe, presumed Governor of the province, had continued to try to accumulate ownership in proprietary shares of the West New Jersey Province after making the initial purchase from the heirs of Edward Byllynge on February 26, 1686/7. Now Dr. Coxe had tired of his efforts to promote and profit from the West New Jersey Province. He had proudly boasted of the vastness of his holdings and of the monetary potential of these interests. But on March 4, 1691/2 he sold most of his interests in West New Jersey to a group of London merchants headed by Sir Thomas Lane, who had organized themselves under the name of the West Jersey Society.[70]

Eventually, it would be determined that the total interests sold to these investors would approximate twenty proprietary shares in the West New Jersey Province, fewer than the number of shares owned collectively by the resident proprietors. However, it is important to note that, unlike the shares of the resident proprietors, the shares of the West Jersey Society included the governing rights to the province because they had originally come from Byllynge.

On April 11, 1692, the West Jersey Society commissioned Andrew Hamilton as Governor of the West New Jersey Province.[71] He was already Governor of the East New Jersey Province. On June 4, 1692, the West Jersey Society commissioned Jeremiah Basse as their land agent in the West New Jersey Province.[72]

In the spring of 1692, when the winter snows melted, there was a sudden flood at the falls of the Delaware River. Numerous settlers at the falls lost their possessions and two settlers died.[73]

While everyone waited for another government to be formed after the accession of William and Mary to the throne in England, most of the business of the province went on as usual. The courts continued to meet. William Biddle served on the bench of the Burlington Court on both May 9, 1692 and June 1, 1692. At the former session he was given a Letter of Administration as executor for the will for the deceased William Ellis. William also served on the bench at the Quarter Court Sessions May 9 through 11, 1692 and August 8, 1692. At the former Quarter Court the rules of the Concessions and Agreements were still in force, for a defendant was allowed to take exception to jurors in the selection of the jury. However, the jury that he approved refused to allow him right to counsel, presumably against an implied right of the Concessions and Agreements for inhabitants of the West New Jersey Province.[74]

On May 30, 1692, William was assigned by the Burlington Quarterly Meeting of Friends to a committee to determine who had pledged and who had given to the fund for the building of the Burlington Meetinghouse.[75]

At the Yearly Meeting for Friends held in Burlington September 7, 1692 and attended by both William and Sarah Biddle, the issue concerning George Keith came to a conclusion. The consensus of the meeting was that Keith should be disowned by the Yearly Meeting. Those present, including William, signed a document to that effect to be sent to the London Yearly Meeting.[76]

George Keith had developed a large following of "Christian Quakers.". He had gained the sympathy of William Bradford, Quaker printer, and Bradford had begun to print pamphlets for him without having them reviewed by the traditional Quakers as stipulated in his contract. The Philadelphia and West New Jersey Quakers had realized by now that freedom of the press was a right that they might want to include in their constitution In spite of the problems with the pamphlets supporting Keith.

The Quakers took Bradford into the Philadelphia courts, but this only led to his moving to New York to publish his pamphlets and books. Daniel Leeds, having become totally convinced that George Keith was right, even encouraged Bradford to publish with him in Burlington.[77] Leeds went further than this. On his waterlot in Burlington, east of High Street, a building was constructed and designated as the Keithian Meetinghouse, a place where Keithian Quakers could meet and worship.[78]

Not long after that time George Keith went to London to appeal the Yearly Meeting decision. The appeal was not accepted and he was disowned by the London Yearly Meeting too.[79] Subsequently he joined the Anglican Church and became a minister for the Society for the Propagation of the Gospel in Foreign Parts.[80] In this position, in later years, he returned to Burlington and assisted in establishing the first Anglican Church in the province, St. Mary's Church in Burlington.

President Thomas Ollive, of the Council of Proprietors of West New Jersey, did not reconvene the council after the meeting of November 3, 1691. It is possible that there was no business that the council could complete because of the change of ownership in the proprietary shares associated with the governing rights of the province or it may have been because of the sickness of the Speaker of the House, Thomas Ollive. His passing would have had a great impact on all those who had, with him, founded the West New Jersey Province. When the General Assembly meeting of November 3, 1692 was called, the usual Speaker of the House, Thomas Ollive, was absent. It soon became apparent that this Quaker of West New Jersey was ill. Thomas Ollive prepared his will on November 8, 1692 and died soon thereafter.[81]

Ollive had lived in West New Jersey for the last fifteen years of his life. Although he and his wife Judith had no children, Thomas did have family surrounding him in West Jersey. Ann Jennings, the wife of Samuel Jennings and Joyce Marriott, the wife of Isaac Marriott, were first cousins of Thomas Ollive. The wife of John Woolston Sr. was a relative of Thomas Ollive, and she was the sister of the wife of Freedom Lippincott, Mary Curtis, a relationship that explains why these families all lived near each other on or near the Northampton River, and why Thomas Ollive mentioned them all in his will. Thomas's wife Judith died in 1688 and after her death he had married Mary, the daughter of his friend Daniel Wills.[82]

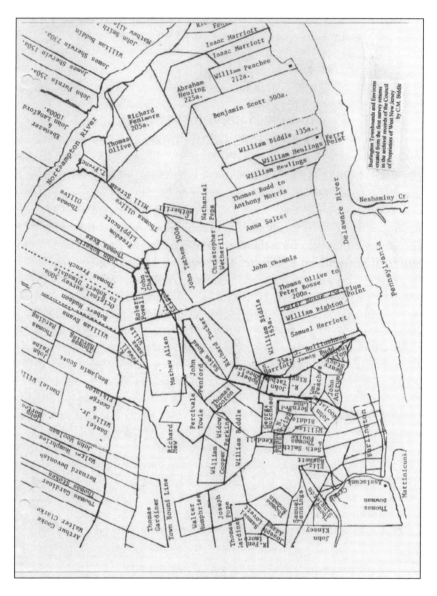

Burlington Townbounds, from first surveys of the properties
approximately 1678 to 1695.

CHAPTER 20

Andrew Hamilton, Governor,
April 11, 1692 – November 1697

On April 11, 1692 Andrew Hamilton was commissioned as Governor of West New Jersey by the West Jersey Society. However, the government of West New Jersey did not begin to function officially and publicly until November 3, 1692. In the interval between these two dates the residents of West Jersey either governed themselves or were counseled by Hamilton on matters of government in private. The residents had remained prepared for the official resumption of their General Assembly and courts. Town meetings were held and general meetings of the inhabitants of the province were continued at least occasionally despite the uncertainty of the legality of doing so.

When it came time for the General Assembly to meet again on November 3, 1692, it was attended by the duly elected Assemblymen who convened with the approval of the new Governor.[1] They elected Francis Davenport as their Speaker and Thomas Revell as their Secretary. The first business completed by the legislative body was the passage of an act that would protect the pacifist rights of the Quaker majority.[2]

Other acts passed by the General Assembly in 1692 further defined the bounds of Burlington and Gloucester Counties and created a fourth county, Cape May County. These actions officially did away with the concept of Tenths that had been established by the Concessions and Agreements. They also established small claims courts which would be held regularly to handle matters of less than forty shillings. These courts would be served by only one justice [3]

This General Assembly, besides attending to matters concerning weights and measures and reestablishing rules against selling rum to Negroes and Indians, addressed the most important issue of the province, the matter of taxation. The legislators agreed to establish a Poll Tax for the province. A tax of 2 shillings, 6 pence was placed on each inhabitant over the age of sixteen. The Governor, Andrew Hamilton, was to be paid £100 yearly from the receipts of this tax. Before they completed their business and adjourned on November 12, 1692 the General Assembly agreed that they would meet only once each year, on the twelfth of May.[4]

It took longer for the courts to be reestablished and officially convened. On November 3, 1692, Justices William Biddle, Edward Hunloke, Mahlon Stacy and Andrew Robeson convened the Quarter Court as that was the customary time for that court to meet. However, the court was adjourned immediately without any business being accomplished.[5] The day was not wasted by William, for he was already in Burlington to attend the opening session of the General Assembly as an Assemblyman from Burlington County. In addition William, as a Justice, acknowledged an indenture of Francis Davenport that day. The deed was witnessed by George Hutcheson, William Hickson and innkeeper Henry Grubb.[6]

The Burlington Quarter Court met again on November 10, 1692, but it was again adjourned before any business was accomplished.[7] William had other business to complete in Burlington that day. He sold a waterlot in the Yorkshire side of the town to William Fryley, carpenter. As Fryley had already constructed his house on the lot, he and William probably had a ground rent agreement on the property prior to that date.[8]

The Burlington Quarter Court was at last officially convened on November 21, 1692. Some or all of the justices may have been appointed by Governor Hamilton which may have been why it took so long to reorganize the judicial system. Some of the justices, if not all of them, were also members of the Governor's Council. Edward Hunloke, Esquire, was commissioned as deputy governor. John Tatham, Esquire, William Biddle, Thomas Lambert, Thomas Gardiner and William Righton, were all commissioned as justices. Daniel Wills, Mahlon Stacy, Francis Davenport and Daniel Leeds were additional justices not present that day. James Hill was attested as sheriff for Burlington County, Daniel Wills was attested as county coroner and James Wills, cooper, was chosen as packer for the county. In addition to there usual duties, the constables who had been previously elected in each township were to serve as collectors of the taxes. Because the tax levied for the building of the new prison had been insufficient to cover the cost, an additional tax was established on the inhabitants of the province to raise sufficient funds to finish the project.[9]

The court met from November 21 through 23, 1692. There was a significant backlog of cases to be heard, and the usual business of assigning responsibility for maintaining the public roads and structures all took time. It would have been of interest to William that the house and lot of William Fryley was seized by the court by a Warrant of Execution brought before the court by Edward Hunloke. The property was to be sold to satisfy the warrant. William Biddle had completed the sale of the land to Fryley less than two weeks before.[10]

The leaders of the Friends of Burlington County met a few days later at Mount Hope for Burlington Quarterly Meeting.[11] They would have been pleased that their province had reestablished an official legislative body and judicial system. This meant that they should be able to continue their religion without fear of unjust rules being made against them. Quakers were still in the majority in the province with a strong presence in the courts and in the Assembly. Their biggest concern at that time was the schism that had been created in their religion by George Keith. Although they took no official action at that meeting, undoubtedly they were perplexed by the expressions of anti-Quaker sentiment by such people as Daniel Leeds, who had gone so far as to construct the Keithian Meetinghouse on his waterlot in Burlington.[12]

On February 20, 1692/3, William had the company of his son on the trip to Burlington. He had to serve on the bench of the Quarter Court while William Jr. served as a member of the Grand Jury at the same courthouse. It was decided that each township have a meeting on or before the first day of the first month of that year to raise taxes to pay for the costs of the constables and to pay for the killing of wolves. The location of the highway going to East New Jersey was officially approved to go through Mansfield Township. James Croft was attested as Mansfield Constable for the upcoming year, and John Shinn was to serve as the Overseer of Highways for the township.[13]

On February 27, 1692/3, Burlington Quarterly Meeting of the Religious Society of Friends was held at Mount Hope. Caleb Wheatley gave testimony to the Friends present of his earlier experience as a Keithian Quaker. By his presence and words he returned to them as a reconvinced Friend.[14]

On March 24, 1692/3, William returned to Burlington to serve as a Justice once again. That day an indenture of sale of the Lessa Point property of Thomas Bowman to Edward Hunloke was acknowledged before William and the other justices. The transaction was actually a mortgage foreclosure ordered by the Burlington Court. At Thomas Bowman's request Edward Hunloke had apparently paid for a considerable number of improvements to the property. Bowman had been unable to reimburse Hunloke for the improvements and thus he forfeited the property to him.[15]

At the Burlington Quarter Court Session held on May 8, 1693, licenses to keep inns and ordinaries in Burlington were granted to Henry Grubb, Richard Basnett, Thomas Kendall and Abraham Senior.[16]

In Burlington, on May 13, 1693, the Council of Proprietors of West New Jersey was reorganized. Thomas Gardiner Sr. was elected as president of the body and his son Thomas Gardiner Jr. also joined the council. William Biddle continued as a Council member.[17] No business was recorded at that organizational meeting and the council reconvened again on May 30, 1693. At that time it recognized that some persons were requesting warrants for amounts of land beyond which they were entitled by their proprietary rights. The council, therefore, required that each person requesting a warrant submit proof to the council of their entitlement to the land rights. The council also doubled the value of the warrants to six shillings each.[18]

In this same session the council noted that some inhabitants of the province had been cutting down trees on unappropriated lands that belonged to the body of proprietors. It requested that the attorneys for the council take action against such trespassers and charge them two shillings per tree. If the trespasser refused to pay the amount, the council gave its attorneys permission to take the parties to court over the matter.[19]

William had most of the summer to concentrate on his homestead and personal business. It was not until August 8, 1693 that he had to return to Burlington to sit on the bench for the Quarter Court Session. Apparently some of the justices had been irregular in attending the Quarter Court sessions, and the court decided to fine them three shillings for each session of the court missed, unless they had an excuse for their delinquency such as sickness or absence from the province.[20]

On August 20, 1693, William sold another parcel of land when Charles Woolverton, husbandman, purchased 100 acres from him for the bargain price of £6. This land was planned to be sold to John Green, a carpenter, for £10, but the final indenture was changed to Charles Woolverton at the lower price. Woolverton had been in close association with William and William Jr., and probably worked for them taking care of their animals at both Mount Hope and at the Oneanickon farm. The reduced price of the sale may have indicated that William owed Woolverton £4 for his labor.[21]

At the Burlington Quarterly Meeting of Friends held August 29, 1693 at Mount Hope, members were appointed to attend Yearly Meeting And included William Biddle along with Thomas Lambert, John Wilsford, Francis Davenport, Robert Young, John Day and Mahlon Stacy. At that meeting women Friends informed the meeting of the financial troubles that New England Friends were experiencing. In addition, a difference that had arisen between the guardians of Nathaniel Pope (Thomas Gardiner and Richard Guy) and Christopher Wetherill, the stepfather of the boy were discussed. The matter, which concerned the rights of the widow Pope to the possessions of her deceased husband, was referred to arbitration by Friends. [22]

William and Sarah had the opportunity to visit Philadelphia when they attended the Yearly Meeting of Friends on September 6, 1693. Sarah, with Thomasin Towle, attended as the official representatives from Burlington Quarterly Meeting. They had a chance to renew their acquaintances with

Abigail Lippincott and Elizabeth Hooten from Shrewsbury, Sarah Sharp from Gloucester County, and Hannah Carpenter from Philadelphia, among others in the meetings. William was able to discuss the matters of the Friends with Edward Wade, Samuel Spicer, Joseph White and William Cooper from Salem and Gloucester Counties in West New Jersey, and also with Thomas Lloyd, Griffith Owen, Samuel Jennings, Thomas Janney, Samuel Carpenter and others from Philadelphia and the other Pennsylvania Quarterly and Monthly Meetings.[23]

On October 6, 1693, while he was in Burlington attending the General Assembly meetings, William signed two indentures with Mary (Wills) Ollive, wife and executrix of the will of Thomas Ollive and daughter of Daniel Wills. The first document confirmed that Thomas Ollive had owned one-fourth of the proprietary share that William had purchased with Thomas Ollive and Daniel Wills on January 22, 23, 1676/7, and the second indenture conveyed ownership of that one-quarter proprietary share to Daniel Wills.[24]

Though the last General Assembly had decided that there would be meetings yearly on May twelfth of each year, apparently no meeting was convened that spring. The General Assembly did meet in Burlington from October 3 through 18, 1693. Francis Davenport was again elected as Speaker of the House. The boundary line between Burlington and Gloucester Counties along the Pennsauken Creek was again discussed but not resolved. A court was established for Cape May County. The coinage and its values for the province were decided.

A Court of Appeals was established for Burlington to be held twice each year and the appeal process that had been established for the province by the Concessions and Agreements was altered.

A Court of "Oyer and Terminer" for cases of capital offenses was established for the province. The Governor would select one judge who would be accompanied by two justices of the involved county to serve on the bench of the court.

The Assembly also set rules for the resurvey of property and allowed for boundary disputes to be settled by arbitration first, and to only involve the court if this method failed.

The tax rate for the province was established. Again the tax was based on land and assets rather than a poll tax: one penny per acre for improved lands or sixpence per one hundred acres of lands unimproved. Taxes were also applied to livestock. Estates of those who lived in town with less visible assets were to be appraised and taxed at the rate of 3 pence per pound. Penalties were established for people who falsified their tax records. With these anticipated revenues the salary for Governor Hamilton was increased to £300 per year.[25]

The General Assembly also ordered the town of Burlington to distribute its unsettled and unclaimed lands. The burgess (mayor) of Burlington was to select two members of his council and with them he was instructed to meet in committee with three members of the Council of Proprietors of West New Jersey. This committee was to see that the unclaimed lands of the town were divided by the proprietary rights, and the ownership assigned proportionally by the proprietary rights to the current owners of the full or fractions of those original twenty London and Yorkshire proprieties. The swamp and wetlands were to be divided from the fastlands (the dry uplands). A charge of 20 shillings per acre for draining the wetlands was to be charged the involved proprietors by their proportion of right to ownership of this previously undesirable land.[26] This act was important for William and Sarah. Since they were the resident proprietors with the largest share of proprietary rights, 1.58 shares, they would be entitled to more of the improved lands than any others, but they would also be billed more than the other proprietors for improving the town.

William attended the traditional Burlington fall Fair on November 1 and 2, 1693. He officiated as a justice on the second day of the fair when he certified an indenture that was drawn up for a transaction made between George Hutcheson and John Langstaffe.[27]

On November 3, 1693, the Burlington Quarter Court reconvened. William Biddle was on the bench with Thomas Revell, Daniel Wills, Francis Davenport, Daniel Leeds and William Righton. The Grand Jury established the tax for the county as one-third of the tax set for the province by the General Assembly. This tax was to be assessed in the same manner, except that now that there no longer was a poll tax in place, an additional tax of one penny per pound of value was placed on negroes for those who owned them. It thereby became more expensive to own slaves. George Hutcheson was appointed treasurer of the county. He was to see that the assemblymen were paid for attending to their duties, a provision that had been stipulated by the Concessions and Agreements. Any surplus in the treasury was to be used to finish the courthouse, a job that apparently had never been completed.[28]

At this session of the court Walter Reeves brought suit against William Biddle. The plaintiff felt that he owned land along the Rancocas Creek that had previously been surveyed to William. William came off the bench to defend himself. Arbitration, the usual manner chosen by William to settle such matters, had apparently failed in this case with the persistent Walter Reeves. The records of the county and proprietors failed to show a recorded deed or a return of survey to the land claimed by Reeves. Daniel Wills also came off the bench and testified that Reeves had been advised not to survey the land since it had been previously surveyed to William

Biddle. The court found in favor of William Biddle and Walter Reeves was ordered to pay the cost of the suit.[29]

Before the day was over the Council of Proprietors of West New Jersey met in Burlington with Thomas Gardiner Sr. and Thomas Gardiner Jr. as well as Francis Davenport, John Reading and William Biddle. The only business that they recorded in the day was receiving twenty shillings from the Council Ranger, John Day, as the half-share of the unmarked horse that he had captured on the unappropriated lands of the proprietors. Since it was late, they adjourned, agreeing to meet the next morning.[30]

The council reconvened with the same members present at eight o'clock in the morning of November 4, 1693. At that session it responded to the request of William Biddle, with George Hutcheson and Francis Collins, to make another purchase of lands from the Indians. There were apparently no other lands suitable for them and others in the original purchase. The council gave the three men permission to make a purchase of no less than ten thousand acres in no more than two tracts from the Indians. The council invited other proprietors who had a right to take up more land to "signify their desires" to join them within twenty-one days of the publication of the announcement of the purchase so long as the other proprietors also paid for their portion of the cost of the purchase.[31]

As their final business for that session the council reiterated that the residents of the province must by law promptly bring their surveys to the county courts for proper inspection and recording.[32]

A few days after returning home William was saddened by the death of his close friend and neighbor Samuel Andrews. Samuel was buried in the cemetery that had been established on the Andrews' lands in Mansfield. William, accompanied by Francis Davenport, John Wilsford and Isaac Horner, took the inventory of the estate on November 10, 1693.[33] To make sure that necessary matters were put in order as quickly as possible for Mary Andrews, William Biddle and Frances Davenport as justices of the Burlington Court recorded the will and inventory with Thomas Revell, Registrar, that same day in a special session of the court. A letter of administration was granted to Mary Andrews and executor Edward Rockhill.[34]

William may have stayed in Burlington that evening at Grubb's Inn, for he served as a Justice with Daniel Wills the next day in certifying an indenture made by John Woolston Jr. to Thomas French in front of witnesses John Shinn and innkeeper Henry Grubb.[35]

William returned to the town again on November 18, 1693 to serve on the bench with fellow justice Thomas Gardiner. That day the will of Thomas Butcher was presented to the court by John Butcher, John Antram and John Shinn Sr. The document was recorded by the Registrar, Thomas

Revell. Also, during that session of the court, William, as the attorney for the estate of William Ellis, completed the sale of a 460-acre tract at Mount Pleasant from the Ellis estate to Richard French.[36]

William was relieved of the trouble of traveling elsewhere to a meeting when Friends gathered at the appointed time for Burlington Quarterly Meeting at Mount Hope on November 27, 1693. On December 2, 1693, he traveled to Burlington for the usual Saturday session of the Burlington Court. With Justice William Righton he received the will and inventory of his friend Richard Guy from the widow, Bridget Guy.[37] On Saturday, January 6, 1693/4, William attended the court session in Burlington as a Justice. That day Edward Rockhill was appointed as guardian of Edward Andrews, the minor child of the deceased Samuel Andrews.[38]

The following week William and Sarah went to Burlington to attend to an important real estate transaction. Knowing that the General Assembly had ordered that the ownership of the town lands be established, William had begun to take inventory of the lots he owned and made plans to sell those lots he did not need for his own use. On January 13, 1693/4 William and Sarah sold two lots to innkeeper Richard Basnett. One lot, three acres, on the south side of Broad Street, was sold to the innkeeper for £9. Another adjacent lot of two acres was sold from the estate of William Ellis, by William Biddle, to Basnett for £6. These lots were part of the now twelve-acre lot owned by Richard Basnett in the center of the town, between High Street and York Street on the south side of Broad Street.[39]

At that same session another deed of sale was completed between William and Sarah and Richard Basnett, of an important water lot, 48 feet wide from Pearl Street to the low-water mark on the river. This transaction completed Basnett's ownership of the 84-foot water lot upon which he had built his home and inn. It was adjacent to the 36-foot lot he had purchased from William Budd, both lots being in the water lot originally assigned to the proprietary rights of Thomas Ollive. The business was probably transacted in the inn of Richard Basnett called The Brew House. Samuel Ogborne, Nicholas Martineau and Thomas Potts were present to witness the indentures that were drawn and recorded by Thomas Revell.[40]

During the month of February William returned to Burlington at least twice. On February 3, 1693/4, he attended the Burlington Court as a Justice with Edward Hunloke and Registrar Thomas Revell. Daniel Leeds was present that day to have an indenture recorded. Joseph Adams may have accompanied William on the trip to Burlington, for he completed a purchase of 500 acres at Mansfield from the William Ellis estate at that session of the court. William acted again as attorney for the estate.[41]

On Tuesday and Wednesday February 20-21, 1693/4, the Burlington Quarter Court met as scheduled. Edward Hunloke, John Tatham, James

Marshall, Nathaniel Westland, Thomas Gardiner, Daniel Wills, Francis Davenport, Mahlon Stacy and William Righton were the other justices on the bench with William Biddle for those sessions. Each of the townships had elected their Constables and Overseers for the year and the court approved these elected officials that day. Several cases involving boundary disputes were settled. A reconciliation was accomplished between a man and wife who had separated.

The justices of the court remained as intolerant of lying. A woman found guilty of slandering a man was sentenced to the severe punishment of whipping. The residents of the town then witnessed the punishment on the second day of the court sessions, Wednesday, between the hours of twelve and two. The whipping took place from the courthouse to the Delaware River on High Street. No more than forty lashes were allowed to be meted out. The guilty woman did not have sufficient funds to pay the court costs. With her permission, for a payment of forty-four shillings to the court, and an additional sixteen shillings to be paid to the woman herself in one year's time, John Antram purchased the indenture of her as his servant for one year.[42]

On February 26, 1693/4 Friends met at Mount Hope for Burlington Quarterly Meeting. It was again brought to the attention of these Quakers that the Friends of New England were in need of financial assistance. It was decided that they would consider sending them aid at the next Quarterly Meeting.[43]

William continued to claim his lots in the undeveloped land in Burlington. In March of 1693/4 he had a lot of one acre ½ rod surveyed for his possession. The lot, fronting 9 perches, 4 yards on the west side of Wood Street, was in the nine-acre tract originally assigned to William and his co-proprietor, Daniel Wills.[44] On March 16, 1693/4, William sold this lot to Isaac Marriott, merchant and joiner, for £5.7s.6d.[45]

On March 22, 1693/4, William, with his upriver neighbor from Whitehill, John Snowden, rode to Burlington by horseback accompanied by Sarah and their daughter Sarah, who was now fifteen years old. They completed their shopping and enjoyed the company of friends in town whom they had not seen very often that winter. In addition, William, acting as attorney for Joseph Helmsley, sold a 1/6th proprietary share to George Hutcheson. The indenture was witnessed by both his wife and daughter and by John Snowden.[46]

William returned to town on April 9, 1694 for a meeting of the Council of Proprietors of West New Jersey. The meeting was also attended by President Thomas Gardiner Sr., Francis Davenport, Thomas Gardiner Jr. and John Reading. It was recognized that the General Assembly at its last meeting had ordered that they appoint three proprietors to join a committee of town officers, to include Richard Basnett, the mayor of Burlington and two others chosen by him, to divide and reclaim the swamp and wetlands of the town. The council appointed William Biddle to this committee along with John Tatham and Isaac Marriott.[47] It may have been during this meeting of the council that surveys of town bound lands of 120 acres and 165 acres and surveys of a one acre lot and one and three-quarter-acre lot east of York Street, between Broad Street and Pearl Street were approved for William.[48]

A pleasant task fell to William on April 12, 1694. He was included among the justices that officiated at the non-Quaker wedding of Ann Revell, daughter of Thomas Revell, to Joseph White. The wedding, which would have been attended by neighbors and friends from throughout the region, was held at the Revell home in Mansfield.[49]

On Saturday, April 21, 1694, William returned to Burlington. That day he sold a water lot on the Yorkshire side of the town to innkeeper and butcher, Henry Grubb for £4. He also sold 100 acres of town bound lands to Samuel Harriott, mariner from Bermuda, for £18.[50]

May 1694 was a busy month for William as he had to attend to business in Burlington on several days. First the Burlington Quarter Court met on May 8, 1694. He was accompanied on the bench by Justices Edward Hunloke, John Tatham, James Marshall, Nathaniel Westland, Thomas Gardiner and Daniel Leeds. At this court the Grand Jury ordered that improvements be made on the road from Crosswicks to Widow Hancock's on the Assiscunk Creek, and to the Yorkshire Bridge, and to the road from the town to Heulings Point. They also cited the town of Burlington for the amount of debris found on the streets of Burlington.[51] The town, through the General Assembly and now through the courts, was ordered to make improvements. Although the Quarter Court adjourned that day, a Court of Appeals was held the next day for a plaintiff who requested an appeal of his prior verdict. The court did not have to be continued, however, for the appeal was withdrawn. While the justices were on the bench they acknowledged an indenture of Richard Basnett to Peter Resnier.[52]

The May Fair Days were held in Burlington as usual, and on Friday May 11, 1694, the Council of Proprietors of West New Jersey met to elect their officers. Thomas Gardiner Sr. continued as president of the council for another year. William Biddle remained on the council as a member and attorney for Burlington County. William Biddle Jr. was appointed as a ranger. The council completed some business and then adjourned to enjoy the day in the town, reconvening at five o'clock that evening. In this second session they recognized the right of Mahlon Stacy to have made an Indian purchase on the northern branch of Sinpinck Creek. They asked that those who were to claim land in the bounds of the purchase should pay Stacy

5 shillings for every one hundred acres claimed so that he would be reimbursed for the purchase.[53]

On Saturday, May 12, 1694, the Burlington justices met with Governor Andrew Hamilton on the bench for the first Court of Oyer and Terminer, a new court established for capital crimes. A woman was accused of killing her newborn child, but after lengthy testimony, the jury found the defendant to be not guilty. The woman, however, had to continue to serve out the time remaining on her indenture to her master, John Bainbridge, and in addition must find someone to pay her court costs of £3.16s. She would then have to extend her servitude to whomever paid the costs.[54] While waiting for the jury's decision William, with Justice Francis Davenport, attended to the usual business of the Burlington Court. They acknowledged an indenture of William Watson.[55]

The session of the General Assembly began on Saturday, May 12, 1694, but then adjourned to continue its business on May 14 through 17, 1694. Francis Davenport was again elected Speaker of the House. Peter Fretwell, one of the younger Quaker leaders, was elected as Treasurer of the province. Thomas Revell was reelected as Recorder. The first business of the Assembly was to set the penalties for whoredom and adultery. The courts had been applying the penalties, but now the General Assembly made their actions the law of the land. Whipping as a punishment was permitted. This could be prevented if a payment of £5 for unmarried and £10 for married offenders was paid with court costs. Defendants were able to petition the court to be indentured to pay off these debts.[56] All of the inhabitants of the province, Quaker and non-Quaker, realized by now that the morals of this new society had to be protected with strong laws. Even though the province had been founded as an idealistic religious experiment, there was some behavior that was antisocial and criminal. That day the Assembly joined the courts in establishing and enforcing the standard of behavior of the citizenry of the territory.

Among other accomplishments of that General Assembly was an act to set the legal interest rate for the province at no more that eight percent per annum. Election days were set for the counties. Cape May was to elect on the sixth of April, Burlington on the tenth day of April, Gloucester on the thirteenth day of April and Salem on the sixteenth day of April annually. To make the Assembly more representative of the population of the province, the old rules of the Concessions and Agreements which sent ten representatives from each Provincial Tenth were changed and now Burlington and Gloucester Counties were to elect twenty members to the Assembly, Salem was to elect ten assemblymen, and Cape May was to send only five elected members. Justices were elected, and William Biddle was reelected as a Justice in Burlington County.[57]

At seven o'clock in the evening on Tuesday, May 15, 1694, the Council of Proprietors met again. The only business conducted concerned Francis Collins. Though he had been given permission to buy land from the Indians with George Hutcheson and William Biddle, he found that the lands that they wanted to purchase were too remote to be useful to him. Considering this, the council allowed Collins to make his own purchase of 1,200 acres from the Indians as long as it was in one tract and not in an area that had been previously purchased from the Indians.[58] It is uncertain if George Hutcheson or William Biddle had exercised their rights to purchase land from the Indians before that time. It was important that the council continue to state and record their right to approve Indian purchases. Later that summer George Hutcheson purchased Stepson Island from Master Thomas Indian Chief.[59] This island would protect the mouth of the Maurice River. William may have been considering or completing land purchases from the Indians around Little Egg Harbor, another potential port of entry for the province.

At six o'clock in the morning of May 18, 1694, the morning after the adjournment of the General Assembly, the Council of Proprietors of West New Jersey met again in Burlington. They first ordered that an instrument be drafted that confirmed and constituted the council, a document that would be sent to the Resident Proprietors for approval or ratification. Secondly, the council elected Thomas Gardiner Jr. as the Surveyor General, and it asked him to deputize other surveyors to see to the orderly continuation of the business of dispersing the proprietary lands of the province. Deputy Surveyors were designated for each area of the province. The fee for surveying was established by the council at no more than eight shillings for a survey of one hundred acres and no more than two shillings and six pence for every hundred acres surveyed afterwards in the same tract.

Jeremiah Basse appeared before the council. He verified that, as the agent of the West Jersey Society, he had made an Indian purchase of all of the lands between the headwaters of the Cohansey Creek and the Prince Maurice River to the Delaware Bay, except for those lands that had been formerly surveyed to John Fenwick. The council allowed the purchase. As was their usual practice, they told Basse that all other Proprietors had the right to survey and claim land within the purchase, so long as they paid their proportion of the cost of the purchase and any other associated charges. He agreed to their terms.[60]

The last meeting of the month was the Burlington Quarterly Meeting of Friends held at Mount Hope on May 28, 1694. Since there was no significant business to discuss, Friends who convened that morning enjoyed each other's company and adjourned to the fourth second day in August.[61]

During the summer months of 1694 William took time out from his life as a public servant and as a Proprietor to enjoy his homestead. Like other leaders in the province William had been spending an extensive amount of time on public work to ensure that West New Jersey was an organized, civil and comfortable place for all to live in.

It was not until August 8, 1694 that he resumed his duties as a Justice. The Burlington Quarter Court met that day and he was joined on the bench by Edward Hunloke, James Marshall, Daniel Wills, Francis Davenport, Daniel Leeds, John Curtis and Peter Fretwell. The court attended to routine matters of debt or trespass of land ownership disputes. In one case William Biddle Jr. was sued by Jacob Spicer, but the charges were improperly made and Spicer was made to pay the cost of the suit. In another case a legal separation and terms for it were finally agreed to for a couple that the court had previously tried to reconcile. The wife returned to England.[62]

William Biddle returned to Burlington on August 11, 1694 and as a Justice he acknowledged an indenture between James Hill and Samuel Oldale. Thomas Revell recorded the agreement.[63]

At the Burlington Quarterly Meeting of Friends held at Mount Hope on August 28, 1694, the only business recorded was appointment of the members who would represent the meeting at the upcoming Yearly Meeting of Friends.[64]

The Friends for Yearly Meeting met in Burlington from September 16 through 19, 1694. The meetings lasted longer than usual. One of the concerns of the elders was for the welfare of the young Friends. It was decided that a stronger effort should be made to bring young Friends together in activities and to educate them in the manner of Friends.[65] They knew that the future of their religion depended on their children growing up and continuing to support Quakerism.

On October 10, 1694 William continued the distribution of his Burlington lots. That day he sold a lot of 3/4 acres on Bread (Third) Street to Mary Myers, widow of the deceased butcher, William Myers, for £4, adjoining the lot on which her house was built. The indenture was witnessed by Joseph White and Joseph Senior and was probably drawn up in the inn of Abraham Senior by Thomas Revell.[66] While he was in Burlington that day William may have seen the progress that had been made in cleaning up the town and draining the swamp lands as had been directed by the General Assembly and the courts. He had been one of those responsible for the implementation of the project.

On November 2, 1694 the Council of Proprietors of West New Jersey met in Burlington. William attended the meeting with Thomas Gardiner Sr., president of the council, Francis Davenport, Thomas Gardiner Jr., John Hugg Jr., George Hutcheson, Christopher Wetherill and John Reading. The first day very little business was recorded. The council adjourned to eight o'clock the next morning, perhaps so that they could enjoy the second day of the fall Fair in Burlington with their friends and families.[67]

Upon reconvening in the morning, the council continued to discuss a matter of great concern to them, carried over from their meeting of September 14, 1694, namely that the East New Jersey Proprietors had made errors in determining the line between the two provinces prescribed by the Coxe-Barclay agreement. It was ordered that the agreement be reread and that measures be taken to rectify the errors. The council also requested that all previous deputy surveyors and the previous surveyor general turn over all documents related to their work with the council.[68]

The Burlington Quarter Court and Court of Common Pleas was called into session late that day, but since it was Saturday and there would not be enough time to finish the work that had to be done, it adjourned to the following Thursday.[69]

The court reconvened on November 8, 1694 and William was on the bench with fellow justices John Tatham, Nathaniel Westland, Francis Davenport, Thomas Gardiner, John Curtis and Peter Fretwell. The Court of Sessions called for members of the Grand Jury, but so many people were ill that the jury could not be filled and the court had to be adjourned to a later date. The Court of Pleas was convened and the jury filled and it continued to deliberate into Saturday, November 10, 1694. Several cases involving lengthy testimony from multiple witnesses were heard. One involved the rightful ownership of a horse. Another involved the person responsible for a fight that took place between two people at Josiah Prickett's house. The third case involved the possible poisoning death of James Budd, the brother of John, William and Thomas Budd. John Tatham, who had been informally accused of the death, but he was cleared of the slanderous charge.[70]

In the fall months of 1694 a disease of some type struck the inhabitants of the province. Burlington was decimated by the illness. Thomas Gardiner Sr., his son John Gardiner, James Marshall, James Hill and Thomas Gladwin, all residing on High Street, died. Richard Basnett, Samuel Ogborne, John Hands and Bernard Devonish from Pearl Street also died during those months. It may not have been restricted to the town of Burlington for Thomas Shinn, John Pancoast, Peter Harvey and his infant daughter, and Thomas Lambert Sr. of rural West New Jersey among others died that fall too. Perhaps the sickness was at least in part due to the fact that the water levels and drainage of surface water in the town were changed by the draining of swamps that year. It is not known if the illness was experienced by the residents of Philadelphia. The Harvey child is reported to have died of smallpox, and it may have been that disease that caused this disaster. Whatever the cause, in Burlington, that fall season, many of the citizens who had been instrumental in founding the town and overseeing its growth died tragically.[71]

Undoubtedly, the seriousness of the situation was discussed at the Burlington Quarterly Meeting of Friends held on November 26, 1694, as Friends prayed for the sick and the bereaved.[72] William was reminded again of the situation when he attended court on December 8, 1694 to receive the will and inventory of Samuel Ogborne from his widow Jane,[73] and again on January 5, 1694/5 when the will and inventory of Thomas Gladwin were submitted to the court by his executors George Hutcheson, Robert Wheeler, Samuel Furnis and Joseph Adams.[74]

William had a break from the unhappiness that shrouded the province when on Wednesday, January 9, 1694 he officiated at the wedding of Nathaniel Cripps to Grace Whitten.[75]

In February William made three trips to Burlington. The first was to attend Saturday court as the attorney for Joseph Helmsley to record an indenture.[76] On the second trip he was accompanied by his son for the Quarter Court Session held on February 20, 1694. William Jr. served on the Grand Jury that day and he also was approved by the court as the newly elected Constable for Mansfield Township. Present on the bench of the court with William were Governor Andrew Hamilton, Edward Hunloke, John Tatham, Jeremiah Basse, Nathaniel Westland, Daniel Wills, Francis Davenport, Mahlon Stacy, John Curtis, Daniel Leeds and Peter Fretwell. Among other matters, the court passed judgment on several social and behavioral problems. One involved the wife of a man living with another man. The second case involved a couple where the woman had become pregnant before marriage. The third cited another couple for having their first child born out of wedlock.[77] The leaders of the West New Jersey Province continued to see that their utopian state had not altered sometimes-aberrant human nature.

Two other matters were brought before the Court of Pleas that day. In the first, Thomas French again presented to the court his claim to lands that he had purchased from John Woolston Sr. These lands were among those first surveyed by Hancock in 1678. William had also traded some lands in the tract with Thomas French. The boundaries of Richard Fenimore's land and the land of Abraham Hewlings were also involved, as well as the validity of the surveying done by Daniel Leeds. Thomas French lost the case and had to pay court costs. In the second matter taken before the court George Porter successfully defended his right to £16 owed to him by the deceased William Ellis. William Biddle as the attorney for the Ellis estate had to pay the money to Porter from the proceeds of the sales of land that he had already completed.[78]

Two days later in Burlington William recorded the sale of a townlot of one and a half acres in Burlington to Daniel Smith for £5. This was land west of High Street and South of Broad Street where Smith was beginning to accumulate a sizeable tract of town land.[79]

Burlington Quarterly Meeting of Friends was held on Monday, February 25, 1694/5 at Mount Hope at ten o'clock in the morning. Peter Fretwell joined the meeting as a member replacing the deceased Thomas Gardiner Sr. Numerous epistles and letters that were important documents for Friends to save were brought to the Meeting to be kept in a book until it was further decided what to do with them. A difference had arisen between Christopher Wetherill and Samuel Furnis that was not an issue for the court to decide. In the manner of the Friends an arbitration panel was selected to solve the problem. Wetherill chose Mahlon Stacy, Francis Davenport and Robert Wilson to support his cause. Furnis chose William Biddle along with Isaac Marriott and John Wilsford to help him.[80]

Apparently William had provided financial support to several persons as they developed their homesteads and businesses in the province. On March 21, 1694/5, it became necessary to foreclose on the mortgage that he had with John Melbourne, blacksmith, of Nottingham. That day the Melbourne property of 165 acres and a house were sold to Caleb Wheatley, weaver, of Chesterfield for £28, and William received most of the proceeds of the sale.[81]

On April 10, 1695, election day in Burlington County, William presided in the court to receive the will of John Skene, prior deputy governor of the province, from his widow Helena Skene.[82]

William returned to Burlington for the Quarter Court and the Court of Pleas on May 8, 1695. Only Edward Hunloke, Daniel Leeds and Nathaniel Westland joined him on the bench that day. There was not much business requiring the attention of the court, so adjournment to the next session came early in the day.[83]

For the next ten days or more of that month William was busy in Burlington. Following the spring Fair Days the General Assembly meetings began on May 13, 1695 and the Council of Proprietors of West New Jersey reconvened on that same day. William also attended to court business, recording indentures on several of the days that he was in town.

Although it appears that the General Assembly did not accomplish much significant business during such a lengthy session, there were probably many political agreements made behind the scenes. Francis Davenport continued as Speaker of the House. The General Assembly was to elect justices as they had done in the past under the Concessions and Agreements. Apparently the Governor would continue to appoint justices too. Since justices were still elected this allowed a greater number of Quaker justices to serve on the bench of the court. Fees were established for elected offices. Burlington and Salem courts were now to hear all cases for fewer than forty shillings, thus reducing the number of cases that would be heard by the County Court of Common Pleas. The need to license all alehouses and tavern keepers was reemphasized. Cohansey was permitted to hold a fair. To reinforce the desire of the Council of Proprietors of West New Jersey to have all deeds and conveyances recorded, a fine of 20 shillings per deed was imposed on those who concealed their documents.[84]

The annual organizational meeting of the Council of Proprietors of West New Jersey was held on May 13, 1695. Those who had been elected to the council were William Biddle, John Tatham, Frances Davenport, Samuel Jennings and Mahlon Stacy for Burlington County and Thomas Gardiner Jr., John Hugg Jr. and John Reading for Gloucester County. John Tatham was elected as president of the council, replacing the deceased Thomas Gardiner Sr. Samuel Jennings and John Reading were appointed as commissioners for granting warrants. Thomas Gardiner Jr. was continued as Surveyor General. John Reading was to serve as Clerk.[85]

At this meeting Samuel Jennings resumed his active political and public life in the West New Jersey Province. In the employ of William Penn, he had lived in Pennsylvania for several years. In November 1693 he purchased the home of Thomas Budd on the west side of High Street in Burlington, along with the Malt House and Brewhouse.[86] Thomas Budd had moved to Philadelphia.

Following their first organizational meeting, the council adjourned to the next day, May 14, 1695, at six o'clock in the evening, after the session of the General Assembly. The council had been and remained concerned about an act of the General Assembly for resurveying lands. They reread the document and set it aside for further study. Governor Hamilton had undoubtedly been made aware of the council's concern about the claiming of land by not only the East New Jersey proprietors, but also by the West Jersey Society. Governor Hamilton submitted a letter to the council at that session in which he made proposals concerning the procedure for claiming and titling of lands of the province. The council read the letter and set the matter aside again for further consideration.[87]

The council then adjourned until four o'clock in the afternoon of the next day. At that session Jeremiah Basse joined the councilmen. Basse, as the agent of the West Jersey Society, claimed that he represented as many as thirty proprietary shares of West New Jersey whose ownership remained in England. He had requested that he be given a seat on the council with the right to cast as many votes as his employers had proprietary shares. Although Basse had made a request for action of the council, no decision was recorded. They adjourned to the next afternoon, May 16, 1695 at five o'clock. Thomas Gardiner, Surveyor General, promised to provide a book in which he would update all surveys and drawings of land that had been made in the province. Also, the council requested that the executors of the deceased Andrew Robeson, the prior surveyor general, return to them all records pertaining to the business of the council.[88]

The council adjourned and reconvened on May 21, 1695. It was at that time that they further considered the request that Jeremiah Basse had made of the council. They all knew that the West Jersey Society had only twenty proprietary shares. It was quite evident that Jeremiah Basse had overstated his case. The council agreed that if Basse could show evidence for the rights to the thirty proprietary shares, that "they shall have liberty to elect as many representatives resident in the province to sit in Council proportionably to thirty proprietys as here are allready persons in the council representing the forty proprieties in the two counties of Burlington and Gloucester." With that decision, the council adjourned to its September meeting. The disagreements between the council leadership and Jeremiah Basse were at least beginning to be defined.[89]

During the summer months William was able to spend most of his time attending to his home and family. Fortunately his son was able to help manage the expanding business of the farmlands that they had claimed and improved. William and Sarah again hosted the Burlington Quarterly Meeting on May 26, 1695.[90] Later in the summer, on June 15 and 22, 1695, William traveled to Burlington to serve as a Justice at the court.[91]

On June 29, 1695, William, with Samuel Jennings, Mahlon Stacy, John Woolston, Isaac Marriott and Peter Fretwell served as an arbitration panel to settle a dispute between Henry Grubb and widow Mary Ollive. Henry Grubb had built his inn on a lot 60 feet by 50 ½ feet on the west side of High Street on the north side of Pearl Street. He had owed Thomas Ollive for the lot, but apparently had not settled his account. The arbitrators agreed to bestow to Mary Ollive the ownership of a corner lot one block to the west in the wharf lot originally assigned to Daniel Wills and William Biddle. Several months later the arrangement was settled. Mary gained ownership to a lot of 73 feet on the west side of Wood Street and 80 feet on the north side of Pearl Street as compensation.[92]

As early as January 2, 1693/4, the members of the Chesterfield Monthly Meeting had requested that the First Day meetings that had been held once each month at Mount Hope be moved to the Chesterfield Meetinghouse that had been constructed for their Monthly Meeting. When asked if they would give up those First Day meetings, William and Sarah had replied that "they want to take it into their consideration." [93] Besides having permission from the Burlington Monthly Meeting to hold them at Mount Hope, William and Sarah, 60 years old now, liked having the First

Day Meetings for Worship at their home so they could avoid the long travel to Chesterfield.

The issue was still not resolved when William attended the Chesterfield Monthly Meeting held July 4, 1695. William, remaining as a member in good standing of the Meeting, was appointed with others to attend the Burlington Quarterly Meeting representing Chesterfield Monthly Meeting.[94]

William returned to Burlington on August 8, 1695 to attend the Quarter Court and Court of Pleas. With him on the bench were Edward Hunloke, John Tatham, Nathaniel Westland, Francis Davenport, Mahlon Stacy, John Curtis, Daniel Wills, Peter Fretwell, and new justices John Adams, Samuel Harriott and John Hollinshead.[95]

William completed an indenture and had it acknowledged and recorded that same day, for the sale of a two-acre town lot to Nathaniel Cripps for £10. The indenture was witnessed by Joseph White and acknowledged by Justices Mahlon Stacy and Thomas Revell.[96] On August 31, 1695, William returned to the town to sell another one-acre lot to James Verier, mason, for £8.[97]

At their meeting on September 5, 1695, the members of the Chesterfield Monthly Meeting again asked that their First Day meetings held once a month at Mount Hope be returned to their Meetinghouse. A committee was appointed to visit William and Sarah again about the matter, but it was not resolved.[98]

William attended the Yearly Meeting of Friends in Philadelphia from September 15 through 18, 1695. He and his friends from the region were able to concentrate on the business matters of the Friends while they reinforced their spiritual lives.

Shortly thereafter their daughter Sarah, not quite seventeen, informed her parents that she had decided to marry a ship's captain, William Righton, who was not a Quaker. On October 3, 1695, the men's Chesterfield Monthly Meeting expressed concern and sent Mahlon Stacy and Francis Davenport to speak with the parents. On the same day, the Women's Meeting asked Esther Gilberthorpe and Sarah Bunting to speak to Sarah Biddle about the proposed marriage. The parents answered the Meeting by stating that "their daughter has been an obedient child and had done nothing in this her marriage without their consent." When asked what answer they should give to the meeting, William answered that they were "men capable to give the answer." The meeting found this answer "altogether unsatisfactory" and referred the rest of the discussion to the next Monthly Meeting.[99]

William and Sarah's daughter Sarah did marry William Righton Jr., Master of the ship *William and Mary*, in a civil ceremony held at Mount Hope on October 21, 1695. Thomas Revell, Edward Hunloke and John

Tatham served as the justices of the peace. Guests included the groom's parents, William and Sarah Righton, his sisters and his brother-in-law Thomas Masters, a merchant of Philadelphia. William Biddle Jr. and his wife Lydia Biddle were present with their young children. Thomas Biddle, the bride's cousin, attended.[100] Other friends of the bride made up the remainder of the wedding party. Despite the criticism that they received about the marriage from the official Quaker Meeting, William and Sarah stood behind their daughter's decision.

William Righton Sr. and his wife Sarah (Murell) Righton had been a part of the small Quaker community in Bermuda before they moved to Burlington about 1689. The father of William Righton Sr., William Righton the elder, had moved to Bermuda as early as 1650. He had been assigned as a preacher and reader for Smythe's and Hamilton Tribes by the Somers Island Company, positions that carried with them lodging and grounds on which he could raise crops to survive. He apparently was not a very good minister and he was relieved of this position perhaps about 1657.[101]

Quaker ministers arrived in Bermuda as early as 1660. William Righton the elder had become sympathetic to them and his son, William Righton Sr., had joined the Quakers. Both father and son had become mariners during this time, participating in carrying cargoes from the whaling industry and the tobacco industries to other ports. It appears that they did not always keep accurate accounts of the imposed shares (the monetary contributions) that they should have paid to the Somers Island Company.[102]

William Righton Sr. was apparently a leader in opposing the established government of the island. He built his own sloops and continued to trade between the islands, England and America. He married a Quaker girl from Bermuda, Sarah Murell, daughter of Thomas Murell. Their son Stephan, named after William Righton's brother, lived in London. Their son William Righton, the bridegroom, went on to learn to be a ship's captain from his father and grandfather. He too was listed as a Quaker while still in Bermuda, and it was probably after he left the island that he stopped practicing that religion.[103]

William Righton Jr. was trusted as a captain by Quakers, including William Penn, when they wanted their cargos shipped across the seas. He had been the Master of the *Mayflower of Philadelphia* prior to becoming the Master of the *William and Mary*.[104] His sister, Sibella, married Thomas Masters from Bermuda, who afterwards became a carpenter and a merchant and mariner of Philadelphia. Undoubtedly William Biddle knew of the Righton family from his experiences as a merchant even before he immigrated to West New Jersey. His daughter Sarah had become acquainted with the ship's captain through his sisters Sibella, Frances and Agnes who were about her age. Sarah Biddle and William Righton Jr. may have met in Burlington or even in Philadelphia as these young girls socialized or continued their educations.[105]

At the Court of Pleas of November 5, 1695, it was revealed that William Righton Jr., in his enthusiasm to be with or near his new bride, had docked his ship, the *William and Mary*, at Burlington without the necessary approvals or payments. Captain Thomas Meach, agent of the Crown for Pennsylvania, seized the vessel. The matter was addressed by the Court of Pleas in the presence of Governor Andrew Hamilton and it ruled that Captain Meach did not have jurisdiction over the port of Burlington. Edward Hunloke was the official collector of duty for his majesty in West New Jersey. Upon release of the vessel, Edward Hunloke seized it, only to let it go immediately when William Righton Jr. posted sufficient bond in the name of the owners of the ship in England.[106] The bridegroom learned that he could not freely take his ship beyond the port of Philadelphia. Later, in England, Jeremiah Basse would capitalize on the act of the Court of Pleas as an example of the improper manner in which Andrew Hamilton had governed the province.[107]

On November 25, 1695, William and Sarah had the opportunity to meet with Quaker leaders again at Mount Hope at the Burlington Quarterly Meeting, although the conflict between the hosts and the Chesterfield Monthly Meeting had not been resolved. It was noted at the meeting that a copy of the *Journal of George Fox* had been obtained for the use of the Meeting. It was to be left in the possession of Peter Fretwell.[108]

On December 5, 1695, the Chesterfield Monthly Meeting met and since they had not received a response to the request to move First Day Meetings from Mount Hope, Edward Rockhill and John Bunting were appointed to visit William and Sarah to obtain an answer. They reported back at the next Meeting that the couple should now "leave it up to Friends to have it where they think fit." The Chesterfield Monthly Meeting immediately appointed those First Day meetings to be held at their Meetinghouse.[109] It is uncertain whether William and Sarah attended the meetings at Chesterfield, or if they continued to have meetings for worship at Mount Hope or, at some other convenient location near Mansfield. The Burlington Monthly Meeting had originally approved the Meetings for Worship at Mount Hope and they had permitted Friends of that location to allow meetings to be held wherever they wanted. It was not until years later that a Preparative Meeting for Worship was officially founded at Mansfield, perhaps as an extension of this permission.

On December 6, 1695, William and Sarah, with their friend George Hutcheson, traveled to Philadelphia. The men had to attend court to receive a letter of administration for Rebecca Bowden, the widow of their friend, Mordecai Bowden, who lived just across the river from William, in

Pennsylvania.[110] The trip afforded the parents their first opportunity to call on their daughter, Sarah Righton, at her new home in the city. Sarah by now had her own furnished home and servants.

On Monday, December 9, 1695, William attended court in Burlington. He acknowledged the indenture between his neighbors Anne and John Snowden and his neighbor-to-be, Richard Allison. Whitehill, the homestead of the Snowdens, situated on a high bluff overlooking the Delaware River just upriver from Mount Hope, was sold, for they had decided to move to Pennsylvania.[111]

On January 16, 1695/6, William sold his 100 acres just down-river from Burlington, in the town bounds, to William Righton Sr., daughter Sarah's father-in-law, for £18.[112]

The Chesterfield Monthly Meeting reopened its discussion of Sarah's marriage to William Righton Jr. at its meeting of February 6, 1695/6. The strong feelings of the clerk are evidenced by the minute book where he recorded that "William Biddle continuing weak and not capable to bring here the answer about their daughter's marriage. Consensus recorded."[113] The meeting did not do what they probably wanted to do. They did not remove Sarah as a member of the meeting for marrying outside of the religion probably because or her parents, William and Sarah.

Friends again met at Mount Hope on February 24, 1695/6 for Burlington Quarterly Meeting. The Meeting began with an expression of concern over not having recorded enough of their records. It was decided that all Friends should be asked to bring in any records or letters that they had which would be appropriate to include in the minutes of the Quarterly Meeting. Peter Fretwell was to be in charge of the task.[114]

On April 2, 1696, the freeholders of Burlington convened at the courthouse to elect town officers as they had been directed to do annually by the General Assembly of October 3, 1693. Those males who were inhabitants of the town who "enjoyed the fee simple" ownership of a house and lot in the town were eligible to vote. Those eligible to vote elected John Hollinshead as Burgess, Thomas Revell as Recorder, Peter Fretwell as Treasurer, John Meredith as Clerk and Samuel Jennings, Edward Hunloke and Benjamin Wheate as Councilmen.[115]

William did not attend the court of May 8, 1696, but he took Sarah to town for the spring Fair. This social time just before the session of the General Assembly allowed the Assemblymen time to consider the matters that they would discuss when in formal session. The General Assembly met from May 12 through May 23, 1696 and William did participate as an Assemblyman at the sessions. Francis Davenport was again elected as Speaker of the House. William Biddle was one of the justices elected to the Burlington Court.[116]

The first acts of the General Assembly were simple matters concerning weights and measures. They also agreed that all summons to court must be delivered at least ten days before the court was to be held. Because of the strong Quaker leadership in the province the leaders had been lax in administering oaths of office. The English Parliament had recently restated the need to take oaths of office. They had also allowed an alternate oath for Quakers. At this session, the General Assembly, with its Quaker majority, passed an act allowing for the use of the alternate oath in the province. The Assembly decided to continue the same rate of taxation for the province, with an added tax on negro slaves. Slave owners were taxed 2 shillings, 6 pence for each of their slaves greater than ten years of age.[117] This may have been intended to provide a further incentive to eliminate or reduce slavery in the province — or it may have been merely another way of taxing wealth, as slaves were still considered possessions.

While the General Assembly meetings were taking place in Burlington, the Council of Proprietors of West New Jersey also held its meetings, in the evenings. The council was reconvened for its annual meeting for electing officers on May 12, 1696. William did not continue as a member. Only Mahlon Stacy, Frances Davenport and John Reading remained on the council as charter members. John Tatham and Samuel Jennings also left the council. John Shinn became a member for the first time. Francis Davenport was elected as president.[118]

In addition to its usual business, the Council of Proprietors expressed concern that they had not recovered the records of Surveyor General Andrew Robeson from his son Samuel Robeson who lived in Philadelphia. They felt also that they needed a restatement of the purpose and legitimacy of the council, and proposed submitting a bill to the General Assembly for "constituting of ye said Council and obliging an observance of ye whole body of proprietors to what shall be by them transacted." Obviously the council was insecure, and despite the justifications that had been received supporting its existence, it felt the need to have this restated by the governing body.[119] Although this bill was undoubtedly discussed by the General Assembly, no action was taken.

William and Sarah met with the leaders of the Friends at Burlington Quarterly Meeting on May 25, 1696 at Mount Hope. At the Men's Meeting they learned that the deceased Thomasin Towle had left the Quarterly meeting a gift of £6.10s. Peter Fretwell was appointed to receive the money from the executors of the estate. With the money and property that the

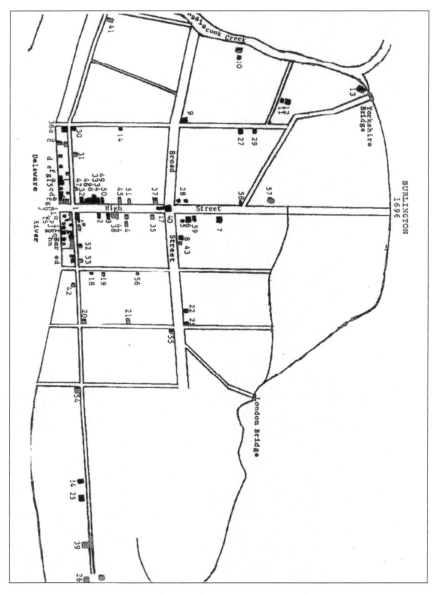

Buildings in Burlington City, 1696

1. Samuel Jennings malt house, brew
   house, bolting house and stable
2. Richard Love's house
3. Thomas Gardiner house
4. James Wills house and cooper shop

5. Thomas Kendall's log cabin
6. Thomas Kendall's townhouse
7. John Cripps townhouse
8. Daniel Smith's townhouse and lot
9. Mariner Robert Hopper's townhouse

10. Nathaniel Pope's house and barns
11. John Smith's house on Pudding Lane
12. Peter Fretwell's house bought from Robert Stacy
13. Peter Fretwell's tanhouse
14. Obediah Hierton's townhouse
15. a. Seth Hill, ferryman, house and lot
    b. George Hutcheson's house occupied by Joseph Adams
    c. Mathew Champion and Percivale Towle's heirs' bakehouse
    d. Percivale Towle's heirs townhouse
    e. Richard Francis's stable
    f. House of mariner Daniel England
    g. George Hutcheson's townhouse
    h. Isaac Marriott's house, kitchen and bakehouse
    i. Isaac Marriott's house
    j. George Hutcheson's house
16. a. Henry Stacy's heirs' house
    b Lawrence and Virgin (Cripps) Morris's house
    c. Lawrence and Virgin (Cripps) Morris's log cabin
    d. Bernard Devonish's house
    e. Mary (Budd) (Gosling) Collins' house
    f. Rebecca Decou's home bought from brewer Nathaniel Ible
    g. James White's house
    h. John Meredith, schoolmaster's, house and lot
    i. Basnett's brickhouse
    j. Elizabeth Basnett's Brewhouse
    k. Bartholomew Minderman's house and lot
    l. Henry Grubb's Inn
    m West Jersey Society's house
    n. West Jersey Society's pottery
    o. John Tomlinson's house
    p. Edward Hunloke's house
    q. John Hollinshead's house
    r. Thomas Bibb's house
17. Marketplace
18. Benjamin Wheate's lot with decaying log cabin of William Brightwin
19. Benjamin Wheate's lot and cabin
20. Joshua Humphries's house
21. William Myers' house
22. Daniel Smith's house

23. Hollinshead - Eves townhouse
24. Thomas Potts' house in Ollive Town
25. Daniel England's lot and house
26. Nathaniel Duggles' pastures and barns
27. William Cooper's lot and cabin
28. Anna Salter's lot and log cabins
29. John Butcher's townhouse
30. Thomas Revell's townhouse
31. Daniel Sutton's house and tailorshop
32. James Marshall's heirs house
33. Isaac Decou's butcher shop
34. Isaac Decou's house
35. Friends Meetinghouse and burial ground
36. a. Nathaniel Westland's inn
    b. Lawrence Morris's townhouse
    c. Thomas Renshaw's butcher shop and slaughterhouse
    d. Jane Riggs' house
    e. Samuel Oldale's house
    f. Daniel Leeds' Keithian Meetinghouse
    g. Samuel Terret's house
37. Christopher Wetherill's house and tailorshop
38. Thomas Raper's house
39. shipbuilder Peter Resnier's house and lot
40. Courthouse
41. John Tatham's house and lot
42. James Satterthwaite's house
43. Daniel Smith's house
44. Thomas Gladwin's heirs' house and blacksmith shop
45. Samuel Furnis's house and saddle shop
46. Robert Wheeler's house
47. Thomas Revell's office
48. Robert Wheeler's store
49. Thomas Raper's house and whitesmith shop
50. Abraham Bickley's house
51. Josiah Prickett's house
52. Benjamin Wheate's house
53. Bernard Lane's house
54. James Verier's house
55. Robert Hudson's townhouse
56. Jonathan West's house
57. Brick kiln
58. Thomas Atkinson's house
59. Thomas Kendall's house

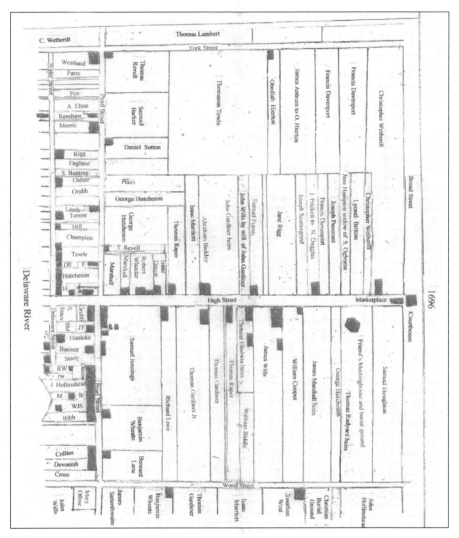

Center of Burlington City, 1696.

Quarterly Meeting had been left by Percivale and Thomasin Towle, the Burlington Quarterly Meeting had an income to help support other Quaker activities. It was noted also that Peter Fretwell had loaned the *Journal of George Fox* to Gloucester Friends, who promised to return it within one year.[120]

Under Sarah's leadership the Women's Quarterly Meeting was becoming more active. Sarah was given permission to purchase a minute book from Mathew Watson, bookbinder, for 10 shillings[121] to better record their actions in the future.

Quarter Court and Court of Pleas was held as scheduled on August 8, 1696. Governor Andrew Hamilton attended. William was accompanied to Burlington by his son that day, for William Jr. had been called to serve on the Grand Jury. With William Sr. on the bench were Mahlon Stacy, Francis Davenport, Daniel Wills, John Hollinshead, John Adams and Peter Fretwell. The appointed non-Quaker justices were conspicuously absent.[122] John Tatham had been excluded from the Council of Proprietors of West New Jersey at its last session. Apparently Governor Hamilton had not reappointed those non-Quaker justices, or they had decided to no longer participate in the courts of the county. Governor Hamilton began to work more closely with the established Quaker political leaders. Jeremiah Basse had been in England since early that year.[123] It was uncertain what was happening with the West Jersey Society by whose authority Andrew Hamilton held his office.

During the court sessions one case was heard and decided by the Traverse Jury of the Court of Pleas. The Grand Jury set the tax for Burlington County at one-third of that of the Province of West New Jersey, and they also established the location of several roads in the county.[124]

Near the end of the summer, on August 31, 1696, William and Sarah again hosted the Burlington Quarterly Meeting of Friends. Those in attendance agreed to have the Quarterly Meeting pay for the Quaker-related books that had been sent to them from England. William and Sarah were both appointed to attend the upcoming Yearly Meeting of Friends.[125]

An important meeting for the interests of the owners of the proprietary rights of West New Jersey occurred on September 22, 1696. In his new alliance with the West New Jersey Quakers, Governor Hamilton had apparently agreed to pay some attention to the concern previously voiced by the Council of Proprietors of West New Jersey that the Coxe-Barclay agreement boundary line between East and West New Jersey was not being honored by the East New Jersey proprietors. William Biddle, with his friend George Hutcheson, met with Governor Hamilton and some of the other East New Jersey proprietors to complete an indenture that would better define the boundary.[126]

On June 6, 1695, Captain Arent Schuyler, one of the Crown's English military officers in New York, purchased 5,500 acres from the Indians, land on both sides of the Pequannock River near to the intersection of the Pompton River.[127] At this place the Pequannock River was the borderline between the two provinces. On November 11, 1695, 4,000 acres of East New Jersey proprietary rights were sold to Major Anthony Brockhills and Captain Arent Schuyler to give them complete ownership of the portion of the Indian purchase which was on the eastern side of the river. The officers paid the East New Jersey proprietors £100 for the rights.[128]

On September 22, 1696, Governor Hamilton personally acknowledged that William Biddle and George Hutcheson had each transferred to Major Brockhills and Captain Schuyler 750 acres of West New Jersey proprietary land rights; the total 1,500 acres represented the West New Jersey portion of the Indian purchase on the western side of the Pequannock River. The indenture was witnessed by East New Jersey proprietors John Barclay, Nathaniel Coagland and Charles Sanders. There is no evidence that George Hutcheson or William Biddle ever received any compensation for these land rights.[129] A later minute of the Council of Proprietors reveals that the transaction was made for the "public good." [130]

The West New Jersey proprietors had acknowledged that the Coxe-Barclay line was the division line between the two provinces. These transactions, also known by the East New Jersey proprietors, proved their intent to continue to agree to that arrangement. Since the political power of Governor Hamilton was under attack by Jeremiah Basse in England, the West Jersey proprietors and Quakers would need every bit of help that they could get to continue to protect the judicial and governing systems that they had established, as well as their land rights.

A surprise was in store for William and Sarah the next day. The Yearly Meeting of Friends was held in Burlington on the morning of September 23, 1696, and it was boisterously disrupted by George Hutcheson and others who had recently become Keithian Quakers.[131] The disturbance was settled without any physical injury, but the emotional impact was undoubtedly strong. Though George Hutcheson was living most of the time in Philadelphia by then, he still owned his luxurious townhouse and gardens on the Burlington riverfront just east of High Street. This Quaker Yorkshire proprietor had been one of the pillars of the founding of the province. He still owned a considerable amount of proprietary rights in the province and he had worked closely with William Biddle to keep the Quaker experiment in democracy viable. Now he had joined the other followers of George Keith in West New Jersey and Philadelphia. After disrupting the Friends Meeting, the Keithian Quakers undoubtedly retired to the riverfront meetinghouse that Daniel Leeds had provided earlier for them on his waterlot.

The Friends continued their meetings for business and worship that day. Although the sessions were brief, one message was sent clearly from the meeting to other Friends of the region. They were advised not to import any more negroes.[132]

Following the fall Fair Days in Burlington, William again sat on the bench of the Quarter Court on November 3, 1696 with Quaker Justices

Francis Davenport, Daniel Wills, John Hollinshead and Peter Fretwell in attendance. John Hollinshead, Mayor of Burlington, presented the applications for licenses for ordinaries (eating and drinking establishments) to the court for Elizabeth Basnett, Henry Grubb, Thomas Kendall, George Willis and Robert Hudson. The licenses were approved. After attending to a few other matters the juries and the court were adjourned.[133]

At the Burlington Quarterly Meeting held at Mount Hope on November 30, 1696, it was agreed that £3 would be paid for books, and James Satterthwaite was paid £2.12s.8d. and Daniel Leeds £5 for maintenance work that they had done for the Chesterfield Meeting. Now that the meeting had a more certain income of its own, more projects for the Friends of the area could be undertaken.[134]

On Thursday, December 10, 1696, William returned to Burlington to record an indenture between himself and James Sherwin. There had been an apparent mortgage or ground rent arrangement between the two, for William had transferred 150 acres of land on the southwest side of the Northampton River in 1687 to Sherwin, who had lived there and built his home there. Now with a payment of £12 the purchase was completed and the deed officially recorded.[135]

On Friday, February 19, 1696/7, William again traveled to Burlington. Justices William Biddle and Francis Davenport acknowledged an indenture for a trade of parcels of land between Mordecai Andrews and Joshua Newbold. John Meredith, school master and town clerk, witnessed the deed and, Meredith recorded the document in the absence of Thomas Revell.[136]

The next morning the Quarter Court and Court of Common Pleas was attended by Andrew Hamilton, Governor, William Biddle, Francis Davenport, Mahlon Stacy, John Hollinshead, Daniel Wills and Peter Fretwell. Each year at the February court the townships submitted their newly-elected Constables and Overseers of Highways, each township having held these elections prior to that court date. The new Constables were approved. Also, the territory above the Assinpink Creek was now officially established as a township called Maidenhead. In November of 1695 the court had ordered that £100 be raised for building a bridge over the Assiscunk Creek at Burlington. This court made more certain arrangements for raising the money and appointed a committee consisting of Francis Davenport, William Wood, Peter Resnier, John Adams and John Hollinshead to decide where the bridge should be built between Peter Fretwell's house and the point near Mr. Tatham's house.[137]

On Monday, February 22, 1696/7, Friends again met at Mount Hope for Burlington Quarterly Meeting. Consistent with the concern of the Yearly Meeting, the Quaker leaders further discussed the many distractions from the Quaker faith that faced the children of the Quaker meetings. It was decided that youth meetings should be held to try to guide the activities and thoughts of the Quaker children, but no decision about the effort was made at that time.[138]

In Burlington on March 9, 1696/7, William received a warrant for 50 acres of unappropriated land from the Council of Proprietors of West New Jersey.[139] Peter Fretwell probably met with William to complete this transaction, for he had been commissioned by the council that year to issue warrants. It is possible that this land was given to Joseph Stewart, as called for by the original terms of the Concessions and Agreements, as payment for indentured services.

At the Quarter Court and Court of Common Pleas held May 8, 1697, again only the Quaker justices were on the bench. Thomas Revell was in court as the attorney for Ralph Hunt. William's neighbors Nathaniel and Moses Petit and Mordecai Andrews were fined that day for selling liquor without a license. The court renewed the licenses for keeping victual houses for Elizabeth Basnett, Henry Grubb, Thomas Kendall and George Willis, completing business from the prior Quarter Court. Thomas French was in court again, having never been satisfied with the previous decision of the court over the bounds of his meadowland. Edwin Shippen presented the debt of widow Elizabeth Basnett to him of over £700. Mrs. Basnett acknowledged the debt and the court was asked to decide how she could make good on the funds owed to Shippen. It would take an act of the General Assembly a few days later to enable the widow to use assets from her husband's estate to settle the debt. John Gosling Jr., son of Mary (Budd) (Gosling) Collins chose Thomas Revell and Thomas Gardiner Jr. as his guardians at this court.[140] Thomas Gardiner Jr. had now moved to Burlington to the home of his late father on the west side of High Street.

After the spring Fair Days the sessions of the General Assembly began on May 12, 1697 and lasted through May 21, 1697. It had been recognized that Francis Davenport was sick when the Council of Proprietors of West New Jersey met on April 9, 1697. Apparently he was still not able to resume his public duties, for Samuel Jennings was elected as Speaker of the House in his place. The Assembly met for a long time, but there were not many official acts passed by the legislative body. A new township of Fairfield was created at Cohansey. It was decided that a road to Cape May from Burlington needed to be built. The Assembly gave widow Elizabeth Basnett control of the Brewhouse and empowered her to sell it if necessary to meet the terms of her husband's will and to pay the debt to Edwin Shippen.[141] This act was necessary, for under English law a widow was entitled to only a third of her husband's estate for her lifetime and could not dispose of real estate.

On May 22, 1697, following the completion of the General Assembly meetings, the Council of Proprietors of West New Jersey met. William, through election, had returned as a member of the council. Although Francis Davenport was present, he apparently did not want to continue as president and the council elected William Biddle as its president for that year. In addition to Francis Davenport the council was made up of Mahlon Stacy, Francis Collins, Thomas Gardiner Jr., Thomas Thackara, Peter Fretwell, John Reading and John Kay. William Biddle Jr. was appointed a ranger for Burlington County. The business that day was routine and they adjourned well before the day ended.[142]

At ten o'clock in the morning of May 31, 1697, the leaders of the Men's and Women's Monthly Meetings met for Burlington Quarterly Meeting. Although no business of importance was noted for the men's meeting, the women's meeting was concerned about the gossiping of one of the members of the Chesterfield Monthly Meeting and began discussions regarding the proper way to handle the situation.[143]

In early 1697 the Board of Trade in London, under Secretary Popple, and the West Jersey Society had decided that Andrew Hamilton was disqualified to be Governor of the New Jersey provinces because the Navigation Act of 1696 made it illegal for foreigners to govern the provinces. Hamilton was Scottish, as were some of the other governors in America. It was on that technicality that Jeremiah Basse persuaded authorities in London to dismiss Governor Hamilton. In June 1697 London proprietors of both East and West New Jersey requested that the Board of Trade approve Jeremiah Basse as the new Governor of both proprietary provinces.[145]

William, with the other Quaker justices, sat on the bench of the Burlington Quarter Court and Common Pleas Court on Monday, August 9, 1697. A special session of the Court of Common Pleas was held on June 11, 1697 to publish the laws passed by the General Assembly and to read the commissions of the justices.[144] Because they did not know how much time that they had before the governorship would change, they wanted these laws to be seen and acknowledged officially as soon as possible.

Burlington Quarter Court also heard another case that day. James Trent had sold three Scottish boys to three residents of the province, who brought the boys to court to determine how long their period of indenture should be. The court determined that each boy should serve his new master for nine years. Another action from the court between Edward Hunloke and John Hammell was held over to August 27, 1697 because the summons and the information about the case had not been delivered ten days prior to the regularly scheduled court. William returned to Burlington on that date to sit on the bench and to help to decide that case, which involved a property dispute.[146] It is clear that their rules of the court were being strictly followed.

Friends met at Mount Hope for Burlington Quarterly Meeting on August 30, 1697. In response to discussions held at previous Quarterly Meetings it was decided that four youth meetings per year should be held to enable young people to get to know each other and to further teach them about their Quaker faith. Following up on prior discussions, the Women's Meeting asked Sarah to inform the woman who had been gossiping of their deliberations and decisions.[147]

By September 4, 1697, William had obtained a warrant from the Council of Proprietors of West New Jersey for 2,000 acres.[148] On that day he further discussed his trips to Little Egg Harbor that summer. Daniel Leeds had completed surveys of 760 acres and 430 acres for him and these were approved by the council, becoming the property of William Biddle.[149]

William and Sarah had the opportunity to travel to Philadelphia again on September 22, 1697 to attend the Yearly Meeting for Friends and they stayed with their daughter Sarah while there. William was able to hear what others knew of the status of the governance of West New Jersey. Attending the meeting were Samuel Carpenter, Griffith Owen, Phineas Pemberton and Thomas Ducketts among others from Pennsylvania, as well as his peers from Burlington Quarterly Meeting and William Cooper and Thomas Thackera from the Gloucester Meeting.[150] This group of Quakers were closely connected to trade and commerce with London and probably were able to discuss with William the latest positions of the Board of Trade and of the West Jersey Society with regard to their Governor, Andrew Hamilton.

By October 1697, Governor Andrew Hamilton was notified by both East and West New Jersey London proprietorships that he was disqualified from being Governor of the Provinces. Jeremiah Basse was appointed by the London proprietors to govern both East and West New Jersey. However, as expected, Basse was unable to obtain sufficient authority from them. He wanted an approbation (a written official approval from the Crown) to solidify his position, but Secretary Popple of the Board of Trade had, perhaps wisely, denied him this degree of approval.[151]

Burlington Quarter Court and Common Pleas Court met as usual the day after the fall Fair Days, November 3, 1697. Despite the notice that had been served to Governor Hamilton, he remained active in his position, not having been formally relieved of his command. With Edward Hunloke, the appointed Customs Officer of the Crown, Andrew Hamilton, through Benjamin Wheate, who was appointed King's attorney, brought suit against the mariner Daniel England for importing sugar from unknown sources. Although the jury found for the defendant, the Governor had acted in the manner expected by the Crown. Also at this session, Peter Indian decided to bind himself to Mordecai Howell for a period of eight years, which the court approved. Several more Scottish boys sold to residents by James Trent were presented to the court to determine how long their indentures should last.[152]

The General Assembly met on November 4, 1697 to finalize the business that had to be done before Governor Hamilton left office. Samuel Jennings continued as Speaker of the House. The Assembly passed an act to allow the bequests from the wills of Percivale and Thomasin Towle to be given to the Burlington Quarterly Meeting. This act was necessary in order to be certain that such a philanthropic gift would be legal and hopefully not taxable. Although the Governor was to continue to receive his same salary, £200, the tax rate for the province was halved; the people did not want to pay taxes for a governing administration that was not their own. Peter Fretwell continued as Treasurer of the Province. He would have to deal with the new Governor and his Councilmen when they discovered that the treasury was nearly empty. With these and a few other acts the General Assembly adjourned, presumably intending to meet again at its usual time, May 12, 1698.[153] The Quaker leaders knew that this might be their last chance to work with and honor Governor Andrew Hamilton. It was very important to them that he had allowed them to continue their Quaker experiment in democracy.

William probably spent most of the first week of November in Burlington. In addition to the Quarter Court and the General Assembly meetings, the Council of Proprietors of West New Jersey met on November 2, 4, 5 and 8, 1697. On the eighth, the council asked Thomas Gardiner to publish the notice to all of the proprietors that accession of a third dividend of land was under consideration, so that the resident proprietors could attend the next meeting of the council in Burlington and bring their requests, or any objections they might have. The meeting was called for March 5, 1697/8 in Burlington.[154] Thus, under the leadership of William as president, the council was trying to take a more aggressive role in acquiring and allocating the provincial lands.

William returned home with no governing responsibilities ahead of him for awhile, other than to attend to the needs of his homestead and his farms. He and Sarah hosted the Burlington Quarterly Meeting of Friends on November 29, 1697.[155]

Since Jeremiah Basse had not arrived from England as Governor by court time, William, with the other Quaker justices, sat on the bench of the Burlington Quarter Court and Common Pleas Court on February 21 and 22, 1697/8. At this session the new Constables were presented from each township for approval. The court agreed to continue the county tax at the same rate as the previous year. It received an accounting from the County Treasurer, Peter Fretwell, and found it in good order. Fretwell owed only eighteen shillings for which he could personally be accountable beyond that date. The justices ordered that all licenses for selling strong liquors must be issued by the Quarter Court. In addition, the justices ordered that any warrants that were issued for any taxes must bear the signatures of at least three justices.[156] The latter provision was probably enacted to prevent the bad experiences most of them remembered so well in England when only one justice was required.

One week later, on February 28, 1697/8 the members of the Burlington Quarterly Meeting read and discussed the minutes of the Yearly Meeting for the benefit of those who had not attended.[157] The Quaker leaders were still waiting fearfully for the Governorship of Jeremiah Basse to begin.

On March 5, 1697/8, the Council of Proprietors of West New Jersey met in Burlington as planned. Since the records had not yet been obtained from Samuel Robeson by Thomas Gardiner, the council appointed John Reading to get them. The council decided to defer the determination of taking a third dividend of land until its next meeting.[158]

On April 2, 1698, elections were held in Burlington in the courthouse. John Hollinshead was reelected as Burgess of the town. Thomas Gardiner was elected as Recorder, Edward Hunloke as Treasurer, John Meredith as Clerk, and Isaac Marriott, Thomas Raper and Benjamin Wheat as Councilmen. The election of the Burgess, John Hollinshead, was attested by Edward Hunloke, who was at that time president of Governor Andrew Hamilton's Council.[159]

On April 7, 1698 Jeremiah Basse returned to the provinces from England, arriving in Perth Amboy. He would not travel to Burlington until April 12, 1698.[160] The Council of Proprietors of West New Jersey had planned its next meeting to take place during that interval, and under the leadership of William Biddle they met on April 9, 1698. The council received and put into safe keeping the books of Andrew Robeson. Now their own records were complete and they would be better prepared to face whatever challenges Jeremiah Basse might present should he question their accuracy or legitimacy. A copy of the records was to be returned to Samuel Robeson as he had requested. Again the council deferred the determination of a third taking-up of land to its next annual meeting scheduled for May 12, 1698.[161]

CHAPTER 21

Jeremiah Basse, Governor,
April 7, 1698 – August 19, 1699

With the onset of the governorship of Jeremiah Basse, the Quaker leaders anticipated problems. Their experience with him when he was a resident among them in Burlington had not been good. He was dishonest with them when he told them that his employers, the West Jersey Society, held more proprietary shares than they really did. He was not supportive of the Quaker ideals for life and government. They realized, however, that it was important that they show outward respect for newly-commissioned governmental authorities even if they did not agree with them. Now they again faced a major test of the preservation of their Quaker experiment in democracy.

Though Governor Jeremiah Basse had arrived at Perth Amboy on April 7,[1] it was not until April 12, 1698 that he traveled to Burlington in West New Jersey to announce his commission from the English West New Jersey Proprietors and the West Jersey Society who had proclaimed him as Governor of the province. His entrance into Burlington County and the town of Burlington was relatively quiet, for the Quaker majority did not bother to greet him on his arrival, a procedure of courtesy usually extended to new governors. Governor Basse presented his commission and letters to his newly appointed Council. John Tatham was appointed president of the council, with John Jewell, Thomas Revell and Edward Randolph as its other members.

Apparently, during those first days in Burlington the Governor's Council presented Jeremiah Basse's papers to Andrew Hamilton and the representatives of the General Assembly of the Province. Since Basse did not have the necessary papers of approbation from the King, Hamilton and the Assembly refused to accept his authority.[2] Probably any further negotiation of the matter was deferred to the time of the next General Assembly meeting.

Despite the presence of Jeremiah Basse in the province, the Quaker justices of West New Jersey peacefully remained on the bench of the Quarter Court when it was convened in Burlington on May 9, 1698. William Biddle, Peter Fretwell, Francis Davenport, Mahlon Stacy, John Hollinshead and John Adams held court that day. Under the law of the land, as allowed by the Concessions and Agreements, a defendant was permitted to object to jurors who were to hear his case.[3]

The residents of West New Jersey had continued their practice of holding elections in each county in April of each year, despite the change in governance. In addition to electing their local officials, the residents of each county must have elected their representatives to the Assembly also, for there is evidence that the General Assembly met May 12, 1698, even though no minutes exist for that meeting.[4] Samuel Jennings was continued as Speaker of the House, and with "near fifty" Assemblymen present, he continued to state reasons why the assumption of the governorship by Jeremiah Basse rested on false grounds. It appears, consequently, that the Assembly voted not to accept Jeremiah Basse as Governor of the Province.[5]

The actions of this group set the tone for the quiet Quaker rebellion that followed. Jeremiah Basse did not intend to use the General Assembly in his government, so the actions of this Assembly were ignored and never recorded. Basse challenged the Quaker representatives by questioning their right to serve without having taken the oath of fidelity to the Crown as required for those who were to hold public office. Basse refused to recognize the oath of the Quaker Assemblymen that had been submitted to England earlier and had been met with no objection.[6]

The Council of Proprietors of West New Jersey also met in Burlington on May 12, 1698. William Biddle, President, was accompanied by Francis Davenport, Mahlon Stacy, Peter Fretwell, Thomas Gardiner and John Reading at that meeting. There was concern expressed about the actions that were being taken by Jeremiah Basse concerning proprietary land rights. Three dinner meetings were held, probably at the inn of Henry Grubb, on the evenings of May 13, 16 and 18, 1698. Gloucester resident proprietors and Council members Thomas Sharp and John Kay joined the group. It was not until the meeting on the last night that they recorded their concern. Apparently, Jeremiah Basse, in the name of the West Jersey Society, had appointed Joshua Barkstead and John Jewell as Surveyors General for the Province. The council members were incensed, for this was a major threat to their right to continue to operate as a valid institution. The members of the council were each assessed to raise money for a defense fund. Thomas Gardiner was to act as attorney for the council. They decided that the case was to be taken to the courts of England, if necessary, to have the matter resolved in their favor. Records show that William Biddle was assessed £2 for the defense fund.[7]

On May 30, 1698, the Burlington Quarterly Meeting of Friends was held at Mount Hope and that day William would have explained to his fellow Quakers the actions that the council might have to take in the near future. At this meeting the trustees for the Percivale Towle Trust were changed. George Hutcheson had left Quakerism, moved to Philadelphia and subsequently died. Peter Fretwell, as the former treasurer of the province, was under the scrutiny of the Basse government. As a result, Samuel Jennings and Thomas Gardiner were made trustees of the trust in their places.[8]

During this period Thomas Gardiner may have angered John Jewell and Joshua Barkstead, for he encouraged settlers in the province to ignore the directions of these two unofficial surveyors general. William Biddle, on the other hand, took an entirely different approach. On June 4, 1698, as the President of the Council of Proprietors of West New Jersey, he granted to Joshua Barkstead a power of attorney so that he could act as surveyor for the lower lands of the province. The document was witnessed by George Willhouse and by John Jewell and Thomas Revell of the Governor's Council.[9] Prior to that time Barkstead was a ranger for the council in the lands below Salem. This document made him a deputy surveyor with the blessing of the president of the council.

On August 8 and 9, 1698, the Jeremiah Basse faction took over the court of the province. Justices appointed to the bench included John Tatham, Thomas Revell, Nathaniel Westland, Thomas Bibb, Anthony Elton, Michael Newbold, John Test, George Deacon, Joshua Ely and William Emley. Only the last three were Quakers.[10]

Jeremiah Basse would govern the province mainly through his council and through his appointed court. At those first sessions of the court held by his appointed justices, most of the business was routine. John Hollinshead, Special Coroner in the place of the deceased Daniel Wills, reported on the accidental drowning death of Joshua Buddin, son of William Buddin who lived on the Northampton River. Jacob Ong appeared to answer a complaint against him for galloping his horse down High Street from the markethouse to the waterfront, but no one appeared to prosecute him, so he was dismissed. Edward Hunloke presented a complaint against John Tatham, but the matter was tabled on a legal formality. A committee was appointed to decide the location of a road to be laid out in Mansfield Township.

The Grand Jury, after being both sworn in, and for those desiring to be certified in a manner acceptable to Friends, attested, deliberated and presented a petition to the court to call Peter Fretwell, the previous Treasurer for Burlington County, to account for the money he received for the county. The bench appointed a committee consisting of Nathaniel Westland, Thomas Revell, John Tatham, George Deacon, Thomas Bibb and Daniel Leeds to audit the account.[11] The last Quaker court had already audited Fretwell's accounts and found them to be in order. The Basse justices reopened the matter.

On August 29, 1698, the Burlington Quarterly Meeting of Friends was convened again at Mount Hope. Samuel Jennings and Peter Fretwell were asked to procure a replacement bond to represent the money that the meeting had previously sent to a needy Friend, the first bond having been found insufficient in amount. Francis Davenport, Samuel Bunting, John Day and Peter Fretwell were appointed official representatives to the Yearly Meeting of Friends. Ann Jennings and Bridget Watson were appointed to attend as delegates for the Women's Meeting. Henry Grubb, Christopher Wetherill, Isaac Marriott, Thomas Pupert, Samuel Furnis and Peter Fretwell were appointed to provide the platforms (temporary bleachers for sitting) for the Yearly Meeting Gallery.[12]

On September 19, 1698, the Council of Proprietors of West New Jersey met with William Biddle presiding. Also in attendance were Mahlon Stacy, Francis Davenport, Thomas Thackera, Peter Fretwell and Thomas Gardiner. It was decided by the council to indemnify Peter Fretwell. He had been the Treasurer for the County and also the person responsible for issuing warrants for unappropriated lands for the Proprietors. He needed the council's support, for he questioned the authenticity of the new authority and had refused to hand over his accounts to the Governor's agents.[13]

On September 21, 1698, the Yearly Meeting of Friends was held in Burlington. Friends from the eastern colonies met and attended to the business issues of their religion and worshipped together. No significant new actions were taken by the Quakers, perhaps in part because they were not then in control of the civil institutions in West New Jersey.[14]

On October 6, 1698, a special town meeting was held in Burlington in the courthouse. John Hollinshead, who had been elected as Burgess of the Town of Burlington on the first fifth day of April, continued to "disown" the present Governor and government of the province. The inhabitants and freeholders of the town of Burlington who attended the meeting, all members of the Basse faction, voted to replace Hollinshead as Burgess. Thomas Bibb was elected as the new Burgess of the town. In addition, the entire slate of officers was reelected. John Meredith became Recorder, Edward Hunloke continued as Treasurer and Thomas Revell, Joseph Adams and Robert Wheeler were elected as Councilmen. The officers were sworn or attested by John Tatham, President of the Governor's Council. The Basse faction had, in this meeting, successfully taken over the governance of the largest town of the province.[15]

Thomas Gardiner, the most skilled surveyor in the province, was spending time in the more remote parts of the province, perhaps to inform rural Quakers of the actions of the Basse government. He surveyed a tract of 100 acres located on Rock Creek at Little Egg Harbor for William Biddle on October 19, 1698.[16]

The Burlington Court met at its usual fall time on November 3, 1698, probably following the fall Fair Days that were customarily held on November 1 and 2. The afternoon session of the court was moved from the courthouse to the inn of Thomas Kendall. The courthouse may not have been suitable if the weather was inclement. The Basse-appointed justices sat on the bench and numerous non-Quakers sat on the juries. Numerous minor offences were tried. The court appointed the new Treasurer for the county, Thomas Bibb. The sessions of the court continued until final adjournment on November 10, 1698.[17]

The Burlington Quarterly Meeting of Friends was held on November 29, 1698 at Mount Hope. Among others in attendance were the Quaker political leaders Samuel Jennings, Peter Fretwell and Thomas Gardiner. At this meeting it was found that Jennings and Fretwell had not yet procured a proper bond to assure the loan they had made to a needy Friend. They discussed the need to decide on what documents to copy into their records and Peter Fretwell was given the task of taking their record books home with him to perform the task. In addition to attending to the business of their religion, these leaders could freely communicate with each other and plan strategy for the political struggle in which they found themselves. Mount Hope had become a safe and convenient place for the out-of-power Quaker political leaders to meet.[18]

On December 17, 1698, William Biddle was again in Burlington to preside over the meeting of the Council of Proprietors of West New Jersey. The meeting was attended by Peter Fretwell, Mahlon Stacy and Thomas Lambert. Only the routine business of the council was attended to since the conflict with Jeremiah Basse, who was still the agent of the West Jersey Society, effectively blocked any ability to work toward another land dividend for the proprietary shares.[19]

In that same month, December 1698, Samuel Jennings held a meeting of the "Quaker Party" at his rural homestead, Green Hill. Those present probably already knew that the West New Jersey Proprietors in England and the West Jersey Society were seeking a new opinion from the Attorney General of England concerning the eligibility of Andrew Hamilton to govern the province. The process to oust Jeremiah Basse from office had begun and at this meeting the resident Quaker proprietors and inhabitants of the province had the chance to prepare their own request for a change in government to send to England. Undoubtedly, they knew that their counterparts in the East New Jersey Province had already taken such action.[20]

The annual meeting of the residents of Mansfield Township was held at eleven o'clock on January 1, 1698/9. The township elected Mordecai Andrews as Constable, William Biddle as Supervisor of Highways, and Isaac Gibbs as Clerk.[21] The elected constables of each township had to be further approved by the Burlington Court. With the court dictating a number of changes in the roads of the township, perhaps it was fortunate that William Biddle would be the one to oversee these changes during the tenure of the Basse government.

On February 20, 1698/9, the Burlington Court met again. At this session each of the townships presented the constables elected at their annual town meetings so that they could be sworn in or attested by the justices of the county. In particular, Thomas Scattergood and James Satterthwaite, Constables of Burlington, presented Thomas Clark and Isaac Decow as their elected replacements.[22]

At this same session William Biddle was criticized by the Grand Jury for not prosecuting Edward Andrews. Even under the laws of the Concessions and Agreements one could forgive a crime, but not a felony. It was discovered that Edward Andrews had stolen two hogs from William Biddle and apparently William had forgiven him without presenting the act formally to the court. Now William was forced to charge his neighbor with the theft. The Grand Jury continued subtle harassment against the Quaker leaders of the province, moving to have former County Treasurer Peter Fretwell audited again.[23]

The leaders of the Friends met at William Biddle's home, Mount Hope, on February 27, 1698/9. They continued to discuss the geographic boundaries for the Chesterfield Monthly Meeting and they completed other routine business.[24]

William had made a decision by this time to begin selling some of the lands that he held in the province. On March 14, 1698/9, he and his son, William Jr., sold the 500-acre tract they had claimed in Springfield Township to John Antrum for £90. The price indicates that either there were some minor improvements on the land, or it was just a valuable farm. The indenture was witnessed by Thomas Bibb, Benjamin Field and John Meredith. The fact that William Jr. also signed the document suggests that his father had intended that the farm would belong to his son some day and had included his name on the deed.[25]

The Burlington Court had been adjourned to that same day, March 14, 1698/9. After opening the session in the courthouse, the court adjourned to the inn of Thomas Kendall. Routine matters were presented, including the locations and conditions of roadways established in Wellingborough and Mansfield.[26]

The court was adjourned until the next day, and at that session Governor Basse was present, accompanied on the bench by Justices John Tatham, Thomas Revell, George Deacon, Nathaniel Westland, Anthony Elton, Daniel Leeds, Joshua Ely and William Emley. This court continued to the next day. In that session it began to take action against the Quaker leaders of the province. John Jewell and Joshua Barkstead brought suit against Thomas Gardiner, who was not present. The court refused to accept Gardiner's written explanation of the case, and a process was begun to determine the size of the damage he would be fined.[27]

In an unrelated matter, Christopher Snowden brought suit against Thomas Gardiner. When the defendant again did not appear, a large fine of £10 plus court costs was levied against him [28]

In another case James Satterthwaite and John Hollinshead were presented for searching the house of Daniel Sutton without a legal warrant. At the time of the offense Satterthwaite had been Constable of Burlington and Hollinshead had been the Burgess, and they had not taken time to obtain the appropriate warrant. For this offense, they were fined severely. Satterthwaite had to pay £5 and Hollinshead, who was also found to have not attended to another matter was fined £10 for both incidents. The two defendants were kept in custody until their fines were paid. They were also kept in custody by the court on another matter. They were found guilty of not bringing Mons Cock (who had been dead for over a year) before the court when they were in office, for selling liquor without a license and selling liquor to the Indians. For this misfeasance they were sent to jail.[29]

The main interest of the court was to finalize its business with Peter Fretwell, the former County Treasurer. Now that the Governor was present, the penalties dealt by the court had become more severe. Fretwell continued his refusal to surrender his accounts of the tax for the county and he was imprisoned for this and for his refusal to recognize the authenticity of the government.[30]

As the intensity of acts against the Quaker leaders of the province increased, it is likely that Governor Jeremiah Basse was unaware that the West New Jersey Proprietors in London had nominated Andrew Hamilton as their Governor to replace him in West New Jersey.[31] Basse had displeased Governor Bellomont of New York early in his term in office, and the New York Governor had never stopped complaining to England about him. He had explained to the Lords of Trade how Jeremiah Basse was unable to convene a meeting of the General Assembly, for he had never received the approbation from the King of England needed to make him the official Governor of the provinces.[32]

Furthermore, the East New Jersey Proprietors of England had also petitioned the Crown to reappoint Andrew Hamilton as the Governor of their Province in late 1698.[33] On January 7, 1698/9 Secretary Popple of the Lords of Trade had asked Thomas Trevor, Attorney General of England, if it was proper for this Scotsman to be governor of the province.[34] An affirmative answer was delivered by Attorney General Trevor on February 2, 1698/9.[35] On March 13, 1698/9 the West New Jersey Proprietors of London, perhaps with the encouragement of the resident Proprietors of West New Jersey, petitioned the Council of Trade and Plantations to reappoint their nominee, Andrew Hamilton, as Governor of the West New Jersey Province.[36] Andrew Hamilton himself wrote to Secretary Popple ten days later trying to expedite the appointment,[37] but the Board was not to be hurried in its decision. All parties were sensing that there would be a change in governorship in the Jersey Provinces, but for now Jeremiah Basse remained in power.

On April 9, 1699, William Biddle presided over the meeting of the Council of Proprietors of West New Jersey, with Thomas Lambert, Mahlon Stacy, Francis Davenport and Thomas Gardiner in attendance. No important business was recorded. They were still awaiting the dissolution of the Basse regime.[38]

On May 8 and 9, 1699, the Burlington Court was convened again with the Basse-appointed justices on the bench. Sentences given to the Quaker leaders were not as harsh at this session which Governor Basse apparently did not attend. Samuel Jennings was presented by the Grand Jury for stating that the Governor's Commission was unlawful, but no sentence was passed against him for this act. James Satterthwaite presented himself to the court, but no one came forth to prosecute him, so he was dismissed. John Hollinshead did not appear to answer a suit against him by John Ogborne, so the court by default made judgment against him for £11.14s.4d. plus £3.10s court costs.[39]

The Council of Proprietors of West New Jersey met on May 15, 1699 for their annual meeting. William Biddle was elected as the president of the council again. Also present at the meeting were Mahlon Stacy, Francis Davenport, Peter Fretwell, Thomas Thackera, Thomas Sharp, John Kay and Thomas Gardiner. William Biddle Jr. was continued as a ranger for the council for Burlington County.[40]

On May 29, 1699 Friends of Burlington County met at Mount Hope for the Burlington Quarterly Meeting. No business was recorded. The residents of the province were waiting to see if there would be another change in the governorship.[41]

On June 3, 1699, William continued to implement the plan of selling the acreage that he owned at a distance from his Mount Hope homestead. On that day he recorded the deed of sale of his 823-acre property with barns and dwelling house near Oneanickon, to John Clayton of Monmouth

County, East New Jersey, for £350. The indenture was witnessed by Thomas Duggles, Nathaniel Duggles and Thomas Revell.[42]

The Burlington Court convened again on August 8, 1699, with Governor Basse present along with several of his appointed justices, John Tatham, Nathaniel Westland, Thomas Revell, John Jewell, George Deacon and Daniel Leeds. Routine matters were attended to by the bench, but the court could not function because not enough residents appeared to serve on jury duty. The court was dissolved until the next session.[43]

The Lords of Trade and the Crown had not produced a decision on the matter of Andrew Hamilton's appointment. On August 19, 1699 the West Jersey Society appointed him as their agent in place of Jeremiah Basse and Nathaniel Westland, and the West New Jersey proprietors in England appointed him as Governor of the province.[44] Despite the fact that he did not have the approbation of the Crown, Hamilton would now replace Jeremiah Basse, who had caused such disarray in the New Jersey Provinces.

A few days after this the Burlington Quarterly Meeting of Friends was again held at Mount Hope. It was too soon for the Friends gathered there to have learned that Andrew Hamilton would be returning. They were concerned about the safety of "Traveling Friends" in the province since there had been adamant feelings against them initiated by Jeremiah Basse. They asked both Chesterfield and Burlington Monthly Meetings to provide suitable Friends to accompany such traveling Friends to East New Jersey and New York. William Biddle, Francis Davenport, John Day, Peter Fretwell, Thomas Gardiner and Robert Murfin were appointed to attend Yearly Meeting. The Women's Meeting selected Grace Hollinshead, Bridget Watson, Ann Jennings and Rebecca (Decou) Davenport to represent them at the Yearly Meeting.[45]

When the Yearly Meeting for worship and business for the Religious Society of Friends was held in Philadelphia on September 16 through 20, 1699, an epidemic of yellow fever in the city greatly reduced attendance.[46] Only John Shinn and Samuel Jennings attended from Burlington County.

On September 29, 1699, William chaired another meeting of the Council of Proprietors of West New Jersey. It was attended by Thomas Thackera, Thomas Sharp, Peter Fretwell and Francis Davenport. The council attended only to routine business. The Proprietors were still unable to proceed in the direction of giving out more land.[47]

The Burlington Quarter Court met again on November 3, 1699 and continued after adjournment on November 4, 1699. Governor Basse attended. His appointed justices, Thomas Revell, Nathaniel Westland, John Jewell, George Deacon, John Test and Michael Newbold completed the necessary business of the province. Several cases were presented to the court by the Grand Jury involving persons having sexual relations outside of wedlock and of cohabitation without marriage. The court demanded an end to the behavior of living together, either by separation or by marriage within a specified period of time. Abraham Carlisle was found guilty of fornicating with someone other than his wife and fined £5. As he had done in other cases Governor Basse, recognized Carlisle's poverty and returned the money to him.[48]

This same court sentenced a prisoner and his Negro accomplice to thirty-nine lashes with the whip at the "cart's tail" for stealing. The penalty seemed harsh by the standard set by the Concessions and Agreements, but the case actually involved multiple thefts and lies that had been told in court. The punishment was carried out behind a cart traveling down High Street to the river and back to the courthouse during the mid-day adjournment of the court.[49]

On Monday November 27, 1699, Burlington Quarterly Meeting of Friends was convened at Mount Hope at ten o'clock in the morning. The group asked that Francis Davenport pay £17 to Samuel Jennings for the Quarterly Meeting contribution to the funds of the Yearly Meeting. With the Percivale Towle Trust they now had an annual income to pay dues to the Yearly Meeting. They discussed the fact that local Friends were now accompanying Traveling Friends throughout the province. They learned that a needy Friend who had borrowed their funds to restore his home after it burned down had sold his homestead and moved to Burlington. Abraham Bickley was asked to visit him and secure the money that he owed to the Burlington Quarterly Meeting.[50]

On December 19, 1699, William and Sarah sold a tract of 430 acres of land and an additional 50 acres of unappropriated land at Little Egg Harbor to their neighbor Mordecai Andrews, for £70.10s. The indenture was witnessed by William Biddle Jr. and John Hancock and acknowledged before Justice Daniel Leeds.[51]

At last, on December 20, 1699, Andrew Hamilton officially resumed his role as Governor and reinstituted the General Assembly of the West New Jersey Province.

CHAPTER 22

Andrew Hamilton, Governor,
December 20, 1699 – May, 1703

On December 20, 1699 Governor Andrew Hamilton had arrived in West New Jersey. He had been living in East New Jersey and had already appointed his Council and called for the reestablishment of the General Assembly, the legislative body that had always served the people of the province. The West New Jersey residents were prepared. The sessions of the General Assembly began on December 20, 1699 and continued through January 1, 1699/1700.

The first business of the Assembly was to establish an appeals court for the province. Originally, by the Concessions and Agreements, all appeals from the courts were made to the General Assembly. In 1693, under Governor Hamilton, an appeals court had been established that could be called as needed, but this had not been successful. Now it was decided that there would be three provincial judges elected each year who would circulate. Twice yearly, in April and in October, at least two of these provincial judges, with at least one justice from a county, would serve as an appeals court in each county. These courts and judges were allowed to charge double the usual fees. For a case to be worthy of appeal it had to be worth £10 or more. In Burlington County the court of appeals was to meet every April and October on the eleventh day of those months.[1]

The General Assembly elected the officers of the West New Jersey Province. Justices were elected for each county. William Biddle, Francis Davenport, Mahlon Stacy, Peter Fretwell and Thomas Lambert Jr. were elected as Quorum Justices to the bench of the Burlington Court, while Ralph Hunt, Joshua Newbold, John Wills, John Adams and Elias Toy were also elected as justices for Burlington County. Samuel Jennings was elected Speaker of the House. Edward Hunloke became Clerk and Recorder of the General Assembly and the Burlington Court in place of Thomas Revell. Thomas Gardiner became King's Attorney. John Wills became County Coroner in the place of his deceased father, Dr. Daniel Wills. Peter Fretwell, after all of his troubles during the years of the Basse government, was elected Provincial Treasurer. Francis Davenport, Edward Hunloke and Jonathan Beer were elected as the first Provincial Judges.[2]

Although the General Assembly lasted for twelve days, there was not much business. The body decided to halve its size by allowing only ten representatives to be elected from Burlington and Gloucester Counties, five from Salem County and three from Cape May County.[3] Probably most of the time was spent in reestablishing the good working relationship that the Quaker majority had previously enjoyed with Governor Hamilton.

During the time of the meetings of the General Assembly William Biddle sold more of his lands. On December 25, 1699 he sold a tract of 500 acres at Little Egg Harbor to Nicholas Brown, a planter, for £60.[4] It appears that William had decided to reduce his land holdings. He began to turn his land assets into cash.

The Quarter Court and Court of Pleas met February 20 through 22, 1699/1700, in Burlington. Of the newly elected justices, only Thomas Lambert and Elias Toy were missing from the bench. Quite a few matters were taken care of in court in those three days. The township of Hopewell was founded and its bounds decided and published. The routes of several roads were altered. Restore Lippincott and John Shinn each brought an Irish boy to court. They had purchased the boys, named Daniel MacCay and John Anderson, as servants until they reached the age of twenty-one, and it was up to the court to decide the boys' ages in order to set the length of their servitude. They were found to be eleven and ten years of age. An apprentice, Thomas Wetherill, brought suit against James Wills, cooper, for not properly teaching him his trade, and was awarded £20 by the court. The guardianship of Benjamin Wheat over Theophila Cripps was concluded, for she had become of age. It was verified by the court that she had received all of her estate, so the bond that Wheat had posted was delivered to him and he was released from his responsibility. At the same court, Peter Fretwell was made guardian of Joshua Tompkins, orphan. Fretwell made a security bond and was given a letter of guardianship.

Peter Fretwell, who was treasurer of the province, asked that those collectors who had not turned over their money or accounts of taxes collected be sent warrants by the court to do so by the next quarter court. It was also ordered that Mathew Watson put a new binding on the court record book. As was usual for that time of year, all of the townships reported the results of their elections for constables and overseers of the highways for the court's approval, which was given. It was interesting that Mansfield presented the recently prosecuted Edward Andrews as their constable.[5]

An event dating back to Jeremiah Basse's time as governor was brought to court that day. At the Brewhouse of Elizabeth Basnett a marriage had quietly taken place between Robert Hickman, a suspected pirate, and Dorothy Tatham, the oldest daughter of John Tatham, Esquire. When widow Basnett had been charged with letting this happen, Benjamin Wheat and Isaac Marriott had bonded her for the court. Now the court found Mrs.

Basnett guilty of allowing the couple to marry and stay with each other in her inn. The £40 recognizance bond was forfeited and the amount was taken out of the goods and chattels of the three, Widow Basnett, Wheat and Marriott. Widow Basnett lost her license to continue to run her tavern.[6]

It was probably at that time that Elizabeth Basnett sold the Brewhouse, her inn and eating establishment to Samuel Jennings. The General Assembly of 1697 had empowered her to sell it but the land on which it stood was to be kept by the widow for the estate of her children. Samuel Jennings modernized or rebuilt the establishment which became known as the New Brewhouse. It was on the waterfront on the north side of River Street with a wharf to accommodate the ships that brought travelers to and from the town. Later it served as a station for the stagecoaches that traveled to points as distant as Perth Amboy. For Samuel Jennings it was a sensible investment. He already owned the brewhouse and malt house where the liquors were made, those having been included in property that he had bought from Thomas Budd. Years later, when the estate of Samuel Jennings was settled, it became apparent that he had owned the New Brewhouse but the land under it had remained in the Basnett family. Samuel Jennings probably helped support Elizabeth Basnett after she lost the license by paying her ground rent for the property, and she may have continued to manage the inn.[7]

Another case heard by the court was a suit brought by Dr. John Robards against John Tatham for not paying his bill. Tatham was defended by Thomas Clark. The defense tried to make the case that the physician was guilty of malpractice in setting the bone of the broken arm of John Tatham's son. Numerous people gave testimony, mostly in support of Dr. Robards the plaintiff, and the court ordered Tatham to pay the £3.2s.debt and also to pay the court costs. With this case the court adjourned.[8] The courts were operating properly again.

Having returned to Mount Hope, William and Sarah, hosted the Burlington Quarterly Meeting of Friends on February 26, 1699/1700. Friends were pleased that they were in control of the legislative and judicial institutions of their province. The only business recorded was that a needy Friend had not given a satisfactory answer to them through Abraham Bickley and had not repaid the money the meeting had loaned to him. They were to insist that he sign a bond, so that he would become legally indebted to them for the amount of the loan.[9]

At the same time, at the Women's Meeting in the next room, Olive Black, who had recently returned to traditional Quakerism, told those present of her experience as a Keithian Quaker.[10]

On March 11, 1699/1700, as spring neared, William continued to sell his lands. That day he sold a 2-acre lot in Burlington to Daniel Smith for £13.[11] The land was part of an 18-acre parcel that Smith was accumulating on the south side of Broad Street, west of High Street.

Hopefully all business that might require his attention at Mount Hope was completed by early May, for William had to spend most of the rest of that month attending to his responsibilities as a public servant in Burlington. Beginning May 8, 1700 and lasting through May 10, 1700, the Court of Pleas and the Quarter Court met. Among other actions, the Grand Jury, through their foreman William Wood, submitted a petition to the bench to be given to the General Assembly suggesting that another method be found for raising taxes in the county and the province. Also the court adopted an "alternate oath" for Quakers, as the standard oath for attestation was based on the sacraments of the Church of England and "swearing". When it came time to attest Daniel Leeds before he was to give testimony in a case, he requested that he be attested only by the oath of "the law of England." Justice Joshua Newbold granted his request.[12]

At the completion of the court hearings the spring Fair Days commenced in Burlington. This year it was a more pleasant time for the Quaker residents of the province since Jeremiah Basse had been relieved of his office. There was less active verbal abuse of the Quakers and the fear of a return to religious persecution was gone.

The General Assembly reconvened on May 12, 1700 and continued through May 25, 1700. As its first business the Assembly held elections and almost all of the officers were reelected to their positions. William Biddle continued as a quorum justice for Burlington County. Richard Ridgway and Robert Wheeler were added as Burlington County Justices and Christopher Wetherill became County Sheriff.[13]

Probably because Governor Hamilton realized that punishments for some crimes in the West New Jersey Province should be similar to those of England, and despite the fact that the Quakers might have felt that the penalties were too violent, the General Assembly passed a new law for punishing burglars. Now, in addition to making four-fold restitution, a burglar was to receive "thirty nine stripes upon the bare back." For a second offence, besides being whipped, the criminal would also have the letter "T" for thief burned on his forehead. For a third offence the criminal would have the letter "T" burned in the cheek and would be imprisoned at hard labor for one year and whipped with thirty-nine lashes monthly for the entire year. The convicted criminal could request transportation from the province and this would be granted. However, for every time that the criminal might return to the province within the next seven years he would need to make four-fold restitution, be whipped and be branded with the letter "T". It was hoped that this law would reduce the incidence of burglary in the province. It would also deter burglars who had faced such harsh treatment in other provinces or colonies from seeking asylum in West New Jersey if they thought they might be treated less harshly there,[14]

Probably the most important task faced by the legislators was the difficult problem of taxation. Before Governor Hamilton left the province in November 1698 the Assembly had reduced taxes. Although the residents of the province must have appreciated lower taxation, it was now time to increase taxes in order to adequately support the maintenance and development of the province. The legislators more than doubled the old rates. They now taxed all freemen who had attained the age of twenty, but they no longer taxed residents for their Negro slaves. The unsurveyed, unappropriated lands of the proprietors were not taxed.[15] Governor Hamilton's salary was increased to £300 per year.

In its final business the Assembly passed an act to enable Elizabeth Basnett, as executrix of the real estate of her deceased husband, Richard, to dispose of £500 of the real estate assets in order to pay his debts and legacies. Richard's legal heir, his son William Basnett, was not yet of age [16] Although the province did not have a law covering this situation, by English Law only the male heir of a deceased person could dispose of the assets of an estate. In the Basnetts' case, the Assembly circumvented this restriction for this specific case.

Before he could leave Burlington that Saturday, May 25, 1700, William had to preside at the annual meeting of the Council of Proprietors of West New Jersey. Governor Hamilton was present at the meeting, which was also attended by Mahlon Stacy, Samuel Jennings, Thomas Gardiner, John Wills, Thomas Thackera, John Kay and John Reading. The Governor carried a brief letter from the West Jersey Society introducing him as their agent in the province. The West Jersey Society claimed only twenty proprietary shares, not the thirty that had previously been claimed by Jeremiah Basse. The Society and Governor Hamilton wanted to work with and through the Council of Proprietors of West New Jersey. They wanted to end disputes and prevent disagreements in the future. They wanted to establish a method for suitably laying out the lands, a method which would make the title to the land "indisputable for ye future." [17]

It was in this spirit of cooperation that William called for elections to be held. Governor Hamilton was elected as president of the council.

William Biddle was elected as vice president, to preside in the absence of the Governor.[18]

William returned to Mount Hope that evening to have First Day Meeting for Worship with his family and neighbors the next day. He and Sarah then hosted the Burlington Quarterly Meeting of Friends on Monday, May 27, 1700. At the latter meeting it was learned that Abraham Bickley had convinced the needy Friend to sign the bond for the money he had borrowed from the meeting.[19]

One month later, on June 25, 1700, the Council of Proprietors met again in Burlington with Governor Andrew Hamilton presiding. The full council was in attendance. It was decided that for the time being all officers elected by the council would be commissioned under the hand and seal of the president of the council. In earlier meetings the council had tried to arrange for a restatement of its legitimacy but the General Assembly had not been willing to make a statement showing by what authority they existed. Now the West Jersey Society and the proprietors in London had renewed their authenticity. This action by Governor Hamilton, who was essentially commissioning their officers, certainly further supported their position as having overall authority concerning land titles in the province.[20]

At that meeting the question of ownership of the islands in the Delaware River also resurfaced. Some West New Jersey residents who had been cutting reeds on an island in the Delaware River had been stopped by government officials from Pennsylvania. The council believed that West New Jersey owned the island but understood that William Penn believed that he owned all of the islands in the Delaware River. William Biddle was familiar with Penn's position on this issue, but it was he, not Penn who had already surveyed and claimed one of these islands, Seppasink. The council did not know that Pennsylvania officials had also stopped their own residents from cutting reeds on the islands. Thomas Fairman of Pennsylvania had become frustrated when he was stopped from cutting reeds on an island that he and his wife Elizabeth (Kinsey) had purchased from the Indians for £54.[21] Penn had returned to Pennsylvania on December 1, 1699 so he was easily accessible to the members of the council. They decided to send a committee consisting of Governor Hamilton, Samuel Jennings and Thomas Thackera to visit with Penn to inquire of the Governor "by what authority he claimes yᵉ said islands." [22]

Undoubtedly William stayed in Burlington that night to discuss the topic of the next meeting with some of the other council members before they reconvened at six o'clock the next morning. Samuel Jennings, John Wills, Thomas Gardiner and John Reading were particularly familiar with

William Biddle's interest in distributing more of the unappropriated provincial land. Now that their position as a council was strengthened, they needed to convince the Governor that proceeding in this way would be to everyone's benefit.

The council met at the appointed hour in the morning. It was recognized that several people had been asking for permission to take up a third dividend of land on their proprietary shares. The council, considering these requests, did "condescend" to them, and ordered a third land dividend of 5,000 acres of unappropriated land per proprietary share to be given to shareholders of record as of November 1, 1701. Appropriate notice of the dividend was to be made so that proprietors in London would be prepared to benefit from the disbursement of the new lands.[23]

The council also noted at that meeting that the previous surveys and land claims that had been made under the authority of John Jewell and Joshua Barkstead, who were said to have been appointed by the West Jersey Society as Surveyors General during the Jeremiah Basse administration, were illegal. Those surveys were declared null and void. Governor Hamilton added to the minutes of the council that tracts of land belonging to the West Jersey Society that had been obtained in the proper manner were not jeopardized by this motion. All other business of the council was relatively easy to accomplish and they were able to adjourn that day.[24]

William returned home to tell Sarah about the actions of the Council of Proprietors. They were still the largest holders of proprietary rights among the resident proprietors but they had been concerned that the political instability would make it impossible for them to obtain their land. With 1.58 proprietary shares they would be entitled to another 7,900 acres of unappropriated land in addition to the 15,232 acres that had already been divided out to them in the two previous dividends. It was estimated at the time of the founding of the province that a proprietary share would be worth about twenty to twenty-five thousand acres per share. This dividend placed them much closer to their hoped-for allotment of land for the investment they had made in the venture.

During the summer months there were far fewer tasks for William to attend to away from Mount Hope. He and Sarah attended Chesterfield Monthly Meeting on July 4, 1700. At the Women's Meeting Sarah, along with Sarah Bunting, had received a bequest from the will of Bridget Guy.[25] The two women presented the money to the Chesterfield Women's Monthly Meeting in the form of a bond, one of the ways that money was transferred in this society that lived without a formal institution for banking.

Their daughter Sarah Righton spent many weeks with her parents that summer, for there was another small outbreak of yellow fever in Philadelphia. William had to miss some of the time with his daughter in order to participate in business matters in Burlington and Gloucester. On July 21, 1700 the trip was short. William, with fellow justices Mahlon Stacy, Peter Fretwell and Francis Davenport granted a letter of administration on the estate of Dr. John Houghton to Colonel William Markham, non-Quaker cousin of William Penn, and the deputy governor of Pennsylvania.[26]

William sat with his fellow justices on the bench of the Quarter Court and Court of Pleas when they met on May 8, 9 and 10, 1700. The Grand Jury presented to the court a plan of taxation for the county. They ordered a tax of approximately one-half of the provincial tax. In addition they resumed the county tax on Negro slaves. The bench accepted the plan, although two non-Quaker members of the Grand Jury dissented. However, residents of the county and the province had long been under-taxed and the tax laws had never been stringently enforced.[27] Many Quaker and non-Quaker residents of the province had learned not to take their responsibility to pay taxes seriously. Because the Crown of England still had not issued an approbation for Governor Hamilton, many inhabitants of the province felt unsure of the authenticity of the government.

The Recorder of the Court, Edward Hunloke, brought to the attention of the bench the poor condition of the county's book of deeds. It was ordered that the book be rebound by Mathew Watson. The court also approved the purchase of books to keep the records of wills and letters of administration, and to record the minutes of the Grand Jury. In a further effort to maintain order in the business of the court, the Grand Jury inspected and updated their report on the accounts of the county treasurer, Peter Fretwell. The courts adjourned on August 10, 1700.[28] William returned to Mount Hope, probably in the company of his neighbor James Craft, who had been serving on the jury.

The Burlington Quarterly Meeting of Friends was held at ten o'clock on the morning of August 26, 1700 at Mount Hope. At the Men's Meeting a "declaration of trust," (a bond) for £23.3s.3d. from Abraham Bickley and Isaac Marriott was presented to the Meeting. This was the bond they had been waiting for concerning the money owed to them by the needy Friend. Now that the Meeting had a significant endowed income, it decided to initiate a yearly contribution of £17 to the Yearly Meeting of Friends. William Biddle, Samuel Jennings, Robert Wilson, Francis Davenport, Peter Fretwell, John Day and Thomas Eves were appointed to attend the upcoming Yearly Meeting as their representatives.[29] In the next room, the

Women's Meeting appointed Sarah Biddle, Hannah (Cooper) Woolston, Frances Antrum and Sarah Bunting to attend the Yearly Meeting.[30]

For the first time in its history the Council of Proprietors of West New Jersey scheduled a meeting at Gloucester. The purpose was to let the members of the council examine the documents that were being kept in that county for the proprietors.[31] Early on the morning of September 3, 1700, Samuel Jennings, William Biddle and Governor Andrew Hamilton were taken down river by ferryman Seth Hill and his Negro, Mingo, to Gloucester where they met with John Reading, Thomas Thackera and John Kay to complete the inspection. Following the meeting and a midday meal, they traveled with the tide back to Burlington, stopping briefly at Pyne Point to discuss issues regarding the islands of the Delaware with William Cooper and his son Joseph.

Yearly Meeting for Worship and Business was held in Burlington from Saturday, September 14, through Wednesday, September 18, 1700. For William and Sarah this was an enjoyable time. Their daughter, Sarah Righton, was able to be with them on the religious visit to Burlington. Also accompanying them were their son, William Jr. and their daughter-in-law, Lydia, who now lived with them, in another house on the homestead at Mount Hope in Mansfield, and their four children: William 3rd, Elizabeth, Sarah and newborn Penelope. Sarah Biddle and Sarah Righton with Lydia's mother, Lydia Wardell, enjoyed helping the busy mother care for and proudly introduce their growing family to their West New Jersey and Pennsylvania friends.

As usual there were in excess of two thousand Quakers gathered for this Yearly Meeting. Friends came from New England and from as far south as Carolina. William and the other delegates from Burlington County met in the business meetings with men from other areas, including Thomas Sharp and John Adams from Gloucester County, Remembrance Lippincott from Shrewsbury, East New Jersey, and Edward Shippen, Griffith Owen, John Bevan, Samuel Carpenter, Nicholas Waln and Hugh Roberts from Pennsylvania.[32] William Penn was within six miles of Burlington, but he was indisposed with a swollen leg and a serious cold, so probably did not attend the meetings.

A special session of the Court of Pleas was held September 19 and 20, 1700 to consider several cases that had required more study by the court and jury than could be allowed by the August court. William, with Mahlon Stacy, Francis Davenport and John Adams served on the bench. The court had to consider a foreclosure on a mortgage and determine the ownership of the property and its value. Attorneys guided them through the legal aspects of the case so that they could reach a fair decision.[33] William and his fellow jurists took their responsibilities very seriously.

While the court proceedings were in recess, William, with fellow Justice Mahlon Stacy, acknowledged an indenture of Francis Collins.[34] Since the court sessions were lengthy, they may have stayed overnight in Burlington so that they could start court the following day early enough to complete the docket. The sessions ended with a court-ordered sale of the 1,000 acre Langford plantation on the west side of the Northampton River, to satisfy a debt owed by deceased merchants Ebenezer and John Langford to Edward Hunloke. The last two cases were dismissed, for neither the plaintiffs or defendants appeared in court. In one of these cases widow Elizabeth Tatham, executrix of the estate of the deceased John Tatham, had brought suit against Jeremiah Basse, who was absent in England [35]

William returned home to Mount Hope for the rest of the harvest season. He was able to assist his son, William Jr., as he directed work on the farmland at the end of the growing season and prepared his land for the oncoming winter months. Grains had to be harvested and prepared for shipping overseas by the merchant Thomas Masters. The cultivated lands were sown with winter grasses. The apples from the orchard were stored, and the potatoes dug and stored in the root cellar. The livestock was inventoried and decisions were made about which animals to slaughter for food for the homestead for the winter. William Biddle, with his son and grandson, were able to enjoy several outings on their property to hunt small game, deer and ducks and geese on the river. Indoweys would now be able to show the youngest William Biddle the efficient hunting methods of the Indians. During this quiet time, William and his son were able to travel to the area above the falls of the Delaware River to examine the lands in that location more closely. They knew that these were the next lands that would be sought by those with proprietary rights.

The fall Fair Days at Burlington was held on Friday and Saturday, November 1 and 2, 1700. The justices were not able to begin the work of the court immediately, for William and the other Quakers had to return home for First Day Worship on Sunday November 3, 1700. When the Quarter Court and Court of Pleas opened on Monday, William was on the bench with Governor Andrew Hamilton, Mahlon Stacy, Francis Davenport, John Adams and Samuel Furnis, now Burgess of Burlington. They were joined by Justice John Wills on the second day. The court approved the license of widow Hancock to keep a victual house. William Cooper from Pyne Point appeared on behalf of his daughter, widow Hannah Woolston, to apply for a seven-year indenture for a young boy, Robert Gannington, who would work for Hannah.

A prisoner, an East New Jersey resident, was presented to the court for disturbing the peace by falsely stating that Governor Hamilton had fled the provinces. He had been unwise enough to make the inflammatory statements in the ordinary (tavern) of George Willis and several who were present testified. He chose to be tried by a jury, which found him guilty, fined him £100 and imprisoned him until he could pay the fine. The justice was swift, but with the help of some West New Jersey residents, the prisoner escaped that day. The person who helped him was arrested and released on an extremely large bail bond of £400 provided by John Hollinshead and Nathaniel Cripps.[36]

The court, in another matter, appointed Thomas Wetherill and Joseph White, coopers, as packers for the county. James Wills, who had been Packer to that time, had become suddenly senile or insane. His son John Wills approved the will that Thomas Gardiner had prepared for his impaired father for the court.[37]

The Court of Pleas was held in Henry Grubb's Inn instead of the courthouse. Perhaps the weather had turned colder that day making the public facility unusable. The matters brought before the court were routine. In one case Thomas Revell acted as an attorney.[38]

William probably stayed at the inn overnight, for he had to attend to the remaining business of the Quarter Court at eight o'clock the next morning. While in town on November 5, 1700, he completed the sale of 100 acres to Mathew Forsyth, yeoman, for £8.[39] The Council of Proprietors may have met informally that day, as they usually convened before or after the court sessions. It was probably while he was in Burlington that day that Samuel Jennings prepared a warrant for 1,500 acres for William Biddle against his existing proprietary rights.[40]

When the Quaker leaders met for the Burlington Quarterly Meeting at Mount Hope on November 25, 1700, there was little to report. Both the Men's and Women's Meetings were mainly social and spiritual gatherings that day.[41]

William and his son had to travel to Burlington in the cold winter days of February 20 through 22, 1700/01 for Burlington Court. William Jr. served on the jury of the Court of Common Pleas. Governor Hamilton was present with the usual Quaker justices. This year, due to the new tax act, they had also received warrants to elect assessors and tax collectors, in addition to other township appointments. Most of the townships had refused to elect these new officials and the tax revolt was becoming more formal.[42]

In another matter, William Biddle was asked to select twelve men who would determine the course of a road to be laid out to the mill in Mansfield as requested by Jacob Decou and John Brown of Mansfield. Also in court, John Ogborn Jr. again asked the court to award him the damages due to him from a judgment awarded against John Hollinshead Sr. by the Basse Court. The court had found that John Hollinshead had falsely arrested John Ogborn while he was Constable and Burgess of Burlington. This Quaker court found that the plaintiff, Ogborn, was proceeding in court illegally and it was judged that he needed a *scire fascia* to continue. They ruled also that the executors of the deceased John Hollinshead were not liable for that matter, as it was an act performed while Hollinshead was carrying out the duties of his office. They ruled that any accountability owed had died with him and ordered that Ogborn make no more demands of them on that matter.[43] Within a year of regaining the court bench, the Quaker justices felt that they, with their Governor, were powerful enough to reverse some of the actions of the non-Quaker courts that had served under Jeremiah Basse.

Court was adjourned before night fall on Saturday, February 22, 1700/01 and William and William Jr. returned to Mount Hope to enjoy their families. First Day Meeting for Worship was the next day, and the Burlington Quarterly Meeting gathered at ten o'clock in the morning of the following day. At the latter meeting it was recognized by those attending that the work of Joseph Smith as a scrivener (writer) was of great value to them. They agreed to have Francis Davenport pay Joseph Smith twelve shillings for copying a number of epistles into their meeting book.[44]

The Quarter Court had been adjourned to a special court held March 3, 1700/01 in Burlington. William attended and was joined on the bench by John Adams, John Wills and Francis Davenport. They decided that they would no longer allow the individual seals of the justices to be used for matters concerning the court. The Privy Seal would be used until a seal for the county was obtained. The justices went on to sign warrants to the constables of several townships ordering them to see to the collecting of the provincial and county taxes. Governor Hamilton entered the court after it had commenced and he sent for Justice Robert Wheeler, requesting that Wheeler join the other justices in signing the warrants. Wheeler did not agree with the taxes, so he refused, and Governor Hamilton, with the advice of the court, discharged him from his office as a Justice.[45]

One week later, on March 10, 1700/01, the Council of Proprietors of West New Jersey met at Burlington with Governor Hamilton presiding.

William Biddle was present with Samuel Jennings, John Wills, John Kay and Thomas Gardiner. The council decided to have Governor Hamilton ask Governor William Penn to meet with them to discuss concerns about Salem County and other areas in the province. The council also heard from Governor Hamilton that the West Jersey Society would like to take up more lands. They all agreed that there would be another purchase from the Indians and that any of the resident proprietors who desired could join them in the Indian purchase. They were to publish their intention so that all proprietors, resident and non-resident, would be aware of it.[46]

On March 18, 1700/01 some residents of West New Jersey, acting as a mob, broke into the county jail to free two men who had been imprisoned for trying to enflame the citizenry.[47] Anger had been aroused in the province, first by the new taxes and now also by sentiment against the governing authority, Governor Hamilton in particular. Some in the mob were from East New Jersey, where feelings were even stronger. Many people felt that the Governor did not have the authority to raise taxes or even to be their Governor. No one was injured in the break-in, for the pacifist behavior of the Quakers still predominated in the province.

It is noteworthy that when the town meeting was held in Burlington on April 3, 1701 to elect town officers, the elected officers were all non-Quakers. Robert Wheeler was elected as Burgess, Thomas Revell, Nathaniel Westland and Joseph Adams as Councilmen, Thomas Revell as Treasurer and John Ogborn as Recorder and Clerk.[48] The Quaker majority in Burlington had lost control of the town government, probably because in their desire to avoid confronting the civil tension, they chose to offer no candidates for the election and not to vote in the election.

The Council of Proprietors of West New Jersey met again on April 8, 1701 with Governor Andrew Hamilton again presiding. William Biddle, Samuel Jennings, Thomas Gardiner, Francis Davenport and Thomas Thackera were present. Samuel Carpenter visited the council to present the proprietary rights of William Welsh to one and one-half shares of propriety in the West New Jersey Province. Samuel Jennings was asked to inspect the records and to report to the council at its next meeting.[49]

They met again in Burlington two weeks later, on April 21, 1701. They had already reelected their members for the year and Francis Collins had joined the council as a new member. Governor Hamilton continued to preside and Thomas Gardiner continued as substitute Clerk for John Reading at this organizational meeting.[50]

The council did not complete any new business at that session, but they did authorize their commissioners to continue accepting surveys and to issue warrants for unappropriated land. On April 29, 1701, William returned to Burlington to have two surveys recorded for his use in the survey book of the council by the Surveyor General, Thomas Gardiner. Both surveys were lands that he had claimed in Amwell. One was for 1,500 acres and the other was for 240 acres.[51] Many of the other proprietors were also beginning to claim lands in that area by survey.

On May 8, 1701, the Burlington Court met as scheduled. Edward Hunloke and Peter Fretwell sat on the bench with John Wills to constitute the three justices required by the Concessions and Agreements. Thomas Gardiner served as Clerk of the Court.[52]

Governor Hamilton had been spending more time in Burlington than in past years. He undoubtedly worked closely with and listened carefully to the advice of his Council on those days just prior to the General Assembly meetings. The council consisted of William Biddle, Edward Hunloke, Thomas Gardiner, George Deacon, John Thompson, Jonathan Beere and Andrew Robeson Jr.[53]

The General Assembly met from May 12 through 21, 1701. William Biddle remained as a quorum justice for the county. Peter Fretwell remained as Treasurer of the Province and Samuel Jennings continued as Speaker of the House.[54]

On the first day of the General Assembly meetings the two political factions of the province began to express their disagreements with each other more boldly. The non-Quakers in the West New Jersey Province had elected their own slate of representatives to the General Assembly but these men were refused admission to the legislative meetings as true representatives. Eighteen of the Quaker assemblymen, headed by the Speaker of the House, Samuel Jennings, joined by the Governor's Council, which included William Biddle, drafted a letter to William III, King of England. In the letter they pointed out that Joshua Barkstead, half-brother of Jeremiah Basse, had tried to incite the people of the province against Governor Hamilton and themselves. They explained the riot that had occurred when the jail was broken into by dissenters. They asked once more for approbation for their Governor, Andrew Hamilton, so that they could stabilize the government of the province. The letter was dated May 12, 1701, but it was not recorded as an official act of the meetings that day.[55]

Having learned of this letter, the non-Quakers responded. Four days later, on May 16, 1701, non-Quakers Thomas Revell, Nathaniel Westland, William Budd, John Jewell, Robert Wheeler, Anthony Elton, Richard Fenimore, John Rudderow and Joseph Adams, among others, wrote another letter to the King of England. In their letter they described the Quakers as anything but pacifists and they expressed support for the previous Governor, Jeremiah Basse. They described the extreme burden that they thought the recent tax had put onto the residents of the province. They asked the King to take over control of the province.[56]

After organizing themselves and electing the officers of the General Assembly, the first business of the Assembly was to pass an act to increase the number of Assemblymen elected yearly. This Assembly was still reduced in size by the law it had passed in 1699. Now they wished to be a more representative body again with the goal of electing more Quaker Assemblymen, for Quakers were still in the majority throughout the province if not in the town. It was decided that Burlington and Gloucester Counties should have twenty representatives, Salem County ten, and Cape May County five.[57]

The remaining business of the General Assembly concerned taxation. First, the legislators explained the need for the tax. Then they appointed tax assessors and collectors for each township, and set the dates and means by which taxes were to be determined and collected and turned over to the provincial treasurer. They set penalties for non-payment of taxes. They gave the power to replace assessors and collectors and to set times of collection to the Governor with two members of his Council. They also allowed an interest rate of ten percent on money owed to any individual if tax collections were not sufficient to pay their bills by the prescribed date of October 20, 1701. The Hamilton-Quaker coalition hoped that having all of the details of taxation clearly defined would help to quell the unrest in the province.[58]

On May 26, 1701, William was unable to attend the Burlington Court because he and Sarah were scheduled to host the Burlington Quarterly Meeting that day. It is interesting to note that William's responsibilities to his Quaker faith were carefully balanced with those of provincial governing. The meeting discussion was completely dominated by the concern that that some of the younger Quakers may have participated in the riot at the jail in March. Each of the Monthly Meetings was instructed to deal with any of their members who might have been involved.[59] Probably all the members present at the meeting knew that several young Quakers really had taken part in the incident. At the Burlington Court that day all of those believed to have caused the disturbance of the peace were named and charged with the crime.[60]

William did not have to attend to public business again that summer until August 8, 1701 when he joined some of the other justices on the bench of the Burlington Court. As requested earlier, William submitted a report made to him on March 4, 1700/1 by twelve men of Mansfield recommending the route for a road to the mill in Mansfield. The rest of the court business concerned mostly domestic matters, or suits to collect debts. William Biddle Jr. served on the jury of the Court of Pleas. The court sessions carried over to August 9, 1701.[61]

Later that month, on August 25, 1701, the Burlington Quarterly Meeting of Friends was held at Mount Hope. William was again selected to be one of their representatives to the upcoming Yearly Meeting. If the subject of Friends involved in the break- in at the prison was discussed, it was not recorded that day.[62]

In England the East and West New Jersey proprietors had been negotiating a surrender of governing rights of the territories to the Crown. A condition was that the property or land rights would be retained by those who owned the proprietary rights. By that time William Penn had been informed that the continuation of his own proprietary rights to the land of Pennsylvania was being questioned by the Board of Trade. He planned to return to England soon to protect his own interests.

On September 24, 1701 William and Sarah went to Philadelphia for the Yearly Meeting for Business and Worship. They had the pleasure of visiting their daughter and staying with her in her city home. The meetings were well attended. Most of the Quakers knew by then that this meeting might be the last one that William Penn would attend with them because of his impending travel back to England. In the company of such Quaker leaders as Samuel Carpenter, Edward Shippen and Joseph Kirkbride, William was able to learn much more about the status of the proprietary governments in America.[63]

At Yearly Meeting, William Biddle would hear more about how William Penn intended to maintain his position as Chief Proprietor of Pennsylvania. William Biddle knew that the political and economic stability in Pennsylvania was more certain than it was in West New Jersey because of William Penn's political strength. The West New Jersey residents had no comparable benefactor unless William Penn would help them too. He did, after all, own twelve percent of the West New Jersey proprietary rights. However, it was obvious to all who witnessed his concern about the affairs in England that he would need to direct his energy first and foremost towards the defense of his Pennsylvania proprietary rights.

Burlington Quarter Court and Court of Pleas was held on November 3 and 4, 1701. William attended with fellow justices Francis Davenport, Samuel Furnis, John Adams and John Wills. The justices found out officially what they already knew had happened with the latest tax collections. The deadline for collection had been October 20, 1701 but by November 3, 1701 almost all of the Assessors and Collectors had failed to collect the taxes due.[64]

The debt of the province was growing and there were not enough funds to support it. The efforts of the "democratic" General Assembly had failed. It was not simply that residents were unwilling to pay a just tax. The main issue was that no one was sure who actually had the right to govern and to impose taxation, and citizens of the province were reluctant to pay their money into an uncertified treasury in an uncertain political climate.

William also knew by then that on October 27, 1701 Andrew Hamilton had been chosen as deputy governor of Pennsylvania by William Penn, a post that was in addition to his West New Jersey office. He would receive a stipend of £200 for the new position.[65] Penn had just left for England to attempt to get an approbation for Hamilton, at least for the Pennsylvania position. Since it was very likely that Andrew Hamilton would not be continued as Governor of the East and West New Jersey Provinces, it was unlikely that he would be willing to take any strong actions against the West New Jersey residents who were ignoring the laws of the General Assembly.

William returned to Burlington on Saturday, November 15, 1701 and spent the morning at court in Henry Grubb's inn with fellow justice Thomas Gardiner. The justices acknowledged an indenture of Benjamin Field.[66]

The Burlington Quarterly Meeting of Friends was held on November 24, 1701 at Mount Hope, but there was no business recorded in the minutes.[67] Undoubtedly the Quaker leaders were concerned about the total disarray of the government and the economics of their province. It would be difficult, if not impossible, to continue the Quaker experiment in democracy in West New Jersey. Their worship and discussions afterwards that day would have focused on the challenges ahead.

The next day William headed to Burlington for two days of meetings. On November 25, 1701, a session of the Court of Pleas was held, having been adjourned from the court of November 4, 1701. Samuel Furnis, John Wills and Thomas Gardiner joined William on the bench. During this session, ferryman Seth Hill used "abusive" language against some of the Magistrates and the court. He refused to find security or bail bonding for his behavior, so the sheriff, Isaac Marriott, imprisoned him by order of the court.[68]

On November 26, 1701 Governor Andrew Hamilton presided over the meeting of the Council of Proprietors of West New Jersey. William was present with Francis Collins, Samuel Jennings, Francis Davenport, John Wills and Thomas Gardiner. The only business recorded was the receipt of fifteen shillings from Ranger Thomas Hooton due to the council for a stray horse that he had captured on the proprietors' land and sold in Evesham Township.[69]

At that meeting Governor Hamilton told the proprietor councilmen what he knew of affairs in England and Pennsylvania. Most of the details of the proposed surrender of the governments of the New Jersey Provinces to the Crown had been known. The plan was to join the two provinces under one government. The rights to the land were to remain in the hands of the proprietors. Also, the exclusive right of the proprietors to purchase lands from the Indians was to be preserved.

Thomas Gardiner and William Biddle acknowledged an indenture for Samuel Jennings while they were there that day,[70] thus saving William another trip to town.

William returned to Mount Hope for the night, but he and Sarah packed to go to Philadelphia the next day. Thomas Biddle was available, so he could take them in his ferry to the city. Their son-in-law, William Righton, had returned to Philadelphia in his ship, the *Hopewell*. The parents probably thought that this would be a good time to visit their daughter and her family. But unfortunately William Righton found himself in court during their visit over matters concerning his ship. Apparently rats had eaten his registration papers and certificate of clearance document from Jamaica. He was made to post bond by the Court of Pleas of Philadelphia of £1,000 until he could secure the proper documents on a return trip to Jamaica.[71]

Also during this trip to Philadelphia in November 1701, William and Sarah purchased a lot and home in the city from Thomas Masters, brother-in-law of William Righton. In 1693 Masters had bought a lot from John Duplovys, who had purchased the land from Nathaniel Allen.[72] Thomas Masters had built houses on the lot and William and Sarah had decided to buy part of the lot which contained a newly-constructed house for £330. The lot was twenty feet wide on Front Street and between the lot of William Sharlow on the south and Jacob Collins on the north. It ran westward two hundred and twenty-two feet to the remainder of the Thomas Masters lot. William would owe a quitrent yearly to Jacob Collins who now owned the remainder of Duplovys' lot and interests.[73] With this purchase William and Sarah had assured themselves that they could move to a safe home in Philadelphia if events in the West New Jersey Province failed to improve.

It was shortly after that visit, sometime after February 5, 1701/2, that William and Sarah learned that their son-in-law, William Righton, had died while on business in Jamaica. Thomas Biddle had been with him and was one of those who witnessed his will. William left a house in Philadelphia with three slaves (Phylis, Hagar and Joan) and his interest in his ship, *Hopewell*, to his wife Sarah and made smaller bequests to his sisters who were the wives of Thomas Masters, Randall Janney and George Claypoole. He appointed Thomas Masters as executor, along with his wife Sarah, executrix.

Thus, Sarah Righton, at age twenty-three, was a widow. The couple had no children.[74]

It was quite cold that February and the river was frozen over, so William and William Jr. had to travel by horseback from Mount Hope to Burlington. Burlington Court was held February 20 and 21, 1701/2. William joined his fellow justices Mahlon Stacy, John Adams, John Wills, Thomas Gardiner, Samuel Furniss and Richard Ridgway on the bench. William Jr. served on the Grand Jury again. Several domestic cases took up much of the court's time. A person found guilty of stealing was sentenced only to four-fold restitution, not to the whipping prescribed by law. Another confessed adulterer was fined instead of whipped. The justices and the juries were in a benevolent mood. Seth Hill, however, received a large fine—£40 and imprisonment—for abuses to the court and to the magistrates.[75]

On Monday February 23, 1701/2, the members of the Burlington Quarterly Meeting of Friends gathered at Mount Hope. Probably because of the social and political unrest in the area more men than usual attended and the parlor of the Mount Hope home must have been crowded. Burlington Monthly Meeting had sent Thomas Raper, Christopher Wetherill, Francis Collins, John Wills, Joshua Humphreys, John Butcher and Richard Ridgeway as official representatives. Others included Samuel Jennings, Isaac Marriott, John Scott, Abraham Bickley, Thomas Gardiner John Shinn, Samuel Bunting, Francis Davenport, John Day and Mahlon Stacy were also there. The Women's Meeting was less crowded. Sarah was joined by Mary Smith and Lydia Horner from Burlington and Sarah Farnsworth and Mary Bunting from the Chesterfield meeting.[76]

It was noted that Abraham Bickley would be leaving the province. His wife, Elizabeth (Gardiner) Bickley, had died and he was moving to Philadelphia to remarry.[77] A new bond was drawn up to cover the debt of the needy Friend that Bickley had been holding and it was assigned to Isaac Marriott and Thomas Raper.[78]

The real worry of the leaders of the Friends was the increase in verbal abuse they were receiving. The minutes of the meeting reveal their level of concern:

> … report being made to this meeting that several persons in this province have abused Friends in their petition directed to the King as also in their petition directed to the Society of proprietors residing in England, therefore the meeting agrees to refer to Samuel Jennings, Mahlon Stacy, Francis Davenport, William Biddle, Thomas Gardiner, John Wills, John Shinn, John Day, Samuel Bunting and John Scott.[79]

Friends who were old enough to remember the days of religious persecution in England could sense the similarity in this situation. They cautioned and advised the younger members to begin action now to prevent this abuse from going any further.

Perhaps there was some relief from the concerns and worries of the Quaker leaders when the elections were held for town officers in Burlington on April 2, 1702. The previous year the non-Quakers had won all of the positions. This year almost all Quakers were elected, including Thomas Gardiner as Burgess, Peter Fretwell as Recorder and Clerk, Thomas Raper as Treasurer, Benjamin Wheat and Samuel Furnis and Edward Hunloke, a non-Quaker, as Councilmen.[80]

In London on April 15, 1702, the inevitable happened. The governments of both New Jersey Provinces were surrendered to the crown by the East and West New Jersey Proprietors in England, including the West Jersey Society. William III had died, pre-deceased by Queen Mary. His sister-in-law, Queen Anne, who succeeded them on the throne, accepted the surrender of the governments on the terms of those who had negotiated the surrenders during the rule of William III.[81]

For the resident proprietors and the Quakers of West New Jersey this was no surprise. They had been kept informed of the progress toward change by the communication network available to them through the Quaker merchants. Two old friends of William and Sarah, Clement Plumstead and Dr. James Wasse, were directly involved with the decisions in London. Now the West New Jersey Quaker leaders would have to learn to work with yet another governing authority, the English Crown. The Quaker residents of the West New Jersey Province had to hope, that despite the loss of their political, legislative and judicial powers, the ideals and patterns that they had established while living under the Quaker Concessions and Agreements would be continued and respected. Those Quaker leaders who served on the Council of Proprietors of West New Jersey quietly took possession of all of their records. These documents included the Concessions and Agreements of West New Jersey, the Tripartite Agreement, the Quintipartite Agreement and all indentures and writings relating to their settling the lands of the territory over the previous twenty-five years. These documents along with their records of land distribution were carefully protected and put safely away. They are still all intact and in November 2005 they were loaned to the New Jersey State Archival Library for further safekeeping and preservation.

As was usual when the governance of the West New Jersey Province changed, especially from such a great distance, there was some delay before the new officials would actually assume office. For more than one year the Quaker justices were able to continue most of their public duties, their institutions and governing. The residents of the province in this waiting period went on with their lives as before. Governor Hamilton had begun his duty as deputy governor of Pennsylvania, but he also continued as Acting Governor of the New Jersey Provinces. Efforts by William Penn to obtain an approbation for Hamilton's Pennsylvania position from the crown continued, and others in London were still working on his behalf.

William did not attend the session of the Burlington Quarter Court and Court of Pleas that was held on May 8, 1702, but that court was attended by all the other Quaker justices. The usual business continued on schedule.[82] May twelfth would have been the usual time for the General Assembly Meeting, but no meeting was held.

The Annual Meeting of the Council of Proprietors of West New Jersey was held in Burlington on May 14, 1702. William did not continue as a council member for the ensuing year. In the absence of Governor Hamilton, Mahlon Stacy was elected as president of the council. Isaac Sharp was a new member from Gloucester County, and William Wood and William Budd were new members from Burlington County. The council considered a charge that John Hutchinson and his father, Thomas Hutchinson, had claimed more land than they were entitled to. John was requested to bring all relevant documents to the next meeting of the council. The council also ordered that Thomas Gardiner, Thomas Foulke Jr., Thomas Lambert, William Emley and William Biddle Jr. "shall with all conveniency" go to the Indians and inspect the land up-river near the falls and try to settle terms and conditions for the purchase of the land for the third dividend.[83]

Despite the surrender of the government rights, the resident proprietors believed that their proprietary land rights and their right to purchases land from the Indians were secure. The council decided to continue their plans to exercise these rights. William Jr. reported the topics of the meeting to his father that night when he returned to Mount Hope, for he had to take the warrant for 100 acres to him that William had requested from the council.[84]

Friends gathered at Mount Hope on May 25, 1702 for Burlington Quarterly Meeting of Friends. The committee appointed to study the situation concerning abuses to local Friends had recommended that all abuses or sufferings be recorded, as had been done in England during the days of religious persecution. The recorded sufferings would be sent to William Penn in England.[85]

On August 8, 1702 court was held in Burlington. Apparently Governor Hamilton had received permission to continue at least temporarily in his position, for he commissioned the justices and other officers of the county. William Biddle, with Francis Davenport, John Wills, John Adams, Samuel Furnis and Richard Ridgway were commissioned as justices. Thomas Raper was commissioned Sheriff and he made his brother-in-law, Henry Grubb, his Deputy Sheriff. Hugh Huddy, son-in-law of the deceased Edward Hunloke, was commissioned as Clerk. The juries were called, but no business was recorded as completed.[86]

Among the members of the Grand Jury called was Eliakim Wardell. The parents of Lydia (Wardell) Biddle had moved from Shrewsbury to Burlington. Another daughter and her husband William Welch, butcher and waterman, had purchased the home and wharf of John Hollinshead on Pearl Street.[87] Eliakim Wardell and his wife had purchased the nine-acre lot, house and out-buildings of Nathaniel Douglas situated on the waterfront at the western edge of the town.[88] The Biddle family was increasing in size in Burlington, West New Jersey.

On August 30, 1702 the Men's Burlington Quarterly Meeting at Mount Hope continued to discuss the abuses to Friends. William was chosen with Francis Davenport, Robert Wilson, Peter Fretwell, Thomas Eves and John Shinn to be representatives at Yearly Meeting held September 23, 1702 in Burlington.[91] Sarah welcomed the Women's Quarterly Meeting. Among the attendees were Elizabeth Fretwell and Frances Antram from the Burlington Monthly Meeting.[89]

On September 2, 1702, William went to Burlington where he visited with Samuel Jennings. He requested and received another warrant for 100 acres of unappropriated land from Jennings, who had continued as the Commissioner for Burlington County for the Council of Proprietors of West New Jersey.[90]

On September 23, 1702, Yearly Meeting was held in Burlington. As usual, Friends from all over the region attended. The sessions only lasted one day that year.[91]

The Burlington Court was reconvened on September 29, 1702. Francis Davenport and Thomas Gardiner joined William that day to make the prescribed three justices on the bench. Because of illness, too many people were missing for the juries to be completed, so the court was adjourned until two o'clock in the afternoon. When reconvened, John Wills had joined the bench. However there was still too much sickness in the province to have full juries, so the court was adjourned until November 3, 1702. The only business completed by the justices was their review of the notes of Edward Hunloke for the May 1702 court sessions. He had died before he had been able to transcribe them into the court record books. The justices corrected the notes and requested that the new clerk, Hugh Huddy, son-in-law of the deceased Edward Hunloke, transcribe them into the official record.[92]

The usual fall Fair Days were held on October 30 and 31, 1702. The social atmosphere of the town must have been somewhat strained that year, for Thomas Revell had surprised the residents of Burlington County by having George Keith as his guest for the weekend. On Sunday, November 1, 1702 Keith, with The Reverend John Talbot, preached in Burlington at the Town House, the public meeting hall, to the members of the Anglican Church, including Governor Andrew Hamilton. Keith had left Quakerism altogether and his sermon was strongly anti-Quaker.[93]

Two days later the Burlington Quarter Court and Court of Pleas were held. William was on the bench with fellow justices Thomas Gardiner, Samuel Furnis and Richard Ridgway; later they were joined by Justice Mahlon Stacy. William attested and charged the Grand Jury. The new clerk, Hugh Huddy, kept court minutes in much greater detail than his father-in-law had done. The attorney, Thomas Clark, was involved in more cases than ever before.[94]

On the fourth second day, Monday November 30, 1702, the Burlington Quarterly Meeting of Friends convened. In the Women's Meeting Sarah enjoyed the company of Mary Wheat and Mary Elkinton from the Burlington Monthly Meeting along with others who joined her from Chesterfield Monthly Meeting and from the area of the falls on the Delaware River. The Men's Meeting reviewed Henry Grubb's accounts of expenses of traveling Friends, expenses incurred chiefly to counter the efforts of George Keith. It was thought necessary to have traveling Friends speak at public meetings throughout the region to speak the truth about Quakerism as Keith often misrepresented their beliefs.[95]

By late fall, Queen Anne had chosen a Governor for the East and West New Jersey Provinces. She prepared instructions on November 16, 1702 and sent a commission on December 5, 1702 to her cousin, Edward Hyde, Lord Cornbury who was to serve as the new Governor of New Jersey. Andrew Hamilton would be relieved of his responsibilities in the colony.[96]

During January 1702/3, George Keith visited Thomas Revell again and delivered another sermon in Burlington. He had introduced Reverend John Talbot to the town, and by the spring of the year the Anglicans would begin construction of their own church building there to be called St. Mary's.[97]

William returned to Burlington to sit on the court bench on February 20, 1702/3. He was joined by Francis Davenport, Samuel Furnis, John Adams and John Wills; later in the day Richard Ridgway joined them. During the midday recess William, with Francis Davenport and Samuel Furnis, acknowledged an indenture of Jacob Ong to Abraham Brown.[98] In the court proceedings most of the business was routine. A license to keep a victual house was issued to John Moore. A thief was required to make four-fold restitution for her crime, and when she proved unable to pay, the court ordered her to be sold into servitude for as long as it took to pay off her debt.[99] Overall the court proceedings were far more formal and lengthy, or at least they appeared so by the manner in which they were recorded.

By now William had served on the Provincial and then the Burlington Court for twenty-one years. His attendance record and length of service were greater than any of his peers. From his vantage point on the bench, coupled with his other civic, proprietary and religious positions, he had observed and understood more about the West New Jersey province than any other resident of the territory. He was nearly 70 years of age, and perhaps he felt the winter chill a little more as he returned by horseback to Mount Hope that night to report the events of his day to Sarah.

Despite the cold weather, the Burlington Quarterly Meeting of Friends hosted by the Biddles was well attended when held at Mount Hope on February 22, 1702/3. Joining William Biddle were the members of the Burlington Monthly Meeting, including George Deacon, William Petty, Richard Smith, Joshua Humphries, John Woolman, John Shinn and John Brown. A letter from James Logan, William Penn's Secretary in Pennsylvania, to the Meeting was read and recorded. Apparently during some of their efforts to stop trespassing on the islands in the Delaware, an issue that had never been resolved with William Penn, Pennsylvania officials had been confronted by some New Jersey Friends with guns. The situation posed a new challenge for Quaker leaders.[100]

The Burlington Quarter Court and Court of Pleas met as scheduled in Burlington on May 8, 1703, but were immediately adjourned to August 8, 1703. Governor Andrew Hamilton had died a few weeks before. The justices present felt that the court should be adjourned and they did so with a prayer for the deceased former governor and his family.[101]

The Burlington Quarterly Meeting was held at Mount Hope at ten o'clock in the morning of May 31, 1703. The men's meeting decided to forgive the debt of the needy Friend of £23.3s.3d. that they had so carefully demanded from him. The involved family, it was felt, had suffered enough.[102] The gathered Quaker leaders knew that the new Governor would appear in the province soon. They hoped for the best.

The Council of Proprietors of West New Jersey continued their business. On June 17 and 18, 1703, they met at the falls of the Delaware River, presumably for some first hand study of the next Indian purchase being negotiated with the Indians. Mahlon Stacy presided at the meetings. He was accompanied by Thomas Gardiner, John Wills, George Deacon, Christopher Wetherill and John Reading.[103]

Apparently the site visit was satisfactory, for on June 25, 1703, an indenture was signed with the Indian sachems (chiefs) Nunham alias Squahikkon, Wammishanaman, Pokehantas Taulaman and Wawaleaseed. William Biddle Jr., Andrew Heath and Joseph Kirkbride signed for the proprietors.[104]

The Council of Proprietors of West New Jersey reconvened in Burlington on June 27 and 28, 1703. Mahlon Stacy presided and the meeting was attended by councilmen Samuel Jennings, Thomas Gardiner, John Wills, Christopher Wetherill, George Deacon and John Reading. The council reviewed the agreements made with the Indians. There were two purchases of land above the falls of the Delaware River. One parcel was negotiated and settled with the Nimahammoe, consisting of land on both sides of the South Branch of the Rariton River, stretching from the Delaware River to the division line between East and West New Jersey. The other tract, between that purchased from the Nimahammoe and another previously purchased by Adlord Bowde, was still under negotiation and the final purchase agreement had not been signed.[105]

The council decided to publish a public notice about the Indian purchase and to invite all those proprietors who were interested in participating in the land dividend to join them in Burlington on July 19, 1703 to learn more.[106]

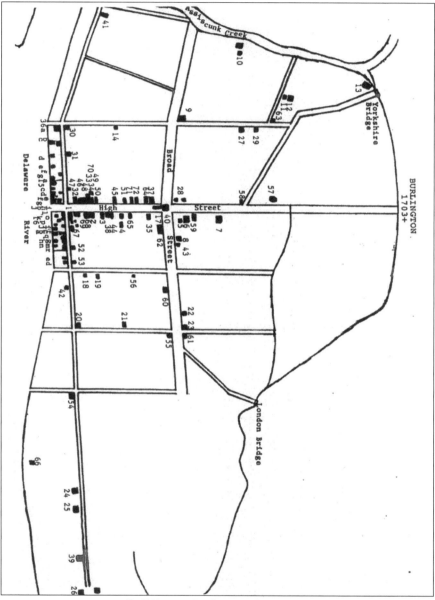

Buildings in Burlington City 1703+

1. Samuel Jennings' malt house, brew house, bolting house and stable
2. Samuel Gibson, baker's, townhouse and shop sold to Daniel Smith in 1705
3. Thomas Gardiner's house
4. James Wills' house and cooper shop
5. Edward Hunloke's heirs' log cabin
6. Edward Hunloke's heirs' townhouse
7. John Cripps' heirs' townhouse
8. Daniel Smith's townhouse and lot

9. Townhouse of mariner Robert Hopper
10. Samuel Jennings' house and barns
11. John Smith's house on Pudding Lane
12. Peter Fretwell's house bought from Robert Stacy
13. Peter Fretwell's tanhouse
14. Obediah Hierton's townhouse
15. a. House and lot of Seth Hill, ferryman
    b. Bear Tavern of George Willis
    c. Mathew Champion's and Percivale Towle's heirs' bakehouse
    d. Percivale Towle's heirs' townhouse
    e. Richard Francis's stable
    f. mariner Daniel England's house
    g. John Hollinshead's townhouse leased to Jeremiah Basse
    h. Isaac Marriott's house, kitchen and bakehouse
    i. Isaac Marriott's house
    j. Christopher Wetherhill's house bought from George Hutcheson
16. a. Henry Stacy's heirs' house
    b. Robert Wheeler's house
    c. Robert Wheeler's log cabin on Potters Alley
    d. Bernard Devonish's heirs' house
    e. Mary (Budd) (Gosling) Collins' house
    f. Samuel Lovett's house
    g. James White's house
    h. House and lot of John Meredith, schoolmaster
    i. Basnett's brickhouse leased by Coll. Daniel Coxe
    j. Samuel Jennings' New Brewhouse
    k. Hugh Huddy's house and shop 1704
    l. Henry Grubb's Inn
    m. West Jersey Society's house
    n. West Jersey Society's pottery
    o. William Bustill's house
    p. Hugh Huddy's warehouse
    q. Lydia and Eliakim Wardell's home
    r. Nathaniel Westland's house
17. Marketplace
18. Benjamin Wheate's lot with decaying William Brightwin's log cabin
19. Benjamin Wheate lot and cabin
20. Joshua Humphries's house
21. William Myers's house
22. Daniel Smith's house
23. Hollinshead - Eves townhouse
24. Thomas Potts' house in Ollive Town
25. Daniel England's lot and house
26. Nathaniel Duggles' pastures and barns
27. William Cooper's lot, cabin and blacksmith shop
28. Anna Salter's lot and log cabins
29. John Butcher's townhouse
30. Thomas Revell's townhouse
31. Daniel Sutton's house and tailorshop
32. James Marshall's heirs house
33. Isaac Decou's butcher shop
34. Isaac Decou's house
35. Friends Meetinghouse and burial ground
36. a. Joseph White's house
    b. Lawrence Morris's townhouse
    c. George Kendall's butcher shop and slaughterhouse
    d. Jane Rigg's house
    e. Lemuel Oldale's house
    f. Daniel Leeds' Keithian Meetinghouse
    g. Daniel Leeds' townhouse
37. Christopher Wetherill's house and tailorshop
38. Thomas Raper's house
39. House and lot of shipbuilder Peter Resnier
40. Courthouse
41. John Tatham's house and lot
42. James Satterthwaite's house
43. Daniel Smith's house
44. Thomas Gladwin's heirs' house and blacksmith shop
45. Samuel Furnis's house and saddle shop
46. Robert Wheeler's house
47. Isaac Decou's office
48. Robert Wheeler's store
49. Thomas Raper's house and whitesmith shop
50. Abraham Bickley's house
51. Josiah Prickett's house
52. Benjamin Wheate's house
53. Bernard Lane's house
54. James Verier's house
55. Robert Hudson's townhouse
56. Jonathan West's house
57. Brick kiln
58. Thomas Atkinson's house
59. John Ogborne's house
60. St. Mary's Church
61 Emmanuel Smith's house
62. Thomas Kendall's Inn (1707)

63. William Petty's house (1709)
64. Thomas and Phoebe Scattergood's
    house
65. Samuel Furnis's house
66. Benjamin and Experience Field's lot
    (burn't house lot)

67. Samuel Jennings' townhouse
68. Daniel Smith's house (1709)
69. Francis Smith's house (1709)
70. Emanuel Smith's house
71. Richard Smith's house
72. Joseph Smith's house

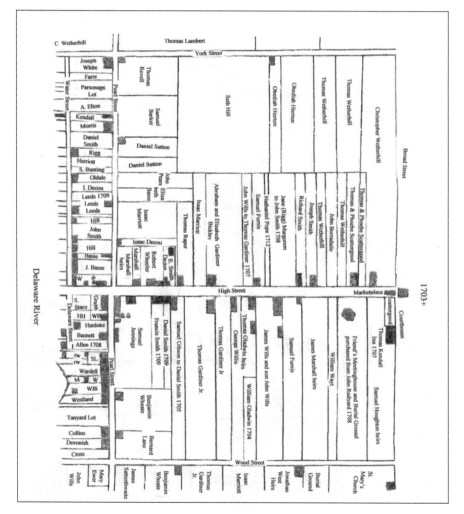

Center of Burlington City, 1703+

After an evening break on June 28, 1703, the council met again. They had written and reviewed the public notice and approved it for printing. Before they could adjourn they had to attend to another matter. The Indian sachem, Mahamickwon, "alias King Charles," had asked the council to consider changing the bounds of the Indian purchases above and below the Rancocas Creek made by the Englishmen in 1677. The deeds called for the lands from the headwaters of the Assinpink, Rancocas and Timber Creeks to be the boundary, but in fact both parties had agreed to a boundary further down stream than that described. Mahamickwon's request was granted.[107]

On July 19, 1703, a meeting of the resident proprietors of West New Jersey took place in Burlington. The Council of Proprietors met with them. It was announced that two Indian purchases were being made. There would be about 150,000 acres of land and the purchase price would be valued at about £700 to be paid to the Indians.[108]

The council announced their intention to inform the absent proprietors living in England and elsewhere of their plan and that there was an opportunity to purchase more land to make a dividend of 5,000 acres available for each propriety. As the agreements had been negotiated to that time, there would be 5,000 acres available for only thirty proprieties from this purchase. Each interested party would have to pay £24 per proprietary share, or whatever was proportional for the fraction of a share owned. Payment was to be made before July 20, 1704 and the council promised to deliver the warrants for the land sometime after October 1, 1704.[109]

The council emphasized that if the absent proprietors did not pay their part of the charge, then the Indian purchase would be divided out only to those resident proprietors who had paid the charges for their portions. In a separate notice the council further encouraged the resident proprietors to pay soon so that the promises to pay the Indians by certain times agreed to could be met. It was suggested that they should pay the first half in silver money to Thomas Gardiner in Burlington by August 1, 1703 and the other half by October 1, 1703.[110]

The council met again the next day, July 20, 1703, just long enough to write and post the letter to the proprietors in England. Then they adjourned, planning to meet again on August 9, 1703. By then, if the resident proprietors responded to their requests, they should have almost one-half of the purchase money in hand. Henry Grubb was asked to prepare a bill for them for the use of his inn.[111]

CHAPTER 23

The Royal Colony of New Jersey
Governor Cornbury August 14, 1703 – December 20, 1708

Governor Cornbury, already serving as Governor of New York, did not receive his formal instructions for his New Jersey governorship from Queen Anne until July 29, 1703, almost six months after they were issued.[1] He left New York on August 10, 1703 and arrived the next day at Perth Amboy, New Jersey where he was met by the East New Jersey Councilmen. He published his commissions there and with most of his East New Jersey commissioners he traveled to Burlington to begin his government in West New Jersey. On August 13, 1703 he called for the first meeting of the Governor's Council to be held on August 14th.[2]

Edmund Andros, many years before that time, had noted the non-militaristic nature of this western portion of the colony. Governor Cornbury made the same observation. He later wrote to the Board of Trade that there were no fortifications or military stores in West New Jersey. He also observed that there was no place for a governor to reside.[3]

In her instructions to Lord Cornbury, the Queen was explicit as to the type of government New Jersey should have and about the rights that the proprietors should retain. The proprietary rights of West New Jersey, of both the resident proprietors and the English proprietors, were to be honored, including their exclusive right to purchase lands from the Indians. The boundary line between the East and West New Jersey provinces was to remain as it had been decided by the proprietors. The Council of Proprietors of West New Jersey was to continue to have the right and authority to regulate land ownership and to lay out lands in their domain. All surveyors were to be appointed by the Council of Proprietors of West New Jersey in their territory. The Board of Proprietors of East New Jersey was to have the right to do the same in their part of New Jersey. No acts of the General Assembly were to lay taxes on lands that lay unprofitable.[4]

Queen Anne showed her understanding of the Quakers, directing that an alternate oath of office be developed by a specific act of the General Assembly, an oath that would allow the Quakers a solemn affirmation which would meet with their approval. This oath was to allow Quakers to hold public office and to participate in jury duty. She further directed that there would be liberty of conscience for all persons except "papists" (Catholics). Realizing that there were inadequate facilities for the practice of religion by members of the Church of England in New Jersey, she encouraged the building of churches for that religion in the colony.[5]

The Queen chose the initial Governor's Council and she reserved the right to approve all future changes in the council. She dictated that there would be complete freedom of debate in the Governor's Council and in the General Assembly.[6]

From West New Jersey those selected for the council were Quakers Samuel Jennings, Francis Davenport and George Deacon, balanced by non-Quakers Thomas Revell, Daniel Leeds and Edward Hunloke.[7] Apparently the fact that Edward Hunloke had died in June 1702 was not known to those who drew up the instructions for the Queen. West New Jersey would be one vote short on the council.

The councilmen from East New Jersey were Lewis Morris, Andrew Bowne, William Pinhorne, Samuel Leonard, Samuel Walker and William Sanford. Robert Quarry was also appointed a councilman, apparently to allow him to better carry out his duties as Judge of the Vice Admiralty Court of Pennsylvania which served the entire Delaware Valley. He would also benefit from this position when he succeeded Edward Randolph the following year as Surveyor General of Customs in America. He was the representative of the Crown in the region and after Governor Cornbury the most important person in New Jersey.[8]

After having been removed as "Acting" Governor of the East and West New Jersey Provinces in 1699, Jeremiah Basse returned to London to look after his own interests. Failing to get the position he wanted on the Governor's Council, he returned to Burlington and was appointed as Secretary of the Colony.[9]

The General Assembly was to continue as the elected house of the legislature. Its meetings were to alternate between Burlington in West New Jersey and Perth Amboy in East New Jersey. The assembly was to consist of twenty four members, one half from each of the former divisions of New Jersey. In West New Jersey two representatives were to be elected by the "inhabitant householders" (those who owned homes in Burlington and lived there) from the town of Burlington and ten by the freeholders (those who owned estates in the territory) of West New Jersey.[10]

The broad electorate that the West New Jersey residents had enjoyed was significantly diminished. To be qualified to vote, a freeholder now must have 100 acres of land, and to hold office it was necessary for a representative to have 1,000 acres.[11] Thus, the Queen's instructions for forming the new government continued the English system of controlling representative government by a wealthy minority. In West New Jersey land had been dispersed widely among the Quaker residents, so many of them were able to meet the voting requirements. Their proprietary years had prepared them to remain politically strong in the colony. Many of the Quaker proprietors would qualify for holding office by virtue of the recent distribution of unappropriated acres to those entitled to receive them. William had sold off many parcels of land recently, but he had retained 1,740 acres surveyed out to him in 1701 above the falls of the Delaware River.

The instructions from Queen Anne required the General Assembly to initiate all acts of taxation. It was to specifically set taxes that would create enough revenue to pay for the expenses of the colony, including the salaries of the governor, other administrative officers, councilmen and assembly-men. The ports of New Jersey would no longer be duty free. Customs points were to be established and import and export taxes comparable to those of New York were to be levied. All acts of the General Assembly and of the colony were to be forwarded to the Crown within three months of their passage, and must be approved by the Crown before becoming law for the colony. The governor was given the right to adjourn sessions of the General Assembly and the council whenever he saw fit. He could also dissolve the General Assembly and call for new elections as he saw fit.[12]

The instructions also directed fundamental changes in the judicial system. All justices were to be appointed by the Governor. No longer would there be any elected justices. An act was to be passed by the General Assembly to define the qualifications of jurors. The Governor was given the responsibility of licensing those services that might be in the public interest, such as printers, ferrymen, or apothecaries. The Governor was to keep an accounting of the people (census), including slaves. He was given the responsibility of forming a defense for the colony, including the right to declare martial law if necessary.[13]

The first meeting of the Governor's Council was held in Burlington on August 14, 1703. It was at that meeting that the new Governor took the oath of office for his commissions.[14] His primary concern was the establishment of law and order in the colony, and particularly establishing a militia in West New Jersey. The first commissions he issued were to William Fisher as Sheriff of Burlington and to John Spay as Sheriff of Gloucester. Alexander Griffith, Attorney General for New Jersey, took his oath of office at that session of the council.[15] The Governor saw to it that his councilmen received their oaths of office. The Quaker councilmen, Samuel Jennings, George Deacon and Francis Davenport, had to help the governor understand the alternate oath of the Quakers, that had been developed and allowed in England in the time of the reign of King William

III. In England, even though they had taken the alternate oath, the Quakers could not hold public office. In New Jersey Queen Anne had made an exception to that law, allowing the Quakers to hold public office provided they took the now-acceptable alternate oath. That day, August 14, 1703, this topic was debated before the Governor. He read and reread his instructions from the Queen, and discovered that Samuel Jennings and his fellow Quakers were quite correct. Those three Quaker members of the Governor's Council were allowed to take the oath appropriate for Quakers that day before Governor Cornbury and they were permitted to serve on the council.[16] Nonetheless, it is likely that non-Quaker officials of West New Jersey were still unable to accept the fact that Quakers were allowed to hold public office or public employment by English Law. Although the Governor allowed the Quaker councilmen to be seated by a Royal edict, he would in the future give non-Quaker public officials the opportunity to interpret the law as they saw fit with regard to other offices.

On August 16, 1703, Governor Cornbury commissioned Daniel Coxe Jr. as Colonel of the militia of Burlington, Gloucester, Salem and Cape May Counties.[17] Colonel Coxe had come into possession of a large part of his father's remaining real estate holdings in New Jersey.[18] He had leased the brick house of Elizabeth (Basnett) Gardiner and lived there when he visited Burlington.[19]. He went on to claim several more lots in the town.[20]. His first assignment, designated by the Governor, was to establish a militia in this territory that was still inhabited by a Quaker majority.

The next day Governor Cornbury commissioned Joshua Newbold as Captain of the militia of foot soldiers under Colonel Coxe in the counties of Burlington, Gloucester, Cape May and Salem.[21] He had chosen his military leaders before he had the permission of an act of the Assembly to do so.

The Governor held daily sessions with his Council from August 18 through 21, 1703. John Jewell for Burlington and John White for Perth Amboy were commissioned as Collectors of the Customs for those ports. The courts were defined. There was to be a Court of Conscience for all cases less than forty shillings, to meet monthly and to be attended by three justices and other officers to be appointed by the town or county. There were no juries or appeals from its decisions. The county courts were to continue as the Court of Pleas, sitting four times yearly and attended by the judge or the first assistant justice accompanied by four assistant justices. These Quarter Courts were not to refer any cases less than £10 to the Supreme Court, except those involving land titles. The Supreme Courts were to meet on the first Tuesday in May at Perth Amboy and the first Tuesday in November at Burlington.[22]

On Friday, August 20, 1703, the justices chosen by Governor Cornbury were commissioned. These included William Biddle, Francis Davenport, Daniel Leeds, George Deacon, Alexander Griffith, Nathaniel Westland, Robert Wheeler, Joshua Newbold, Ralph Hunt, Roger Parke, William Emley, William Wood, Michael Newbold, William Budd, Richard Ridgway, William Hewlings, Samuel Jennings, Thomas Revell and Jeremiah Basse. John Jewell was commissioned as the Clerk of the Burlington Court the same day.[23] Only seven Quakers were appointed to the bench, so now they were in the minority on the court in a county where they had a majority of the population and voting power. Cornbury did, however, commission Samuel Jennings as Judge of the Court of Common Pleas of Burlington,[24] and he gave the Quaker leader control of that most important court of the county.

Before adjourning the meetings of the Governor's Council at Burlington on August 20–21, 1703, the council ordered that all constables who had been serving in that position of authority on August 9, 1703 should continue in office "until further order." Constables were to be chosen at the Quarter Courts by the justices and they would be appointed in that manner at the next Quarter Court in each county. The sheriffs had been appointed for each county and they were ordered to immediately proclaim the Governor's commission in each county. In addition, they were to see to it that an election was held in each division of New Jersey to select representatives to the General Assembly.[25]

On Sunday, August 22, 1703, Burlington became a two-church town when St. Mary's (St. Anne's) Anglican Church on Broad Street, west of Wood Street, was dedicated.[26] The Reverend George Keith delivered the first sermon in the new church building.[27] The Governor and all but one of his council were present for the dedication service, and the service was well attended, for there were numerous members of the Church of England in the town and county now. The proprietary province that the Quakers had founded had always allowed religious freedom for all, but there had been no interest in building an Anglican church or formalizing the presence of that religion until it was actively requested by Queen Anne.

On Monday, August 23, 1703, before he left Burlington to return to Perth Amboy, Governor Cornbury designated Samuel Jennings and Thomas Revell to administer the oath of office to those he had commissioned.[28] It is not certain what happened in the courts after that time, for John Jewell, clerk of the court, did not record the minutes. The records of the court from September 1703 to December 1704 were kept in a separate bundle by Hugh Huddy, who replaced Jewell as clerk. Eventually

Huddy turned these records over to Governor Cornbury and they were lost.[29] The local officials, led by Thomas Revell, Daniel Leeds and Jeremiah Basse, interpreted English law as it was practiced in England. No Quakers using alternate oaths could serve in public office or places of public employment. Despite the orders from Queen Anne, there is no evidence that any of the Quaker justices, including Judge Samuel Jennings, although commissioned, ever received their oaths of office or were allowed to sit on the bench.[30]

The Quakers of West New Jersey had to have been shocked by events that accompanied the governorship of Lord Cornbury. The Province that they had so carefully founded and prepared as an example of a better society was being torn apart. They were now excluded from participation in the judicial system that they had built and run fairly. They no longer had a voice in the selection of those who were administrating law enforcement in their territory. They stood a good chance of being harassed by and taxed for a military system that was being forced upon them. They could anticipate that there would be many more ways in which the government would regulate their lives and try to control their future.

On August 30, 1703, the leaders of the Friends met at Mount Hope for the Burlington Quarterly Meeting of Friends. Undoubtedly the discussion concerned the new government of the colony and what it would mean for their lives and religion. Those chosen to attend Yearly Meeting were William Biddle, Francis Davenport, Robert Wilson, Peter Fretwell, Thomas Raper, John Day and John Wills.[31]

The Council of Proprietors of West New Jersey had planned to adjourn to August 9, 1703, the day that would usually have been the Burlington Quarter Court. With the takeover of the government by Governor Cornbury, the court did not meet and it is probable that the council did not meet either. They did meet on September 11, 1703, Mahlon Stacy presiding, with Councilmen Samuel Jennings, George Deacon, John Wills, Christopher Wetherill and Thomas Gardiner.[32] Although William was not a member of the council, he may have attended the meeting, for he was granted a warrant for 100 acres of unappropriated land.[33] Mahlon Stacy had reason to be pleased that day, for his grandson, Mahlon Kirkbride, had been born a few days earlier.

Two recorded matters were discussed by the council. Joseph Kirkbride, son-in-law of Mahlon Stacy, presented a problem with which he needed their assistance. He had come into ownership of 5,000 acres of land that had been surveyed by Andrew Robeson and John Barclay in an area along the South Branch of the Rariton River that had not been properly purchased from the Indians. Bonds had been drawn up using the land as collateral and therefore his title had to be perfected to make the bonding good. The matter was deferred by the council until they met again with more members present. In other business the council acknowledged that they needed more money in order to complete the second purchase agreement with the Indians. So far the resident proprietors had not brought in sufficient funds.[35] They ordered that "papers of publication be forth with put up to give ye note to ye proprietors to bring in their parts of ye said purchase money."

Yearly Meeting of the Religious Society of Friends was held in Philadelphia from September 22 through 28, 1703. William was pleased to see Caleb Pusey and John Blunston from Chester Monthly Meeting and Anthony Morris from Philadelphia Monthly Meeting, fellow Friends that he had not seen for several years.[36]

William and Sarah had the chance to visit with their daughter, widow Sarah Righton, for the entire week and to meet the many friends that she had made in Philadelphia. In particular she introduced them to one special young man, Clement Plumstead, who later would become her husband.

On October 27, 1703, William returned to Burlington with William Murfin to complete an indenture in which he sold 100 acres of unappropriated land rights to the young Murfin for £4. The indenture was witnessed by Thomas Biddle, Isaac Marriott and John Wills,[37] but it was not acknowledged before a justice as had been the policy before the Cornbury government took office. Now William Murfin could select his own farmland and he owned enough acreage to make him eligible to vote in the next election.

Elections for assemblymen were ordered at the meeting of the Governor and his Council of August 21, 1703. They were probably held in early November about the time of the usual fall Fair Days in Burlington. Governor Cornbury had called for a meeting of the General Assembly, so it was necessary to get the new electorate out to vote. Two members would be elected from the town of Burlington, but the rest of the assemblymen would be elected by those eligible to vote in the entire Western Division of New Jersey, thus giving the Quaker majority of Burlington County the advantage they needed. Assemblymen elected from West New Jersey included William Biddle, Peter Fretwell, Thomas Gardiner, Restore Lippincott, John Kay, John Hugge Jr., Joseph Cooper, Thomas Lambert, William Stevenson, William Hall, John Mason and John Smith.[38] Every one of them was a Quaker.

On November 2, 1703, the Council of Proprietors of West New Jersey met at Burlington with George Deacon presiding. Mahlon Stacy had experienced the joy of the birth of his grandson, Mahlon Kirkbride, in September, but there followed the pain and sorrow of the death of his daughter, Sarah Kirkbride, on September 29, 1703.[39] Mahlon's health apparently began to fail after that and he was not able to continue to serve on the council. George Deacon was elected president of the council in his place.[40]

The Council of Proprietors ordered that John Wills, William Biddle Jr. and John Reading, or at least two of them, go to the Indians above the falls to complete the land purchases. The lands being purchased from the Caponockous had to be marked and the deed for them had to be signed. The Indians were to receive partial payment now and the residual owed them would be paid in the spring. In addition, the members of the excursion were to go to the wigwam of the Nimhammoes to mark their lands and to pay part of the purchase price to them. It was suggested that they take Thomas Foulke, Andrew Heath, or some other qualified person, to interpret for them.[41]

On November 11, 1703, the second indenture for the land for the "Lotting Purchase" was signed by William Biddle Jr., Andrew Heath, William Albertus, Benjamin Furnis and Mahlon Stacy Jr. The Indian sachems signing the agreement with their mark were Caponakonkikkon, Lurkanntaman, Kelalaman and Chekanshakaman. The land lay on the Delaware River and ran from the mouth of the Loakalong Creek, along the 1688 purchase line of Adlord Bowde and northwards to the Indian purchase of June 25, 1703, below the South Branch of the Raritan River.[42]

The first General Assembly Meeting under Governor Cornbury was held in Perth Amboy from November 10 through December 13, 1703. Thomas Gardiner, Quaker, of West New Jersey was elected Speaker of the House. Gardiner requested that the governor grant certain privileges to the Assembly. First, that members and their servants were to be free from arrest or molestation during sessions of the Assembly. Second, that Assemblymen have free access to call on the Governor when necessary. Third, that there was to be liberty of speech and debate in the Assembly. As these were standard requests of English assemblies, the Governor had no problem granting them to the legislators.[43]

The Governor could not accept a fourth privilege that Thomas Gardiner requested, namely that when misunderstandings arose between the Governor's Council and the General Assembly, a committee of the council and a committee of the house be appointed to reconcile such differences. Such an arrangement would reduce the power of the Governor, and Cornbury, after labeling the idea "an innovation," refused the request.[44]

The General Assembly session was lengthy, longer than William had ever been away from home before. Presumably, the West New Jersey Assemblymen were able to return the nearly fifty miles to their homes on weekends if weather permitted. Fortunately, William had the companionship of his fellow Quakers who were on the Governor's Council and on the Assembly.

Although there was much business that the Queen had wanted the General Assembly to complete, most of the efforts of the Assembly went into the formation of new political coalitions. A proprietor-Quaker alliance developed, opposed by an anti-proprietor party. The proprietor majority tried to establish a bill that would guarantee their rights, as had been requested by the Queen, but their effort proved unsatisfactory in the way it was drawn up. Knowing that the Governor wanted a tax bill, the Assembly attached the tax bill to the proprietary rights bill. However, first, the West New Jersey members of the Assembly wanted payment of the tax owed during the Governor Hamilton years in West New Jersey. Some of them were owed money at ten percent per annum interest for money that they had advanced to the government to meet its obligations. It was estimated that the tax for 1700 and 1701 combined amounted to £1,400 which was largely still owed to the West New Jersey treasury. Even the fact that the quitrent of twenty nobles per year owed to the Crown had not been paid was brought into the debate; for the forty years since the proprietary grant had been made, the debt to the Queen would be in excess of £270 sterling. Eventually the proprietor-Quaker alliance managed to agree to a tax of £1,000 attached to the bill defining the proprietors' rights. By then the Governor was so frustrated or confused that he rejected all of the bills except one.[45]

One act that they all agreed to had been demanded by the Queen. It concerned the proprietary rights. No man was allowed to receive land from the Indians after December 1, 1703 without certification from the recorder of the proprietors. In addition, it was required that a license for the purchase be obtained from the Governor. The penalty for failure to comply was forty shillings per acre. Moreover, all deals made previously with the Indians illegally had to be covered by a proprietary right or be forfeited within six months. This bill partially protected the proprietary rights. It was agreed upon and sent to the printer, William Bradford. Governor Cornbury adjourned the session on December 13, 1703.[46] All in all, the Quaker minority in the Assembly had been successful in their efforts to block the legislative acts that were inconsistent with their beliefs about what was right for their colony. William finally was able to return home to enjoy the more peaceful winter months.

Upon his arrival home William and Sarah had much to talk about. He had missed the Burlington Quarterly Meeting of Friends held at Mount Hope on November 29, 1703,[47] and for the first time she had to host the meeting without him. William was surprised to find that his daughter, widow Sarah Righton, was visiting when he arrived and that she had brought a guest with her — Clement Plumstead. They announced their engagement to William, since her mother, Sarah, already knew. The parents advised their daughter to follow the proper procedure of the Society of Friends to request permission to marry. It was necessary for both Sarah and Clement to request a certificate of clearness to marry from their Meeting, the Philadelphia Monthly Meeting. They wanted to be married at Mount Hope, the home of her parents, which, as required by the Friends, qualified and served as a place of worship for Quakers of the area. They would be married there under the care of the Chesterfield Monthly Meeting.

The certificates of clearness were forwarded to the Chesterfield Monthly Meeting and on February 3, 1703/4 William and Sarah Biddle accompanied their daughter and her husband-to-be to attend worship at Chesterfield Monthly Meeting.[48] In her letter to Philadelphia Monthly Meeting Sarah Righton explained her previous disregard of their wishes when she married William Righton Jr. as "a failing of my youth." [49] The standard procedure was followed by the monthly meeting and a committee was formed to look into the matter and to report back to the next monthly meeting.

Although William Biddle did not attend the meeting, the Council of Proprietors of West New Jersey met in Burlington on February 14, 1703/4. As Mahlon Stacy was still absent, John Wills was elected president in his place. Mahlon died shortly after that date.[50] The council discussed the Indian purchase and their need to get the remaining money owed to the Indians from the resident proprietors.[51]

William learned of the business of the meeting when he went to Burlington the next day. On February 15, 1703/4 he sold 120 acres in the townbounds of Burlington to Bernard Lane for £40. The indenture was witnessed by William Bustill, John Carlisle and Thomas Gardiner.[52]

The Burlington Quarterly Meeting gathered at Mount Hope on February 28, 1703/4, but no important business was recorded at that time.[53]

Friends representing Chesterfield Monthly Meeting would have had the chance to discuss with William and Sarah their thoughts about the proposed second marriage of their daughter.

At ten o'clock in the morning of March 2, 1703/4, William Biddle, accompanied by Clement Plumstead and Sarah (Biddle) Righton, attended the Chesterfield Monthly Meeting. The committee gave a favorable report to the Meeting, and since there were no objections by other members, the couple was given permission to marry under the care of the Chesterfield Monthly Meeting at Mount Hope.[54]

Opposite page (transcription below):
Sarah (Biddle) Righton's letter to the Philadelphia Monthly Meeting

Friends of the Monthly Meeting in Philadelphia

    I Having spent Great Part of my Time since it pleased God to Take my Dear husband from me as a resident amongst you find myself obliged to acquaint you of my proposed intentions of marrying my friend Clement Plumstead and in order thereunto I request a certificate from you to satisfie Friends of the monthly meeting at Chesterfield to which I formerly belonged of my clearness of all others and what further you shall so convey unto.

    But because my former marriage have given offense and that it may be an example unto others I find myself concerned to acquaint you that I am sincerely sorry that I made any procedure therein contrary to the good order used amongst Friends and I desire it may be explained as a failing of my youth and not as a slight or contempt of the method and order of that Holy profession I am now under And this I can truly say hath been for a considerable time the real thoughts of my heart and is not now brought only to serve the proposed occasion.

    So hopeing through Divine Assistance to walk more circumspectly for the future I subscribe

Philadelphia 24 11: mo[nth] 1703

                        Your Friend
                        Sarah Righton

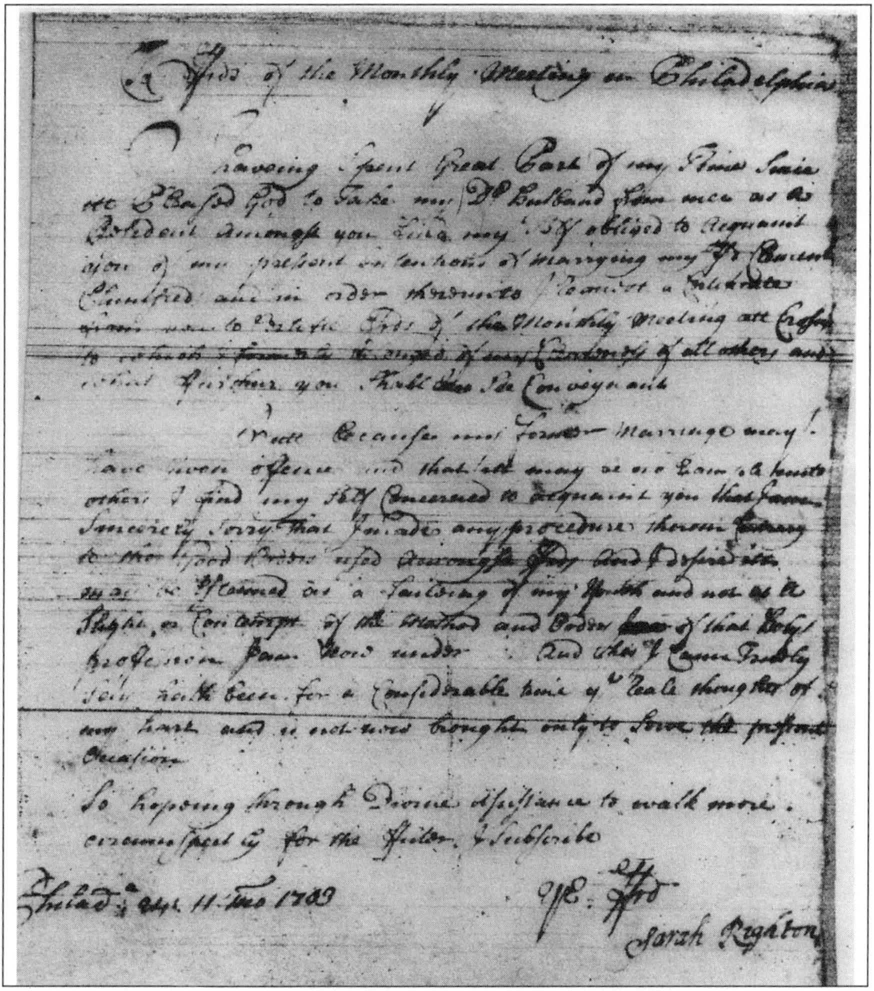

Sarah (Biddle) Righton's Letter

The trio returned to Mount Hope, where Sarah's parents would now freely approve of the marriage and began to finalize plans. Early the next morning William, with his daughter and future son-in-law, set out for Burlington to transact land business for William and perhaps to shop for wedding essentials. The first business to be completed after their arrival in the town was a transaction William had previously arranged. He sold another portion of his High Street lot to William Gladwin, blacksmith, son of the deceased Thomas Gladwin, for £3.4s. The lot had a 50-foot front on Wood Street and ran eastward halfway to High Street, backing up to the lot on High Street that William Gladwin's father had previously bought from William Biddle. Sarah Righton and Clement Plumstead with John Wetherill served as witnesses to the indenture.[55]

While in Burlington William probably learned from Samuel Jennings about his experience as a member of the Governor's Council. Samuel had been unable to continue as Judge of the Court of Pleas, for the anti-Quakers persisted in not permitting the alternate oath that would allow a Quaker to hold office. He had been removed from that appointment by Governor Cornbury.[56]

Now it was time to take a break from the political tensions of the times. For William and Sarah it was perhaps the happiest day of their lives. The social event about to take place among the finest ever seen in West New Jersey. The Biddle family, their friends and their extended family, the servants and slaves, were to experience a wedding and the celebration following, probably very much like described below:

March 14, 1703/4 was the day of the wedding of Sarah Biddle Righton and Clement Plumstead. An impressive list of guests began to arrive at Mount Hope.[57] The religious tone of the wedding was set by the Friends who were appointed to attend by their Monthly Meetings. Burlington Monthly Meeting sent Samuel Jennings, John Wills, Thomas Raper, Samuel Furnis and Peter Fretwell, all longtime associates of William Biddle. Chesterfield Monthly Meeting sent Samuel Bunting, Edward Rockill and his wife Mary, Robert Wilson and Francis Davenport. Samuel Carpenter attended for Philadelphia Monthly Meeting, which would be the couple's home meeting after they were married. He was accompanied by his daughter Hannah Fishbourn, a close friend of Sarah Righton and her husband William Fishbourn, who later served as mayor of Philadelphia from 1719 to 1722.

There were so many friends of Sarah Righton and Clement Plumstead (who also served as a mayor of Philadelphia, in 1723, 1736 and 1741) coming from Philadelphia, that arrangements had been made for Cousin

Guest list of the wedding of
Clement Plumstead and Sarah (Biddle) Righton
March 14, 1703/4

Mary Warder	Benjamin Wright	Samuel Jennings	William Biddle
Sarah Dimoche	John Sanders	William Penn Jr.	Sarah Biddle
Susan Marriott	Daniel Radley	Roger Mompesson	William Biddle Jr.
Mary Wheat	Samuel Bunting	George Roch	William Hall
Mary Rockhill	Joseph Usher	Samuel Carpenter	Lydia Biddle
Phoebe Scattergood	Thomas Lambert	Francis Davenport	Thomas Biddle
Susan Harwood	Edward Rockhill	Robert Wilson	Thomas Masters
Rebecca Briant	William Satterthwaite	Joseph Kirkbride	Randall Janney
Ann Satterthwaite	Thomas Raper	John Parsons	Agnes Righton
Ann Buckley	Thomas Scattergood	James Sansom	Sarah Hall
Hannah Scott	Samuel Wilson	Abraham Scott	
Mary Lambert	James Craft	Thomas Murray	
Ann Davenport	Hugh Huddy	Samuel Furnis	
Susan Decou		Tobias Dimoche	
Bridget Davenport		Peter Fretwell	
Ann Wood		John Wills	
Elizabeth Gardiner		William Fishbourne	
Hannah Fishbourne		Isaac Marriott	

— From the records of the Chesterfield Monthly Meeting, p.59

Thomas Biddle to bring some of them in his ferry. Besides Samuel Carpenter and the Fishbourns, other passengers included George Roch (future mayor of Philadelphia in 1713), Benjamin Wright, John Sanders, Daniel Radley, Joseph Usher, John Parsons, James Sansom and Thomas Murray. Because there was not enough room on the ferry for all of those who wanted to come, Thomas Masters (future mayor of Philadelphia in 1707), husband of Sibella (Righton) Masters, had his servants take some of the guests with them in one of his boats. That party included Randall Janney and his sister-in law, Agnes Righton and Susan Harwood, Mary Warder and widow Ann Bulkley.

For guests coming from Bucks County the trip was easy. Joseph Kirkbride, widower of Sarah Stacy, was joined by Tobias and Sarah Dimoche. They traveled to Pennsbury, where they met William Penn Jr. and his guest Roger Mompesson (barrister, recently appointed to the New Jersey Supreme Court and future Chief Justice of the Supreme Courts of New Jersey and Pennsylvania). Penn and Mompesson had stayed an extra night at Pennsbury so that they could attend the wedding.[58] These guests crossed the Delaware River to Mount Hope in William Penn's barge.

Robert Wilson and his son, Samuel, accompanied Ann Wood, eldest daughter of William and Mary (Parnell) Wood, traveling by horseback from Chesterfield. Assemblyman Thomas Lambert Jr. escorted his sister, Mary Lambert, by horseback from Nottingham for the festivities.

A larger group arrived from Crosswicks. Frances Davenport, councilman, escorted his daughters, Ann and Bridget, and his stepdaughter, Susan Decou. His son-in-law, assemblyman William Hall (brother-in-law of Clement Plumstead) and his daughter Sarah (Davenport) Hall had come to visit Francis several days earlier. Samuel Bunting loaned his extra horses to the Halls and he accompanied them as they all rode to the wedding together. Edward and Mary Rockhill met William and Ann Satterthwaite on the trail, and they arrived together from the farmlands southeast of Mount Hope along with nearby neighbor James Craft.

All of the guests were greeted by the bride's proud parents, William and Sarah Biddle.

Perhaps the most dificult trip to the wedding was made by guests coming from Burlington. Although the roads were not quite ready for carriages, Hugh Huddy (son-in-law of the deceased Edward Hunloke) had promised Elizabeth (Basnett) Gardiner that he could transport her to the gathering in his horse-drawn coach with special foods for the party that she could not bring ahead of time. She was accompanied in the carriage by widow Hannah (Lambert) Scott, Phoebe (Wetherill) Scattergood, Rebecca (Collins) Briant, Susan (Field) Marriott and Mary Wheate. The young men, Thomas Scattergood, Isaac Marriott Jr. and Abraham Scott, accompanied the jostling carriage on horseback, helping to steady it and to free it from potholes when necessary. The older men, Councilman Samuel Jennings with Peter Fretwell, Thomas Raper, John Wills and Samuel Furnis rode on horses separately.

Everyone had arrived by the appointed hour, ten o'clock in the morning. As opposed to the separation of men and women in the Quarterly Meeting business meetings, at this wedding ceremony men and women filled both rooms together. The door between the rooms was left open. Two chairs had been placed there and Clement Plumstead waited by one of them.

The guests quieted when Sarah, with several of her closest friends, began to descend the stairway from the rooms above. Sarah followed her friends into the rooms and seated herself in one chair next to Clement. After a period of silence, Clement and Sarah stood and faced each other. In turn they said their wedding vows to each other, taking each other in matrimony before their friends, in the traditional manner of the Society of Friends.

When the couple finished and sat down, the silent Meeting for Worship continued until it was interrupted by remarks of the prominent Quaker minister, Samuel Jennings. Samuel Carpenter, Elizabeth Gardiner, Samuel Bunting and Sarah Hall also spoke to contribute thoughts to the occasion.

When Samuel Jennings and Samuel Carpenter shook hands, it was a signal to all that the formal ceremony was over. The bride and groom stood and began to receive the congratulations of their guests. The servants who had been watching from the doorways hurried from those places to prepare to serve the food, as the guests spread out into the hallway and onto the porch.

Indoweys observed that there was some similarity in the way Indians and Quakers marry each other. Indians also place the couple to be married in a circle of their family and friends. The male gives the female a bone, signifying that he will provide the meat to nourish them. The female gives him an ear of corn, indicating that she will provide the bread and starches for the family.[59]

The servants attended the tables prepared with food and drink. Fine wine from Europe had been brought from Philadelphia for the occasion. Ample servings of ham and beef were offered. Indoweys had supplied the best delicacy for the occasion: the first of the spring shad had just appeared off the island, and there was plenty of shad roe for everyone. The tables were full of delicacies, as well as many kinds of potatoes and breads. However, the biggest surprise was unveiled last. Now everyone could see why Elizabeth Gardiner needed to take the stagecoach to the wedding. She secretly had had Samuel Gibson, baker and her neighbor in Burlington, bake a wedding cake for the couple.

The party was enjoyed by all. Never had such a festive occasion taken place in West New Jersey. The guests continued to mill about, chatting in an atmosphere of happiness and joy. It was Thomas Biddle who had to suggest an end to the celebration. About an hour from dusk, he asked the guests to prepare to leave so that they would get home safely and they all departed on the routes and in the manner that they had come to Mount Hope. Clement and Sarah Plumstead left with Thomas Biddle to go to Philadelphia where they would live in her father's house, on Front Street, between Chestnut and Walnut.

For William and Sarah, left alone in the twilight, all seemed too quiet after such an important day in their lives. Neither one of them could have imagined a few years before that time that such elegance could be brought to this wilderness. Non-Quakers, Roger Mompesson and Hugh Huddy, had learned more about the ways of the Friends. Indians, Negro slaves, councilmen, assemblymen, justices, merchants, farmers and young men and women from the newly developing Philadelphia society had mingled and enjoyed each other's company, all friends with whom Sarah Jr. and Clement and Sarah and William wanted to share this special occasion. The parents knew that this new son-in-law would be respected and successful.

Now it was time to return to the necessary work of the springtime on the farm. Fields must be prepared for planting. Livestock had been breeding and the newly born young animals would require attention.

When they were in Burlington for the spring Fair Days, on May 10, 1704, Thomas Biddle and John Wills, before Justice Thomas Revell, confirmed that William Biddle had sold 100 acres to William Murfin.[60] The indenture was finally properly recorded in the books of the county.

On May 11, 1704, William Biddle attended the annual meeting of the Council of Proprietors of West New Jersey, having been reelected to the council that April. He joined Samuel Jennings, Thomas Gardiner, Christopher Wetherill, John Wills and George Deacon at the session. William had probably planned to remain retired from the council, for now he was seventy-one years old, but, the councilmen realized that they needed him as their president. Mahlon Stacy had died. George Deacon would be busy on the Governor's Council. John Wills did not want to take the job. When elected by the others, William accepted the position of president of the council again. All other officers were to "continue till further order." [61]

The council members may have known that some of the London Proprietors were growing alarmed by the fact that they, as a Council of Proprietors, were proceeding with plans to purchase lands from the Indians and to take lands only for themselves. The London Proprietors had sent a letter to Governor Cornbury. In the letter, received April 6, 1704, they asked the governor to put a stop to the activities of the Council of Proprietors until they proceeded by the terms agreed to by the original proprietors.[62]

Friends gathered at Mount Hope for the Burlington Quarterly Meeting on Monday, May 29, 1704. The meeting was well attended. The Quakers were beginning to worry about the ownership of their meetinghouses and burial grounds and therefore they decided that the deeds for all the meetinghouses in Burlington County should be recorded in the public record.[63] They realized that Jeremiah Basse, as Secretary of New Jersey, was responsible for the records of the colony. Until then they had not recorded the sites of their religious buildings in official public documents, just as they had not done so in England when they were under religious persecution.

After a quiet summer the Burlington Quarterly Meeting convened at Mount Hope on August 28, 1704. George Deacon, who was among the members attending from Burlington Monthly Meeting, informed William and the other Quaker leaders of the activities of the Governor's Council since they last met. Hannah (Cooper) Woolston, Elizabeth Fretwell, Mary Myers and Ann Satterthwaite were among the members joining Sarah Biddle that day in the Women's Meeting.[64]

On September 7, 1704 Governor Cornbury convened the second session of the first General Assembly of New Jersey in Burlington. William attended with the other elected assemblymen. Governor Cornbury asked the legislators to attend to necessary business, such as acts for taxation, militia and highways and, if there was time, for an act to protect the rights of all of the proprietors. The assemblymen did earnestly work on appropriate bills but, their efforts failed to meet with the approval of Governor Cornbury.[65]

William did not attend every meeting, for on September 19, 1704 he went to Philadelphia to complete an important transaction. That day he deeded his Philadelphia property, worth over £330, to his daughter Sarah and her new husband Clement Plumstead "for and in consideration of the natural love and affection which he hath and beareth unto the said Clement and Sarah and for and towards a Marriage portion unto the said Sarah." His friend Abraham Bickley was among the witnesses to the indenture.[66]

The Friends' Meetinghouse, Burlington, West New Jersey, where
Yearly Meeting was held September 1704.

The Yearly Meeting for Friends was held in Burlington at the same time that the sessions of the General Assembly were taking place. This was the first time that there had been a conflict in scheduling between religion and government in the history of the territory. The Quakers went on and conducted their business from September 20 through 25, 1704 at the Burlington Meetinghouse.[67] At the same time the legislators met almost next door at the Town House, the public meeting hall in the courthouse on the corner of High Street and Broad Street. The Quaker assemblymen, including William, undoubtedly attended both meetings. On September 28, 1704, three days after the conclusion of the religious meetings, Governor Cornbury abruptly and without warning dissolved the General Assembly, calling for new elections and another meeting of the legislative body to be held in Burlington on November 13, 1704.[68]

The Council of Proprietors of West New Jersey met in Burlington on October 11, 1704, with William Biddle presiding. Samuel Jennings, George Deacon, John Wills, Christopher Wetherill, Thomas Gardiner and John Reading also attended the meeting. The council ordered Thomas Gardiner to find out what goods were still needed to pay for Nimahammoe's Indian purchase and to procure those goods immediately. If not the full council, then at least William Biddle Jr. and John Reading, with Thomas Foulkes, were to go up to the lands to mark the Indian purchase and to tell the Indians to come to Burlington to receive their payment.[69] Plans were made then to complete at least the first portion of that Lotting Purchase.

On November 8, 1704, Thomas Biddle, mariner, cousin of William, married Rachael Groesbeck at the First Presbyterian Church in Philadelphia.[70] Rachael was of Dutch descent. Her father had purchased a tract of 106 acres in Pennsylvania from Joseph Growden in 1696, fronting on the Delaware River, next to the homestead of the Vandergrift family, near the Neshaminy Creek. He paid £50 for the land and paid an annual quit rent to Growden of 2 shillings, 6 pence.[71] When Growden purchased the land from William Penn, he owed only 1 shilling per 100 acres on it as annual quit rent due to Penn.[72] Apparently it was possible to make a profit not only on the land itself, but also on the quit rent attached to it. West New Jersey land owners had long before abandoned this feudal system. The newlyweds were to live with her family, a location that was very convenient for Thomas as a ferryman.

William received a warrant from the Council of Proprietors of West New Jersey for 220 acres of unappropriated land on Tuesday, November 14, 1704,[73] to cover two tracts of land that he was selling. The first was 170 acres sold to Thomas Sheperd, yeoman, from Cohansey in Salem County, for £14.12s. That same day the deed was witnessed, acknowledged and recorded in the Burlington Common Pleas Court, by Justice Jeremiah Basse, Joshua Barkstead, who served as a witness, and Judge of Common Pleas Court, Thomas Revell.[74] The second tract of land was 50 acres sold to John and Eve Sheperd of Cohansey for £4.5s., the indenture for which was completed in Burlington Court the following day before the same three people.[75]

Since the Cornbury courts had been commissioned, William had not taken his deeds directly to the Court of Records to be entered in the public books because he and others were not sure that their business would be handled properly. If it was not, there could be the expense of doing warrants, deeds, and surveys a second time. On November 14, 15, 1704, William tested the system by taking his documents to the Court of Records, which was under the care of non-Quaker justices Jeremiah Basse, Joshua Barkstead and Judge Revell. As the President of the Council of Proprietors of West New Jersey, it was William's responsibility to be sure that the system designed for this business was still working. He used his own proprietary rights to test the rights both of the Council of Proprietors of West New Jersey to issue land warrants, and of a proprietor (himself) to sell those unappropriated acres to others.

If Jeremiah Basse or Thomas Revell had really intended to disrupt the system of ownership and distribution of land in New Jersey, they had the opportunity to do so that day. By doing nothing to object, they created a precedent that the West New Jersey proprietors could use in the future if they needed it.

Jeremiah Basse, Secretary of New Jersey, now lived in Burlington with his wife Elizabeth and their daughters Catherine and Ann. Secretary Basse had leased the beautiful George Hutcheson house, grounds, gardens and orchards on the waterfront east of High Street, from John Hollinshead Jr., who had purchased the property from the Hutcheson estate.[76]

Elections were held for assemblymen and William did not stand for reelection. He probably did not want to continue in office this time, because of his age and other responsibilities to the proprietors. Elected from the West New Jersey part of the territory were Restore Lippincott, John Hugg, John Kay, John Smith, William Hall, John Mason, Thomas Bryan, Robert Wheeler, Peter Fretwell, Thomas Lambert, Thomas Gardiner and Joshua Wright.[77]

The newly elected General Assembly met on November 13, 1704 in Burlington and its sessions continued until December 12, 1704. Peter Fretwell was elected by the Assembly as Speaker. At the suggestion of non-

Quaker assemblymen Daniel Leeds and Thomas Revell, Governor Cornbury arbitrarily dismissed Thomas Gardiner, Thomas Lambert and Joshua Wright from the Assembly, claiming that their estates were not sufficient to allow them to hold office.[78] This unjust maneuver changed the proprietor-Quaker political coalition to a minority by one vote in the house, facilitating the enactment of laws that Governor Cornbury wanted.

The first act passed by the Assembly laid a tax on the colony of £2,000 annually for two years. Tax rates were set on many services, including ferry rides, stage coaches, mills, shops and sales of goods, particularly alcoholic beverages. The tax called for an assessment on each man, including his lands, domestic animals and slaves. One provision called for assessment on all lands that were held by survey, deeds, or patents, and had been settled in any manner in the province at £10 per 100 acres. Assessors and Collectors were appointed for each county. The timetable for assessing, tabulating the assessed value, setting the annual tax rates, preparing the tax bills, delivering them, payment dates for taxes and penalties for concealment and failure to pay were all specified by the law. This tax program would continue for two years, 1705 and 1706.[79]

Besides the assessment that they would receive on their Mount Hope homestead, William and Sarah would be assessed an additional £174 if they had settled any servants on the unproductive 1,740 acres surveyed to them in Amwell. The perpetrators of this law had miscalculated the severe effect on the West Jersey Society with its thousands of surveyed acres, and on other London proprietors who might have settled people on their lands. An explanation to the proprietors who lived in London would have to be made. West New Jersey inhabitants who had refused to pay taxes when Andrew Hamilton was governor would now have to pay a tax that was at least thirty percent higher.

Another act of the General Assembly created a militia for the colony. Captains were to be appointed in each township. Every male between the ages of sixteen and sixty was to be listed, designated as a foot soldier or a horse soldier and outfitted accordingly. The act allowed exceptions for Quakers, who would be objecting on the basis of religion. To qualify for exception each Quaker had to get written verification of his belief from six members of the Monthly or Quarterly Meeting and he had to pay 20 shillings per year into the public fund. If the money was not paid, the Captain of the Militia would deliver a warrant to the Constable to seize the goods and chattels of the involved Quaker and to sell these belongings in order to obtain the funds owed by that person.[80]

This act would have been disheartening to the Quakers of West New Jersey. They had hoped for and tried to create an idealistic and peaceful society. They knew that it had not worked perfectly, but this sudden thrust of militarism into their lives seemed so unnecessary. William could remember back to the days of his father, before 1660, when one owed allegiance to the Lords of the Manors in England. Moreover, now son and grandsons would be subject to the requirements of serving in the militia.

A third act passed by this assembly concerned the improvements that had to be made for highways and bridges. Several main highways, including the road from the Perth Amboy ferry to Burlington and beyond to Salem were to be six rods, ninety-nine feet wide. Other common public roads were to be only four rods, sixty-six feet wide. The act appointed commissioners for the highways in each county, to be responsible for laying out the roads, building them and maintaining them according to specifications and standards established by the Assembly. In February and March the justices of the Quarter Session Courts in each county were to nominate and appoint two overseers for the highways for each town or precinct in their county. These overseers were to determine what equipment and manpower were needed to complete the work on the roads and bridges and then they could enlist the help of the residents and their wagons and teams of horses and oxen to complete the work. A person so designated could send a servant or some other person in his place.[81]

When the roads of New Jersey were originally laid out and cleared, they had been prepared for transportation of passengers or goods by horses and carts, not by stages or carriages. Now the government was demanding that the overland transportation system of the colony be upgraded to a level comparable to that of England. This act would mean that more land would be taken from farms to widen the roads and make new ones. For the rural Quakers it represented another form of taxation, as they now had to give time and energy to complete the work of building roads they didn't think they needed. This new act was perhaps creating a greater burden or expense than necessary. No separate appropriation of money was made to implement it.[82]

Other acts passed by this General Assembly included one that set penalties for immoral behavior. Another act forgave all of the inhabitants of the Jersey provinces their crimes committed before August 13, 1703, with the exception of serious offenses such as murder or treason. Another act changed the distribution of assemblymen elected in West New Jersey. Two would be elected from Burlington, two from Burlington County, three from Gloucester County, four from Salem County and one from Cape May

County. It enabled all freeholders of a county to vote. It required that a representative live in the county or town from which he was elected.[83]

Perhaps the most disturbing act was the one that regulated Negro, Indian and mulatto slaves within New Jersey. This law set more severe penalties for crimes committed by slaves than the penalties set for white people. For thefts of less than five shillings the slave was whipped with forty lashes. For thefts of greater proportion the slave would receive the forty lashes and would be burned on the cheek near the nose with the letter "T". The act denied that baptism of slaves was reason enough for giving them their liberty. It forbade any children of freed slaves from inheriting or purchasing any lands or tenements in New Jersey.[84] This law disenfranchised those Negroes who had inherited land.

The Quakers of West New Jersey were very disturbed by the passage of the acts concerning the treatment of slaves. At this time the Yearly Meeting of Friends from throughout the region were working their way toward a policy against slavery. In the courts designed by the Quakers, the penalty for crimes was the same for people of all races. The Quaker government in effect before this time had allowed freedom for slaves and it permitted them to purchase and inherit lands. A freed slave, by hard work or inheritance, could become a freeholder of the province. In New Jersey many slaves had already been freed by their masters/owners. Samuel Andrews of Mansfield had left one of his Negroes twenty acres in his will,[85] and Abigail Lippincott had freed two of her slaves through her will.[86] This new act, if allowed to continue, would severely reduce the human rights of all dark-skinned people of New Jersey. It would deny freedom to those slaves and their children who had already won or earned the status of being free.

The General Assembly continued until December 12, 1704. Fortunately all of the acts that it passed had to be forwarded to England for final approval. but this did not stop the government from beginning to implement and enforce them.

Before the General Assembly adjourned, Governor Cornbury issued commissions to persons who were to provide services involving the public. On December 11, 1704 he commissioned Thomas Biddle to operate a ferry between Burlington and Philadelphia. John Reeves, Henry Tuckness and William Bagley received similar commissions to run ferries on the same route. Christopher Snowden was granted permission to continue ferry service between Burlington and Bristol in Pennsylvania.[87] Travel between New Jersey and Pennsylvania was growing steadily.

While the General Assembly had been in session in Burlington, the life of the Quakers went on as usual. The Burlington Quarterly Meeting of Friends was held at Mount Hope on November 27, 1704. William and the Friends from Nottingham and Chesterfield were joined by Thomas Raper, Thomas Smith, Thomas Scattergood, Joshua Humphries, John Woolman and John Day from Burlington. Joining Sarah at the Women's Meeting were Frances Antram, Margaret Hunt, Mary Bunting, Rebecca (Decou) Davenport and others.[88] Friends discussed the events of the General Assembly in Burlington, but there was little they could do at that time to reverse or stop the actions taken. It was important that the Monthly Meetings quickly prepare the documents needed to keep the men from being drafted into military service. They began to estimate what the cost at twenty shillings per adult male would be yearly if they agreed to participate as the act required. They would need to try to determine what the cost would be to them economically and emotionally if they decided not to cooperate with such a law.

The Burlington Court of General Quarter Sessions was held Tuesday, December 12, 1704. Thomas Revell, President, was on the bench with Justices Nathaniel Westland, William Budd, Joshua Newbold and Michael Newbold. The grand jury was summoned. The non-Quakers were sworn in the usual manner. The Quaker jurors William Hollinshead, Joseph Pancoast, William Hascor, Joseph Decou, William Hackney, Christopher Wetherill, John Wills and John Hollinshead were attested.[89] In Burlington County it had been decided by the judge and justices that the Quakers would be allowed to take the alternate oath and serve as jurors. This was not the case in some of the other counties of the colony.

The Court of Pleas was held in Burlington the following day. Judge Thomas Revell was on the bench with Justices Nathaniel Westland, William Budd, Joshua Newbold, Robert Wheeler and William Hewlings. William Biddle Jr. was fined ten shillings for failing to respond to a summons to the Grand Jury. Joseph Kirkbride had made statements about Reverend John Talbot, and he was ordered to publish a retraction on "three of the most public places in the town": the gate of the Quaker burying ground, at the market place and at George Willis's ordinary (tavern).[90]

On January 1, 1704/5, a meeting of the Mansfield Township citizens was held at the home of John Hancock. To implement the new tax law, six Assessors were chosen. William Biddle Jr. was one of them, along with James Croft Sr., Abraham Brown Sr., John Brown Smith, William Foster and Isaac Gibbs. At the same meeting Richard Allinson and John Pancoast were elected as collectors and John Hancock was chosen constable for the year.[91]

The winter of 1704/5 was severe, with more snow than usual. Even the deer had to come into the barnyard to find food.[92] William and Sarah had wanted to visit their daughter, Sarah Plumstead, in Philadelphia, but the weather prevented their trip. Sarah and Clement were expecting their first child, who was to be born in the spring.

Despite the weather, the Burlington Quarterly Meeting was held on February 26, 1704/5. Samuel Furnis, Thomas Raper, Joshua Humphries, Thomas Eves and Richard Ridgway were among those who attended the meeting. Katherine Champion and Mary Wheat joined Sarah Biddle, Rebecca Davenport and Hannah Overton at the Women's Meeting. The men reviewed an abstract of the minutes of the last Yearly Meeting of Friends.[93] The men discussed the fact that Governor Cornbury had issued a warrant and license for the Friends' burial ground in Burlington to Samuel Jennings, Francis Davenport, George Deacon, Peter Fretwell and other Friends.[94] In England Friends had not registered their burial grounds for fear that they would be taken away from them.

William returned to Burlington on March 15, 1704/5 to preside at the meeting of the Council of Proprietors of West New Jersey. Samuel Jennings, George Deacon, Thomas Gardiner, John Wills, Christopher Wetherill and John Reading attended the meeting. The council ordered Samuel Jennings, Thomas Gardiner, John Wills and John Reading to return to the Indians to work out more details about the Indian Purchase. Apparently the first deed had been accidentally burned before it was recorded and the terms of the agreement had to be renegotiated. Either a second deed had to be drawn up, or the terms of the first had to be agreed upon again. The council adjourned, intending to meet on April 25, 1705.[95] No minutes exist to tell if that meeting ever took place.

While in Burlington for the council meeting, William attended to some personal business. He sold six acres of land in the town of Burlington to Samuel Jennings for £40. The indenture was witnessed by council members George Deacon, John Wills and Thomas Gardiner.[96]

Sarah Biddle had finally been able to go to Philadelphia to be with her pregnant daughter. On the way to join her, William stopped in Burlington on May 10, 1705 to call on Jeremiah Basse, who was now Secretary of New Jersey. Basse acknowledged the indenture by which William had sold 120 acres in the townbounds to Bernard Lane on February 15, 1703/4, which had never been officially entered on the books of the colony.[97]

William joined his wife, daughter and son-in-law later that day in Philadelphia and found that Sarah was having problems with her pregnancy. On May 14, 1705 newborn William Plumstead, William's grandson, died. Sarah Plumstead was very sick following the delivery and it was questionable if she would survive.

Sarah Biddle stayed with her daughter. William left to return to Mount Hope to attend to business matters there. He hosted the Burlington Quarterly Meeting by himself, when it was held on May 28, 1705. Lydia Biddle probably filled in for her mother-in-law. No business was recorded from the meeting.[99] William Jr. would oversee the Mount Hope property while his father returned to Philadelphia to join his mother and sister, to try to help with that serious situation. The parents stayed in Philadelphia through most of the summer. All of their plans and hopes for their daughter ended on August 17, 1705 when Sarah (Biddle) Plumstead died of consumption (tuberculosis).[100] The family's grief was enormous.

Ten days later, on August 27, 1705, they were consoled by their friends when the Burlington Quarterly Meeting was held at Mount Hope. Sarah was joined by Elizabeth Day, Frances Antram, Rebecca (Decou) Davenport and Ann Abbott, among others. William was joined in the Men's Meeting by Thomas Gardiner, Thomas Eves, John Butcher, Isaac Marriott, George Elkinton, Richard Ridgway, Samuel Jennings, Francis Davenport, Robert Wilson, John Day and Peter Fretwell. The men asked Samuel Jennings to write to England to request copies of epistles that might be "worthy" to copy into their minute book. William Biddle was among those asked to attend the upcoming Yearly Meeting, representing the Burlington Quarterly Meeting.[101]

William and Sarah returned to Philadelphia for the Yearly Meeting of Friends in September 1705.[102] They stayed with their son-in-law, Clement Plumstead, and they visited Sarah's grave.

Back home for the fall months of the year, William and Sarah were fortunate to have their son and his family living near them on the homestead. Their grandchildren visited them frequently and this must have helped to take their mind off their loss. Joseph, the youngest, was barely able to walk. Sarah, the grandmother, began to spend more time with her older granddaughters, Elizabeth and Sarah, teaching them to cook and to sew.

On November 24, 1705 William and William Jr. attended an organizational meeting of Mansfield Township, held at the house of Edmund Wells. William Jr. was elected clerk of the township for the next year. Hugh Hutchins was selected as constable. Joseph English and Samuel

Gibson were chosen as overseers for the poor and a tax of 1s.5d. per £100 of assessed value was levied for relief of the poor of the township. William Hoffer and Jacob Decou were chosen as overseers of highways. Hugh Hutchins and David Curtis were to serve as assessors for the township.[103]

Friends met at Mount Hope on November 26, 1705 for Burlington Quarterly Meeting to strengthen one another through worship and to deal with matters of concern in their religion and government. The Men's Meeting discussed what should be copied into their minute book.[104] (It is important to note that record-keeping and contents of their minute books were a high priority for early Quakers, a dedication which has been carried on ever since then.)

On December 5, 1705 William went to Burlington to complete another real estate transaction, selling to Thomas Gardiner the last portion of his lot on the west side of High Street, a six-foot strip running from High Street to Wood Street. Gardiner paid him £3 for the land. The indenture was witnessed by William Biles of Bucks County, Pennsylvania, William Hall and John Reading.[105] These five proprietors undoubtedly attended to other business for the Council of Proprietors of West New Jersey, probably concerning the Indian purchase above the falls of the Delaware River. Also, William Hall was probably arranging for the sale of some of the proprietary rights he had purchased from James Wasse in England, to William Biles of Bucks County, Pennsylvania.[106]

The winter months were uneventful. On February 25, 1705/6 Friends again met at Mount Hope for the Burlington Quarterly Meeting. Sarah was joined by Ann Watson and Mary Bunting from Chesterfield Monthly Meeting and Hannah Surkett and Mary Elkinton from Burlington Monthly Meeting. Among those attending the Men's Meeting were Thomas Raper, Samuel Furnis, Richard Smith, Joshua Humphries, George Elkinton, John Day and John Brown. Six men were appointed to inspect the minute book of the Quarterly Meeting.[107]

William had been summoned to grand jury duty. On March 5, 1705/6 he traveled to Burlington to the courtroom for that purpose. The bench was occupied by Thomas Revell, President, and Justices Jeremiah Basse, Daniel Leeds, Nathaniel Westland, Robert Wheeler, Joshua Newbold, Michael Newbold and Roger Parks. William was attested as a juror and the charge was given to the grand jury by Thomas Revell, Esquire. There was little work for the grand jury that day so they were dismissed with thanks from the bench and the court adjourned for one hour.[108]. The non-Quaker justices adjourned together to George Willis's ordinary, as was their custom.

William probably went to Henry Grubb's inn or the New Brewhouse of Samuel Jennings for his lunch before returning to Mount Hope. It was likely that he would find his friends there. He might have seen Richard Smith that midday and learned that Deputy Governor Richard Ingoldsby had issued a license to Dr. Smith that morning, authorizing him to practice the science of Chirurgery (surgery) and Physic in New Jersey.[109]

On April 11, 1706 Governor Cornbury issued a patent to Hugh Huddy of Burlington, giving him the right to run all of the stage coaches, wagons and carriages that transported passengers or freight from Perth Amboy to Burlington and back. This was to include the right to travel all of the roadways that might be used to get from either town to the other. No other person or persons were to enjoy the same privilege.[110]   If interpreted strictly, this meant that one could not travel or ship goods in any wagons other than those owned by Mr. Huddy on the roads that connected the two capitals of the province. The creation of such a monopoly aroused the anger of the inhabitants of the province.

Apparently there were no meetings of the Council of Proprietors of West New Jersey that spring, or if there were, the minutes no longer exist. The members and officers of the council continued in place as ordered by the last election. William was able to devote his attention to the chores of Mount Hope, helping, or accompanying his son and grandson as they went about the spring planting.

The Burlington Quarterly Meeting convened at Mount Hope on May 27, 1706. Joining Sarah at the Women's Meeting were Mary Wood, Mary Rockhill, Hope Wills and Abigail Raper. William was joined by Isaac Marriott, Samuel Furnis, John Day, Richard Ridgway, Thomas Eves and John Wills and other members from Chesterfield Monthly Meeting. The members from Burlington Monthly Meeting reported that, with the help of Samuel Jennings, they had started to record the sufferings of their members as they had done in England.[111]

Although the minutes of the Quarterly Meeting suggest that the Quakers were having problems in the colony under Cornbury's governorship, the simplicity of the record, and probably their fear of having their words revealed to the authority, greatly understated the true experience of some of the Friends. The new laws of the province had been implemented even before comment had been received on them from England, and they were being used to harass and hurt the Quakers whenever possible.

The Highway Improvement Act had become a real problem for the rural Quakers. Their properties had been disrupted by the widening of the roads and laying out of new roadways. Fences and buildings found to be in the way were torn down by the road officials without just compensation. In one reported case a road was made to run out of its way to destroy the mill and mill pond of a Quaker farmer, despite his offer to build the road himself in a more appropriate location for the county. There appeared to be no fairness in the process of deciding where the roadways would be built. After the locations for the roads were set, the Quakers were further bound by the law to work on them or to provide workers in their place.[112]

The greatest inequity occurred against the Friends when the militia act was implemented. The Friends had, by conscience, decided that they could not show any degree of cooperation with the act. This meant that the authorities had to take legal action against them to collect the 20 shillings per annum owed for those who did not participate in the military. When a captain of the militia served a constable with warrants to seize the goods and chattels of the Quakers, the warrant included the right to seize as many of the goods and chattels of the guilty party as he saw fit to take. Unfortunately, the act had not stipulated that the goods taken had to represent the amount due, nor did it say that any "overplus" was to be returned to the guilty party.

Constables who did seize the goods and chattels of the Quakers did so aggressively. This occurred particularly in Salem County under Sheriff Dare. As a group, the Quakers may have suffered a loss of possessions as great as £1,000 per year while the act was in force. It became apparent that the Tax Act had not appropriated enough funds for the military and that these fines or value of goods taken from the Quakers were going to be used to support the war effort. This caused anguish among the Quakers, who by their consciences could not support the military in any way.[113]Most of the residents of New Jersey refused to buy the goods that had been seized from their Quaker neighbors under these circumstances, so they accumulated in storage. It was said that a house in Burlington became filled with the goods of the Quakers. Because of their support of the Quakers, eight of the constables of Burlington County had to be taken before the Supreme Court for failure to serve the warrants of the Captains of the Militia.[114]

William Biddle Jr. was able to witness this harassment of Friends when he sat on the Grand Jury of the Burlington Court on June 4, 1706. Constable Joseph Parker of Northampton was fined ten shillings for not appearing, and an additional thirty shillings for refusing to receive the warrants for obtaining twenty shillings worth of goods from each of the Quakers in his township as required by the Military Act.[115]

William and Sarah greeted the leaders of the Friends at their home again on August 26, 1706 for the Burlington Quarterly Meetings. Francis Davenport was instructed to pay £17 to the Yearly Meeting. William was among those appointed to attend Yearly Meeting.[116]

The Yearly Meeting for Friends was held September 18, 1706 in Burlington. It was well attended, no doubt in part because of the challenge that Quakers were again facing in New Jersey. With William from Burlington County were Francis Davenport, John Wills, John Sirket, Robert Wilson, Thomas Gardiner and Peter Fretwell. Friends coming from Pennsylvania included Samuel Carpenter, Rowland Ellis, Anthony Morris, William Preston, Thomas Walton, Thomas Storey, Caleb Pusey, John Blunstone and Nicholas Walne. Gloucester and Salem Counties sent John Haines, Richard Dorkin, John Kay and John Estaugh. The men discussed the unsatisfactory state of the Friends' burying grounds. It had been the custom to have very simple grave markers, but this tradition was not being kept by everyone. To solve the problem, it was ordered that the gravestones be removed from all of the Friends' burying grounds.[117]

Governor Cornbury called two more sessions of the second elected General Assembly. They met October 15 through November 8, 1705 and October 25 through November 1, 1706.[118] No significant business was accomplished. He dissolved the General Assembly at the last session, calling for elections and the meeting of the third General Assembly in April 1707 in Burlington. The Governor had hopes that this election would give him a majority of anti-proprietary, anti-Quaker members in both the Assembly and the council. If his plan succeeded, he would be able to control the politics of the colony and direct the legislation to always suit his purposes.

Governor Cornbury was so confident of his future political strength that he sent a letter to the Council of Proprietors of West New Jersey, challenging their existence. He did this despite the clear instructions that he had received from Queen Anne when he took office that he should accept the council. In his summons of November 14, 1706, the Governor required the members of the council to meet with him in Burlington on April 29, 1707 to answer three questions: "Who were the members of the Council of Proprietors for the last year," "Who was chosen for the year 1707," and "What were the powers that the council 'pretended' to have and by whom were these powers granted." In that November 14, 1706 memorandum, the governor ordered that the council stop issuing land warrants, distributing land and purchasing land from the Indians.[119]

William was thankful that there was no new business that required any commitments from him when the Burlington Quarterly Meeting convened at Mount Hope on November 25, 1706,[120] or at the Mansfield Township Meeting held Saturday, November 30, 1706.[121] As the President of the Council of Proprietors of West New Jersey, he had to see to it that a proper answer was prepared for the Governor.

The Council of Proprietors of West New Jersey met on January 22, 1706/7 in Burlington with William Biddle presiding. Samuel Jennings, George Deacon, John Wills, William Hall, Christopher Wetherill and John Kay all attended the meeting. The council discussed the summons from the Governor and made plans to prepare an answer. On another matter, they were concerned that the Indian purchase was still incomplete. They asked Christopher Wetherill to speak with William Biles, Joseph Kirkbride, widow Stacy and Thomas Lambert and anyone else that had information about that purchase.[122]

Sometime after that council session a meeting of all of the resident proprietors was called. The result of the meeting was that a notice was sent to the Governor stating that they, the resident proprietors, were not pleased with the fact that he had disrupted their business. They had paid a large amount of money to the Indians for their land and he should not interfere with that purchase.[123] The resident proprietors probably were told that the council planned to strengthen its position by including the agent of the West Jersey Society, Lewis Morris, as a member.

The actions of Governor Cornbury gave the resident proprietors and Quakers warning that they needed to make changes in their efforts to protect their rights in the colony. Samuel Jennings realized that he was ineffective as a member of the Governor's Council. He tendered his resignation and stood for election to the General Assembly.[124] The Council of Proprietors of West New Jersey realized that the last time they had such problems they combined their interests with those of the agent of the West Jersey Society, Andrew Hamilton, and the problem was solved. Now that Lewis Morris was that agent of the West Jersey Society they opened a discussion with him. Agreement was made to form a coalition of the East New Jersey proprietors, the West Jersey Society proprietary interest, and the Quaker West New Jersey resident proprietary interests. Lewis Morris would become a member of the Council of Proprietors of West New Jersey,[125] and he would also stand for election to the General Assembly in East New Jersey.[126] The members of all three groups hoped that acting together would give them strength to protect their interests and to provide encouragement to the electorate.

The elections were held in East and West New Jersey. Lewis Morris was elected to the General Assembly in his division of the colony. In West New Jersey Samuel Jennings was elected and sent to the General Assembly with Peter Canson, William Hall, Richard Johnson, John Thomson, Bartholomew Wyatt, John Wills, Thomas Bryan, Thomas Gardiner, John Kay and Philip Rawle.[127] When the General Assembly was convened on April 5, 1707, it was apparent that Governor Cornbury did not have the majority of non-Quakers that he had hoped for.

Either before then, or at the usual Burlington County election day, the resident proprietors of West New Jersey reelected their Council. The council members for 1707 were William Biddle, Samuel Jennings, Lewis Morris, George Deacon, John Wills, John Kay, John Reading, Thomas Gardiner and William Hall.[128]

When the General Assembly convened in Burlington on April 7, 1707, Samuel Jennings was elected Speaker of the House. Governor Cornbury gave his opening address, telling the assemblymen what he wanted them to do. They then went into session, as a committee of the whole, to prepare their grievances against the Governor.[129]

On May 8, 1707, in the next session of the General Assembly, Samuel Jennings delivered the "remonstrance" that the Assembly had prepared and agreed upon to the Governor in person.[130] Jennings took full advantage of the freedom of speech and debate that Queen Anne had guaranteed them. He delivered the speech forcefully and effectively to the Governor in the presence of his Council and the full General Assembly, despite the objections and attempted interruptions of the Governor.

In the remonstrance, Samuel Jennings accused the Governor of misgovernment in a number of specific ways:

He was absent from the colony too often to properly attend to the business of the territory.

He had interfered inappropriately with the decisions of the courts.

He was guilty of having a very expensive and inefficient government.

It was pointed out that the secretarial duties of the colony were being handled in only one office, whereas two offices were needed with the approval of the Governor. Jeremiah Basse was doing all his work in Burlington, which meant that there was serious delay in completing work for East New Jersey residents.

Governor Cornbury had awarded only one commission for a stagecoach between Perth Amboy and Burlington, to Hugh Huddy, thus creating a monopoly which was against the laws of England.

Cornbury was further chastised for placing the records of the East New Jersey proprietors in the hands of Peter Sonmans. This situation interfered with the East New Jersey proprietors' business.

He was censured for preventing the West New Jersey proprietors from granting warrants for unappropriated land in their portion of the colony. This was an attempt on his part to shut down the work of the West New Jersey proprietors, something that Queen Anne had instructed him not to do.

Assemblyman Jennings informed him that it was commonly known that he had received a bribe in the form of a large amount of money, as payment for dissolving the first elected General Assembly. These monies had led to his dismissal of Thomas Gardiner, Joshua Wright and Thomas Lambert, at the suggestion of Thomas Revell and Daniel Leeds, even though it could be demonstrated that the men dismissed were qualified to serve and had been legally elected to the Assembly. He had refused to let these three Quakers sit in the second elected General Assembly. His inappropriate actions had reduced the number of Quakers voting in the Assembly and this situation had led to the passage of the disastrous acts of the legislative body.[131]

The impact of Jennings' forceful speech led to a virtual uprising in the Assembly against the Governor's deviant and autocratic behavior. Samuel Jennings had begun the process of trying to get rid of this very bad governor. With the delivery of this speech, Jennings became one of the first truly great statesmen of America, according to the accounts written.

A few days later, on May 12, 1707, Governor Cornbury returned to the General Assembly to give his rebuttal. His presentation was orderly and logical, but his audience was not convinced of his sincerity. He did nothing to correct the errors that they had pointed out to him.[132] A stalemate ensued. The Assembly refused to pass an act of taxation until he addressed their grievances.

During that session of the General Assembly the representatives had finally seen the records of Peter Fauconier, the Receiver General of the colony. The tax act of the government had been enforced and the residents of New Jersey had paid in nearly £2,000 per year for two years. Burlington County, where the Friends resided in the greatest numbers, had by far the greatest tax burden, greater than £400 for each year of the act. This would have been less serious if the money had been used for purposes that would benefit the colony but three-quarters of the money was paying for the salaries and expenses of the Governor, Lieutenant Governor and other appointed officials of the colony. When requested by the Assembly to provide them with copies of his vouchers for the expenditures, the Receiver General of the Colony and the Governor refused to do so.

The residents of the colony, and particularly the majority of their elected representatives, realized the seriousness of the poor governance of Lord Cornbury. They continued to refuse to renew any of the legislative acts that had expired. On May 16, 1707 the Governor adjourned the General Assembly.[133]

On May 30, 1707, the representatives of the Council of Proprietors of West New Jersey presented their answers to Governor Cornbury and his council in Burlington. Samuel Jennings, Lewis Morris, Thomas Gardiner, William Hall, John Wills, Christopher Wetherill and John Kay met with the Governor to defend the council and its rights. William Biddle had stayed home. He had been responsible for presiding over and leading the council to this point, but at seventy-four he did not need to become involved in this dispute. The councilmen presented a strong case that the Governor had no authority to question their right to continue their business.[134]

Unfortunately their associate Francis Davenport, who had worked with them so diligently over the years, had died a few weeks prior to the meeting.[135]

That month William and Sarah received papers confirming that William had become the owner of his father's property back in England. His older brother, Thomas, had died without children and Thomas's wife was now deceased. The ownership had therefore reverted to William as the second son of the family. Documents arrived to be signed to sell the property to Edward Roberts of Birlingham. It was necessary for all parties with an interest in the property who were of age to sign, so William and Sarah and their son William Jr. and his wife Lydia all signed and the papers were sent back to England. William could expect £60 for the sale. Had he been the oldest son in the family and remained in England, their lives would have been much different.[136]

On May 26, 1707 Burlington Quarterly Meeting was held at Mount Hope. Joining William at the Men's Meeting were Isaac Marriott, Samuel Furnis, Thomas Raper, John Shinn Jr., Samuel Lippincott, George Elkinton and Thomas Eves. At the Women's Meeting with Sarah were Mary Myers, Ann Watson, Sarah Bunting, Frances Antram and Elizabeth Fretwell. The events of the General Assembly must have been discussed by the men, but no important business was recorded.[137]

The summer months were relatively quiet. William and Sarah could enjoy Mount Hope and each other almost without distraction. Of course their grandchildren were under foot, but that was a pleasure. William Jr. and

Lydia had their seventh and last child, John Biddle, that year. Lydia, living nearby, appreciated the help that her mother-in-law could give her with the children. It was also a help to have her own mother, Lydia Wardell, living on the waterfront in Burlington.

On August 25, 1707 Friends gathered for the Burlington Quarterly Meeting at Mount Hope. Samuel Jennings brought epistles from London to the meeting so that they could decide what should be copied into the minute book. William was appointed as one of the members to attend the Yearly Meeting representing the Quarterly Meeting. Sarah was joined by Hannah Surkett, Frances Antram, Mary Rockhill and Ann Abbott in the Women's Meeting. She was instructed to donate ten shillings to the Women's Yearly Meeting, a gift that was possible largely because of the bequest the meeting had received from Bridget Guy.[138]

The Friends of both the Men's and Women's Meeting probably were unaware that Governor Cornbury had taken the wills of Percivale and Thomasin Towle and Bridget Guy into his possession. He was trying to decide if a bequest could be made to an institution that was not a "corporate body." [139] St. Mary's Church had been incorporated to prevent just such a problem for that congregation.[140]

William and Sarah attended the Yearly Meeting for Friends in Philadelphia on September 23, 1707. William and his New Jersey friends enjoyed the company of Caleb Pusey, Thomas Story, Griffith Owen, Rowland Ellis, Anthony Morris and others in the business meetings.[141]

While he was in Philadelphia, William attended to other important business. He arranged for the apprenticeship of his grandson, William 3rd, with Mr. Griffiths, a merchant.[142] He had never been able to give his own son such special training and he remembered the apprenticeship his father had arranged for him. If young William could learn to be a merchant, he might some day become a very successful and wealthy man.

On November 24, 1707, Friends appointed to attend the Burlington Quarterly Meeting gathered at Mount Hope with William and Sarah Biddle. The minutes of the last Yearly Meeting were read. The Burlington Quarterly Meeting, having been asked to provide an amount to defray the expenses of the Yearly Meeting, agreed and directed Samuel Bunting to pay the amount requested. Peter Fretwell was asked to write to Anthony Morris to obtain a copy of the Yearly Meeting epistle concerning discipline and to bring it to the next meeting.[143]

Peter Fretwell, being one who was familiar with the activities of the legislators, informed the leaders of the Friends at this meeting of the events of the recent General Assembly meeting held at Perth Amboy from

October 23 through 31, 1707. The Assembly, with their speaker, Samuel Jennings, had published a rebuttal of Governor Cornbury's answer to them. The Assembly tried to pass more laws, particularly acts that would secure the rights of the Quakers and the Proprietors but Jeremiah Basse, Secretary of New Jersey, blocked their attempts. Governor Cornbury had refused to receive the rebuttal of the Assembly in person. He had also received a copy of a "memorial" sent from the West New Jersey proprietors in London to the Commissioners for Trade and Plantations, which expressed strong criticism of him. Realizing that no useful business would be completed by the Assembly, the Governor adjourned the legislative body, planning to reconvene it in the spring of the year in Burlington.[144]

On February 11, 1707/8, William sold more of his land. He sold or mortgaged 140 acres of the 240-acre survey near Amwell to William Alburtus.[145]

William was joined at Mount Hope February 23, 1707/8. by Samuel Jennings, Thomas Gardiner, Peter Fretwell, Samuel Furnis, Isaac Marriott, John Surket, John Day, Richard Ridgway, John Wills, Joshua Humphries and other Friends for the Burlington Quarterly Meeting. The transcribing of the Quarterly Meeting minute book was left to the care of Samuel Jennings, Peter Fretwell and Thomas Gardiner. William Biddle produced minutes relating to the Quarterly Meeting that he had saved and these were given to Peter Fretwell to be put into the meeting book.[146]

On March 4, 1707/8, William attended the Chesterfield Monthly Meeting. At the request of the Meeting, William returned the deed to the burial ground that had been established on the land of Samuel Andrews in 1686 and John Bunting took it into his care.[147]

William returned to Burlington on April 9, 1708 to attend to more business for the proprietors. He received a warrant from the council that day for 200 acres of unappropriated land.[148] This was done despite the orders of Governor Cornbury, suggesting that his order was not being enforced.

Burlington Quarterly Meeting was held at Mount Hope on May 31, 1708. William was joined by Isaac Marriott, Thomas Raper, John Surkett, John Shinn, John Day, John Wills, Joshua Humphries, Thomas Gardiner and Peter Fretwell from Burlington Monthly Meeting. Other Friends joined them from Chesterfield Monthly Meeting and from the area at the falls of the Delaware River. Samuel Jennings was absent due to serious illness. Sarah was joined by Hannah Lippincott and Frances Antram from Burlington and Mary Rockhill and Sarah Scholey from Chesterfield.[149]

At the Men's Meeting it was discussed that the minute books were not yet complete. Those overseeing the transcribing of the book were encouraged to continue. It was brought to the attention of the group that George Willocks, son-in-law of the deceased Thomas Rudyard, on behalf of Thomas's son John Rudyard, had laid "claim to the lands whereon the meetinghouse and graveyard are planted in Burlington." Peter Fretwell and Thomas Gardiner were asked to inquire into the validity of the claim.[150] William would have known that Andrew Robeson, as land agent for Thomas Rudyard, had been asked many years ago to settle the matter of the ownership of those lands and apparently had not accomplished that task.[151]

Assemblyman John Wills presented the latest details of the recent General Assembly meetings to the gathering at Quarterly Meeting. Governor Cornbury had reconvened the General Assembly in Burlington on May 5, 1708. Because Samuel Jennings was not present, Cornbury had insisted that they elect a new speaker and Thomas Gordon from East New Jersey was elected. On May 12, 1708, the new speaker delivered their grievances to the Governor once again. They complained of the unfair practices that had developed in the judicial system. The secretary, Jeremiah Basse, still refused to assist them in creating legislation. They refused to revive the Military Act, which had expired. They had been prevented from taking action to confirm the proprietors' rights and to define the requirements for Quaker jurists. Governor Cornbury, realizing that they were in a stalemate, adjourned the Assembly.[152]

The Quaker leaders realized that the tactics used by the proprietor-Quaker coalition had successfully prevented the passage of any further legislative acts that were counter to their interests. Those legislative acts that had concerned them, such as the Military Act and the Tax Act, had expired at the end of 1706, and they had not been renewed. The Quakers had finally regained some control of the government.

On August 13, 1708 William returned to Burlington to sell more of his property. He sold 46 unappropriated acres either in or out of the town bounds and a 23-perch lot in town on Wood Street to Hugh Huddy for £9; Charles Huddy was among the witnesses to the deed.[153] This town land, near St. Mary's Church, was adjacent to the William Myers house, which Hugh Huddy had purchased from Thomas Gilberthorpe.[154] Reverend John Talbot lived in the house and eventually purchased it from Hugh Huddy.[155]

On August 30, 1708, the Burlington Quarterly Meeting convened at Mount Hope. It was reported that transcription of the minute book was continuing. Thomas Gardiner and Peter Fretwell had looked into the matter of the claim to the meetinghouse and graveyard grounds and found it valid.

They arranged to purchase the land from John Rudyard for £60 "West New Jersey money at or before the 20th d. of 8th m. next." A deed was first to be made out by John Rudyard to Thomas Gardiner, Peter Fretwell, Samuel Bunting and Thomas Raper. Samuel Bunting paid the £6.1s. charges incurred by Gardiner and Fretwell and he was also authorized to pay £17 to the person collecting funds for Yearly Meeting.[156]

At this Quarterly Meeting Thomas Gardiner and John Wills informed the Quaker leaders that Queen Anne had dismissed Governor Cornbury. She had appointed John Lord Lovelace, Baron of Hurley, as the new Governor of New Jersey[157] and they could expect his arrival sometime in the fall of 1708. They had struggled with Governor Cornbury since August 1703 and now they had to prepare to work with yet another governor. Hopefully they would be able to regain the rights they had lost in the past five years. Perhaps they would be able to implement some of the new governing ideas that they wanted to see in the new colony.

On September 9 and 10, 1708, William presided over meetings of the Council of Proprietors of West New Jersey. The elections that had been held in the spring placed William Biddle, Lewis Morris, Samuel Jennings, George Deacon, John Wills, Thomas Gardiner, Richard Bull, John Reading and William Hall on the council. In May, when Lewis Morris was in Burlington for the General Assembly meetings, the annual organizational meeting of the council was held. Lewis Morris had been elected president of the council and William Biddle was elected vice president.[158]

At the meeting on September 9, 1708, it was clear by the actions of the Proprietors Council that they assumed that their rights to purchase lands and to divide and survey them for distribution to those with proprietary rights had been restored. They ordered that the recent Indian purchases be resurveyed to determine the amount each proprietor owed toward the purchase price. Colonel Morris was permitted, as the agent for the West Jersey Society, to survey two tracts of land above the recent Indian purchase, one of 40,000 acres and a contiguous tract of 60,000 acres. The council gave him permission to make the necessary Indian purchase for these lands. Thomas Byerly, on the proprietary rights of Robert Squibb and John Rudyard and George Willocks, on the proprietary rights of Thomas Rudyard and John and Thomas Clarke, from Hempstead, Long Island, were cleared by the council to receive warrants for unappropriated land.[159]

The last topic discussed and decided before adjournment concerned the further taking-up of land in the old Indian purchases. The council decided that "any proprietor having right to take up land in the new purchase shall be permitted and have liberty to take up their respective rights in the old purchase formerly made if they so please, and that upon their application to the council they shall have warrants granted for the survey of the same." The council adjourned until nine o'clock the next morning.[160]

At its meeting the next day, the Council of Proprietors decided to draw lots among their members for claiming the lands in the new purchase. John Rudyard, son of the deceased Thomas Rudyard, was told that he could have the inherited land rights of his father surveyed to him if he brought his deeds to the council. He appeared before William Biddle and the rest of the council, who inspected his indentures and, knowing that Thomas Rudyard had never exercised those rights in West New Jersey, issued warrants to his son.[161]

The Yearly Meeting for Friends was held in Burlington on September 21, 1708.[162] William and Sarah did not attend as representatives to the business meetings. However, as participants they focused on the spiritual value of the gathering that year. Most of the people from their generation who had come from England for this Quaker experiment in democracy had died. Of those who actively participated in the civic duties of the province, only Francis Collins and Isaac Marriott were still alive.

On September 29, 1708, Jonathan Davis, a Baptist preacher, asked the justices of the peace for permission to establish a Baptist Church in Burlington as allowed under the Act of Toleration. Justices Thomas Revell, Daniel Leeds, Robert Wheeler, William Budd, John Rudroe and William Bustill agreed to the request. There were now three religions in the town. The house of Jonathan Davis would serve as the interim church building for the Baptists.[163]

William Biddle, Vice President, convened the next meeting of the Council of Proprietors of West New Jersey on November 2, 1708. Joining him were Councilmen George Deacon, Thomas Gardiner, Richard Bull, John Reading and John Wills. The council announced that they would proceed to grant warrants for surveys of land in the old Indian purchases to those who requested them and brought evidence of their rights to the council, showing who had paid their shares of the new Indian purchase. The resident proprietors who had paid for the new Indian purchase before that meeting would now also receive land for their money.[164]The council adjourned until the morning of November 3, 1708. With the same members present they debated about the fee that the clerk should receive for preparing the warrants. Unable to reach a decision, they adjourned until nine o'clock on the morning of November 4, 1708. By then the council had made its decision and with the same members present they began to issue the warrants for land in the old Indian purchase. Andrew Heath received a warrant for 500 acres and other warrants were issued to Christopher

Wetherill, Henry Peeps, Philip Paul, John Easton, William Budd, John Budd, Jeremiah Langhorn, William Biles, Jonathan Stoute, Samuel Furnis and Mary Hancock.[165]

The council reconvened the next morning, November 5, 1708. More warrants were issued to John Reading, John Ladd, Richard Bull, Samuel Carpenter who was serving as attorney for Amos Strettell, Nathaniel Pope, Mathew Medcalf, George Deacon, William Biddle (for 833 $1/3$ acres for the $1/6^{th}$ share of propriety that he purchased from Samuel Clay on August 21-22, 1684) and Amos Ashead. Joseph Kirkbride had a problem with 5,000 acres on the south branch of the Raritan River from the first and second dividends for which he already had a return of survey (validated survey) from Andrew Robeson and John Barclay. He had purchased the land from Michael Russell, who had purchased it from Luke Forster, but apparently it had not previously been purchased from the Indians. The council granted Kirkbride a warrant for the land which would entitle him to correct the survey. Before adjourning the council proceeded to elect rangers for each county, and announced their intention to meet again on the first Tuesday in February.[166]

The Burlington Quarterly Meeting gathered at Mount Hope on November 29, 1708. It was recorded that the meetinghouse grounds in Burlington had been purchased from John Rudyard.[167] William was able to report to the Friends who joined him that the Council of Proprietors had begun to function again. It would appear that for now the proprietary rights of the residents of West New Jersey were valid. However, Governor Lovelace, who would be arriving in the territory shortly, could challenge these rights. The Friends were now without the man who had been perhaps their most important leader politically and spiritually, for Samuel Jennings had died that fall. His wife, Ann, had also died.[168] Samuel Jennings had been a forceful spokesman for the Quaker settlers in West New Jersey and throughout the region. His voice would be sorely missed both in Quaker Meetings for Worship and in the halls of Government and the Courts.

CHAPTER 24

Governor John Lord Lovelace
December 20, 1708 – May 1709

The new administration of the government of New Jersey commenced on December 20, 1708, when the Royal Governor, Lord Lovelace, Baron of Hurley, met his Council in Bergen, New Jersey. He published his commission that day. Even though elections had been held already that fall for a new General Assembly, the Governor refused to recognize the results of that election, and he called for the election of another General Assembly which was to meet in Perth Amboy in the spring.[1] Governor Lovelace had replaced Governor Cornbury as Governor of both New York and New Jersey; the incumbent Lieutenant Governor, Richard Ingoldsby, remained in office. William and Sarah knew several of those who had been appointed by the Crown to sit on the Governor's Council, including George Deacon, Roger Mompesson, Lewis Morris, Hugh Huddy and William Hall.[2]

The Council of Proprietors of West New Jersey continued their business as planned, despite the presence of the new Governor, and they met in Burlington on Wednesday, February 2, 1708/9. William Biddle presided in the absence of Lewis Morris. Thomas Gardiner, John Wills, John Reading and George Deacon made up the necessary quorum for the council.[3]

Warrants were issued by the Council of Proprietors to Henry Ballenger, William Hewlings and Christopher Wetherill for their third-dividend lands to be taken up in the old Indian purchase, as allowed by the action of the council meeting of November 2, 1708. Thomas Foulke had previously made an Indian purchase of land along the Rariton River and now the council granted him a warrant for surveying 350 acres anywhere he chose in one tract in his Indian purchase, so long as he quit his claim to any of the other lands in that purchase, thus making them available to other proprietors.[4]

The council then acted to try to protect, or at least to clarify, their right to purchase lands from the Indians. John Reading was given permission to make a purchase of land from the Indians on the western bank of the Rariton River between the Assiskonetkong and the Mineankoing Brooks. This land, approximately 300 acres, was adjacent to the recent Indian purchase made by the council, but had not been included in that purchase.

The council issued a certificate for Reading to take to Governor Lovelace to receive from him the necessary license to allow the Indian Purchase.[5]

In the last business completed by the Council of Proprietors that day, William Biddle was also given permission to make a purchase of 800 acres from the Indians. This represented land that had already been surveyed to him, but not purchased from the Indians. It was located near Little Egg Harbor. He presented the one-quarter proprietary share purchased from Thomas Hutchinson on May 20, 1686 against which he made the claim for this land. The council made out another certificate to Governor Lovelace, requesting that he license or approve this Indian purchase.[6] These last two actions would test the new Governor's willingness to allow the council to continue to do business. They then adjourned until the next morning.

William may have stayed in Burlington the following two nights in order to prepare for the next two council meetings. His presence in town with that of the other council members would allow resident proprietors the opportunity to ask questions and better understand their right to claim more land. The certificates to the Governor Lovelace had to be prepared and the warrants had to be written; Thomas Gardiner and John Reading would see to those matters. Any new documents submitted by other proprietors must be inspected. The records of the proprietors had to be searched to verify the indentures used to claim new lands. The presence of the council members busy at work would certainly show the inhabitants of the province, as well as the public officials, that the proprietors intended to continue their work.

The Council of Proprietors reconvened February 3 and 4, 1708/9. Warrants were issued to John Reading on behalf of John Clark, to John Reading on behalf of William Biles, attorney for William Crouch and James Wasse in England, to John Wills on behalf of Samuel Lippincott, son of the deceased Freedom Lippincott and to Joshua Wright, John Abbott, Christopher Snowden and Thomas Lambert on their own rights. All of the lands were to be taken up in the old Indian purchase. No lands had been released or surveyed in the new Indian purchases. The council then adjourned to March 22, 1708/9.[7]

Friends of Burlington County gathered at Mount Hope on February 28, 1708/9 for Burlington Quarterly Meeting. Joining Sarah at the Women's Meeting were Mary and Sarah Bunting from Chesterfield Monthly Meeting and Hope Wills, Mary Elkinton, Frances Antram, Abigail Raper, Susanna Marriott and Elizabeth Hill from Burlington Monthly Meeting. Besides those who attended from Chesterfield, Mansfield and Nottingham, William was joined by Isaac Marriott, Christopher Wetherill, John Wills, Thomas

Eves, John Day and John Butcher from Burlington. The minutes and records of the Quarterly Meeting were now in proper order and Samuel Bunting was ordered to pay for the binding of the minute book.[8]

The first session of the fourth General Assembly commenced in Perth Amboy on March 3, 1708/9. In a spirit of cooperation with the new Governor and his Council the Assembly passed a number of acts. The first was a tax bill to support the government with a tax amounting to £1722,10s,4½d. Again about twenty percent of the tax would be raised in Burlington County. The Governor was to receive £800 but no housing allowance appears to have been included. Lieutenant Governor Ingoldsby would receive £200 and the treasurer, Miles Forster, was to receive a salary of £50. He was to be bonded and his receipts were to be accountable to the General Assembly. His disbursements were to be only those allowed by the act and only by warrants signed by the Governor in the presence of his Council. The elected representatives were to be paid six shillings per diem.[10] The tone of the proceedings and the accomplishment of the legislative body gave everyone hope that the problems present during the prior administration were now in the past and could be avoided in the future.

Another act passed by the Assembly concerned the creation, or continuation, of the militia. Each male between the age of sixteen and fifty was eligible for the military. The troops were to be mustered for one day twice yearly on the third Friday in March and September. Any man who did not appear would be fined 5 shillings per day of absence, and if he did not pay the fine, a warrant could be issued to seize his goods and chattels for sale. However, the overplus from the sale was to be returned to the offender. This bill allowed the inhabitants of the colony to act by their own consciences. It prevented the abuse of the power of seizure of goods and chattels. The Quakers could more easily afford to meet the requirements of the bill even though they might be in opposition to it.[11]

The Assembly also passed an act to officially continue the post offices that had existed in the colony before that time. Offices were to continue to exist in Perth Amboy and Burlington. The act defined the duties of the postal service and it set the rates for posting letters and packets. A person could send a single-sheet letter to London for four pence, half penny, or a packet of letters to the same destination for nine pence.[12]

Another act changed the qualifications of electors and the elected in the colony. Now freeholders of towns or counties had to have 100 acres or £50 of personal worth to vote, a decrease from prior requirements. To be elected a person had to have 1,000 acres or £500 of personal worth. In the Western Division there were to be two representatives from each of the four counties and two more from each of the towns of Burlington and Salem. This would protect against another arbitrary episode like the one to which Governor Cornbury and his Council had subjected them by declaring that Thomas Lambert, Thomas Gardiner and Joshua Wright were not qualified to sit in the assembly. The act emphasized that the properly elected and seated House of Representatives would judge on the qualifications of their own members.[13]

Other acts of the Assembly concerned the establishment of taxation by townships for relief of the poor; an act for defining some of the East New Jersey land grants of Phillip Carteret when he was Governor; an act for setting bounties for killing wolves, panthers, crows, woodpeckers and blackbirds; an act prohibiting swine to run loose; and an act for regulating ordinaries (taverns).[14] For the inhabitants of the territory, the business completed by the Assembly defined the government's expectations for proper function and support of the colony.

The Quakers among the legislators hoped, of course, that their right to participate in the courts as jurors and jurists would be protected by an act that would expand the use of the alternate oath, but this did not happen. The proprietors of New Jersey also wanted legislation to protect their real estate interests. That had not been completed either, but the work of the Council of Proprietors of West New Jersey would eventually bring those rights to the Governor's attention. The General Assembly meetings lasted until April 4, 1709 when they adjourned, with plans to meet again on September 28, 1709.[15]

The Council of Proprietors of West New Jersey met again in Burlington on March 22, 1708/9, but adjourned for eight days, until March 30, 1709, without completing any business.[16] That day the Burlington Quarter Court and Court of Common Pleas met for the first time since Governor Lovelace had taken office. No Quaker justices appeared on the bench. John Wills was needed at the Council of Proprietors' meeting but could not be there because he was foreman of the Grand Jury.[17]

On March 30, 1709, the Council of Proprietors of West New Jersey reconvened in Burlington. William presided, and he was joined by councilmen Thomas Gardiner, William Hall, John Wills and John Reading. That day the council granted warrants for taking up land in the old Indian purchase to Nathaniel Pope and to John Reading on behalf of John Brearly.[18]

The council adjourned for the night and met again in the morning of March 31, 1709. George Deacon joined the others for that meeting. Warrants for land in the old Indian purchase were granted to William Hall,

William Biles, Thomas Wetherill, Edward Kemp, Annanias Gaunt and Christopher Wetherill. The council then adjourned until the next morning.[19]

When the Council of Proprietors reconvened on the morning of April 1, 1709, Lewis Morris, Council President, had arrived in Burlington from Perth Amboy, where he had been attending the meetings of the Governor's Council. Morris chaired the meeting with William Biddle, George Deacon, William Hall, Thomas Gardiner, John Wills and John Reading present. It was agreed that the new Indian purchase above the falls of the Delaware River would remain undivided until another purchase could be made from the Indians of the land further north of that purchase. The council had already approved Indian purchases for Lewis Morris for two tracts, accounting for 100,000 acres which would cover the third-dividend lands of the West Jersey Society at 5,000 acres per propriety. They had failed to provide Morris with the permission to obtain a license from the Governor for the Indian purchase, however. When the entire 250,000 acres was in their possession, it would be divided to the benefit of the resident and London proprietors.

The Council of Proprietors recognized that the division line between New York and New Jersey would have to be determined as their purchase of land from the Indians might be affected by that line. The council allowed Colonel Morris, Colonel Coxe, Mr. Byerley and Mr. Willocks to negotiate with the East New Jersey proprietors and to bring the matter to the attention of Governor Lovelace. Thomas Gardiner, Surveyor General, was designated to survey the line. Public notice was to be given to the proprietors that money was needed for the Indian purchase. It was agreed that all of those who had already advanced money towards the undivided purchase, as well as those who would advance money toward the next purchase, would be paid interest commencing on April 12th at the rate of eight percent per annum until the whole purchase was divided. The meeting adjourned with the issuance of a warrant for the first and second dividends for one proprietary share for George Willocks.[20]

The Council of Proprietors reconvened the next morning, April 2, 1709. Lewis Morris had returned to Perth Amboy, so William Biddle chaired the meeting. The council granted warrants to Henry Peeps and John Steel for land to be taken up in the old Indian purchase. They then adjourned until the first Tuesday in May, with instructions to John Reading to prepare the public notice.[21]

William would have been quite pleased with the events of the last four days. The work of the council was proceeding efficiently again. They had a plan for implementing the third dividend of land, so he knew that additional acreage would be available for him to claim and sell very soon.

For the first time since his arrival in West New Jersey 28 years before, William, now 76 years old, did not have any responsibilities to attend to. He was no longer a justice. Thanks to his efforts, the affairs of the Council of Proprietors were in the best condition that they had ever been. The affairs of his religion were in order. His son and grandchildren were doing all of the work necessary to run the farm. He had asked John Reading to get his license for the Indian purchase from the Governor when he went to get his own. When that was returned to him he could go to Little Egg Harbor to negotiate with the Indians for the land. Now he could relax and watch William Jr. prepare the farm for planting. He had time to visit his neighbors. Horseback trips to the William Wood farm, his old farm, the Clayton farm, the Newbold farm and the homestead of William Satterthwaite could be enjoyed. He could even take trips with Sarah to Philadelphia by Thomas Biddle's ferry, to shop or to visit their friends in the city. Some days Thomas Biddle would bring his wife and two children, Thomas and Sarah, to visit them, the elder Biddles. Other days Sarah would enjoy her granddaughters, Elizabeth, Sarah, Penelope and Lydia. William would go shad fishing with his grandsons, Joseph and John. William III could not join them for he was away in Philadelphia serving his apprenticeship, but he would return to Mount Hope periodically to give them reports on what he was learning.

It is not known whether there was any warning, such as a sign of illness or infirmity, but on April 27, 1709, Sarah Biddle died. She was in her seventy-first year of life.[22] William and Sarah had been married for forty-four years. Though there is no record of it, she was probably buried in the Friend's Burial Ground at Mansfield. This land had been acquired for the Friends by William from Samuel Andrews and it had been overseen by him for years. It is probably the ground on which a part of the graveyard of the Mansfield Preparative Meeting was founded in 1731,[23] which is still in existence. That site is about two miles from the Mount Hope homestead.

Sarah Biddle had experienced a long and full life. She had been raised in London, one of the most modern cities of that time. The economic advantages that she enjoyed there could have given her a comfortable position in London society. Instead she chose the path of a religious non-conformist, first as a Puritan and then as a Quaker. When she converted to Quakerism, joining her husband in that religious movement, she developed a strong convincement that lasted the rest of her life.

Women had few rights in society in the seventeenth century, but Sarah had, in her religion and in her marriage, more rights than most other women of her time. Through the unusually strong communication and understanding that existed in her relationship with her husband, William, she contributed to the decisions that they made throughout their lives together.

Following Sarah's death, William, now 76 years old, continued to live at Mount Hope.

CHAPTER 25

William Biddle's Final Years
May 1709 – November 26, 1711

When the Council of Proprietors of West New Jersey met May 3 - 6, 1709, for their annual meeting, William did not participate. The council carried on its business for the year with only eight members seated. Lewis Morris continued as president of the council; George Deacon became vice president in William Biddle's place; and William Stevenson took the place of Samuel Jennings, his deceased father-in-law.[1] William's grief was too great to allow him to continue the responsibility of working on the council.

In early May 1709, the colony experienced another unexpected event, when Governor Lovelace died. The government was automatically placed in the hands of Lieutenant Governor Richard Ingoldsby, who had served in that capacity under Governor Cornbury.[2] Understandably, the Quakers of West New Jersey feared that the governing policies of the Cornbury era might return.

On May 26, 1709, Lieutenant Governor Ingoldsby held a special meeting of his Council and called for a meeting of the General Assembly at Perth Amboy. Queen Anne intended to send a military force against the French in Canada, and New Jersey was to provide two hundred men and money to support the expedition. It was the task of the elected legislators to plan how this obligation to the English Crown would be met. The meetings to discuss this issue and others facing them continued until June 30, 1709 [3]

On May 30, 1709, the Burlington Quarterly Meeting of Friends was held at Mount Hope. Perhaps out of respect for the deceased Sarah Biddle, more women than usual had been asked to attend the meeting by the Monthly Meetings. Those attending from the Burlington Monthly Meeting included Frances Antram, Mary Wheat, Susanna Marriott, Mary Butcher, Hope Wills and Elizabeth Woolman. Women attending from Chesterfield Monthly Meeting included Mary Myers, Ann Abbott, Rebecca Warren and Sarah Murfin.[4]

The Men's Burlington Quarterly Meeting was attended by William Biddle, Christopher Wetherill, John Surkett, Thomas Raper, John Day, John Butcher, Thomas Eves and George Elkinton from Burlington, and others from Chesterfield. The group discussed the fact that the Yearly Meeting committee of Ministers and Elders wanted to change the place of their meetings from Burlington to Philadelphia. The Quarterly Meeting members realized that one of the strongest members of that group, the late Samuel Jennings, had been one of the reasons that the meetings had continued to be held in Burlington. The meeting asked Christopher Wetherill and John Surkett to report to the Meeting of Ministers and Elders their concern about the plan to remove their meetings from Burlington.[5]

Thomas Raper, as a member of the General Assembly, was able to inform the Friends of the request that would be made of them to support the Crown's war efforts against Canada. The ten Quakers who were Assemblymen would have to use great political skill to create legislation that would be acceptable to the Friends of New Jersey.

William may have visited the Little Egg Harbor region that June. He had to make an Indian purchase, and he needed to inspect his lands in that location. It was probably during that trip that he visited Mordecai Andrews. Mordecai's house had burned along with his original indenture to his property bought from William and Sarah in 1699. It may have been William's advice that caused Mordecai Andrews to return to Burlington on June 20, 1709 to receive a replacement indenture for his property. The document was signed by William and witnessed by William Biddle Jr. and John Hancock before Daniel Leeds, Assistant Justice of the court.[6]

The General Assembly Meetings were concluded on June 30, 1709. A means of fulfilling the Queen's request had been found. Three bills had been passed. First a bill to raise £3,000 over two years was enacted, and assessors and collectors were to be appointed to implement the tax. Second, 200 men were to volunteer to serve in the army that was to be formed and sent to fight against Canada. To encourage men to volunteer, the terms of the duty, including rates and method of pay, were decided and advertised. The third act of the assembly concerned the creation of Bills of Credit. Notes of five pounds, forty shillings, twenty shillings, ten shillings, and five shillings were to be issued as paper currency, backed by the resources of the citizens of the colony.[7]

On July 9, 1709 William made his way back to Burlington to sell 100 acres of unappropriated land rights to John Tuly for £12.[8] He undoubtedly enjoyed visiting with his friends in the town before returning to Mount Hope.

On August 29, 1709 Friends gathered at Mount Hope for Burlington Quarterly Meeting. Among the men attending were Thomas Gardiner and Thomas Raper. As Assemblymen they told the Friends about the discussions and compromises that had gone into forming the acts of the Assembly.[9] For those Friends who refused to pay the tax because it was used to support the war, their property could be seized to pay the tax and the fine. However, a clause had been inserted into the act requiring the constable to return any overplus to the offender after he had a distress sale of his goods. The Quaker leaders had to be greatly relieved that the army was to be composed of volunteers. Each Quaker male would be able to choose freely whether or not to be involved in the effort.

On Tuesday, September 13, 1709, the Court of Quarter Sessions was held in Burlington. The Grand Jury and the Court appointed the tax assessors and collectors for each township. They assigned the amount of tax to be raised by each township to pay for the act of the legislature previously passed for destroying wolves, panthers, crows, blackbirds and woodpeckers. Mansfield Township was taxed £4, and William Biddle Jr. was appointed Collector.[10]

One week later, on September 20, 1709, William had the opportunity to visit Philadelphia for the Yearly Meeting of Friends. Although he was no longer an official representative of the Quarterly Meeting, he was able to enjoy the company of his many friends gathered there for business and worship.

In the fall months of that year William had time to enjoy his homestead and his neighboring friends. His grandson, Joseph, was old enough now to accompany him and the Negro servant to the cove on the north end of Seppasink Island, where they would hunt for geese and ducks. Other days they would hunt upland game along the gorges that traversed the property. It was a pleasure to visit his son, William Jr., and his neighbors, William Satterthwaite, William Wood at Oneanickon and Samuel Bunting at Chesterfield, as they attended to the chores of the fall harvest.

By the time that the Burlington Quarterly Meeting was held at Mount Hope on November 28, 1709, it was apparent that William was still struggling with the grief that he felt over the loss of Sarah. The meeting agreed to loan to him the large Journal of George Fox that William Meade had sent to them from London.[11]

Reading this book, William had time to review the goals that he and Sarah had made for their lives. George Fox had meticulously recorded the events and thoughts that led to the development of Quakerism. William was reminded of the life that he had experienced since becoming a Quaker in 1654. The terrible environment of Quakers in England under religious persecution was vividly recalled. He remembered Newgate prison. He could easily recall why he and his friends and their wives and families had devoted themselves to planning for the Quaker experiment in democracy away from England.

William was reminded by reading the Fox book that the individual and his manner of conducting himself, was the essence of Quakerism. He knew that Sarah and he had both conducted their lives properly, serving as role models for their society. He realized yet again that Sarah and he had done the right thing in coming to West New Jersey and in staying by their original decision to remain loyal to the teachings of George Fox.

In September Lieutenant Governor Ingoldsby called for elections for a new General Assembly to be held that fall. The Assembly convened on November 21, 1709 at Burlington and the session continued until January 31, 1709/10. Ten acts were passed, but they were minor pieces of legislation required to more effectively administer the colony business.[12]

When Burlington Quarterly Meeting gathered at Mount Hope on Monday, February 27, 1709/10, Thomas Raper, Isaac Marriott, John Surkett, John Day, John Shinn, Thomas Eves and George Elkinton from Burlington Monthly Meeting joined William Biddle and others from Chesterfield Monthly Meeting. The only business recorded was the clearance for Samuel Bunting, the Treasurer, to pay the annual share to the Yearly Meeting.[13] For William it was pleasing to have so many of his friends attending the meetings and warming his home for a few hours. There was barely room for those who attended the Women's Meeting in the kitchen room of the house. Among those who gathered that winter day were Elizabeth Day, Hannah Lippincott, Hope Wills, Elizabeth Woolman, Frances Antram, Susanna Marriott, Sarah Bunting, Mary Rockhill, Ann Abbott and Frances Nicholson.[14]

On March 20, 1709/10 William was accompanied on his trip to Burlington by his son and daughter-in-law. Perhaps he needed their assistance to get there, but his intention was to show them the procedure for selling land, recognizing that at his death his significant real estate holdings would come into their possession. That day William sold 500 acres of land at Little Egg Harbor to Thomas Wooley of Shrewsbury for £125; William Jr. and Lydia witnessed the indenture.[15] They then went to visit and have lunch with Lydia's parents, Lydia and Eliakim Wardell, at their townhouse on Pearl Street (previously the home of John Hollinshead Sr.) before returning to Mount Hope.

On May 29, 1710 the Burlington Quarterly Meeting was held again at Mount Hope. Thomas Gardiner was among those who attended the meeting.[16] He informed William and the others present of the business of the Council of Proprietors of West New Jersey. At the annual meeting held May 2, 1710, nine members had been again elected to the council. George

Deacon did not continue on the council. Christopher Wetherill and William Budd took the two vacant Burlington County seats.

Lewis Morris, agent of the West Jersey Society, was continued as president, despite the problems he had created for them by not following the rules of land transfer. The council had never issued Lewis a certificate for purchasing the 40,000- and 60,000-acre tracts of land from the Indians. By the law of 1703, he needed such a certificate signed by the Recorder of the council to present to the Governor in order to receive the license needed to complete the purchases. Lewis Morris had merely taken a copy of the minutes of the council to Lieutenant Governor Ingoldsby to get the license. Thomas Gardiner had to write to both Lieutenant Governor Ingoldsby and Lewis Morris informing them of their error and explaining to them the right way to proceed by the law of the Colony.[17] William was interested to hear of this business from Thomas Gardiner. The law and the method of obtaining permission to make an Indian purchase had been established while he was an Assemblyman and while he was presiding over the council and it was good to hear that the laws were being followed.

Friends again joined William at Mount Hope on August 28, 1710 for Burlington Quarterly Meeting. At the request of the overseers of the Yearly Meeting, the Quarterly Meeting prepared to submit a status report. They reported "that things in a general way are pretty well and care is taken to keep up the discipline of the church and to verify anything that is disorderly." [18]

The Friends gathered at Mount Hope that day discussed what they knew about Robert Hunter, the newly-appointed Governor of New York and New Jersey. Governor Hunter had called for elections to be held for a new General Assembly. His Governor's Council had been appointed by the Crown and among the members of his council were George Deacon and Thomas Gardiner,[19] who would look out for their Quaker interests.

They hoped that their rights which had been taken from them during the Cornbury administration would be returned. The initial instructions given to the colony at the time of the surrender to Queen Anne had not been fulfilled. Quakers were not allowed to serve as justices or judges and, except in those counties where they were in great numbers, they were not permitted to serve on juries, all because the Quakers refused to take standard oaths to the Crown.

Although he was not appointed as an official representative from the Quarterly Meeting, William, with his son and daughter-in-law and grandchildren, attended Yearly Meeting for Friends when it was held in Burlington on September 19, 1710. Perhaps the main business of the meeting was a decision it made to send £100 to Boston to help Friends there build their meetinghouse.[20] While in Burlington William had the opportunity to talk to his son-in-law Clement Plumstead and to meet Clement's second wife, Elizabeth (Palmer) Plumstead and their new son William.[21]

Burlington Quarterly Meeting convened at Mount Hope on November 27, 1710. The meeting received an application through Chesterfield Monthly Meeting from Friends at Stony Brook for permission to start a Meeting for Worship in that location, which they allowed.[22]

Finally, the government of the Colony was reestablished. Governor Robert Hunter convened his Council and the newly elected Sixth General Assembly of New Jersey met at Burlington on December 6, 1710. The session continued until February 10, 1710/11. Governor Hunter addressed the Assembly and directed them to complete the legislative acts necessary to the Colony and to work towards solutions for the sharp differences that had developed between political factions.[23]. Governor Hunter knew that he could not govern effectively unless the struggles of the past between the Quaker-proprietary factions and the anti-proprietary anti-Quaker factions were reduced or resolved.

William had a very pleasurable experience on January 31, 1710/11 when he attended the wedding of Ann Wood. The eldest daughter of Mary (Parnell) Wood and William Wood was married to Thomas Lambert at the Chesterfield Monthly Meeting.[24] It was rewarding to see the daughter of the servant that Sarah and he had brought from England marry Thomas Lambert, a member of the second generation of the Lambert family, who had become one of the Quaker leaders and an Assemblyman.

William again enjoyed the company of his friends when they met at Mount Hope on February 26, 1710/11 for Burlington Quarterly Meeting. The meeting decided that the Chesterfield and Burlington Monthly Meetings would need to raise £17 for the gift to the Friends of Boston. A committee was formed to solicit donations.[25]

At the Burlington Quarterly Meeting held at Mount Hope May 28, 1711, it was decided to seek subscriptions to encourage Friends in both meetings to raise money for the construction of the meetinghouse for the Friends of Boston since those funds were still needed.[26]

Perhaps the most interesting part of his day was when John Wills informed William of the actions of the Council of Proprietors of West New Jersey when they met May 2, 1711 in Burlington. Lewis Morris was reelected as president of the council. John Wills continued as vice president, Thomas Gardiner as Surveyor General and John Reading as Clerk and

Recorder. Christopher Wetherill and Richard Bull had left the council. House Speaker John Kay and young John Gosling had taken their seats. The council continued to issue warrants for third-dividend lands, but the lands were not surveyed out yet. This meant that William could get his warrants for the third-dividend lands that he owned at any time. Also, agreeable discussions that would help them continue their business were had with Lewis Morris when he came to Burlington for the Governor's Council meetings which began in December.

Other business had been completed by the Council of Proprietors at that meeting. The Mattinuck Island was finally claimed by the proprietary rights of the West Jersey Society and a moiety (half) by the other members of the council. It was then totally transferred to Governor Robert Hunter, although the land use was not to change. The council had finally issued a certificate to Lewis Morris so that he could obtain from the Governor a license to purchase the lands above the falls from the Indians. When this purchase was completed, the third-dividend lands could be released by survey.

The council also discussed how they would proceed to more formally incorporate themselves.[27] From the report of John Wills, William understood that the proprietors believed that this new Governor would allow them to continue their land business. William had spent a great deal of time and effort trying to protect those rights. It seemed that the anti-proprietor, anti-Quaker political faction was beginning to lose some of its power.

By now William realized that his life could not go on forever. He was fully aware of how he wanted the assets that Sarah and he had accumulated to be distributed at the time of his death. He completed and signed his will on June 23, 1711. His legal heir was his son William, but he favored his eldest grandson, William III, by leaving him the Mount Hope homestead and farm and Seppasink Island after the death of his parents. He left 500 acres of unappropriated land to his other grandsons, Joseph and John, and another 500 acres of unappropriated land rights to his cousin Thomas Biddle. He made bequests of £75 to his grandson, William, and £37.10s.to each of the other six grandchildren. The money was to be "put forth at interest" by his executors at the proper risk of the grandchildren and to their use and to be paid to them at their full age of twenty-one years, or, in the case of the granddaughters, at the time of their marriages if they were younger than twenty-one. Legacies of £7.10s were left to the three children of Thomas Biddle and to William Plumstead, the son of Clement Plumstead husband of his deceased daughter Sarah. He also left 100 acres of unappropriated land rights to William Satterthwaite and to his cousin, Dorothy Sherwin. All the rest of his estate was left to his son William. He selected Samuel Bunting and John Wills and his son, William, as the executors of his will.[28]

The Burlington Quarterly Meeting convened at Mount Hope on August 27, 1711. Lydia Biddle was one of the appointed representatives of the Chesterfield Monthly Meeting that day.[29] The committee had successfully raised the £17 for the Boston Friends. Isaac Marriott had delivered the money to Samuel Carpenter of Philadelphia and returned a receipt to the meeting. The Quarterly Meeting received the status reports from the monthly meetings as requested annually by the Yearly Meeting. The more urban Burlington Monthly Meeting reported "things are not so well as we could desire but hope they will be better and we are ..." The more rural Chesterfield Monthly Meeting reported "that things are pretty well amongst them."[30] This merely reflected the ability of the Friends to continue the pureness of their religious lives in those more remote areas where they did not have to meld with other elements of society.

Thomas Biddle probably transported William with his son and daughter-in-law and his grandchildren to Philadelphia for Yearly Meeting on September 18, 1711. William was one of the older elders there. He was then seventy-seven years of age. It was good to see that the next generations of Quakers were continuing their work.

Shortly before November 26, 1711, William Biddle died.[31] The Burlington Quarterly Meeting was held that day for the last time at Mount Hope. The Women's Meeting was attended by Mary (Parnell) Wood, Sarah Farnsworth, Elizabeth Horner, Hannah Nicholson, Hannah (Cooper) (Woolston) Surkett, Abigail (Perkins) Raper, Hannah Lippincott, Phebe (Wetherill) Scattergood, Mary Elkinton and Anne (Jennings) Stevenson. The Men's Meeting was attended by Thomas Raper, John Surkett, Samuel Smith, John Butcher, Restore Lippincott, John Wills, George Elkinton, William Wood, Joshua Humphries and others from the Chesterfield Monthly Meeting.

A Meeting for Worship and memorial service for the departed William would have been held before the business meeting.[32] Presumably he was buried in the Quaker burial ground at Mansfield with Sarah.

Thomas Raper, William Wood and Joshua Humphries took the inventory of William's estate on the day of the Quarterly Meeting. As the meeting ended and those attending left, these three Friends began their inspection of the property as was customary after a death. Noted in their inventory were domestic animals, cattle, horses, sheep and hogs restrained in their enclosures. In the basement of the house they inventoried an old Negro male, an Indian woman and two children.[33]

The three appraisers entered the front door of the house. They first recorded the chairs stacked in the hallway which had been used over and over again by those who attended the quarterly meetings. The first room to the right was the living room. It contained a couch, a looking glass and a table. The fire shovel, andirons and tongs were in their usual positions at the fireplace. On the table were earthen plates and drinking glasses left from the Quarterly Meeting. In the kitchen and dining room brass, copper and iron pots hung on the pot racks. A chest of drawers and other chests were positioned against the walls away from the fireplace. In the chest of drawers they found pewter utensils along with plates and serving pieces. The spice box rested on the chest of drawers.[34]

Returning to the hallway, they went up the stairway to the second floor. Each of the four bedrooms contained one bed. The largest, a double bed, was in William's bedroom. Also in this main chamber was a chair and bureaus, one containing William's clothes and in the other sewing silk and silverware that had belonged to Sarah. Other possessions of hers — wool and homespun and linens, and remnants of cloth — were found about the house, reminders of his wife that William had not been able to part with after her death. In his bedroom was a collection of books, some from England that they had brought with them, and undoubtedly some reprinted in Philadelphia as directed by the Yearly Meeting.[35]

The appraisers next went to the barn where they found a small amount of wheat and Indian corn. In the work shop was a keg of nails, some lumber and an old cask. They noticed that William Biddle Jr. was wearing his father's watch, but because it had been given to him before his father's death, it would not count in the inventory. William's generation was the first one to wear watches. They also inquired about the proprietary shares owned by William that he had transferred to his son before his death

William Jr. presented his father's account books for their inspection. The accounts were in good order. Over £500 in notes were owed to William. He had extended credit to a number of individuals and he probably was owed money by the proprietors. There was less than £24 money on hand. The inventory was completed that day, November 26, 1711.[36] The estate was evaluated at £864.12s.7½d.[37]

On February 25, 1711/2, at the request of William Biddle Jr. and Lydia, the court appointed John Wills of Northampton and Samuel Bunting of Chesterfield as guardians for their children under fourteen years of age, Penelope, Joseph, Lydia and John.[38]

On March 3, 1711/2, the will of William Biddle Sr. was probated by the Surrogate, Jeremiah Basse, Esquire.[39]

An Inventory of the goods chattels and credits of William
Bidle late of the Township of Mansfield in the County
of Burlington deceased as the same was appraised
by us whose Names are hereunto subscribed

	£	s	d
Imprimis To his purse and Apparrell	024	00	00
To money due by bonds bills and mortgage	500	12	5 ½
To one old negro male one Indian woman and two children		00	00
To neat cattell and horses	57	00	00
To a Cart and Plough and other utensils for husbandry	16	00	00
To a parcell of sheep	13	00	00
To a small parcell of wheat in the barn & some Indian corn	8	00	00
To a parcel of swine	8	00	00
To a parcel of pewter	8	12	06
In the Kitchen to brass copper and iron vessels	9	00	00
To a pair of steelyards and pot racks and other lumber	1	14	00
In the hall to parcel of chairs	4	00	00
To a chest of drawers one spice box and three chests	4	13	06
To one table and one couch and a looking glass	2	10	00
To some earthen plates some drinking glasses a fire shovel and tongs and andirons	2	00	00
To a parcel of linen	10	00	00
To some plate and a parcel of sowing silk	15	02	00
In the shop a parcell of Nails	7	10	00
To parcel of homespun cloth	4	00	00
To two beds and furniture one old	18	00	00
To an old warming pane and a parcell of books	4	08	00
To a Trunk and some old remnants of stuff	4	00	00
To some old cask and other lumber	1	10	07
In the Chambers to one bed and furniture and one chair and one table	18	00	00
To one bed and one table	10	00	00
To a parcell of wool	3	00	00
To a parcell of lumber goods and huslements	10	00	00
	864	12	1½

The twenty sixt of November 1711
Then the above appraisment was made by us
William Wood
Thomas Raper
Joshua Humphries

*New Jersey State Archives, Department of State/Secretary of State's Office,
Wills and Inventories 253 – 260C. William Biddle Sr. 1711*

Left:

The William Biddle House, Mount Hope, about 1939.

Epilogue

Since the death of William and Sarah Biddle in the early 1700s many of the governmental, religious and business institutions that were started during their lives have continued.

The Burlington Quarterly Meeting has continued to meet in different locations and it conducts business and worship in the same manner today. Quaker Meetings for Worship and Business continue to be held in Meetinghouses throughout Burlington County. The Religious Society of Friends continues to thrive and the Philadelphia Yearly Meeting has over 12,000 members.

The features of the government and judicial systems that the Quakers developed and brought with them from England have endured. It is said that the features of their constitution, The Concessions and Agreements of West New Jersey, served as a model for the formation of the Bill of Rights of the Constitution of the United States.

Their home, Mount Hope, which was located in what is now Mansfield, Burlington County was one of the oldest houses in which religious services were held in the State of New Jersey. The architecture of its virgin timber frame, its brick-filled walls, and its formal entrance with dutch doors was meticulously recorded by the Historic American Buildings Survey (HABS) in 1939. Unfortunately the house was demolished in 2008.

The Council of Proprietors of West New Jersey still oversees the distribution of the unappropriated land of the West New Jersey territory. The proprietary shares and rights of William and Sarah descended first to their son William Jr. then to their grandson John and then to his son Clement. Each of them claimed and sold land to others using those rights until there were no land rights remaining after the sixth dividend in the mid-1700s. On the eve of the Civil War the Council of Proprietors declared a seventh dividend of land. Knowing that there were more land rights available for the Biddle shares, ownership to a fraction of their remaining rights was proven and on May 1, 1984 the council issued a new warrant for unappropriated land rights for that fraction of a share. Land from that warrant was used in 1995 to perfect a title of land in what had been the West New Jersey territory. This type of real estate transaction can continue even today.

The current Council of Proprietors of West New Jersey owns all of the documents and records that pertained to the land matters of West New Jersey. These include the Concessions and Agreements of West New Jersey, the Tripartite Agreement, the Quintipartite Agreement, matters concerning purchases of land from the Indians, returns of surveys, issued warrants for land, evidence of proprietary rights and many other records pertaining to distribution of unappropriated lands of West New Jersey. In November of 2005 they loaned the documents to The Archival Library of the State of New Jersey for permanent safekeeping and preservation.

The Council of Proprietors of West New Jersey continues to meet and elect their members yearly; five members from Burlington County on April 10th at the Corner of Broad and High Streets in Burlington and four members from Gloucester County on April 13th under the buttonwood tree on the Delaware River bank in Gloucester City. When they gather for their annual meeting on the first Tuesday in May, 2012 at their office in Burlington, New Jersey, they will have met for 324 continuous years.

There are many descendants of William and Sarah Biddle throughout the United States and the world, some with the same surname and many without. In each new generation there have been many descendants who have become prominent and distinguished in their vocation, profession or in their community life. These descendants know that William and Sarah Biddle were their most important ancestors. They brought us to America.

It took many strong, intelligent, dedicated people to establish a new society with major improvements in human rights and values over that of England in the 17th century. These beliefs were reflected in the judicial system, in land ownership, in individual rights and in the freedom of conscience and religion. Descendants of all members of this community, including Biddle descendants have benefited and are still benefiting from their accomplishments.

William and Sarah truly planted a seed of democracy in this rich new land called New Jersey.

BIBLIOGRAPHY AND ABBREVIATIONS

Anniversary Book
Nicholas Biddle, compiler, Biddle Anniversary Celebrating the 250th Anniversary of the Arrival in America of William and Sarah Kempe Biddle, November 12, 1931 (The Engle Press, Philadelphia).

Barbour and Roberts
Hugh Barbour and Arthur O. Roberts, *Early Quaker Writings 1650 – 1700* (Wm. B. Erdmans Publisher, Grand Rapids, Michigan, 1973).

Basse BS
Jeremiah Basse collection of recorded surveys.

Besse
Joseph Besse, *A Collection of the Sufferings of the People called Quakers* (London, 1753).

BCB
The Burlington Court Book, A Record of Quaker Jurisprudence in West New Jersey 1680-1709, ed. H. Clay Reed and George J. Miller (Kraus Reprint Co., Millwood, N.Y., 1975).

BCD
Burlington County Deeds, Mount Holly, New Jersey.

Bisbee, *Burlington Island*
Henry H. Bisbee, *Burlington Island The Best and Largest on the South River 1624 to 1972* (Heidelberg Press, Burlington, N.J.).

Bisbee, *Burlington Town Book*
Henry H. Bisbee and Rebecca Bisbee Colesar, eds., *The Burlington Town Book 1694-1785* (Burlington, N.J., 1975).

Bisbee, John Tatham
Henry H. Bisbee, "John Tatham alias Gray," *PMHB*, 83:253 – 270.

BMM
Burlington Monthly Meeting minutes, records, births, deaths, marriages.

BQM
Burlington Quarterly Meeting minutes, records.

Braithwaite, *Beginnings*
William C. Braithwaite, *The Beginnings of Quakerism* (London 1912).

Braithwaite, *Second Period*
William C. Braithwaite, *The Second Period of Quakerism,* 2d. ed., Henry J. Cadbury, ed. (Cambridge, 1961).

CCHS
>Camden County Historical Society.

Commissions
>New Jersey Commissions.

CMM
>Chesterfield Monthly Meeting minutes, records, deaths, miscellaneous.

CPWJ
>Council of Proprietors of West Jersey, minutes, surveys and records.

EJD
>East Jersey Deeds.

Fox
>Norman Penny, editor, *The Short Journal and Itinerary Journal of George Fox* (Cambridge University Press, Philadelphia Friends Book Store, 1925).

GMNJ
>*The Genealogical Magazine of New Jersey.*

HABS
>Historic American Building Survey

Haverford
>Haverford Friends' Library

HBD
>Henry Drinker Biddle, *Notes of the genealogy of the Biddle Family* (Philadelphia, W.S. Fortescue & Co., 1895).

Hinshaw
>William Wade Hinshaw, *Encyclopedia of American Quaker Genealogy*, 6 vols. (Ann Arbor, Mich., 1936-1950).

H & M Comm.
>Pennsylvania Historical and Museum Commission

Hotten
>John Camden Hotten, *The Original Lists of Persons of Quality ... Who Went from Great Britain to the American Plantations, 1600-1700* (New York, 1931).

HSP
>Historical Society of Pennsylvania, Philadelphia.

HSP Penn Papers
>Historical Society of Pennsylvania, William Penn Papers.

Jennings, Samuel
>*Two West New Jersey Tracts With Appendix: "The Case Put & Decided" and "Truth Rescued from Forgery & Falshood"* (reprinted 1880 and 1881, Collins Printing House, Philadelphia).

Jones, *American Colonies*
>Rufus M. Jones, *The Quakers in the American Colonies* (London, 1911).

JFHS
>Journal of the Friends Historical Society.

L&S
>Aaron Leamng and Jacob Spicer, *The Grants, Concessions, and Original Constitutions of the Province of New Jersey*, second edition (Somerville, N.J., 1881).

Leeds BS
>Leeds' Book of Surveys

Lefroy
>J. H. Lefroy, *Memorials of the discovery and early settlement of the Bermudas of Sommers Islands 1515-1685*, Vol. 2, second edition (1932).

L&MQM
>Register of the London and Middlesex Quarterly Meeting, Birth, Death and Marriage records.

London YM
>London Yearly Meeting minutes and records.

MTM
>Mansfield Township Meeting minutes and records.

Milbourne, *Testimonies*
>Thomas Milbourne, *An Abstract or Abbreviations of som few of the Many (Later and Formerly Testimonys from the Inhabitants of New Jersey, and other Eminent Persons Who have Wrote particularly concerning the Place* (London, 1681).

Myers, Albert Cook, *Narratives*
>*Narratives of Early Pennsylvania, West New Jersey and Delaware 1630-1707*, Albert Cook Myers, editor (February 1912).

NJA
>New Jersey Archives

NJSAL
>New Jersey State Archival Library, Trenton

N. J. Wills
>New Jersey Will records listed by county.

PA
>Pennsylvania Archives

Penn-Logan
>Correspondence Between William Penn and James Logan, *Memoirs of the Historical Society of Pennsylvania*. Vols. IX and X (Philadelphia, 1870).

Pepys
O. F. Morshead, editor, *Everybody's Pepys, The Diary of Samuel Pepys 1660-1669* (Harcourt Brace & Co., New York, 1926).

PGM
Pennsylvania Genealogical Magazine.

PMHB
Pennsylvania Magazine of History and Biography.

Pomfret, West Jersey
John E. Pomfret, *The Province of West New Jersey, 1609 – 1702* (Princeton, 1956).

PWP 1
Mary Maples Dunn and Richard S. Dunn, editors, *The Papers of William Penn,* Vol. 1 (Philadelphia, 1981).

PWP 2
Richard S. Dunn and Mary Maples Dunn, editors, *The Papers of William Penn,* Vol. 2 (Philadelphia, 1982).

PWP 3
Marianne S. Wokeck, Joy Wiltenburg, Alison Duncan Hirsch, and Craig W. Horle, editors, *The Papers of William Penn,* Vol. 3 (Philadelphia, 1986).

PWP 4
Craig W. Horle, Alison Duncan Hirsch, Marianne S. Wokeck and Joy Wiltenburg, editors, *The Papers of William Penn*, Vol. 4 (Philadelphia, 1987).

PWP 5
Edwin B. Bronner and David Fraser, *The Papers of William Penn,* Vol. 5, *William Penn's Published Writings, 1660–1726: An Interpretive Bibliography* (Philadelphia 1986).

Revell's BS
Revell's Book of Surveys

Rickman, L.L., Manuscript
Lydia Lewis Rickman, unpublished manuscript, Historical Society of Pennsylvania, Genealogical Society of Pennsylvania Manuscript Collection.

Rickman, L.L., Esther Biddle
L. L. Rickman, "Ester Biddle and her Mission to Louis IV," *Friend's Historical Journal,* Vol. 47:38-45.

Rickman, Lydia L., William Biddle
"The Source of William Biddle's English Fortune," *PGM.* 19:127-129.

Sheppard
Walter Lee Sheppard, Jr., ed., *Passengers and Ships Prior to 1684* (Genealogical Publishing Co., Baltimore, 1970).

Smith, Samuel, *Nova Caesaria*
> Samuel Smith, *The History of the Colony of Nova-Caesaria or New Jersey*, second ed. (Trenton, N.J., 1877).

Snyder, *Civil Boundaries*
> John P. Snyder, *The Story of New Jersey's Civil Boundaries 1606-1968*, (Trenton, 1969).

Stillwell
> John E. Stillwell, *Historical and Genealogical Miscellany* (Baltimore: Genealogical Publishing Co., 1970).

Swarthmore FL
> Swarthmore Friends Library.

Tanner
> Edwin P. Tanner, *The Province of New Jersey 1664-1738* (London 1908).

Trevelyan
> G. M. Trevelyan, *History of England* (Longmans, Green and Co., London, New York, Toronto, 1929).

TWM
> Two Weeks Meeting, London.

WJD
> West Jersey Deeds.

WMQ
> *William and Mary Quarterly*

YM
> Philadelphia Yearly Meeting minutes, records.

NOTES

CHAPTER 1: BIRLINGHAM, WORCESTERSHIRE, ENGLAND 1633-1650

1. *PGM*, 19:73-90, and Rickman, L.L., manuscript, pp.11-12.
2. *PGM*, 19:77-79, and Rickman, L.L., manuscript, p.17.
3. *PGM*, 19:77 and Rickman, L.L., manuscript, pp.20-24.
4. *PGM*, 19:78-79.
5. *PGM*, 19:75-77.
6. *PGM*, 19:75-76.
7. *PGM*, 19:79-80.
8. Rickman, L.L., manuscript, pp.11, 24.
9. Rickman, L.L., manuscript, pp.11-12.
10. *PGM*, 19:77 and Rickman, L.L., manuscript, p.17.
11. Rickman, L.L., manuscript, pp.12-13.
12. Rickman, L.L., manuscript, pp. 12a, 25-26.

CHAPTER 2:: London, Apprenticeship as a Cordwainer, Conversion to Quakerism, 1650-1660

1. *PGM*, 19:76, 78.
2. *PGM*, 19, appendix; and Rickman, L.L., manuscript, p.5.
3. *PGM*, 19:81; Rickman, L.L., manuscript, pp.6-7.
4. Rickman, L.L., Esther Biddle, pp. 38-45.

CHAPTER 3: London and Early Persecution 1660-1665

1. Braithwaite, *Beginnings*, pp.241-278.
2. Braithwaite, *Beginnings*, pp. 273, 471.
3. Braithwaite, *Second Period*, pp.4-6.
4. Braithwaite, *Second Period*, p.9.
5. Braithwaite, *Second Period*, p. 12.
6. Besse, *Sufferings*, p. 366.
7. Braithwaite, *Second Period*, p.7.
8. Braithwaite, *Second Period*, pp. 22-25.
9. Braithwaite, *Second Period*, pp.5-7.
10. Braithwaite, *Second Period*, p.7.
11. Pepys.
12. *PGM*, 19:82n.
13. Rickman, L.L., manuscript, p.7.
14. L&MQM births and deaths, HBD, p.79, and Besse, p.482.
15. Jones, *American Colonies*, pp.84-89.
16. Jones, *American Colonies*, pp.357-358.
17. Pomfret, *West Jersey*, p.94.
18. Braithwaite, *Second Period*, p.16.
19. Sowle, *Sufferings*, 2:299.
20. Pepys, pp.278-322.
21. Register, L&MQM deaths

CHAPTER 4 : Marriage to Sarah Kempe 1665/6

1. *PGM* 19:82; Rickman, L.L., manuscript, p.6.
2. Register L&MQM marriages
3. *PWP*, 1:411-414.
4. Rickman, L.L., manuscript, pp.28-44.
5. *PGM*, 19:88-90; Rickman, L.L., manuscript, pp.28-44.
6. *PGM*, 19:88-90, Rickman, L.L., manuscript, pp.28-44; Rickman, L.L., William Biddle, pp.127-129.
7. *PGM*, 19:88.
8. Besse, *Sufferings*, p.532.
9. Rickman, L.L., William Biddle, pp.127-129.
10. Rickman, L.L., manuscript, pp. 28-44.
11. *PGM*, 19:81.
12. *PGM*, 19:81 and Besse, *Sufferings*, 1:p.690,692.

CHAPTER 5 : Strengthening Quakerism, Family, Inheritance, Planning for a Quaker Province in America 1666-1676

1. Braithwaite, *Second Period*, p.253,291.
2. Braithwaite, *Second Period*, p.253.
3. Braithwaite, *Second Period*, pp.290-292.

4. Braithwaite, *Second Period*, p.276,360.
5. TWM minutes
6. Braithwaite, *Second Period*, pp.69-74.
7. *PGM*, 19:87.
8. *PGM*, 19,77-78.
9. *PGM*, 19,77-78.
10. Besse, *Sufferings*, p.430.
11. Besse, *Sufferings*, p.431.
12. London YM minutes.
13. Jones, *American Colonies*, p.111.
14. Braithwaite, *Second Period*, p.596.
15. Jones, *American Colonies*, pp.357-361 and Jones, *George Fox*, 2:515n.
16. Jones, *American Colonies*, pp.536-538.
17. London YM minutes.
18. Braithwaite, *Second Period*, p.59.
19. *PGM*, 19:87.
20. Besse, *Sufferings*, multiple examples of goods taken in excess of fines, Vol. I, p. 445, 449.
21. London YM minutes.
22. *PGM*, 19:87.
23. Besse, *Sufferings*, discussions of Devonshire House
24. Braithwaite, *Second Period*, p.527.
25. L&S, pp.46-48.
26. Caroline Robbins, "William Penn, Edward Byllynge and the Concessions of 1677," in *The West Jersey Concessions and Agreements of 1676/77*, A Roundtable of Historians, Occasional Papers No. 1 (Trenton, N.J.: New Jersey Historical Commission, 1979), p.17.
27. *PWP*, 1:383 and pp.649-651.
28. London YM minutes.
29. *PWP*, 1:651-653, NJA 1s. XXI:559-565, NJA 1s. I:413-415, Pomfret, *West Jersey*, pp.69-72; Jones, *American Colonies*, p.366.
30. Jones, *American Colonies*, p.366 and Pomfret, *West Jersey*, pp .69-72.
31. NJA 1s. XXI:565.
32. NJA 1s. I:413-415 and Pomfret, *West Jersey*, pp .69-72.
33. London YM minutes
34. London YM minutes
35. London YM minutes
36. *PWP*, 1:653.
37. L&S, pp.61-72.

CHAPTER 6 : The Concessions and Agreements of West New Jersey

1. Barbour & Roberts, pp.411-421 and *PWP*, 1:387-416.
2. Pomfret, *West Jersey*, pp.92-93.
3. Pomfret, *West Jersey*, pp. 93-96 and Barbour and Roberts, pp.411-421.
4. *PWP*, 1:390.
5. *PWP*, 1:403.
6. *PWP*, 1:403,406.
7. Richard P. McCormick, *Experiment in Independence* (Rutgers University Press, 1950), p.70.
8. *PWP*, 1:404.
9. *PWP*, 1:393-394.
10. *PWP*, 1:396.
11. *PWP*, 1:395-396.

12. *PWP*, 1:398 399.
13. Braithwaite, *Second Period,* pp. 69-74.
15. *PWP*, 1:398-399.
16. *PWP*, 1:407 408.
17. *PWP*, 1:409n, 410n, 411-418.

CHAPTER 7: PROMOTING, MARKETING AND SETTLING THE WEST JERSEY PROVINCE
1. *PWP*, 1:414-415.
2. *PGM*, 19:appendix.
3. *PWP*, 1:414 and CMM miscellaneous records, Certificate of Removal from Devonshire Monthly Meeting not previously known to exist. The document had been placed in the records of the Chesterfield Monthly Meeting by William and Sarah after they moved to Mansfield and established their allegiance to that monthly meeting.
4. *PWP*, 1:417.
5. *PWP*, 1:418-421.
6. *PWP*, 1:391-393.
7. Pomfret, *West Jersey*, p.87 and WJD BBB-115.
8. WJD AAA-74,228,267, B-52,63,131,138,330,332,681, BBB-,115, M-14, 29, 79, 109, 162, 188.
9. Pomfret, *West Jersey*, p.87, and appendix pp.285-289.
10. WJD B-624.
11. WJD BBB-115.
12. WJD B-330 and HDB, pp.69-71.
13. WJD B-23 and HDB, pp.63-67.
14. WJD B-332.
15. HDB, pp.69-71.
16. WJD B-1,6,18,26,50,52,62,63,80, M-8,9,11,29,32,162,164, AAA-267.
17. WJD B-131,138.
18. *PGM*, 19:87.
19. *PWP*, 1:410n and Pomfret, West Jersey, p.92.
20. Barbour & Roberts, pp.495-496.
21. London YM minutes.
22. WJD B-25.
23. WJD B-23.
24. Smith, *Nova Caesaria*, pp.92-93 and Pomfret, *West Jersey*, p.103.
25. Pomfret, *West Jersey*, pp.103-104
26. Smith, *Nova Caesaria*, pp.94-97.
27. Noble's Map of Burlington. A copy is in the possession of Senator Henry Haines, President of the Council of Proprietors of West Jersey
28. Noble's Map.
29. Noble's Map.
30. CPWJ Survey Book A, pp. 203-205.
31. Snyder, *Civil Boundaries*, pp.2-3.
32. Smith, *Nova Caesaria*, pp.100-102.
33. Basse BS, p.220.
34. Commissions, AAA-29, *PGM*, 16:185 and Revell's BS, p.132.
35. Hotten, p.404.
36. Pomfret, *West Jersey*, p.104.
37. *PGM*, 27:(3),pp.139-159.
38. Pomfret, *West Jersey*, p.109 and BCB, pp.1-4.

CHAPTER 8: LONDON 1676/7 TO 1681

1. London YM minutes
2. Braithwaite, *Second Period*, pp.100-01
3. Milbourne, testimonies, pp.17-18.
4. Smith, *Nova Caesaria*, p.102.
5. *NJA* 1s. I:413-415.
6. Milbourne, testimonies, pp.17-18.
7. London YM minutes.
8. *PGM*, 19:87.
9. HDB, pp.71-72.
10. WJD B-109.
11. HDB, pp.71-72.
12. HDB,. pp.71-72.
13. London YM minutes.
14. Hotten, p.452 and Besse, *Sufferings*, II:288,316.
15. CPWJ Survey Book A:203-205 and Smith, *Nova Caesaria*, p.104.
16. Milbourne, testimonies, pp.17-18 and Smith, *Nova Caesaria*, pp.115-116.
17. London YM minutes.
18. Smith, *Nova Caesaria*, pp.124-125.
19. WJD AAA-74,267, B-1,6,623, AE-403.
20. Samuel Jennings, p.46.
21. L&S, p.417.
22. BCB, p.xxxii.
23. WJD M-14.
24. Smith, *Nova Caesaria*, pp.124-125.
25. Smith, *Nova Caesaria*, pp.124-125.
26. Revell's BS, p.1.
27. TWM minutes, February 7, 1680/1
28. PWP, 2:103-104.
29. NJA 1s. I:457.
30. PWP, 2:85-87.

CHAPTER 9: EMIGRATION TO WEST NEW JERSEY — SUMMER 1681

1. Besse, *Sufferings*, p.442.
2. Sheppard, *Passengers and Ships*, p.144.
3. Margaret Sefton-Jones, *Old Devonshire House by Bishopgate London*, Swarthmore Press Ltd.
4. Albert Cook Myers, *Narratives*, pp.191-195.
5. London YM minutes May 24, 1681.
6. Marion Balderston, ed., *John Claypoole's Letter Book* (1681-1684 and Philadelphia, 1967), p.45, and Sheppard, *Passengers and Ships*, p.80n.
7. *PGM*, 27:85.
8. WJD B-23 margin notes and Revell's BS p.33.
9. CMM miscellaneous records.
10. Myers, *Narratives*, p.194.
11. Register L&MQM birth and death records and HDB, p.79.
12. HDB, pp.72-74.
13. Penn to Logan, X:3, 15, 63, 67, 73, 104, 108, 293, 322.
14. HDB, pp.72-74.
15. Sheppard, *Passengers and Ships*, pp.146-147.
16. *PGM*, 27:85.
17. Samuel Jennings, p.47.
18. George M. Haines, *Ancestry of the Haines and other Families*, p.253.

19. *NJA* 1s. XXI:414.
20. *NJA* 1s. XXI:414.
21. WJD B-215.
22. Hinshaw, p.213.
23. Sheppard, *Passengers and Ships*, p.146 and *PGM*, 27:85.
24. Sheppard, *Passengers and Ships*, p.146.
25. Marion Balderston, ed., *John Claypoole's Letter Book* (The Huntington Library, San Marino, California, 1967), p.45.
26. Hotten, pp.458 and 485.
27. Hotten, p.452 and Besse, Sufferings, II:288,316.
28. Besse, *Sufferings*, II:288,316; Harriet F. Durham*, Caribbean Quakers* (Hollywood, Florida, 1972), pp.36-37, and Meetings for Sufferings Book of Cases, Book #1 1661 – 1695.
29. Hotten, p.446.
30. BCB, p.3, WJD B-33 and *NJA* 1s. XXIII:119.
31. WJD B-13.
32. YM Minutes
33. Samuel Jennings, p.47.
34. Barbour & Roberts, p.47.
35. L&S, p.433.

CHAPTER 10: BURLINGTON, WEST NEW JERSEY — 1681

1. BMM minutes August 7, 1682.
2. WJD B-13.
3. WJD B-633.
4. WJD B-673.
5. L&S, pp.423-436.
6. L&S, pp.423-436.
7. *PWP*, 2:87n.
8. L&S, pp.423-425.
9. L&S, p.436.
10. L&S, p.433.
11. L&S, pp.437-441.
12. L&S, PP.437-441.
13. BMM minutes December 5, 1681.
14. Hinshaw, II:186.

CHAPTER 11: SURVEYING AND CLAIMING LAND 1681-1682

1. Revell's BS, p.24.
2. HSP Penn papers, 10.735 p.933, and Penn-Logan, I:163, 166, 211.
3. Revell's BS, p.23.
4. Revell's BS, p.23.
5. CPWJ February 9, 1741/2 and HDB, p.86.
6. Revell's BS, p.23.
7. WJD B-68.

CHAPTER 12:: THE STORY OF THE SEPPASINK ISLAND CONTROVERSY

1. Bisbee, Burlington Island, p.8.
2. Bisbee, Burlington Island, p.12.
3. Bisbee, Burlington Island, p.12.
4. PA 2s. XII:769-770.
5. PA 2s. V:673.

6. PA 2s. V:710.
7. PA 2s. V:709 and NJA 1s. III:286.
8. P 2s. XII:726.
9. NJA 1s. I:347.
10. WP 2:261-263.
11. L&S p.455.
12. PWP 2:392-394.
13. PWP 2:398-400.
14. L&S pp.480-481.
15. PWP 2:493.
16. PA 2s. V:739.
17. NJA 1s. I:457.
18. *Autobiography of Charles Biddle 1745-1821* (Philadelphia: E.Claxton and Co., 1883), pp.363-364.
19. PWP 2:493.
20. HSP Penn papers, 5.593, p.728, October 10, 1686, 10.735, p.933 and 11.178, p.870.
21. CPWJ minutes June 25, 1700.
22. Penn-Logan, II:293.
23. Bisbee, *Burlington Island*, p.20 and Samuel Smith, *Nova Caesaria*, p.69.
24. HDB, p.15.
25. Laws of the State of New Jersey revised and published under the authority of the Legislature (Trenton, printer Joseph Justice, 1821), pp.57-59.
26. PWP 2:577n.

CHAPTER 13: BURLINGTON 1682 – 1684, WITH SAMUEL JENNINGS AS DEPUTY GOVERNOR

1. L&S pp.463-464.
2. L&S pp.435-436.
3. PMHB 61:88.
4. Jennings, Samuel, p.47.
5. WJD B-114.
6. WJD B-548.
7. WJD B-178.
8. WJD B-112.
9. Samuel Smith, *Nova Caesaria*, p.156 and EJD A-4-12.
10. Samuel Smith, *Nova Caesaria*, pp.156-157.
11. Samuel Smith, *Nova Caesaria*, p.157.
12. Samuel Smith, *Nova Caesaria*, pp.166-167.
13. L&S pp.443-444.
14. WJD B-33.
15. L&S pp.451-452.
16. L&S pp.442-443.
17. L&S pp.443-444 and 448-449.
18. L&S p.446.
19. BMM minutes August 7, 1682.
20. YM minutes September 6, 1682.
21. BCB pp.11-12.
22. BCB p.12.
23. L&S p.455.
24. L&S p.454.
25. BMM minutes September and October, 1682 and marriage records.
26. BMM minutes November 6, 1682.
27. BMM minutes November 7, 1682.

28. L&S pp.456-458.
29. L&S p.458-468.
30. PMHB 17:195-199.
31. L&S p.457 and Pomfret, West Jersey, p.137.
32. L&S pp.468-471.
33. L&S p.472.
34. WJD B-96.
35. L&S p.470.
36. WJD EF-135.
37. NJA 1s. I:413-415.
38. WJD B-624.
39. WJD B-623.
40. L&S pp.472-473.
41. BCB pp.15-18.
42. BCB pp.18-19.
43. BCB p.19.
44. PWP 2:390-394.
45. YM minutes September 4, 1683.
46. L&S p.480.
47. CPWJ miscellaneous records
48. L&S pp.477-479.
49. L&S pp.479-481.
50. WJD M-8,10,111,114.
51. BCB pp.21-23.
52. Revell's BS p.46 and NJA 1s. XXI:356, November 8, 1683.
53. Revell's BS p.43 and NJA 1s. XXI:355.
54. WJD B-222.
55. L&S pp.482-484.
56. WMQ 3s. V(1948):102-105.
57. HDB p.86 and WJD Q-220.
58. HDB p.89.
59. L&S p.482.
60. PMHB 14:89.
61. BMM minutes April 7, 1684.
62. WJD B-36.
63. BMM minutes March 3, 1683/4.
64. L&S p.485.
65. L&S pp.486-487.
66. L&S p.488.
67. L&S p.489.
68. BMM minutes April 7, 1684.
69. WJD B-386.

CHAPTER 14: THE HOMESTEAD, MOUNT HOPE, MANSFIELD, WEST JERSEY

1. *PMHB* 4:330-342.
2. *PMHB* 15:346 and *GMNJ* 24::51-56.
3. WJD B-118.
4. BMM minutes October 5, 1685.
5. BCB p.125.
6. BCB p.125.
7. BMM minutes April 7, 1684.
8. *PMHB* 4:330-342; miscellaneous inventories of wills and deeds used to estimate values.

CHAPTER 15: THOMAS OLLIVE - DEPUTY GOVERNOR, APRIL 5, 1684 – NOVEMBER 3, 1685

1. L&S pp.489-492.
2. WJD B-23 (margin notes) and Revell's BS p.33.
3. Revell's BS p.111.
4. L&S pp.490-491.
5. L&S p.494.
6. L&S pp.492-496.
7. BCB pp.25-30.
8. BCB p.29.
9. BCB p.30.
10. BCB pp.30-32.
11. WJD B-353 and HDB pp.75-77.
12. HDB pp.78-79.
13. HDB pp.78-79.
14. PWP 2:638.
15. BCB pp.32-34.
16. YM minutes September, 1684.
17. BCB p.34.
18. Pomfret, *West Jersey*, p.133 and L&S p.445.
19. WJD B-528.
20. BCB p.35.
21. L&S p.497.
22. Samuel Jennings, pp.2-10.
23. Fox pp.93, 94, 95, 97, 99, 102, 103, 105, 112..
24. Pomfret, West Jersey, pp.146-147.
25. BCB p.35.
26. WJD B-69.
27. WJD B-68.
28. WJD B-70.
29. BCB pp.35-41.
30. WJD B-70.
31. BCB p.41.
32. BCB p.41.
33. Pomfret, West Jersey, p.159.
34. BMM minutes March 2, 1684/5.
35. CPWJ records, Ellis Book p.15.
36. BCB p.43-45.
37. WJD B-98.
38. Besse, *Sufferings*, I:449,445,450.
39. Besse, *Sufferings*, I:453.
40. Besse, *Sufferings*, I:461,473,479-480.
41. L&S pp.498-502.
42. WJD B-91.
43. Stillwell 2:9.
44. CPWJ surveys, Leeds Bk.A, p.3 and Revell's BS p.72.
45. WJD B-246.
46. NJA 1s. XXXI:474.
47. Stillwell 2:10.
48. BCB p.46.
49. BCB p.178.
50. BCB p.47.
51. YM minutes September 5, 1985.

52. BMM minutes October 5, 1685.
53. BCB pp.47-48.

CHAPTER 16: EDWARD BYLLYNGE, GOVERNOR, JOHN SKENE, DEPUTY GOVERNOR, NOVEMBER 3, 1685 - JANUARY 16, 1686/7

1. L&S p.472.
2. L&S pp.502-503.
3. L&S p.504.
4. L&S pp.503-506.
5. BCB pp.48-49.
6. CMM minutes
7. CMM minutes January 7, 1685/6.
8. WJD B-242.
9. BCB pp.49-54.
10. BCB p.51.
11. WJD B-435.
12. WJD B-102.
13. WJD B-93.
14. WJD B-91 and HDB pp.79-81.
15. CMM minutes April 1, 1686.
16. Besse, *Sufferings*, p.479.
17. Besse, *Sufferings*, p.479,480,482.
18. Register L&MQM births
19. Register L&MQM deaths
20. Rickman, L.L., Esther Biddle
21. Sanders on Barbadoes and other deaths London.
22. *PGM* 19:78.
23. *PGM* 19:78.
24. BCB p.54.
25. BCB pp.54-56.
26. CCHS Library, file No. NB6 L.S. and State of New Jersey Archival Library, unpublished minutes of the General Assembly, May 12-15, 1686, microfilm, Trenton.
27. CCHS Library, File No. NB6 L.S.
28. CCHS Library, File No. NB6 L.S.
29. CCHS Library, File No. NB6 L.S.
30. CCHS Library, File No. NB6 L.S.
31. CCHS Library, File No. NB6 L.S.
32. CCHS Library, File No. NB6 L.S.
33. NJA 1s. I:522-523.
34. Program of the 300th Anniversary of the Board of Proprietors of East New Jersey, April 9, 1985.
35. Pomfret, *West Jersey*, p.152.
36. WJD B-104.
37. CPWJ records, Ellis Book p.14.
38. BCB pp.56-59.
39. Stillwell 2:37.
40. CMM minutes September 2, 1686.
41. WJD B-106.
42. CPWJ records, Ellis Book p.14.
43. BMM Minutes p. 26 and 28.
44. YM minutes September 8, 1686; and PMHB VII:263, Amelia Grummere, 1883

45. BCB pp.59-60.
46. CPWJ records, Ellis Book p.14.
47. WJD B-118.
48. HSP Penn letters 5.542, September-October, 1686.
49. *PMHB* 4:330-342.
50. CPWJ records, Ellis Book p.15.
51. Revell's BS p.86.
52. BCB pp.61-62.
53. WJD B-112,113,114.
54. BQM minutes November 29, 1686.
55. BQM minutes February 22, 1686/7.
56. CMM minutes January 6, 1686/7.
57. CCM minutes February 3, 1686/7.
58. CMM death records.
59. WJD M-8,10,133,135.
60. WJD M-8,12,257,259.
61. WJD M-8,10,133,135.
62. WJD M-8,10,140,142,65,67
63. Pomfret, *West Jersey*, p.153.
64. NJA 1s. I:522.
65. NJA 1s. I:522.
66. Register L&MQM deaths and Pomfret, West Jersey, p.150.
67. CPWJ minutes March 26, 1689, April 11, 1689 and Samuel Jennings, p.7.

CHAPTER 17: Dr. Daniel Coxe, Governor, February 26, 1686/7 – August 18, 1688

1. WJD B-157.
2. BCB p.63.
3. WJD M-8,9,25,26,8,10,140,142.
4. BCB pp.63-69.
5. WJD B-120.
6. NJA 1s. I:24-25.
7. Pomfret, *West Jersey*, p.153, Samuel Smith, *Nova Caesaria*, pp.195-196 and John Clement, *The Province Line*, p.137.
8. CMM death records.
9. *PGM* 27:88.
10. *PGM* 27:89.
11. *PGM* 27:88.
12. BCB p.69.
13. WJD B-150,233.
14. BCB p.70.
15. WJD B-150.
16. NJA 1s. XXXI:440
17. WJD B-233.
18. WJD B-150,231.
19. WJD B-150,231.
20. WJD M-447.
21. Samuel Smith, *Nova Caesaria*, p.195.
22. WJD B-219.
23. WJD B-233.
24. Pomfret, *West Jersey*, pp.157-158.
25. BQM minutes August 29, 1687.
26. YM minutes September 7, 1687.

27. Samuel Smith, *Nova Caesaria*, pp.190-194.
28. Samuel Smith, *Nova Caesaria*, pp.190-194.
29. CPWJ records, Ellis Book p.15.
30. PMHB 7:336.
31. PMHB 7:336-337.
32. PMHB 7:336-337.
33. Samuel Smith, *Nova Caesaria*, pp.199-201 and CPWJ minutes February 14, 1687/88.
34. Samuel Smith, *Nova Caesaria*, pp.199-201 and CPWJ minutes February 14, 1687/8.
35. BQM minutes February 27, 1687/8.
36. WJD B-179.
37. WJD B-181.
38. WJD B-202.
39. WJD B-203.
40. Samuel Smith, *Nova Caesaria*, pp.202-203 and CPWJ minutes.
41. BCB p.82,89.
42. BCB p.88.
43. BCB pp.87-88.
44. BCB p.84.
45. WJD B-255.
46. WJD B-224.
47. WJD B-222.
48. WJD B-210.
49. WJD B-469
50. Pomfret, *West Jersey*, p.160.
51. Pomfret, *West Jersey*, pp.159-160.
52. BCB p.89.

CHAPTER 18 : SIR EDMOND ANDROS, GOVERNOR OF THE DOMINION OF NEW ENGLAND UNDER KING JAMES II OF ENGLAND, AUGUST 18, 1688 - APRIL 18, 1689

1. Pomfret, *West Jersey*, p.160 and Carlos Godfrey, *When Boston was New Jersey's Capitol*, Proc.NJHS 51:1-23.
2. Pomfret, *West Jersey*, p.160.
3. Pomfret, *West Jersey*, pp.160-161.
4. Pomfret, *West Jersey*, p.161 and Godfrey, *When Boston was New Jersey's Capitol*, Proc.NJHS 51:1-23.
5. BQM minutes August 27, 1688.
6. YM minutes September 5, 1688.
7. PWP 3:357n.
8. YM minutes September 5, 1688.
9. Samuel Smith, *Nova Caesaria*, pp.196-198 and Snyder, *Civil Boundaries*, pp.10-11.
10. CPWJ minutes February 6, 1782.
11. CPWJ minutes September 6, 1688 and Samuel Smith, *Nova Caesaria*, pp.201-203.
12. CPWJ minutes September 6, 1688 and Samuel Smith, *Nova Caesaria*, pp.201-203.
13. WJD B-278.
14. WJD B-247.
15. Samuel Smith, *Nova Caesaria*, p.203 and CPWJ minutes September 18, 1688.
16. CPWJ minutes October 10-12, 1688 and Samuel Smith, *Nova Caesaria*, pp.204-207.
17. BCB pp.91-93.
18. BCB pp.91-93.
19. WJD B-365.
20. WJD BBB-81.

21. Trevelyan, p.472, Pomfret, *West Jersey*, p.161 and Godfrey, *When Boston was New Jersey's Capitol*, Proc. NJHS 51:13-14.
22. BCB pp.95-97.
23. PWP 3:35n and Bisbee, *John Tatham*, PMHB 82:253-70.
24. WJD B-503,509.
25. WJD B-487.
26. WJD B-509,510,525.
27. Hills, p.11, WJD D-317, Leed's BS
28. BCB pp.95-96.
29. CPWJ minutes February 14,15, 1688/9.
30. WJD B-512.
31. CPWJ minutes February 22, 1688/9 and HSP manuscript file AM.456.
32. CPWJ minutes February 23, 1688/9.
33. Revell's BS p.67,68.
34. BQM minutes February 25, 1688/9.
35. CPWJ minutes April 11, 1689 and Samuel Smith, *Nova Caesaria*, pp.201-202.
36. CPWJ minutes March 25,26, 1689.
37. CPWJ minutes March 25, 1689.
38. CPWJ minutes March 26, 1689.
39. CPWJ minutes April 11, 1689.
40. CPWJ minutes April 11, 1689 and epistles in appendix.
41. CPWJ minutes April 11, 1689.
42. Carlos Godfrey, When Boston was New Jersey's Capitol, Proc.NJHS 51:13-14 and Pomfret, *West Jersey*, p.161.
43. Carlos Godfrey, When Boston was New Jersey's capitol, Proc.NJHS 51:14.

CHAPTER 19: DR. DANIEL COXE GOVERNOR: APRIL 11, 1689 TO MARCH 1, 1691/2

1. WJD D-103.
2. CPWJ surveys, Leed's BS p.17.
3. NJA 1s. XXIII:238.
4. CMM minutes May 2, 1689.
5. BCB pp.98-100.
6. Revell's BS p.87.
7. CPWJ surveys, Leed's BS p.43 and Revell's BS p.145.
8. WJD B-644.
9. WJD AAA-63,350.
10. WJD B-659.
11. WJD B-359.
12. CPWJ minutes May 13,14, 1689.
13. Revell's BS p.87,145.
14. CPWJ surveys, Leed's BS p.20.
15. Revell's BS p.86 and CPWJ surveys, Bk.A, p.12.
16. Braithwaite, *Second Period*, p.153.
17. BQM minutes August, 1689.
18. Hinshaw 2:222.
19. WJD B-495.
20. CPWJ minutes November 4, 1689.
21. CPWJ minutes December 22, 1689.
22. WJD EF-388.
23. EJD E-365.
24. HSP manuscript file AM .456.
25. CPWJ minutes February 14, 1689/90.

26. CPWJ minutes February 14, 1689/90.
27. CPWJ minutes February 6, 1782
28. BCB p.101.
29. BCB p.10l.
30. BCB p.112 and NJA 1s. XXI:422.
31. CMM minutes July 3, 1690.
32. BCB pp.112-115.
33. BQM minutes August 25, 1690.
34. PWP 3:639n and PWP 5:3.
35. YM minutes September 10, 1690.
36. Trevelyan, p. 476.
37. Trevalyan, p. 476.
38. PWP 3:357n.
39. PWP 3:357n.
40. Braithwaite, *Second Period*, pp.433-435.
41. CPWJ surveys, Leed's BS p.41.
42. E.M Woodward, *History of Burlington County, N.J.* (1883, reprinted, BCHS,1980), pp.108-109.
43. CPWJ minutes October 13, 1690.
44. PWP 2:481n, PWP 3:41n, and PMHB XXXV:199-210.
45. CPWJ minutes October 13, 1690.
46. CPWJ minutes November 1, 1690.
47. CPWJ records, Ellis Book p.15.
48. BCB pp.115-117.
49. CMM minutes February 5, 1690/01
50. BCB pp.128-129.
51. WJD B-656.
52. WJD DD-263.
53. WJD B-17.
54. YM minutes, September, 1691.
55. BQM minutes August 31, 1691.
56. YM, Women's, September, 1691.
57. WJD B-340.
58. CPWJ minutes November 3, 1691.
59. BCB pp.129-130.
60. CMM minutes November 5, 1691.
61. Stillwell 2:17.
62. WJD B-278.
63. *PGM* I:67.
64. *PGM* VII:170.
65. For Isaac Perkins, see Sybil Noyes, Charles Thornton Libby and Walter Goodwin Davis, *Genealogical Dictionary of Maine and New Hampshire* (Portland, Maine, 1928–1939; reprinted Baltimore, 1972), 541-542.
66. The most recent and accurate account of Thomas Wardwell and his family appears in Robert Charles Anderson, *The Great Migration: Immigrants to New England 1634–1635,* Volume VII, T – Y (Boston: Great Migration Study Project, New England Historic Genealogical Society, 2011), 236-238. Wardwell was not a Huguenot as has been claimed in some sources, and in fact many of the Great Migration immigrants came to New England from Alford and surrounding parishes. Eliakim's younger brother Samuel, born at Exeter (N.H.), in 1643, married Sarah (Hooper) Hawkes and in 1692 he and his wife were accused and convicted in the Salem Witchcraft Hysteria of that year.

67. Jones, *American Colonies*, p.108,372.
68. Jones, *American Colonies*, p.372.
69. WJD M-8,9,25,26,8,10,140,142,65,67.
70. WJD G-177 and NJA 1s. II:41.
71. NJA 1s. II:87.
72. NJA 1s. II:92.
73. Samuel Smith, *Nova Caesaria*, p.208.
74. Stillwell 2:17 and BCB pp.136-145.
75. BQM minutes May 30, 1692.
76. YM minutes September 7, 1692.
77. Jones, American Colonies, p.378.
78. WJD BBB-277.
79. London YM minutes.
80. Pomfret, *West Jersey*, p.262.
81. NJA 1s. XXIII:346.
82. *PGM* 27(3):139-159.

CHAPTER 20: ANDREW HAMILTON, GOVERNOR, APRIL 11, 1692 – NOVEMBER 1697

1. L&S pp.507-513.
2. L&S p.507.
3. L&S pp.507-513.
4. L&S pp.510-512.
5. BCB p.145.
6. WJD B-303.
7. BCB p.145.
8. NJA 1s. XXI:444.
9. BCB pp.145-146.
10. BCB p.148.
11. BQM minutes November 28, 1692.
12. WJD BBB-277.
13. BCB pp.148-152.
14. BQM minutes February 27, 1692/3.
15. WJD B-324.
16. BCB pp.152-154.
17. CPWJ minutes May 13, 1693.
18. CPWJ minutes May 30, 1693.
19. CPWJ minutes May 30, 1693.
20. BCB pp.154-156.
21. WJD B-361.
22. BQM minutes August 29, 1693.
23. Men's and Women's YM minutes September 6, 1693.
24. WJD B-337.
25. L&S pp.514-527.
26. L&S pp.523-527.
27. WJD B-474.
28. BCB pp.156-159.
29. BCB pp.157-158.
30. CPWJ minutes November 3, 1693.
31. CPWJ minutes November 4, 1693.
32. CPWJ minutes November 4, 1693.
33. NJA 1s. XXIII:14.
34. Stillwell 2:20.

35. WJD B-352.
36. Stillwell 2:20 and WJD B-352.
37. Stillwell 2:20.
38. BCB p.159.
39. WJD B-369.
40. WJD B-369 and WJD BB-201.
41. WJD B-377,480.
42. BCB pp.159-164.
43. BQM minutes February 26, 1693/4.
44. Revell's BS p.113.
45. WJD B-437.
46. WJD B-427.
47. CPWJ minutes April 9, 1694.
48. Revell's BS p.103,104, and Basse BS p.28,58.
49. Stillwell 2:41.
50. WJD B-383,384.
51. BCB pp.164-166.
52. WJD B-387.
53. CPWJ minutes May 11, 1694.
54. BCB pp.166-167.
55. WJD B-391.
56. L&S pp.527-535.
57. L&S pp.527-535.
58. CPWJ minutes May 15, 1694.
59. WJD B-617.
60. CPWJ minutes May 18, 1694.
61. BQM minutes May 28, 1694.
62. BCB pp.167-170.
63. WJD B-398.
64. BQM minutes August 28, 1694.
65. YM minutes September 16-19, 1694.
66. WJD B-427.
67. CPWJ minutes November 2, 1694.
68. CPWJ minutes November 3, 1694.
69. BCB p.171.
70. BCB pp.171-175.
71. NJA 1s. XXIII: pp.28, 178, 180, 280, 306, 347.
72. BQM minutes November 26, 1694.
73. Stillwell 2:22.
74. Stillwell 2:23.
75. Stillwell 2:43.
76. WJD B-427.
77. BCB pp.175-177.
78. BCB pp.178-180.
79. WJD B-498.
80. BQM minutes February 25, 1694/5.
81. WJD B-598.
82. Stillwell 2:24.
83. BCB pp.180-181.
84. L&S pp.535-543.
85. CPWJ minutes May 13, 1695.
86. WJD GG-184.

87. CPWJ minutes May 14, 1695.
88. CPWJ minutes May 15,16, 1695.
89. CPWJ minutes May 21, 1695.
90. BQM minutes May 26, 1695.
91. Stillwell 2:25.
92. WJD B-515 and BCD N4-582.
93. CMM minutes January 2, 1693/4.
94. CMM minutes July 4, 1695.
95. BCB pp.181-182.
96. WJD B-521.
97. WJD B-540.
98. CMM minutes September 5, 1695.
99. Men's and Women's CMM minutes October 3, 1695.
100. NJA 1s. XXII:47 and Stillwell 2:42.
101. Lefroy, *Bermuda*, 2:55, 56, 68, 77, 85, 99, 122, 551, 561, 650, 659, 663, 665.
102. Lefroy, *Bermuda*, 2:311-312, 374, 377, 436, 453, 454, 162, 165, 202, 247, 261, 359, 419, 484, 485, 487, 491, 514, 515, 518, 525, 554, 568, 741.
103. JFHS 54(1):3-11, will of Thomas Murrell, Bermuda Will Book 1:216, will of Stephen Righton, Bermuda Will Book 2:101, 3:197, and will of Isabella Righton, Bermuda Will Book 4:1.
104. NJA 1s. XXI:212.
105. CMM miscellaneous records.
106. BCB p.183.
107. Pomfret, *West Jersey*, p.191.
108. BQM minutes November 25, 1695.
109. CMM minutes December 5, 1695 and January, 1695/6.
110. *PGM* XIX:265.
111. WJD B-588.
112. WJD B-667.
113. CMM minutes February 6, 1695/6.
114. BQM minutes February 24, 1695/6.
115. Bisbee, *Burlington Town Book*, p.7.
116. L&S pp.544-551.
117. L&S pp.544-551.
118. CPWJ minutes May 12, 1696.
119. CPWJ minutes May 12, 13, 15, 19, 20, 22, 1696.
120. BQM minutes May 25, 1696.
121. Women's BQM minutes May 25, 1696.
122. BCB p.187.
123. Pomfret, West Jersey, p.191.
124. BCB pp.188-190.
125. BQM minutes August 31, 1696.
126. WJD B-565.
127. EJD E-306.
128. EJD E-233.
129. WJD B-565.
130. CPWJ minutes April 28, 1716.
131. YM minutes September 23, 1696.
132. YM minutes September 23, 1696.
133. BCB p. 190.
134. BQM minutes November 30, 1696.
135. WJD B-618.

136. WJD B-611.
137. BCB pp.191-192.
138. BQM minutes February 22, 1696/7.
139. CPWJ records, Ellis Book p.15.
140. BCB pp.192-195.
141. L&S pp.552-557.
142. CPWJ minutes May 22, 1697.
143. Men's and Women's BQM minutes May 31, 1697.
144. BCB p.195.
145. Pomfret, *West Jersey*, p.192.
146. BCB pp.195-198.
147. BQM minutes August 30, 1697.
148. CPWJ records, Ellis Book p.14.
149. CPWJ surveys, Leed's Book A p.28.
150. YM minutes September 2, 1697.
151. Pomfret, *West Jersey*, pp.192-193.
152. BCB pp.198-201.
153. L&S pp.557-563.
154. CPWJ minutes November 2,4,5,8, 1697.
155. BQM minutes November 29, 1697.
156. BCB pp.201-203.
157. BQM minutes February 28, 1697/8.
158. CPWJ minutes March 5, 1697/8.
159. Bisbee, *Burlington Town Book*, p.7.
160. Pomfret, *West Jersey*, p.194 and NJA 1s. II:207-209.
161. CPWJ minutes April 9, 1698.

CHAPTER 21: JEREMIAH BASSE, GOVERNOR, APRIL 7, 1698 - AUGUST 19, 1699

1. Pomfret, *West Jersey*, p.194.
2. NJA 1s. II:207-209.
3. BCB pp.203-205.
4. Samuel Jennings, p.56.
5. Samuel Jennings, pp.66-67.
6. Samuel Jennings, pp.58, 13.
7. CPWJ minutes May 12,13,16 and 18, 1698.
8. BQM minutes May 30, 1698.
9. WJD B-618.
10. BCB pp.205-206.
11. BCB pp.206-208.
12. BQM minutes August 29, 1698.
13. CPWJ minutes September 19, 1698.
14. YM minutes September 21, 1698.
15. Bisbee, *Burlington Town Book*, p.8.
16. CPWJ surveys, Leed's Book A p.35.
17. BCB pp.208-212.
18. BQM minutes November 29, 1698.
19. CPWJ minutes December 17, 1698.
20. Samuel Jennings, p.57, and 12-13 and NJA 1s. II:249.
21. MTM minutes January 1, 1698/9
22. BCB pp.212-213.
23. BCB pp.214-215.
24. BQM minutes February 27, 1698/9.

25. WJD AH-167.
26. BCB p.215.
27. BCB p.216.
28. BCB p.218.
29. BCB pp.217-218.
30. BCB p.219.
31. Pomfret, *West Jersey*, p.201.
32. Pomfret, *West Jersey*, pp.203-204.
33. Pomfret, *West Jersey*, p.201.
34. Pomfret, *West Jersey*, p.201.
35. Pomfret, *West Jersey*, p.201.
36. Pomfret, *West Jersey*, p.201.
37. Pomfret, *West Jersey*, p.201.
38. CPWJ minutes April 9, 1699.
39. BCB pp.219-222.
40. CPWJ minutes May 15, 1699.
41. BQM minutes May 29, 1699.
42. WJD B-647.
43. BCB p.222.
44. Pomfret, *West Jersey*, p.202.
45. Men's and Women's BQM minutes August 28, 1699.
46. YM minutes September 16-20, 1699.
47. CPWJ minutes September 29, 1699.
48. BCB pp.222-226.
49. BCB pp.224-225.
50. BQM minutes November 27, 1699.
51. WJD AAA-350 and HDB pp.83-85.

CHAPTER 22: ANDREW HAMILTON, GOVERNOR, DECEMBER 20, 1699 - MAY, 1703

1. L&S pp.563-568.
2. L&S pp.566-567.
3. L&S pp.567-568.
4. WJD B-659.
5. BCB pp.226-231.
6. BCB p.229.
7. WJD AAA-416,420.
8. BCB pp.230-231.
9. Men's BQM minutes February 26, 1699/00.
10. Women's BQM minutes February 26, 1699/00.
11. WJD B-725.
12. BCB pp.233.
13. L&S pp.569-570.
14. L&S pp.573-574.
15. L&S pp.574-576.
16. L&S pp.576-577.
17. CPWJ minutes May 25, 1700.
18. CPWJ minutes May 25, 1700.
19. BQM minutes May 27, 1700.
20. CPWJ minutes June 25, 1700.
21. PWP 3:611-613.
22. CPWJ minutes June 25, 1700.
23. CPWJ minutes June 26, 1700.

24. CPWJ minutes June 26, 1700.
25. Women's CMM minutes July 4, 1700.
26. Stillwell 2:30.
27. BCB pp.234-237.
28. BCB pp.234-237.
29. Men's BQM minutes August 26, 1700.
30. Women's BQM minutes August 26, 1700.
31. CPWJ minutes September 3, 1700.
32. YM minutes September 14-18, 1700.
33. BCB pp.237-238, 245-246.
34. WJD B-678.
35. BCB pp.238-240, 245.
36. BCB pp.240-243.
37. BCB pp.242-243.
38. BCB pp.241-245.
39. WJD BBB-103.
40. CPWJ records, Ellis Book p.14.
41. BQM minutes November 25, 1700.
42. BCB pp.246-251.
43. BCB pp.248-251.
44. BQM minutes February 24, 1700/1.
45. BCB p.251.
46. CPWJ minutes March 10, 1700/1.
47. Pomfret, *West Jersey*, p.207, NJA 1s. II:360, 368-380 and BCB pp.xxxvi-xxxvii, 252-253.
48. Bisbee, *Burlington Town Book*, p.10.
49. CPWJ minutes April 8, 1701.
50. CPWJ minutes April 21, 1701.
51. CPWJ surveys, Leed's Book A p.48.
52. BCB p.251.
53. NJA 1s. II:377-380.
54. L&S pp.578-580.
55. NJA 1s. II:376-380, 380-384.
56. NJA 1s. II:380-384.
57. L&S p.581.
58. L&S pp.581-587.
59. BQM minutes May 26, 1701.
60. BCB pp.252-253.
61. BCB pp.253-258.
62. BQM minutes August 25, 1701.
63. YM minutes September 24, 1701.
64. BCB pp.258-260.
65. PWP 4:48.
66. WJD B-704.
67. BQM minutes November 24, 1701.
68. BCB p.260.
69. CPWJ minutes November 26, 1701.
70. WJD B-703.
71. PWP 4:126-127,129n.
72. *PGM* 7:170.
73. H&M Commission, Book E-3, 5:459-461.
74. HDB pp.16-17.

75. BCB pp.260-265.
76. Women's and Men's BQM minutes February 23, 1701/2.
77. BQM minutes February 23, 1701/2.
78. BQM minutes February 23, 1701/2.
79. BQM minutes February 23, 1701/2.
80. Bisbee, *Burlington Town Book*, p.10.
81. Pomfret, *West Jersey*, p.213 and Samuel Smith, *Nova Caesaria* pp.211-220.
82. BCB pp.265-269.
83. CPWJ minutes May 14, 1702.
84. CPWJ records, Ellis Book p.14.
85. BQM minutes May 25, 1702.
86. BCB pp.269-270.
87. WJD B-709.
88. WJD B-667.
89. Women's and Men's BQM minutes August 30, 1702.
90. CPWJ records, Ellis Book p.14.
91. YM minutes September 23, 1702.
92. BCB p.265, 270.
93. Pomfret, West Jersey, p.263.
94. BCB pp.270-281.
95. Women's and Men's BQM minutes November 30, 1702.
96. Samuel Smith, *Nova Caesaria*, pp.220-230, 230-261.
97. Pomfret, *West Jersey*, p.263.
98. WJD B-727.
99. BCB pp.281-291.
100. BQM minutes February 22, 1702/3.
101. BCB p.291.
102. BQM minutes May 31, 1703.
103. CPWJ minutes June 17,18, 1703.
104. WJD AAA-443.
105. CPWJ minutes June 27,28, 1703 and WJD AAA-434, 443.
106. CPWJ minutes June 27,28, 1703.
107. CPWJ minutes June 28, 1703.
108. CPWJ minutes July 19, 1703.
109. CPWJ minutes July 19, 1703.
110. CPWJ minutes July 19, 1703.
111. CPWJ minutes July 20, 1703.

CHAPTER 23: THE ROYAL COLONY OF NEW JERSEY: GOVERNOR CORNBURY
AUGUST 14, 1703 - DECEMBER 20, 1708

1. NJA 1s. III:1.
2. NJA 1s. III:
3. NJA 1s. III:6.
4. Samuel Smith, *Nova Caesaria*, pp.230-261.
5. Samuel Smith, *Nova Caesaria*, p.231, 232.
6. Samuel Smith, *Nova Caesaria*, p.231.
7. Samuel Smith, *Nova Caesaria*, p.231, 276.
8. Samuel Smith, *Nova Caesaria*, p.276.
9. Pomfret, West Jersey, p.209, 214.
10. Samuel Smith, *Nova Caesaria*, pp.234.
11. Samuel Smith, *Nova Caesaria*, pp.234-235.
12. Samuel Smith, *Nova Caesaria*, pp.237-239, 250-252.

13. Samuel Smith, *Nova Caesaria*, p.243, 245, 247, 254.
14. NJA 1s.III:301.
15. *PGM* 6:181 and NJA 1s. III:302.
16. NJA 1s. III:1-4, 301-302.
17. *PGM* 6:181.
18. CPWJ records confirm this
19. WJD BB-153-154.
20. NJA 1s. XXX:118-120.
21. *PGM* 6:186 and NJA 1s. III:4-5.
22. NJA 1s. III:302-306.
23. *PGM* 6:182.
24. *PGM* 6:182.
25. NJA 1s. III:305-306.
26. Pomfret, *West Jersey*, p.265.
27. Pomfret, *West Jersey*, p.265.
28. *PGM* 6:182.
29. NJA 1s. III:357.
30. BCB pp.291-344.
31. BQM minutes August 30, 1703.
32. CPWJ minutes September 11, 1703.
33. CPWJ records, Ellis Book p.14.
34. Hinshaw 2:962.
35. CPWJ minutes September 11, 1703.
36. YM minutes September 22-28, 1703.
37. WJD AAA-40.
38. Samuel Smith, *Nova Caesaria*, p.276.
39. Hinshaw 2:963.
40. CPWJ minutes November 2, 1703 and Samuel Smith, *Nova Caesaria*, p.95.
41. Samuel Smith, *Nova Caesaria*, p.95.
42. WJD AAA-434.
43. Samuel Smith, *Nova Caesaria*, p.276.
44. Samuel Smith, *Nova Caesaria*, p.277.
45. Samuel Smith, *Nova Caesaria*, p.280.
46. NJA 3s. II:5-6.
47. BQM minutes November 29, 1703.
48. CMM minutes February 3, 1703/4.
49. CMM minutes February 3, 1703/4.
50. CPWJ minutes February 14, 1703/4.
51. CPWJ minutes February 14, 1703/4.
52. WJD AAA-111.
53. BQM minutes February 28, 1703/4.
54. CMM minutes March 3, 1703/4.
55. WJD AAA-49.
56. Commissions, AAA-19.
57. CMM marriage records p.59 and Willis P. Hazard, *Watson's Annals of Philadelphia*, Volume III (Philadelphia: Edwin S. Stuart, 1857), pp.:87-88.
58. Penn-Logan, IX:278-279.
59. Samuel Smith, *Nova Caesaria*, p.140.
60. WJD AAA-40.
61. CPWJ minutes May 11, 1704.
62. NJA 1s. III:50-51.
63. BQM minutes May 29, 1704.

64. BQM minutes August 28, 1704.
65. Women's BQM minutes August 28, 1704.
66. H&M Commission Book E-3 5:473-475.
67. YM minutes September 20-25, 1704.
68. Samuel Smith, *Nova Caesaria*, p.283.
69. CPWJ minutes October 11, 1704.
70. *PGM* 5:27 and *PGM* 19:84n.
71. Bucks County Pennsylvania Deeds, Doylestown, Book 2 p.157, 1697.
72. Bucks County Pennsylvania Deeds, Doylestown, Book 2 p.157, 1697.
73. CPWJ records, Ellis Book p.14.
74. WJD AAA-71.
75. WJD AAA-70.
76. WJD AAA-100.
77. Samuel Smith, *Nova Caesaria*, p.284.
78. Samuel Smith, *Nova Caesaria*, pp.283-284.
79. NJA 3s. II:11-15.
80. NJA 3s. II:15-21.
81. NJA 3s. II:23-26.
82. NJA 3s. II:23-26.
83. NJA 3s. II:21-22, 26-27, 27-28.
84. NJA 3s. II:28-30.
85. NJA 1s. XXIII:14.
86. NJA 1s. XXIII:293, NJA 1s. XXI:270 and Monmouth Wills.
87. Commissions AAA-27.
88. Women's and Men's BQM minutes November 27, 1704.
89. BCB p.292.
90. BCB pp.292-293.
91. MTM minutes January 1, 1704/5.
92. PMHB 15:110.
93. Women's and Men's BQM minutes February 26, 1704/5.
94. Commissions AAA-29.
95. CPWJ minutes March 15, 1704/5.
96. WJD O-256.
97. WJD AAA-111.
98. Hinshaw 2:407.
99. BQM minutes May 28, 1705.
100. Hinshaw 2:407.
101. Women's and Men's BQM minutes August 27, 1705.
102. YM minutes September, 1705.
103. MTM minutes November 24, 1705.
104. BQM minutes November 26, 1705.
105. WJD BB-148.
106. CPWJ minutes November 4, 1705.
107. Women's and Men's BQM minutes February 25, 1705/6.
108. BCB pp.310-311.
109. Commissions AAA-67.
110. Commissions AAA-67.
111. Women's and Men's BQM minutes May 27, 1706.
112. NJA 1s. III:280-281.
113. NJA 1s. III:p.280.
114. Tanner, p.567.
115. BCB pp.313-314.

116. BQM minutes August 26, 1706.
117. YM minutes September 18, 1706.
118. Samuel Smith, *Nova Caesaria*, p.284.
119. NJA 1s. III:158-159.
120. BQM minutes November 25, 1706.
121. MTM minutes November 30, 1706.
122. CPWJ minutes January 22, 1706/7.
123. NJA 1s. III:164-165.
124. Samuel Smith, *Nova Caesaria*, p.288 and Tanner p.263.
125. Samuel Smith, *Nova Caesaria*, p.286.
126. Samuel Smith, *Nova Caesaria*, p.288 and Tanner p.263.
127. Samuel Smith, *Nova Caesaria*, p.288.
128. Samuel Smith, *Nova Caesaria*, p.286.
129. Samuel Smith, *Nova Caesaria*, p.288.
130. Samuel Smith, *Nova Caesaria*, pp.288-295.
131. Samuel Smith, *Nova Caesaria*, pp.288-294.
132. Samuel Smith, *Nova Caesaria*, pp.296-311.
133. Samuel Smith, *Nova Caesaria*, pp.311-312 and NJA 1s. III:350-356.
134. Samuel Smith, *Nova Caesaria*, pp.285-288.
135. NJA 1s. XXIII:129.
136. *PGM* 19:79-80.
137. Women's and Men's BQM minutes May 26, 1707.
138. Women's and Men's BQM minutes August 25, 1707.
139. NJA 1s. III:358.
140. YM minutes September 23, 1707.
141. *Autobiography of Charles Biddle 1745-1821* (Philadelphia, E. Claxton & Co., 1883), p.1.
142. Women's and Men's BQM minutes November 24, 1707.
143. Samuel Smith, *Nova Caesaria*, pp.312-345.
144. WJD EF-309 and GMNJ 13:75.
145. BQM minutes February 23, 1707/8.
146. CMM minutes March 4, 1707/8.
147. CPWJ records, Ellis Book p.14.
148. Women's and Men's BQM minutes May 31, 1708.
149. Men's BQM minutes May 31, 1708.
150. PWP 3:85, 87n.
151. Samuel Smith, *Nova Caesaria*, pp.348-352.
152. WJD AAA-273.
153. WJD AAA-274.
154. WJD AAA-375.
155. BQM minutes August 30, 1708.
156. Samuel Smith, *Nova Caesaria*, p.355.
157. CPWJ minutes September 9,10, 1708.
158. CPWJ minutes September 9, 1708.
159. CPWJ minutes September 9, 1708.
160. CPWJ minutes September 10, 1708.
161. YM minutes September 21, 1708.
162. BCB p.336.
163. CPWJ minutes November 2, 1708.
164. CPWJ minutes November 3,4, 1708.

165. CPWJ minutes November 5, 1708.
166. BQM minutes November 29, 1708 and WJD AAA-385.
167. NJA 1s. XXIII:259 and Samuel Smith, *Nova Caesaria*, pp.352-354.

CHAPTER 24: GOVERNOR JOHN LORD LOVELACE: DECEMBER 20, 1708 – MAY 1709

1. NJA 1s. XIII:307 and Samuel Smith, *Nova Caesaria*, pp.354-355.
2. NJA 1s. III:309, 317.
3. CPWJ minutes February 2, 1708/9.
4. CPWJ minutes February 2, 1708/9.
5. CPWJ minutes February 2, 1708/9.
6. CPWJ minutes February 2, 1708/9.
7. CPWJ minutes February 3,4, 1708/9.
8. Women's and Men's BQM minutes February 28, 1708/9.
9. Samuel Smith, *Nova Caesaria*, pp.355-359 and Tanner, pp.311-312.
10. NJA 3s. II:45-49.
11. NJA 3s. II:49-51.
12. NJA 3s. II:51-53.
13. NJA 3s. II:53-54.
14. NJA 3s. II:54-59.
15. NJA 1s. III:328-329.
16. CPWJ minutes March 22, 1708/9.
17. BCB p.336.
18. CPWJ minutes March 30, 1709.
19. CPWJ minutes March 31, 1709.
20. CPWJ minutes April 1, 1709.
21. CPWJ minutes April 2, 1709.
22. CMM death records.
23. T. Chalkley Matlack, notebooks, Swarthmore Friends Library, p. 179. Matlack compiled pictures, drawings and histories of all of the Friends Meetinghouses of the Delaware Valley.
24. *PGM* 19:83-87 and N.J. Wills, Burlington County, New Jersey State Archives, Trenton, 253C-260C.

CHAPTER 25: WILLIAM BIDDLE'S FINAL YEARS: MAY 1709 – NOVEMBER 26, 1711

1. CPWJ minutes May 3-6, 1709.
2. Samuel Smith, *Nova Caesaria*, p.359.
3. NJA 1s. III:329-383.
4. Women's BQM minutes May 30, 1709.
5. Men's BQM minutes May 30, 1709.
6. WJD AAA-350 and HDB pp.83-85.
7. NJA 3s. II:63-70.
8. WJD W-462.
9. BQM minutes August 29, 1709.
10. BCB p.340.
11. BQM minutes November 28, 1709.
12. Samuel Smith, *Nova Caesaria*, p.355 and NJA 3s.II:73-85.
13. BQM minutes February 27, 1709/10.
14. Women's BQM minutes February 27, 1709/10.
15. WJD BB-416.
16. BQM minutes May 29, 1710.
17. CPWJ minutes May 2, 1710.

18. BQM minutes August 28, 1710.

19. Samuel Smith, *Nova Caesaria*, p.370.

20. YM minutes September 19, 1710.

21. Hinshaw 2:624.

22. Women's and Men's BQM minutes November 27, 1710.

23. Samuel Smith, *Nova Caesaria*, pp.370-371.

24. NJA 1s. XXII:661.

25. BQM minutes February 26, 1710/11.

26. BQM minutes May 28, 1711.

27. CPWJ minutes May 2, 1711.

28. N.J. Wills, Burlington County, N.J. State Archives, Trenton, 253C-260C and *PGM* 19:83-85.

29. Women's CMM minutes August, 1711.

30. Women's and Men's BQM minutes August 27, 1711.

31. N.J. Wills, Burlington County, N.J. State Archives, Trenton, 253C-260C.

32. Women's and Men's BQM minutes November 26, 1711.

33. *PGM* 19:86. and a copy of the Will from the New Jersey State Archives

34. *PGM* 19:86.

35. *PGM* 19:86.

36. *PGM* 19:86.

37. *PGM* 19:86 and N.J. Wills, Burlington County, N.J. State Archives, Trenton, 253C-260C.

38. NJA 1s. XXIII:37 and N.J. Wills, Burlington County, N.J. State Archives, Trenton, lib. 1, p.335.

39. Ibid.,. 1, p. 338.

Explanation of Proprietary Shares and Rights

The concept of proprietary rights is difficult to understand. The territory, *Nova Caesaria* (New Jersey) had become owned by England. Other territories owned by the Crown, such as the ownership of Pennsylvania, were given to William Penn for the debt owed to his father, and a group of eight English Lords were made proprietors of the Carolinas. The King of England through his brother, James, Duke of York, had given the New Jersey territory to two people to whom he was indebted, Sir John Berkeley and Sir George Carteret. They each owned half of the territory.

Berkeley sold his ownership rights basically to Edward Byllynge and the land came under the ownership of Quakers. The Byllynge indebtedness, apparently mostly to Quakers, was then overseen by the trustees, William Penn, Gawen Lawrie and Nicholas Lucas and they developed the right to sell these proprietary shares.

The territory was divided into ten Tenths and there were 100 proprietary shares, ten in theory to be assigned to each Tenth. The West New Jersey half of the territory contained approximately 2,800,000 acres. So eventually each full proprietary share might be equal to the rights to claim or sell 28,000 acres.

The trustees sold full proprietary shares, but sometimes shares were sold to a group of people. This practice, along with the resale of fractions of shares by other shareholders, led to ownership by many people of full or fractions of proprietary shares.

The land had to be purchased from the Indians before it could be distributed. Not all of the land of West New Jersey was purchased at one time. It was negotiated for and surveyed and bought in many parcels.

Once purchased, distribution of the land was overseen first by the newly created Land Commissioners and later by the Council of Proprietors of West New Jersey. To claim land one had to first pay the amount owing for the purchase from the Indians. Then the claimant would receive a warrant for the correct number of acres, based on ownership of proprietary rights. The land then had to be surveyed and the survey submitted to the regulatory body, which had to verify its validity. When this process was complete, the proprietor could either settle the land for himself or sell it to another person. If sold, a deed had to be prepared and submitted to the proper official for recording.

The Land Commissioners began the process of distributing land by dividends. The first dividend was for 5200 acres per proprietary share and it was given out in two portions. The first portion for 3200 acres was announced on March 19, 1678/9. There were a total of seven dividends in the proprietorship, which still exists today.

Land Transactions of William and Sarah Biddle

Proprietary Shares

Shares Bought/Sold	Date	Price	Seller/Buyer
one half	January 22, 23, 1676/7	£200	Byllynge Trustees
one quarter	April 1, 1677	£37 10s	Helmsley and Pearson
one sixth	October 30, 1676	?	Nicholas Bell
(one sixth)	October 6, 7, 1679	?	(Robert Chinton)
one quarter	August 9, 1684	£45	Joseph Helmsley
one sixth	August 22, 1684	£48.15s	Samuel Clay
one quarter	May 20, 1686	£80.6s	Thomas Hutchison
two twelfths	November 10, 1691	500 acres = £50	Anna Salter
Total 1.58 shares		£461.11s	

Entitled Acres

Date	Survey acres	Warrants	Acres	Price	Purchaser	Location
First portion of First Dividend: 3200 acres per proprietary share declared prior to March 19, 1678/9 = 4512 acres						
March 19, 1678/9	1600					Rancocus Creek
August 3, 1681			300	£20	Richard Baynum	Rancocus Creek
December 17, 1681	278					Seppasink Island
December 20, 1681	135					Burlington Townbounds
January 10, 1681/2	500					Mt. Hope Homestead
February 21, 1681/2			50	?	John Dewsbury	Assiscunck Creek
March 22, 1681/2	322					Springhill
October 13, 1682			500	?	Dr. Robert Dimsdale	Rancocus Creek
May 10, 1684			100	£10	Thomas Williams	Pennsauken Creek
November 1, 1684			150	£15	William Evans	Rancocus Creek

Date	Acres	Lot / Note	Name	Price	Location
November 18, 1684	500		John Underhill	£50	Springhill
March 1, 1684/5	50		John Calowe	£14	First Tenth
		48-foot waterlot, 100			Burlington
April 9, 1685					? Indenture payment
May 10, 1685	200	500	John Silver	£20	Second Tenth
July 5, 1685			John Neuman		Oneanickon
July 25, 1685	100		Walter Pumphary	£8	Second Tenth
August 4, 1685		40-foot townlot	James Hill	?	High Street Burlington
January 20, 1685/6	100		Isaac Horner	£10	Second Tenth
April 14, 1686	500		John Rodman	£50	Chester Township
June, 1686		500			
September 6, 1686	100		Joseph Ambler	£9	First Tenth
September 7, 1686		100			
September 13, 1686		50	? Indenture payment		
October 6, 1686		300	Anna Salter agreement		
October 1686		270			
April 7, 1687	500		John Langford	£54	Springfield Township
August 2, 1687	150		Charles Read	£18	West of Rancocus Creek
November 3, 1687	mortgage	150	James Sherwin		First Tenth / West of Rancocus Creek

Second portion of first dividend: 2000 acres per proprietary share declared February 13, 1687/8 = 2820 acres

Second dividend: 5000 acres per proprietary share declared prior to April 1, 1688 = 7900 acres

Date	Acres	Lot / Note	Name	Price	Location
April 10, 1688	100		Hance Monsieur	£10	Second Tenth
June 10, 1688	150	40 foot waterlot	James Satterthwaite	£23	Second Tenth / Burlington
July 10, 1688	600		Samuel Andrews	£63	Mansfield Township
September 12, 1688	100		William Satterthwaite	£10	Mansfield Township
November 10, 1688	50		John Feake	£5	First Tenth
December 10, 1688	75		Samuel Furnis	£15	Burlington Townbounds

Date	Survey acres	Warrants	Acres	Price	Purchaser	Location
February 15, 1688/9			100	£12	Anthony Woodward	First Tenth
April 23, 1689		58' townlot		£6.11s	Thomas Gardiner	High Street Burlington
May 1689	500					Little Egg Harbor
June 1689	230					Springfield Township
June 1689	323					Oneanickon
November 11, 1689			100	£14	Thomas Harding	Rancocus Creek
April 29, 1690			50	£6	Sarah Scholey	First Tenth
October, 1690		3-acre lot southside of Broad Street				Burlington
October, 1690		45-foot waterlot east of York Street				Burlington
November, 1690		50		?	William Nichols	? Indenture payment
August 18, 1691			50	£5	William Dean	First Tenth
February 9, 1691/2		12' waterlot		£1.10s	John Hollinshead	Burlington
February 25, 1691/2		33¼" waterlot	500	£50	Peleg Slocum	In first Indian Purchase
November 10, 1692				?	William Fryley	Burlington
August 20, 1693			100	£6	Charles Woolverton	First Tenth
January 13, 1693/4		3-acre town lot		£9	Richard Basnett	South of Broad Street
January 13, 1693/4		48' waterlot		?	Richard Basnett	Burlington
March, 1693/4		1 acre half rod town lot				Wood Street Burlington
March 16, 1693/4		1 acre half rod town lot		£5.7s	Isaac Marriott	Wood Street Burlington
April 1694	120					Townbounds
April 1694	165					Townbounds
1694	1 acre townlot					East of York Street
1694	1¾ acre townlot					East of York Street
April 1694		35 unappropriated acres		?	Samuel Harriott	Townbounds
April 21, 1694	35' waterlot			£4	Henry Grubb	Burlington
April 21, 1694			100	£18	Samuel Harriott	Townbounds
October 10, 1694		¾-acre townlot		£4	Mary Myers	Talbot Street
February 22, 1694/5		1½-acre townlot		£5	Daniel Smith	Burlington

Date				Grantee	Location
March 21, 1694/5		house + 165 acres	£28	Caleb Wheatley	Nottingham
		represents a mortgage foreclosure on John Melbourne			
August 8, 1695	2-acre townlot		£10	Daniel Cripps	Burlington
August 31, 1695	1-acre townlot		£8	James Verier	Burlington waterfront
January 16, 1695/6			£18	William Righton	Townbounds
September 22, 1696	750 acres "for the public good"	100		Major Brockhills & Capt. Schuyler	Pequannick River
December 10, 1696		150	£12	James Sherwin	West of Rancocus Creek
March 9, 1696/7	50		?	Joseph Steward	? Indenture payment
May 22, 1697	2000				
September 4, 1697		760			Little Egg Harbor
September 4, 1697		430			Little Egg Harbor
October 19, 1698		100			Little Egg Harbor
March 14, 1698/9		500	£90	John Antrum	Springfield Twp. Farm
June 3, 1699		823	£350	John Clayton	Oneanickon Farm
December 19, 1699		480	£70.10s	Mordecai Andrews	Little Egg Harbor
December 25, 1699		500	£60	Nicholas Brown	Little Egg Harbor
March 11, 1699/1700	2-acre townlot	100	£13	Daniel Smith	Burlington
November 5, 1700					
November 10, 1700	1500		£8	Mathew Forsyth	Burlington County
April 29, 1701	1500				Amwell
April 29, 1701	240				Amwell
May 14, 1701	100				? Indenture payment
September 2, 1702	100				? Indenture payment
October 27, 1703		100	£4	Robert Murfin	unappropriated land
February 15, 1703/4		120	£40	Bernard Lane	Townbounds
March 3, 1703/4	40' townlot	220	£3.4s	William Gladwin	Burlington
November 14, 1704					
November 15, 1704		50	£4.5s	John & Eve Shepherd	Cohansey River
November 15, 1704		170	£14.12s	Thomas Shepherd	Cohansey River

Date	Survey acres	Warrants	Acres	Price	Purchaser	Location
March 15, 1704/5		6-acre townlot		£40	Samuel Jennings	South of Broad Street
December 5, 1705		6' strip of land		£3	Thomas Gardiner	High Street
February 11, 1707/8			140	?	William Aburtus	Amwell
April 9, 1708		200				in or out of Townbounds
April 13, 1708		23-perch townlot and 46 unappropriated acres		£9	Hugh Huddy	
November 5, 1708		833.33				
February 2, 1708/9		Permission received to purchase 800 acres from the Indians				Little Egg Harbor
July 9, 1709			100	£12	John Tuly	unappropriated land
March 20, 1709/10			500	£125	Thomas Wooley	Little Egg Harbor
November, 1711			1700		bequests in will	
Total entitled acres	Retained surveyed acres	warrants disbursed lands	Acreage sold	Money realized	Total Claims, Warrants, Sold acres	
15,232 acres	2873	950	11,428	£1472.19s	15,251	

Townbound acres: Entitled 564 acres; Sold 576

Waterlots: six sold = 216' 4" waterfront

City lots sold = 19.1 city acres

Bequeathed to William Biddle 3rd: Mt. Hope and Seppasink Island = 728 acres

Retained in possession: 2 city lots, 1 waterlot, 1600 acres at Amwell, 360 acres at Egg Harbor.

Council of Proprietors of West New Jersey

1687/8
Thomas Ollive, Pres.
Samuel Jennings
William Biddle
Elias Farre
Mahlon Stacy
Francis Davenport
Andrew Robeson, S.G.
William Roydon
John Reading
William Cooper
John Wills

1688/9
Thomas Ollive, Pres.
John Tatham
George Hutcheson
William Biddle
Thomas Gardiner Jr.
Samuel Jennings
Andrew Robeson, S.G.
William Roydon
John Reading

1690
Thomas Ollive, Pres.
Andrew Robeson, S.G.
William Biddle
William Roydon
Thomas Gardiner Sr.
Thomas Gardiner Jr.
Thomas Lambert
John Reading
George Hutcheson

1691
Thomas Ollive, Pres.
William Biddle
Andrew Robeson, S.G.
Thomas Gardiner Sr.
Thomas Gardiner Jr.
William Roydon
John Reading

1692
No meetings

1693
Thomas Gardiner, Sr. Pres.
Andrew Robeson, S.G.
William Biddle
Thomas Gardiner Jr.
John Reading
Francis Davenport
George Hutcheson
John Hollinshead
John Day

1694
Thomas Gardiner Sr. Pres.
William Biddle
Francis Davenport
George Hutcheson
Thomas Gardiner Jr. S.G.
John Hugg Jr.
Christopher Wetherill
John Reading, Clerk
John Hollinshead

1695
John Tatham, Pres.
Francis Davenport
William Biddle
Samuel Jennings
Mahlon Stacy
Thomas Gardiner Jr. S.G.
John Hugg Jr.
John Reading, Clerk
John Hollinshead

1696
Francis Davenport, Pres.
Thomas Gardiner, S.G.
John Shinn
Mahlon Stacy
Peter Fretwell
Christopher Wetherill
John Reading, Clerk
John Hugg Jr.
John Hollinshead

1697
William Biddle, Pres.
Francis Davenport
Mahlon Stacy
Francis Collins
Thomas Gardiner, S.G.
Thomas Thackera
Peter Fretwell
John Reading, Clerk
John Kay

1698
William Biddle, Pres.
Francis Davenport
Mahlon Stacy
Thomas Gardiner, S.G.
Peter Fretwell
John Reading, Clerk
John Kay
Thomas Sharp
Thomas Thackera

1699
William Biddle, Pres.
Mahlon Stacy
Francis Davenport
Peter Fretwell
Thomas Thackera
Thomas Sharp
John Kay
Thomas Gardiner, S.G.

1700
Andew Hamilton, Gov., Pres.
William Biddle, V. Pres.
Mahlon Stacy
Samuel Jennings
Thomas Gardiner, S.G.
John Wills
Thomas Thackera
John Kay
John Reading, Clerk

1701
Andew Hamilton, Gov., Pres.
William Biddle
Mahlon Stacy
Francis Davenport
Samuel Jennings
Francis Collins
Thomas Gardiner, S.G.
John Wills
Thomas Thackera

1702
Mahlon Stacy, Pres.
Thomas Gardiner, S.G.
Thomas Lambert
Isaac Sharp
John Reading, Clerk
Peter Fretwell
William Wood
William Budd
Samuel Jennings

1703
Mahlon Stacy, Pres. 1
George Deacon, Pres. 2
John Wills, Pres. 3
Samuel Jennings
Thomas Gardiner, S.G.
Christopher Wetherill
John Reading
John Hugg
Isaac Sharp

1704
William Biddle, Pres.
Thomas Gardiner, S.G.
Samuel Jennings
George Deacon
Christopher Wetherill
John Wills
John Reading
William Hall
John Kay

1705
Meeting held
No records exist

1706
William Biddle, Pres.
Samuel Jennings
George Deacon
John Wills
William Hall
Christopher Wetherhill
John Kay
John Reading
Francis Collins

1707
Lewis Morris
John Reading, Clerk
Thomas Gardiner, S.G.
William Biddle
Samuel Jennings
George Deacon
John Wills
John Kay
William Hall

1708
Lewis Morris, Pres.
William Biddle, V. Pres.
Thomas Gardiner, S.G.
John Reading, Clerk
Samuel Jennings
George Deacon
John Wills
Richard Bull
William Hall

1709
Lewis Morris, Pres.
George Deacon, V. Pres.
Thomas Gardiner, S.G.
John Reading, Clerk
John Wills
William Stevenson
Richard Bull
John Budd

1710
Lewis Morris, Pres.
John Wills, V. Pres.
Thomas Gardiner, S.G.
John Reading, Clerk
William Budd
William Stevenson
Christopher Wetherill
Richard Bull
John Budd

1711
Lewis Morris, Pres.
John Wills, V. Pres.
Thomas Gardiner, S.G.
John Reading, Clerk
William Budd
John Kay
John Budd
William Stevenson
John Gosling

Known Attendees at the Men's Quarterly Meetings
at Mount Hope

1686
Thomas Budd
William Biddle
John Borton
Thomas Barton
John Woolston
Robert Wilson
John Horner
Thomas Lambert
Mahlon Stacy
Samuel Andrews
Francis Davenport
Thomas Butcher
William Brightwen
Percivale Towle
William Peachee

1687
Samuel Jennings
Thomas Ollive
Francis Davenport
Samuel Andrews
Mahlon Stacy
Thomas Lambert
William Biddle
John Wilson
Robert Wilson
John Horner
Percivale Towle
Thomas Barton
James Marshall

1688
Percival Towle
John Day
Richard Guy
William Watson
John Wilsford
William Biddle
Mahlon Stacy
Thomas Lambert
Robert Wilson
John Horner
Thomas Gilberthorpe
Thomas Barton
John Shinn

1689
Henry Grubb
John Woolston
Percivale Towle
Charles Read
William Biddle
Thomas Lambert
William Watson
Thomas Gilberthorpe
John Wills
Richard Guy
John Shinn
Thomas Gardiner
John Wilsford
John Horner
Robert Wilson
Francis Davenport
Edward Rockhill
Samuel Bunting
John Bunting
John Curtis

1690
Henry Grubb
Robert Young
John Woolston
Percivale Towle
Charles Read
William Biddle
Richard Guy
John Shinn
Thomas Gardiner
William Watson
John Snowden
Edward Rockhill
Francis Davenport
Samuel Andrews
Thomas Gilberthorpe
John Curtis
Robert Murfin
John Hollinshead
John Butcher
Thomas Evans

1691
William Biddle
Richard Guy
Percivale Towle
William Watson
Francis Davenport
John Woolston
John Browne
Thomas Gardiner
Thomas Butcher
Samuel Bunting
Thomas Gilberthorpe
Samuel Andrews

1692
William Biddle
Mahlon Stacy
John Wilsford
William Watson
Francis Davenport
John Shinn
Christopher Wetherill
Robert Young
Isaac Marriott
John Woolston
John Day
Samuel Andrews
Richard Guy
Henry Grubb
Peter Fretwell

1693
Thomas Lambert
John Woolston
Francis Davenport
Robert Young
John Day
Mahlon Stacy
William Biddle
Samuel Bunting
Thomas Foulke
Robert Wilson
John Bunting
Samuel Andrews
Richard Guy
Thomas Gardiner
Henry Grubb
John Shinn
John Skene
Peter Fretwell

1694
Peter Fretwell
William Biddle
Francis Davenport
Mahlon Stacy
Robert Wilson
John Woolston
Isaac Marriott
Daniel Wills
John Wilsford
Thomas Gardiner
John Shinn
John Day
Benjamin Wheate

1695
William Biddle
Peter Fretwell
William Watson
Thomas Foulke
Robert Wilson
Francis Davenport
Thomas Gilberthorpe
Daniel Wills
Henry Grubb
John Shinn
John Day
Richard Love
Samuel Jennings
John Woolston

1696
Peter Fretwell
William Biddle
Francis Davenport
Mahlon Stacy
George Deacon
John Day
John Shinn
John Hollinshead
Daniel Wills

1697
William Biddle
Francis Davenport
Samuel Bunting
John Day
William Watson
John Bunting
John Warner
Benjamin Field
Robert Wilson
Edward Rockhill
George Deacon
John Wills
Samuel Furnis
Richard Love
Thomas Raper
Abraham Bickley
John Scott

1698
Samuel Jennings
Peter Fretwell
Francis Davenport
William Biddle
Samuel Bunting
John Day
John Hollinshead
Benjamin Wheate
Richard Love
Thomas Raper
Joshua Humphries
John Wills
Christopher Wetherill
John Browne

1699
William Biddle
Francis Davenport
John Day
Peter Fretwell
Thomas Gardiner
Robert Wilson
Samuel Jennings
John Shinn
Restore Lippincott
John Woolman
Thomas Eves
Isaac Marriott
John Hollinshead
Daniel Smith
Henry Grubb
Samuel Furnis
John Wills
John Butcher
John Paine
George Elkinton
Thomas Gardiner
Thomas Raper
Joshua Humphries
Christopher Wetherill
John Browne
Richard Ridgway

1700
Francis Davenport
Robert Wilson
Samuel Jennings
William Biddle
Peter Fretwell
John Day
Thomas Eves
Samuel Bunting
Benjamin Field
John Bunting
Caleb Wheatley
Thomas Gardiner
Thomas Raper
Samuel Furnis
John Shinn
John Browne
Joshua Humphries
Henry Grubb
Christopher Wetherill
John Scott
Richard Ridgway
John Wills
George Elkinton
Isaac Marriott
Abraham Bickley
Restore Lippincott

1701
Robert Wilson
John Day
John Wills
Thomas Gardiner
Samuel Jennings
Mahlon Stacy
Francis Davenport
William Biddle
John Shinn
Samuel Bunting
John Scott
John Hudson
Mathew Champion
John Woolman
William Hunt
Isaac Marriott
Daniel Smith
Thomas Raper
Christopher Wetherill
John Butcher
William Gabitas
Richard Ridgway
John Paine
George Elkinton
Francis Collins
John Browne
Thomas Eves

1702
Samuel Jennings
Thomas Gardiner
Robert Wilson
Peter Fretwell
Thomas Eves
John Wills
Francis Davenport
Mahlon Stacy
John Shinn
Samuel Bunting
John Day
William Biddle
John Scott
Thomas Raper
Christopher Wetherill
Francis Collins
Joshua Humphries
John Butcher
Richard Ridgway
Henry Grubb
Thomas Scattergood
Restore Lippincott
George Elkinton
John Browne

1703
Mahlon Stacy
Peter Fretwell
John Day
Francis Davenport
William Biddle
Thomas Foulke
George Deacon
Richard Smith
John Woolman
John Browne
Isaac Marriott
Restore Lippincott
Robert Wilson
Thomas Raper
John Wills
Samuel Bunting
William Wood
William Petty
Joshua Humphries
John Shinn
Samuel Furnis
George Elkinton
Thomas Eves
Christopher Wetherill
John Butcher

1704
Robert Wilson
Samuel Bunting
John Bunting
Thomas Raper
John Day
Isaac Marriott
John Wills
William Biddle
Samuel Furnis
Thomas Scattergood
Thomas Eves
John Browne
Peter Pington
John Woolman
Joshua Humphries
John Butcher
William Stevenson
George Deacon
Richard Ridgway
Thomas Smith

1705
Francis Davenport
William Biddle
Robert Wilson
Thomas Gardiner
Peter Fretwell
John Surkett
John Day
Samuel Jennings
Thomas Eves
Samuel Furnis
Thomas Raper
Joshua Humphries
Richard Ridgway
Isaac Marriott
George Elkinton
John Woolman
John Shinn
John Butcher
John Browne

1706
John Shinn
Robert Wilson
Thomas Gardiner
Peter Fretwell
John Day
Francis Davenport
William Biddle
Thomas Raper
Samuel Furnis
Richard Smith
Joshua Humphries
George Elkinton
John Woolman
John Browne
Isaac Marriott
Richard Ridgway
John Wills
Thomas Eves
Samuel Fretwell
John Butcher
John Hollinshead
Samuel Smith
John Surkett
Samuel Jennings

1707
William Biddle
Robert Wilson
Thomas Gardiner
Peter Fretwell
John Surkett
John Day
Samuel Jennings
Samuel Furnis
Thomas Raper
Samuel Smith
John Shinn
George Elkinton
John Woolman
Isaac Marriott
John Shinn Jr.
Samuel Lippincott
Thomas Eves
John Butcher
Mathew Champion
John Hudson
Samuel Fretwell
John Hollinshead
Richard Ridgway

1708
Samuel Jennings
John Woolman
John Butcher
John Shinn
John Hudson
George Elkinton
Joshua Humphries
Richard Ridgway
Samuel Furnis
John Surkett
Isaac Marriott
John Day
John Wills
Edward Rockhill
Robert Wilson
Thomas Raper
Samuel Bunting
Thomas Gardiner
Peter Fretwell
William Biddle

1709
John Surkett
Christopher Wethrill
Thomas Gardiner
Peter Fretwell
George Deacon
John Wills
Samuel Bunting
Edward Rockhill
Robert Wilson
William Biddle
Benjamin Field
William Murfin
John Warren
Richard French
Thomas Scholey
John Abbott
William Wood
John Bunting
Isaac Marriott
Thomas Raper
Thomas Eves
John Day
John Butcher
George Elkinton
John Browne
Richard Ridgway

1710

Isaac Marriott
Thomas Raper
John Butcher
Edward Rockhill
John Bunting
Thomas Scholey
William Biddle
Thomas Gardiner
Peter Fretwell
John Wills
Richard Ridgway
Samuel Bunting
William Wood
Richard French
John Warren
Isaac Horner
John Sykes
William Murfin
John Abbott
John Surkett
John Day
John Shinn
Thomas Eves
George Elkinton
Joshua Humphries
Restore Lippincott
William Hackney

1711

William Biddle
William Wood
John Warren
William Murfin
John Cheshire
John Bunting
John Sykes
John Abbott
Isaac Horner
Thomas Scholey
Isaac Marriott
Thomas Raper
Daniel Smith
William Pancoast
Thomas Eves
Hugh Sharp
John Surkett
John Wills
Samuel Lippincott
John Day
Mathew Champion
Richard Ridgway
John Woolman
Samuel Smith
Restore Lippincott
George Elkinton
Joshua Humphries
John Butcher

Known Attendees of the Women's Quarterly Meetings held at Mount Hope

1691
Sarah Biddle
Mary Andrews

1693
Bridget Watson
Mary Rockhill
Sarah Biddle
Mary Foulke
Thomasin Towle

1695
Susannah Farnsworth
Bridget Watson
Rebeccah Davenport
Sarah Biddle

1696
Rebeccah Davenport
Ann Watson
Mary Andrews
Susannah Farnsworth
Sarah Biddle

1697
Bridget Watson
Ann Watson
Susannah Farnsworth
Mary Rockhill
Anne Murfin
Experience Field
Rachell Bunting
Elizabeth Gardiner
Ann Jennings
Lydia Horner
Sarah Biddle

1698
Hannah Overton
Rebeccah Davenport
Sarah Bunting
Mary Bunting
Rachell Bunting
Susannah Farnsworth
Mary Rockhill
Sarah Biddle
Ann Jennings
Elizabeth Day

1699
Ann Watson
Sarah Biddle
Sarah Bunting
Mary Rockhill
Rachell Bunting
Rebeccah Davenport
Mary Bunting
Elizabeth Fretwell
Hannah Woolston

1700
Ann Watson
Rebeccah Davenport
Mary Myers
Sarah Biddle
Susannah Farnsworth
Bridget Watson
Mary Rockhill
Elizabeth Day
Elizabeth Fretwell
Hannah Woolston
Frances Antrum
Hannah Lippincott

1701
Lydia Horner
Elizabeth Frewell
Elizabeth Day
Hannah Woolston
Elizabeth Humphries
Elizabeth Woolman
Sarah Biddle
Sarah Bunting
Rebeccah Davenport
Mary Bunting
Mary Wood
Ann Watson
Hannah Overton
Susannah Farnsworth
Experience Field
Mary Rockhill

1702
Susannah Farnsworth
Mary Bunting
Mary Myers
Mary Rockhill
Ann Watson
Sarah Biddle
Lydia Horner
Mary Smith
Hannah Lippincott
Elizabeth Fretwell
Francis Antrum
Mary Elkinton
Mary Wheate

1703
Hannah Woolston
Frances Antrum
Elizabeth Fretwell
Lydia Horner
Hester Humphries
Mary Wheate
Sarah Biddle
Susannah Farnsworth
Rebecca Davenport
Mary Myers
Mary Wood
Mary Rockhill
Ann Satterthwaite

1704
Mary Myers
Rebeccah Davenport
Susannah Farnsworth
Ann Satterthwaite
Mary Bunting
Sarah Biddle
Elizabeth Gardiner
Hannah Woolston
Mary Wheate
Hannah Lippincott
Elizabeth Fretwell
Frances Antrum
Margaret Hunt

1705
Katherine Champion
Mary Wheate
Susanna Furnis
Elizabeth Woolman
Elizabeth Day
Frances Antrum
Hannah Surkett
Sarah Biddle
Rebeccah Davenport
Hannah Overton
Ann Abbott
Mary Bunting

1707
Hannah Surkett
Elizabeth Hill
Frances Antrum
Elizabeth Fretwell
Susanna Marriott
Sarah Biddle
Mary Bunting
Mary Rockhill
Mary Myers
Ann Watson
Sarah Bunting

1708
Mary Rockhill
Sarah Scholey
Susannah Farnsworth
Mary Bunting
Sarah Bunting
Sarah Biddle
Frances Antrum
Elizabeth Hill
Hannah Lippincott
Abigail Raper
Elizabeth Woolman
Mary Hudson

1709
Hope Wills
Mary Elkinton
Frances Antrum
Abigail Raper
Susanna Marriott
Mary Butcher
Elizabeth Hill
Mary Wheate
Elizabeth Woolman
Hannah Surkett
Hester Humphries
Margaret Hunt
Phoebe Scattergood
Sarah Biddle
Mary Bunting
Sarah Bunting
Mary Rockhill
Mary Myers
Ann Abbott
Rebecca Warren
Sarah Murfin
Mary Wood
Sarah Scholey
Rebecca Briant
Susannah Farnsworth
Elizabeth Horner

1710
Sarah Bunting
Mary Rockhill
Ann Abbott
Frances Nicholson
Mary Myers
Mary Wood
Rebecca Briant
Hannah Nicholson
Mary Bunting
Sarah Scholey
Rebecca Warren
Elizabeth Day
Hannah Lippincott
Hope Wills
Elizabeth Woodman
Frances Antrum
Susanna Marriott
Hannah Surkett
Mary Butcher
Phoebe Scattergood
Margaret Hunt
Mary Smith
Mary Elkinton
Abigail Raper
Lydia Wardell

1711
Mary Eves
Frances Antrum
Katherine Champion
Hannah Lippincott
Abigail Raper
Phoebe Scattergood
Elizabeth Burr
Mary Smith
Hope Wills
Ann Stevenson
Mary Elkinton
Mary Butcher
Susanna Marriott
Elizabeth Fretwell
Hannah Surkett
Mary Wood
Rebecca Warren
Ann Abbott
Rebecca Briant
Mary Bunting
Sarah Scholey
Ann Lambert
Allyce Stuart
Sarah Wheatley
Lydia Biddle
Joannah Sykes
Susannah Farnsworth
Elizabeth Horner
Hannah Nicholson

Men's Yearly Meeting Delegates
when William was a Delegate

September 5, 1688
Burlington

Percival Towle
John Day
Richard Guy
William Watson
John Wilsford
William Biddle
Christopher White
Phineas Pemberton
Thomas Fitzwater
Thomas Budd
George Keith
John Hampton

September 1, 1689
Philadelphia

John Shinn
John Wilsford
William Biddle
Percivale Towle
Robert Turner
John Eccley
William Preston
Phineas Pemberton

September 7, 1692
Burlington

William Watson
William Biddle
Francis Davenport
John Wilsford
John Shinn
Mahlon Stacy
Robert Young
John Woolston
Thomas Thackera
Christopher White
John Thompson
Phineas Pemberton
Nicholas Walne
James Fox
Samuel Carpenter

September 6, 1693
Philadelphia

Thomas Lambert
John Wilsford
Richard Guy
Robert Young
John Day
Mahlon Stacy
William Biddle
Edward Wade
Joseph White
Samuel Spicer
William Cooper
Alex Beardsley
William Southbee
James Fox
Samuel Carpenter
Anthony Morris
Phineas Pemberton
Nicholas Walne
John Goodson

September 15-19, 1694
Burlington

Thomas Gardiner
Samuel Wade
John Smith
George Deacon
Francis Davenport
Mahlon Stacy
William Biddle
John Wilsford
Daniel Wills
James Fox
Alexander Beardsley
Samuel Richardson
Samuel Carpenter
Nicholas Walne
Phineas Pemberton
Morgan Druit
Samuel Hollingsworth

September 15-18, 1695
Philadelphia

Francis Davenport
William Biddle
Francis Collins
Peter Fretwell
Daniel Wills
Nicholas Walne
William Biles
Alexander Beardsley
Samuel Carpenter
James Fox

September 23, 1696
Burlington

George Deacon
Francis Davenport
Peter Fretwell
William Biddle
Mahlon Stacy
John Day
Thomas Thackera
Edward Shippen
James Fox
George Gray
Alex Beardsley
Joseph Paul
Richard Townsend
William Howell
Phineas Pemberton
John Tilton
John Lippincott

September 27, 1697
Philadelphia

Edward Shippen
Samuel Carpenter
Griffith Owen
Thomas Ducketts
Robert Owen
John Roberts
Joseph Paul
Samuel Richardson
Phineas Pemberton
William Biddle
Francis Davenport
Samuel Bunting
John Day
Thomas Thackera
William Cooper

September 14-18, 1700
Burlington

Edward Shippen
Griffith Owen
John Bevan
T. Hammon
Samuel Carpenter
Hugh Roberts
William Howell
Samuel Jennings
Peter Fretwell
John Day
Thomas Eves
William Biddle
Francis Davenport
Robert Wilson
Remembrance
  Lippincott
George Curtis

September 24, 1701
Philadelphia

Francis Davenport
William Biddle
Robert Wilson
John Day
John Wills
Thomas Thackera
Thomas Gardiner
William Evans
John Hance
Obediah Allen
Remembrance
  Lippincott
William Paxton
Richard Hough
Joseph Kirkbride
Ezra Crosdale
Edward Shippen
Samuel Carpenter
Nicholas Walne
John Kinsey
Hugh Roberts
John Bevan
William Howell
Everard Bolton
Reese Thomas

September 23, 1702
Burlington

William Biddle
Francis Davenport
Robert Wilson
Peter Fretwell
John Adams
Nicholas Walne
Rowland Ellis
Samuel Carpenter
William Hudson
Griffith Owen
Joseph Kirkbride
Ezra Crosdale
Thomas Harding
Richard Hough

September 22-28, 1703
Philadelphia

Francis Davenport
Robert Wilson
William Biddle
John Day
Thomas Raper
Peter Fretwell
John Wills
Rowland Ellis
Joseph Paul
Reese Thomas
Anthony Morris
George Morris
Caleb Pusey
John Blunstone
John Lee
William Borton
Thomas Raines
Tobias Dimmock
Richard Hough
John Adams
Thomas Sharp

September 1705
Philadelphia

Francis Davenport
Richard Wilson
William Biddle
John Day
Thomas Gardiner
Peter Fretwell
Thomas Eves
Edward Shippen
Nicholas Walne
Reese Thomas
John Roberts
William Howell
Everard Bolton
Anthony Morris
Pentacost Teague
Tobias Dimmock
Thomas Wilson
William Paxton
Thomas Baynes
Remembrance
  Lippincott

September 18, 1706
Burlington

Robert Wilson
William Biddle
Thomas Gardiner
Francis Davenport
Peter Fretwell
John Wills
John Surkett
Rowland Ellis
William Preston
Thomas Walton
Thomas Storey
Samuel Carpenter
Nicholas Walne
Anthony Morris
John Blunstone
Caleb Pusey
Thomas Mayson
John Haynes
Richard Dorkin
John Kay
John Estaugh

September 23, 1707
Philadelphia

William Biddle
Robert Wilson
Thomas Gardiner
Peter Fretwell
John Surkett
John Day
Nicholas Walne
Griffith Owen
Thomas Storey
Rowland Ellis
Caleb Pusey
Anthony Morris
John Kinsey
Remembrance
  Lippincott
John Woolly

Women's Yearly Meeting Delegates
when Sarah was a Delegate

1691

Sarah Goodson
Hannah Carpenter
Mary Andrews
Sarah Biddle
Elizabeth Kay
Alice Wood
Ann Dilworth
Jane Biles
Elizabeth Limcock
Lydia Wade
Abigail Lippincott
Margaret L.

1693

Thomasin Towle
Sarah Biddle
Hannah Carpenter
Sarah Sharp
Elizabeth Hooten
Abigail Lippincott

1696

Ann Jennings
Sarah Biddle
Ellen Spicer
Margaret Cooper
Abigail Lippincott

1700

Sarah Biddle
Hannah Watson
Elizabeth Kay
Ann Thackera
Jane Biles
Grace Langhorne
Margaret Cock
Hannah Carpenter
Margaret Blunstone
Elizabeth Hooten
Jane Birden

West New Jersey Government, Judiciary and Land Managers

GENERAL ASSEMBLY

Thoms Ollive, Speaker	Bernard Devonish
Mahlon Stacy	Isaac Marriot
Joshua Wright	William Peachee
John Lambert	William Cooper
Thomas Lambert	Mark Newbie
William Emley	Thomas Thackera
Godfrey Hancock	Robert Zane
Daniel Leeds	James Nevill
Thomas Wright	Richard Guy
Samuel Borden	Mark Reeves
Robert Stacy	Richard Hancock
Thomas Budd	John Smith
Daniel Wills	John Pledger
Thomas Gardiner	Edward Wade
John Cripps	George Deacon
John White	Samuel Hedge
John Chaffin	Andrew Thompson

OFFICIALS ELECTED BY GENERAL ASSEMBLY MAY 2-15, 1683

Governor's Council	*Justices*	*Land Commissioners*
Samuel Jennings, Dep. Gov.	William Biddle	William Biddle
William Biddle	John Skene	Thomas Lambert
Thomas Budd	Henry Stacy	William Emley
John Skene	James Nevill	Thomas Budd
John Gosling	Mahlon Stacy	Thomas Gardiner
Mark Newbie	Thomas Gardiner	Francis Collins
Thomas Gardiner	Thomas Budd	Mark Newbie
Henry Stacy	Elias Farre	John Gosling
James Nevill	Mark Newbie	John Skene
Elias Farre	John Gosling	James Nevill
Mahlon Stacy	Thomas Ollive	
	Richard Guy	
	Edward Wade	
	Andrew Thompson	
	William Emley	

GENERAL ASSEMBLY

First Tenth	*Second Tenth*
John Hooton	Thomas Ollive, Speaker
William Emley	Thomas Budd
Mahlon Stacy	John Gosling
Thomas Lambert	Daniel Wills
Percivale Towle	Thomas Gardiner
William Biddle	William Peachee
Elias Farre	John Skene
Joshua Wright	John Chaffin
Thomas Wright	John Borton
John Woolston	Isaac Marriott

Salem Tenth
John Fenwick
Andrew Thompson
Richard Guy
James Nevill
John Thompson
John Maddocks
Edward Wade
Edward Bradway
Michael Berroone
George Deacon

Third Tenth
William Cooper
Mark Newbie
Henry Stacy
Francis Collins
Samuel Coles
Thomas Howell
William Bates

OFFICIALS ELECTED BY GENERAL ASSEMBLY MAY 12-14, 1684

Governor's Council
Thomas Ollive, Dep. Gov.
William Biddle
Robert Stacy
Robert Dimsdale
John Gosling
Elias Farre
Richard Guy
William Emley
Daniel Wills
Robert Turner
Christopher White

Justices
William Biddle
Robert Stacy
Thomas Gardiner
Elias Farre
Francis Davenport
Thomas Lambert
Robert Dimsdale
John Gosling
Francis Collins
Thomas Thackera
James Nevill
George Deacon
Edward Bradway
Andrew Thompson
(*councilmen also were justices*)

Land Commissioners
Richard Guy
William Biddle
William Peachee
Daniel Wills
Robert Turner
Henry Wood
Isaac Marriott
William Cooper

GENERAL ASSEMBLY

First Tenth
George Hutcheson
Robert Stacy
William Biddle
Francis Davenport
Elias Farre
Richard Guy
Percivale Towle
Mahlon Stacy
William Emley
Godfrey Hancock
Salem Tenth
William Braithwaite
John Smith
Christopher White
Roger Carary
Christopher Saunders
John Pledger
Thomas Smith
Roger Milton
George Haselwood
Francis Forrest

Second Tenth
Thomas Ollive, Speaker
Robert Dimsdale
Thomas Gardiner
John Gosling
Daniel Wills
William Peachee
Benjamin Scott
Isaac Marriott
John Borton
Richard Basnett
Third Tenth
William Cooper
Robert Turner
Francis Collins
Henry Tradway
Henry Wood
Marcus Lawrence
William Bates

OFFICIALS ELECTED BY GENERAL ASSEMBLY MAY 12, 13, 1685

Governor's Council	*Justices*	*Land Commissioners*
Thomas Ollive, Dep. Gov.	Robert Stacy	Richard Guy
William Biddle	Thomas Lambert	William Biddle
William Emley	John Gosling	William Peachee
Robert Stacy	Thomas Gardiner	Daniel Wills
James Budd	Francis Davenport	Robert Turner
Francis Davenport	Elias Farre	Henry Wood
George Hutcheson	William Peachee	Isaac Marriott
Daniel Wills	Francis Collins	William Cooper
Robert Turner	Robert Dimsdale	
John Gosling	Thomas Thackera	
Robert Dimsdale	Andrew Robeson	
(*also justices ex officio*)	George Deacon	
	Andrew Thompson	
	Edward Bradway	
	Christopher White	

GENERAL ASSEMBLY

First Tenth	*Second Tenth*
Thomas Barton	Thomas Ollive, Speaker
George Hutcheson	Robert Dimsdale
Percivale Towle	John Gosling
Francis Davenport	Daniel Wills
Robert Stacy	Thomas Gardiner
John Pancoast	William Peachee
Mahlon Stacy	John Borton
John Horner	William Evans
William Biddle	James Budd
William Emley	Richard Basnett

Salem Tenth	*Third Tenth*
John Mattocks	Robert Turner
Richard Johnston	Thomas Sharp
William Penton	Samuel Coles
Joseph White	Samuel Carpenter
Roger Carary	Richard Russell
Hypoet Leseaver	Richard Arnold
Roger Milton	William Albertson
George Haselwood	
Richard Tindall	*Forth Tenth*
Samuel Bacon	Peter Dalboe
	William Warner

OFFICIALS ELECTED BY GENERAL ASSEMBLY NOVEMBER 25, 1685

Governor's Council	*Justices*	*Land Commissioners*
Edward Byllynge, Gov.	George Hutcheson	William Biddle
John Skene, Dep. Gov.	Mahlon Stacy	Richard Guy
William Emley	Francis Davenport	Daniel Wills

OFFICIALS ELECTED BY GENERAL ASSEMBLY NOVEMBER 25, 1685 (*continued*)

William Biddle
Richard Guy
James Budd
Governor's Council
George Hutcheson
Thomas Gardiner
Andrew Robeson
Samuel Carpenter
Elias Farre
Francis Davenport
(*also justices ex officio*)

Elias Farre
James Budd
Robert Dimsdale
Justices
Thomas Ollive
Thomas Thackera
Francis Collins
Andrew Robeson
Richard Lawrence
Caleb Carmen
George Deacon
Andrew Thompson
Samuel Carpenter
Samuel Bacon

William Peachee
Robert Turner
Henry Wood
Land Commissioners)
Anthony Nealson
George Hutcheson
James Budd
Andrew Robeson, surveyor gen.

GENERAL ASSEMBLY

First Tenth
Mahlon Stacy
Thomas Lambert
William Emley
William Biddle
Francis Davenport
Joshua Wright
George Hutcheson
Elias Farre
Robert Stacy
Richard Guy

Second Tenth
Thomas Ollive, Speaker
Samuel Jennings
Robert Dimsdale
Thomas Budd
Daniel Wills
James Budd
Thomas Gardiner
John Borton
William Peachee
William Budd

Third Tenth
Robert Turner
Francis Collins
John Hugg
Thomas Howell
William Bates
John Reading
Robert Zane
Thomas Thackera
John Kay
William Cooper

Forth Tenth
Andrew Robeson
Israel Helme
Woola Dalboe
Anthony Nealson
Benjamin Bramma
John Wood
Richard Lawrence
William Warner
Henry Tradway
Thomas Mathews

Salem Tenth
George Deacon
Edward Wade
James Nevill
Joseph White
Edward Bradway

Samuel Hedge
John Worlidge
Samuel Carpenter
Mark Reeves
William Braithwaite

OFFICIALS ELECTED OR CONTINUED BY THE GENERAL ASSEMBLY
MAY 12-15, 1686

Governor's Council	*Justices*	*Land Commissioners*
Edward Byllyge, Governor	Same as Nov. 25, 1685	Same as Nov. 25, 1685
John Skene, Dep. Gov.	Richard Lawrence resigned;	
	John Wood took his place in the Forth	
Same as Nov. 25, 1685	Tenth. The Third and Forth Tenths	
	established their own courts.	

GENERAL ASSEMBLY
Same as November 25, 1685 except Richard Tindall replaced
Samuel Carpenter in the Salem Tenth and Thomas Sharp replaced
Thomas Howell in the Third Tenth.

OFFICIALS ELECTED OR CONTINUED BY THE GENERAL ASSEMBLY May 12, 1687

Governor's Council	*Burlington County Justices* *May 12, 1787 to August 8, 1688*	*Land Commissioners*
Edward Byllyng, Governor	John Skene	The General Assembly
died January 16, 1686/7	Edward Hunloke	suggests that the financial
Dr. Daniel Coxe, Governor	Richard Basnett	obligation of land matters
February 26, 1686/7	James Marshall	be assigned to the proprietors
John Skene, Dep. Gov.	William Myers	of West New Jersey. This led
	Robert Stacy	to the formation of the
	Elias Farre	Council of the Proprietors of
Governor's Council	Richard Guy	West New Jersey on February
the same as	William Emley	14, 1687/8. That new land
November 25, 1685	Thomas Lambert	management was formed and
	Daniel Wills	took into its possession all of
	Mahlon Stacy	the records related to land
	William Biddle	matters of the territory.

Edmond Andros, Governor
August 18, 1688 to April 18, 1689

*Justices serving the Burlington Court
commissioned under Governor Andros
August 18, 1688 to May, 1689.*

John Skene	William Biddle
Edward Hunloke	Richard Basnett
James Marshall	William Myers
William Emley	Daniel Wills

Daniel Coxe, Governor
April 1689 to March 1, 1691/2
John Skene, acting Deputy Governor

*Justices serving the Burlington Court
May 1689 to November 1692*

John Skene	William Emley
Edward Hunloke	Thomas Lambert
James Marshall	Mahlon Stacy
Richard Basnett	William Biddle
William Myers	Daniel Wills

Andrew Hamilton, Governor
April, 1692 to November 1697
Edward Hunloke, Deputy Governor
Governor's Council
John Tatham
George Deacon
Thomas Revell
Nathaniel Westland
John Worlidge

Justices Commissioned and serving the
Burlington Court November 21, 1692

Edward Hunloke	Mahlon Stacy
John Tatham	Daniel Wills
William Biddle	Thomas Revell
Thomas Lambert	James Marshall
Thomas Gardiner	John Worlidge
William Righton	Nathaniel Westland
Daniel Leeds	Francis Davenport

Justices serving on the Burlington Court May 12, 1694 to May 12, 1695

Edward Hunloke	Mahlon Stacy	Daniel Leeds	Francis Davenport
James Marshall	John Curtis	John Tatham	Thomas Gardiner
William Biddle	Peter Fretwell	Nathaniel Westland	Jeremiah Basse
Daniel Wills	Governor Andrew Hamilton		

Justices serving on the Burlington Court May 12, 1695 to May 12, 1696

Andrew Hamilton	John Curtis	John Hollinshead	Nathaniel Westland
Mahlon Stacy	Daniel Wills	Edward Hunloke	Peter Fretwell
Francis Davenport	John Adams	John Tatham	Andrew Hamilton Gov.
William Biddle	Samuel Harriott	Thomas Revell	Daniel Wills

Justices serving on the Burlington Court May 12, 1696 to May 12, 1697

Andrew Hamilton	Daniel Wills	Francis Davenport	Peter Fretwell
Mahlon Stacy	William Biddle	John Adams	John Hollinshead

Justices serving on the Burlington Court May 12, 1697 to May 12, 1698

Mahlon Stacy	Daniel Wills	Francis Davenport	John Hollinshead
William Biddle	Peter Fretwell	John Adams	

GENERAL ASSEMBLY May 12, 1697

Quakers		*Non-Quakers*
Samuel Jennings, Speaker	William Cooper	John Holmes
Francis Davenport	John Hollinshead	John Reading
William Biddle	Peter Fretwell	George Taylor
Mahlon Stacy	Jonathan Beere	Andrew Robeson Jr.
Daniel Wills	Benjamin Wheate	Timothy Brandreth
Thomas Gardiner	John Thompson	Samuel Hedge
Thomas Thackera	William Bate	Jacob Dayton
Richard Heritage	Archibald Mickle	Joseph Woodroofe
John Taylor	Freedom Lippincott	John Shaw
James Atkinson	Robert Wilson	John Rambo
Samuel Spicer	William Wood	Peter Matson
John Adams	George Deacon	Benjamin Bramma
Thomas Raper	John Hugg	John Ashbrook
Joshua Humphries	Mathew Metcalf	John Crawford
Thomas Lambert	John Woolston	
John Scott	John Day	
Henry Ballinger	Samuel Wade	
Richard Dorkin	John Hugg Jr.	
Hananiah Gaunt	William Hall	
Joseph Cooper	Joseph Browne	
John Wright		

Governor's Council

Jeremiah Basse, Governor
April 1698 to August 1699

John Tatham, President
John Jewell
Thomas Revell
Edward Randolph

Governor's Council

Andrew Hamilton, Governor
December 20, 1699 to May 1703

Edward Hunloke
William Biddle
Thomas Gardiner
George Deacon
John Thompson
Jonathan Beere
Andrew Robeson Jr.

*Justices serving the Burlington Court
August 8, 1698 to November 4, 1699*

Jeremiah Basse	Joshua Newbold
John Tatham	William Hewling
Thomas Revell	Daniel Leeds
Nathaniel Westland	John Jewell
George Deacon	John Test
William Emlley	Michael Newbold
Thomas Bibb	Joshua Ely
Anthony Elton	

*Justices elected to serve the Burlington Court
December 20, 1699 to May 12, 1700*

Andrew Hamilton	Ralph Hunt
Mahlon Stacy	Joshua Newbold
Francis Davenport	John Wills
Peter Fretwell	John Adams
William Biddle	Elias Toy
Thomas Lambert	

*Justices elected to serve the Burlington Court
May 12, 1700 to May 12, 1701*

Andrew Hamilton	William Biddle	John Wills
Mahlon Stacy	Joshua Newbold	John Adams
Francis Davenport	Richard Ridgway	Thomas Lambert
Peter Fretwell	Robert Wheeler	Joshua Ely
		Elias Toy

*Justices elected to serve the Burlington Court
May 12, 1701*

Andrew Hamilton	Thomas Gardiner	Samuel Furnis
Mahlon Stacy	William Emley	Michael Newbold
Francis Davenport	John Wills	John Adams
William Biddle	Richard Ridgway	Joshua Ely

GENERAL ASSEMBLY May 12, 1701

Thomas Thackera	John Kay	Samuel Jennings, Speaker
Mahlon Stacy	Archibald Mickle	John Reading, Clerk
Francis Davenport	Samuel Hedge	John Scott
Restore Lippincott	William Hall	Thomas Wilkins
John Hand	John Woodroofe	Simeon Ellis
John Rambo	John Bacon	Philip Paul

The governments of East and West Jersey are surrendered to Queen Anne, April 15, 1702

Justices Commissioned by Governor Andrew Hamilton August 8, 1702

Francis Davenport	Samuel Furnis
William Biddle	Richard Ridgway
John Wills	Thomas Gardiner
John Adams	Mahlon Stacy

Governor's Council

Edward, Lord Viscount
Cornbury, Governor of
New York and New Jersey

Edward Hunloke
Lewis Morris
Andrew Bowne
Samuel Jennings
Thomas Revell
Francis Davenport
Willian Pinhorne
Samuel Leonard
George Deacon
Samuel Walker
Daniel Leeds
William Sanford
Robert Quarry

*Justices Commissioned by Governor Cornbury
August 20, 1703*

Francis Davenport
Daniel Leeds
George Deacon
Alexander Griffith
Nathaniel Westland
Robert Wheeler
Joshua Newbold
Ralph Hunt
Roger Parke
William Emley
William Wood
William Biddle
Michael Newbold
William Budd
Richard Ridgway
William Heuling
Samuel Jennings
Thomas Revell
Jeremiah Basse

GENERAL ASSEMBLY NEW JERSEY
*November 10 to December 13, 1703
First Assembly First Session
Held in Perth Amboy
West Jersey Delegates*

Thomas Lambert
William Biddle
William Stevenson
Restore Lippincott
John Kay
John Hugg, Jr.
Joseph Cooper
William Hall
John Mason
John Smith
Peter Fretwell
Thomas Gardiner, Speaker

GENERAL ASSEMBLY NEW JERSEY
*September 7 to 28, 1704
First Assembly Second Session
Held in Burlington*

same delegates

When these terms ended William Biddle did not serve again except as a member and leader of the Council of Proprietors of West New Jersey until 1709.

Proprietary Transactions of the Heirs
of William and Sarah Biddle

March 17, 1711/12	A warrant is granted to William Biddle Jr. for 7500 acres of the third dividend on his proprietary shares	CPWJ Minutes
August 25, 1713	William Biddle Jr. sells 100 acres to John Budd at Little Egg Harbor for £15	WJD DD-158
May 1 & 2, 1714	William Biddle Jr. sells 1665 acres at Amwell to Charles Woolverton for £350	WJD BBB-429
June 5, 1714	Dorothy Sherwin and her husband, Richard Marriott, sell to Thomas Smith rights to 100 acres that were given to Dorothy in the will of William Biddle Sr. for £5.	CPWJ Minutes
November 30, 1714	A warrant is granted to William Biddle Jr. for 7500 acres in the fourth dividend of his proprietary rights.	CPWJ Minutes
March 19, 1715/16	William Satterthwaite surveys two tracts of land (80 and 20 acres) which he received as land rights in the will of William Biddle Sr.	Basse BS: 154
March 24, 1715/16	William Biddle Jr. conveys to Jeremiah Basse the remaining two lots in Burlington City.	WJD A-1:. 277 Basse BS, 154
April 8 & 9, 1719	William Biddle Jr. sells to Daniel Howell 200 acres of his lands left from his father's estate.	Leeds BS:372 WJD D-76
1721	An indenture between William Biddle Jr. and William Biddle 3rd allows William Biddle 3rd to sell the Mount Hope property.	WJD D-76
April 14, 1721	William Biddle Jr. and Lydia and William Biddle 3rd sell 24 ¼ acres of the Mount Hope property to John Brown for £23.12s. Penelope (Biddle) witnesses the indenture.	WJD BB-433
July 8, 1722	William Biddle 3rd sells to Thomas Newbold *et al* 200 acres of the Mount Hope property for £120.	WJD D-76
	William Biddle 3rd sells to Penelope (Biddle) Whitehead and to James Whitehead, her husband, 14 acres of the Mount Hope property.	WJD Q-220
	William Biddle 3rd sells to Joseph Shreve 100 acres of the Mount Hope property.	WJD Q-220

	William Biddle Sr. had sold in his lifetime 7 ½ acres of the Mount Hope property on a stream and the river to Henry Stacy in 1682.	WJD Q-220
October 5, 1724	John Biddle is given the 625 acres of land assigned to him by William Biddle Sr. in his will, by an indenture (a moiety of a 1250-acre tract of land that William Biddle Jr. received in the fourth land dividend from the Council of Proprietors of West Jersey) located above the branches of the Raritan River.	Haverford College Library Allinson Collection File #968
November 28, 1724	William Biddle 3rd mortgages to John Holme of Philadelphia the remaining Mount Hope property for £75.	WJD DD-36
October 30, 1726	John Holme sells the Mount Hope property back to William Biddle 3rd for £83.	WJD DD-238
September 10, 1727	Elizabeth Biddle, spinster, sells to James Whitehead 250 acres in Hunterdon County that she had purchased from Charles Woolverton for £30.	WJD DD-12
June 10, 1728	William Biddle Jr. sells to James Craft property rights for 25 acres to correct his resurvey.	CPWJ Surveys Book E-64
July 30, 1728	William Biddle Jr. sells to William Fowle of Amwell, blacksmith, 687 acres for £60.	WJD DD-172, 174
December 5, 1729	William Biddle Jr. sells rights to 425 acres of land to William Pancoast for £22	CPWJ Surveys Book M-156-7
November 3, 1730	William Biddle Jr. surveys for himself 200 acres of land in Hunterdon County	CPWJ Surveys Book M-182
December 9, 1730	Lydia Biddle visits the Council of Proprietors of West Jersey to inform them that the 563 acres of land that they assigned to William Biddle Jr. in their third dividend is in the East Jersey territory. One month later the Council issued a new warrant for this land to her.	CPWJ minutes p. 2
May 6, 1731	William Biddle Jr. sells land rights to William Scholey for 400 acres in Hunterdon County.	CPWJ Surveys Book M-154

November 6, 1732	William Biddle Jr. gives to his daughter Lydia (Biddle) Imlay and his son-in-law Peter Imlay of Mansfield 1150 acres of land.	WJD DD-311
December 21, 1734	William Biddle Jr. gives to his daughter Penelope (Biddle) Whitehead and son-in-law James Whitehead, innholder of Mansfield, a tract of 1350 acres.	WJD E-275
November 24, 1734	William Biddle Jr. sells to Samuel Johnson 1250 acres of land for £160.	WJD EF-463
June 11, 1735	Peter Imlay sells to Charles Woolverton 315 acres at Amwell for £50.	WJD E-197
August 22, 1735	James Whitehead, innholder, and his wife Penelope (Biddle) sell to Samuel Johnson, sadler, from Trenton, 1350 acres for £150.	WJD E-275
February 4, 1736/7	William Biddle Jr. gives to John Biddle, his son, 1 ½ proprietary shares of West Jersey.	WJD E-275
April 9, 1736	John Biddle receives a warrant from the Council of West Jersey for 600 acres.	CPWJ Surveys Book M-213
April 9, 1737	John Biddle assigns rights to 200 acres at Amwell to Benjamin Smith.	CPWJ Surveys Books M-213, 275, 294; S6-159-160
May 5, 1737	John Biddle is granted a warrant for 7500 acres on the fifth dividend from the Council of Proprietors of West Jersey.	CPWJ Minutes p. 5
November 1, 1737	John Biddle sells the rights to 200 acres in Gloucester to James Steel.	CPWJ Surveys Book A-240
November 4, 1737	John Biddle sells the rights to 1000 acres to Aaron Leaming.	CPWJ Surveys Book E-181
February 9, 1737/8	John Biddle is given a warrant for 7225 acres from the Council of Proprietors of West Jersey representing the residual land rights of his father.	CPWJ Minutes p. 5
March 2, 1738	John Biddle sells rights to 800 acres to Joseph Cole.	CPWJ Surveys Book A-324
April 6, 1738	John Biddle sells rights to 1800 acres to William Harrison.	CPWJ Surveys Book A-324
April 21, 1738	John Biddle sells rights to 500 acres to Joseph Cole.	CPWJ Surveys Book A-355
June 8, 1738	John Biddle sells rights to 420 acres to James Steel.	CPWJ Surveys Book M-220

June 12, 1738	John Biddle sells rights to 1000 acres to Jonathan Wright.	CPWJ Surveys Book M-356, 357, 358, 346, 265
July 4, 1738	John Biddle sells rights to 1000 acres to Abraham Chatten.	CPWJ Surveys Book M-225
September 8, 1738	John Biddle sells 300 acres to Henry Wood in Gloucester County for £9.	WJD EF-203
July 2, 1739	John Biddle sells rights to 600 acres to Martin Ryerson for £32.	WJD EF-19
August 1, 1739	John Biddle sells rights to 78 acres to Abraham Long of Gloucester County.	CPWJ Surveys Book M-347
November 5, 1740	John Biddle sells rights to 730 acres to James Steel	CPWJ Surveys Book M-313
February 3, 1741/2	William Biddle Jr. and William Biddle 3rd sell 150 acres of the Mount Hope property to Thomas Biddle, yeoman, Mansfield, including the Mount Hope homestead for £350.	HDB pp. 87-92
February 9, 1741/2	William Biddle 3rd requests a resurvey of the Mount Hope property. It is revealed that there are 881 acres in the original survey, an overage of 381 acres.	CPWJ Minutes HDB p. 86
June 25, 1742	John Biddle sells rights of 100 acres of land to Samuel Rain, Gloucester County, against the 7225 warrant of February 9, 1738/9.	Deed in possession of heirs of James Biddle Yarnall
September 20, 1742	John Biddle sells rights to 381 acres to William Biddle 3rd to clear the title of the Mount Hope property for £25.	WJD GH-550
April 24, 1744	John Biddle sells 550 acres to Peter Matson, Gloucester County, for £23.7s.	WJD H-90
May 2, 1744	John Biddle returns the warrant for 7225 acres to the Council of Proprietors of West Jersey at their request. A total of 140 acres were said to have been sold against that warrant. John received a new warrant for 5000 acres and a promise of an additional warrant to be issued later.	CPWJ Minutes p. 121
September 28, 1745	John Biddle sells rights for 420 acres located in Morris County to Edward Rockhill.	CPWJ Surveys Book BB-98
November 7, 1745	John Biddle sells rights for 96 acres in Morris County to Edward Rockhill.	CPWJ Surveys Book BB-32

November 6, 1746	John Biddle sells to Jonathan Robison 415 acres, keeping for himself 415 acres of an 830 survey located in Morris County.	CPWJ Surveys Book BB-99
June 15, 1747	The survey for a 50-acre tract of land that William Biddle Jr. had sold to Henry Oxley is rerecorded.	CPWJ Surveys Book BB-223
November 4, 1747	John Biddle sells to Aaron Leaming rights to 1000 acres located in Cape May County.	CPWJ Surveys Book BB-214
May 23, 1749	William Biddle 3rd, merchant of Philadelphia, and his wife, Mary, sell to their brother-in-law Peter Imlay of Mansfield, all of the Seppasink Island and the remaining tract of land of Mount Hope for £2000.	WJD Q-283
August 2, 1749	John Biddle is given a warrant from the Council of Proprietors of West Jersey for 2102 acres.	CPWJ Minutes p. 213
May 8, 1751	John Biddle sells rights to Samuel Tucker Jr. for 500 acres	CPWJ Surveys Book S6-5
February 27, 1752	William Biddle 3rd, shopkeeper, and his wife, released to Samuel Smith *et al*, merchants of Philadelphia, creditors of William Biddle 3rd, 1250 acres of land that William Biddle 3rd received as legal heir to his father's estate. His father died intestate. The land was located in Warren County.	WJD S-217
September 6, 1753	John Biddle surveys for himself an 89-acre tract in Amwell, Hunterdon County, next to Dr. John Rodman.	CPWJ Surveys Book S6-92
October 3, 1753	John Biddle sells rights to Daniel Smith Jr. of Burlington for 1000 acres for £65.	WJD L-320; CPWJ Surveys, Book S6-162, 193, 201, 216
March 19, 1754	John Biddle sells to John Rodman 300 acres to correct his property rights on resurvey. He had an overplus of 555 acres.	CPWJ Surveys Book S6-201
October 3 & 4, 1758	An indenture between Lydia (Imlay) Scull and James Scull, of Philadelphia, and Thomas Biddle of Mansfield, for 1/6th rights to the Imlay property, a total of 261 acres and all of the island at Mansfield, Mount Hope.	WJD Q-220
September 8, 1759	John Biddle sells rights to remainder of 2102-acre warrant to Joseph Hollinshead, Burlington.	CPWJ Surveys W-288, S6-331

May 1, 1760	Heirs of Peter Imlay sell the remainder of Mount Hope plus all of the island minus 1/6th part previously sold to Thomas Biddle to Caleb Newbold for £3667.	WJD Q-220
January 7, 1771	The executors of William Imlay, brother of John Imlay and first cousin of Clement Biddle, settle the property of William Imlay.	WJD AE-55
November 3, 1779	John Biddle is granted a warrant on the sixth dividend of proprietary shares for 1000 acres.	CPWJ Minutes Book 8 p. 214
March 20, 1780	John Biddle gives the rights to his 1000 acres to his son Clement Biddle who is living in the Township of Newton, Sussex County in his home which had been the home of Joseph Barton. Clement has two tracts surveyed there for 425 acres and 125 acres. The land is on the Lawrence Line which divides East and West New Jersey.	CPWJ Surveys Q-365 and R-105
February 2, 1782	Clement Biddle presents to the Council of Proprietors of West Jersey his possession of 1 and ¾ proprietary shares of West Jersey. He asks for the remaining warrant for the sixth dividend. A warrant is given to him for 1125 acres.	CPWJ Minutes p. 255
1984 May 1st	C. Miller Biddle presented the Council of Proprietors his ownership of 2/32nd proprietary shares that he has quitclaimed from the heirs of Clement Biddle. He paid the Council $2.40 (a penny an acre) and received a warrant for 240 acres under the seventh dividend which had been distributed on the eve of the Civil War.	CPWJ Deed Book 2 p. 89
1995 January 17th	C. Miller Biddle sells 1.1 acres of unappropriated land rights to correct a gore in surveys in the West Jersey territory using the lands from the warrant he owns from the proprietary shares originally owned by William and Sarah Biddle.	CPWJ Deed Book 2 p. 120

INDEX

The following index is selective. All personal names are included, with married women indexed under both maiden and married names if known. Unknown maiden names are shown thus: (—). The names of William and Sarah (Smith) (Kempe) Biddle are not included, as they appear too frequently for an index to be helpful. Some place names in England are included, and a very few subjects, but except for personal names the index is not intended to be comprehensive. The chronological arrangement of the book and the titles of the chapters will be most useful to the reader for finding events and places of historic or family significance.